THE LIFE of MOZART by EDWARD HOLMES

EVERY MAN WILL GO WITH THEE BE THY GVIDE

INTHY MOST NEED TO GO BY THY SIDE

LONDON: PUBLISHED by J. M. DENT & SONS L?? AND IN NEW YORK BY E. P. DUTTON & CO

INTRODUCTION

THE name of Edward Holmes is probably not very well known
to the general musical public of to-day; but he was one of the
most capable writers upon music in the early part of the last
century, and his *Life of Mozart* is one of the very few pieces
of English musical literature—one might almost say the only
one—of that epoch that is worth reprinting at the present
time. Born in 1797, he was a schoolfellow of Keats at Mr.
Clarke's Academy in Enfield. His friendship with the poet
continued until the latter's death. After leaving school he
was apprenticed to one Seeley, a bookseller of Fleet Street.
Shortly afterwards, however, he became acquainted with
Vincent Novello (the founder of the present firm of Novello
& Co.), who saw his love for music and took him as his pupil.
" In order to facilitate the more assiduous study of the young
man," says Vincent Novello's daughter, Mrs. Cowden Clarke,
in her biography of her father, " Mr. Novello received Edward
Holmes as an inmate of his own house, so that at all hours
left free by other avocations he could superintend the progress
of his pupil in theory and practice. Mr. Holmes became
thoroughly versed in harmony, and was for many years
organist at Poplar Church, and at Holloway Chapel. He was
not only a sound musician, but his taste for letters gave him
that polished vigour of style which distinguishes his writings
upon the art. From his schoolfellowship with John Keats and
Charles Cowden Clarke, Edward Holmes had early acquired
a strong predilection for literature, and his becoming a resident
under Vincent Novello's roof confirmed the bent." The
literary society at Novello's house, 240 Oxford Street, was an
exceptionally brilliant one; Charles and Mary Lamb, Shelley,
Keats, Hazlitt, and Leigh Hunt were regular visitors; and it
is no doubt to these influences that Holmes owed a distinction
of style that was exceedingly rare among the musical writers
of his day.

He was a teacher of the pianoforte as well as an organist;
and when the *Atlas* newspaper was started he became its

musical critic, in which capacity he quickly made a reputation for sound knowledge, patient research, and an agreeable manner of writing. In 1827 he travelled on the continent, and the following year produced his first book, *A Ramble among the Musicians of Germany*, which went into a third edition. He quitted the *Atlas* to join the *Spectator;* and it was during his engagement on the latter journal that he compiled his *Life of Mozart*, which was published in 1845. It at once made its mark. This and the *Ramble* seem to have been his only books, though he wrote a great deal in *Fraser's Magazine* and the *Musical Times*, and the *Life of Purcell* that he contributed to the latter journal in 1847 was afterwards issued with Alfred Novello's second edition of that composer's sacred works. He married the grand-daughter of Samuel Webbe, the glee-composer, but died in America after little more than two years of wedded life, on 28th August 1859. The same number of the *Musical Times* (1st October 1859) that gave the announcement of his death contained also a brightly written article from his pen on " Domestic Music," evidently intended to be the first of a series.

Otto Jahn, in the preface to his copious *Life of Mozart*, points out that it was a Frenchman, Fétis, and an Englishman, Holmes, who first reduced the known facts of Mozart's life to order and made them interesting to the general reader. Holmes's book, indeed, was the first adequate thing of its kind. The material for it existed in various scattered publications. Shortly after the death of the composer in 1791 there appeared the necrology of Schlichtegroll, that was followed by the memoirs of Niemetschek (Prague, 1798), Arnold (Erfurt, 1803), Beyle (Paris, 1814) (stolen from Schlichtegroll and published under the pseudonym of Bombet), and Nissen (Leipzig, 1828). The last-named book, by the Danish councillor who married Mozart's widow and settled in Salzburg, where he died in 1826, was, of course, richest of all in original matter, but unskilfully arranged and weak on the musical side, for Nissen was no musician. Holmes was the first to make a connected story out of all these reminiscences and letters, and to give the world a picture of Mozart in the round. Not content with mere documentary records, he sought out various people—the old Abbé Stadler, for instance—who had known Mozart personally; and he made a careful examination of the scores in the possession of André of Offenbach, who had purchased all Mozart's manuscripts from the widow for £500. Included among these was the thematic catalogue of his works that Mozart had made on his own account since 1784. Holmes's performance is doubly creditable when we remember the difficulties in the way of any foreign inquirer working, as it were, so far from his base. The best tribute to his work is that of Jahn himself, who speaks of it thus in the preface to his own much larger book:

"The task of compiling a compendious and readable biography of Mozart by a proper arrangement and redaction of the really interesting part of Nissen's material was performed by Edward Holmes (*The Life of Mozart, including his Correspondence*: London, 1845). Here the vital part of the correspondence is arranged and combined with a narrative based on the then accessible literature with such discernment and insight that there results a coherent whole, giving a trustworthy and, so far as was possible, a complete survey of Mozart's life. Holmes has moreover made good use of André's published catalogue of Mozart's compositions, and the information these contain as to the date of origin of the works; during a journey through Germany he examined the original manuscripts in André's possession, and gleaned oral traditions here and there; he also made himself acquainted with musical literature, and produced a work that is without a doubt the most reliable and serviceable biography that could be achieved by the skilful use of the material generally accessible."

Jahn, of course, had special advantages in the way of research from the mere fact of his being resident in Germany; and his 1700 pages necessarily add largely to our knowledge of Mozart's life. But a comparison of his work with that of Holmes shows that the difference is only a matter of expansion of detail, not of alteration of the essential lines and colours of the portrait. There is something valuable even in Holmes's temporal limitations. He wrote at a time when there was not a suspicion of the vast changes that were to come over music in the second half of the nineteenth century; when his book appeared, Beethoven had been dead only eighteen years, and Wagner's "Tannhäuser" was only just being completed. Holmes therefore lets us see the old music as it must have appeared to the most cultured and liberal musical minds of the period just before the modern dawn. It must be remembered, too, that he was really doing pioneer work; for Mozart, as appears from the note to p. 73, was comparatively little known in England in the early part of the nineteenth century. Holmes's book was the first complete and adequate account of the composer to appear in English; there had been nothing before it but a translation of the very imperfect Schlichtegroll-Bombet and a few scattered magazine articles.

On few points does he need correcting, even in the light of the assiduous research that has gone on since his day. He was doubtful (p. 101, note) as to the authenticity of the so-called "Twelfth Mass," though inclined on the whole to accept it as Mozartian. Its spuriousness is now universally recognised. He was in error in thinking that the full score of the "Requiem" that was discovered in 1839 (p. 280, note), and is now in the Vienna Hofbibliothek, is in Mozart's handwriting. It is in part a successful imitation of Mozart's script by his pupil Süssmayer, who completed the "Requiem" from Mozart's indications. Süssmayer's share in the "Lacrymosa," the "Sanctus," the "Benedictus," and the "Agnus Dei" of the "Requiem" is now generally admitted. To Holmes's account of the strange circumstances attending the composition of the "Requiem" it needs only to be added that the mysterious stranger was one Leutgeb, steward to the eccentric Count Franz von Walsegg of Ruppach. The Count's wife had died, and he was anxious not only to have a requiem sung in her memory, but to get the honour of having composed it himself. He actually made a copy of the score, inscribed his own name on it as composer, and had it performed on the 14th December 1793. To the paragraph (p. 70) referring to the quartets Mozart wrote in 1773, and the influence of Haydn upon his style after their meeting in 1781, we may add that the six quartets of 1773 were apparently written after he had met with some of the quartets of Haydn. Holmes's conjecture (p. 258), that Mozart's letter to a certain baron must have been written in 1789 is correct so far as it goes; the date is settled by the fact that Mozart gives a similar account of the Hässler episode in a letter dated Dresden, 15th April 1789. It should be added, however, that Jahn and others do not admit the complete authenticity of the letter (to "the Baron von P.," not "the Baron V.," as Holmes gives it), which was first published by Rochlitz in volume xvii. of the *Allgemeine Musikalische Zeitung*. Jahn gives the date of the birth of Mozart's sister Maria Anna as the 30th July 1751, not 29th August as in Holmes (p. 4). The oratorio referred to on p. 30 was "Die Schuldigkeit des ersten Gebotes;" only the first part was by Mozart, the second being by Michael Haydn, and the third by Adlgasser. In the passage on p. 247, referring to Mozart's extra accompaniments to "Every Valley," "clarinets" is apparently a slip of the pen; it should be "flutes." Holmes's taste and judgment, too, are at fault—perhaps for the only time in the book—in his estimate of Gluck (p. 237). But after all it is surprising how little that is really essential has to be added to or deducted from his work, which is still the best, as it is the most concise, English life of Mozart for the general reader.

ERNEST NEWMAN.

BIBLIOGRAPHY

A Ramble among the Musicians of Germany, 1828; The Life of Mozart, 1845; Analytical and Thematic Catalogue of Mozart's Pianoforte Works, 1852; Critical Essay on the Requiem of Mozart, 1854.

CONTENTS

PART I

PAGE

HIS INFANCY 3

PART II

HIS BOYHOOD 33

PART III

HIS YOUTH 70

PART IV

HIS MANHOOD 138

APPENDIX 283

INDEX 299

PREFACE

THE only biographical notice of Mozart in English is a translation from the French of Bombet (M. Beyle), itself a translation
from the German of Schlictegroll—a sketch too short and scanty
to satisfy the interest of the subject, although quite enough to
pique public curiosity.   With the exception of occasional fragments in magazines and reviews, little more is known in England
of the life of the musician, its struggles, varied incidents, and
influence upon art; or of the brilliant reputations that clustered
round him.   The object of the following pages is to supply this
deficiency.

To Nissen, who married the widow of Mozart, we are indebted
for an elaborate collection (in the original German) of the
musician's correspondence, in which his character and genius
are revealed with the most charming candour and simplicity.
But this work is valuable chiefly for its materials; the compiler
undertook it in his old age, when he had lost his memory, and
was incapable of reducing his papers to a systematic arrangement.   He died over the book and left it in confusion.   All the
essential details of that publication are carefully preserved in
their natural order in this volume; and the author's highest
ambition will be gratified, if it be found that nothing of value or
interest has been suffered to escape.

Every available source of information has been diligently
explored to render this memoir complete; and the author has
endeavoured throughout, as much as possible, to let Mozart tell
his own story.   By the collation of André's catalogue with
Mozart's own catalogue, and other scattered memoranda, a full
account of Mozart's compositions is here, for the first time, given
to the public; the original MSS. have been personally inspected;
various fresh channels of inquiry have been opened up; all published authorities, including incidental references in fugitive
periodicals, have been consulted; and the narrative of his life,
gathered from every quarter, is thus conducted uninterruptedly
to the close.

A

THE LIFE OF MOZART

PART I

HIS INFANCY

LEOPOLD MOZART, the father of the great musician, was the son of a bookbinder at Augsburg. He was born December 14, 1719, and was in due time removed to the University of Salzburg, where he studied jurisprudence; whether with undecided views of a profession, is doubtful—for he had already made himself skilful in music, and was an admirable performer on the violin. On leaving the university he was received into the family of Count von Thurn, a canon of the cathedral, and by him afterwards recommended to the notice of the Archbishop of Salzburg, who entertained him in the capacity of valet-musician.

This appointment, however degrading it may appear to modern ideas of the dignity of art, offered at that time the best prospect of preferment in the establishments of the great; and Leopold Mozart found it so, for he was by degrees removed from the meaner servitude, made one of the court musicians, and subsequently vice kapellmeister.[1] Among names distinguished in music and enrolled in the service of the court of Salzburg, are those of Eberlin, Michael Haydn, etc. The emoluments of a post in the orchestra of the archbishop, from the highest member of it to the lowest, were incredibly small; but the country was cheap, there was sufficient for a simple, contented life, and the musician's widow was provided for at his death.

In his 21st year Leopold Mozart made himself advantageously known by the production of six violin trios, which, being too poor to publish them in the ordinary way, he *engraved* himself. These trios and a collection of twelve pieces for the clavier,[2] under the

[1] Composer, and conductor of the orchestra.
[2] The clavier, a keyed instrument (as its name implies), was the precursor of the pianoforte. Though weak in tone, it possessed the same power of sustaining sounds, and was capable of delicate expression. Mozart often used the term " clavier " indifferently for itself and the pianoforte.

3

quaint title—" The Morning and Evening melodiously and harmoniously introduced to the Inhabitants of Salzburg "— pieces which it seems were daily performed at the times alluded to, by a band on the fortifications, are the only compositions that he ever published. But until convinced of the great superiority of the genius of his son, he was a most industrious composer, as his MSS. evince. Before he surrendered the pen to abler hands, he had accumulated twelve oratorios, besides a great variety of pieces for the church and theatre, several pantomimes, more than thirty grand serenades, many symphonies, concertos for wind instruments, trios, etc.

He did much to raise the character of the archbishop's musical establishment. His style of composition is described as having been contrapuntal and solid; consequently better adapted for ecclesiastical than secular purposes. But as a composer he remained within the trammels of the fashion of his day—subject to all its stiffness and formality; and it was only as his son's genius opened, and his different manner of writing became apparent, that the father discovered his own talent to lie rather in the didactic than the inventive part of music.

No sooner was Leopold Mozart fairly established with the archbishop, than he married a young person to whom he had long been attached, named Anna Bertlina, a ward of the institution of St. Gilgen. The newly-married pair were so conspicuous for beauty of form, that it was said at the time so handsome a couple had never before been seen at Salzburg. Of seven children, the issue of this union, a girl and a boy alone survived the period of infancy. The girl, named Maria Anna, was born on the 29th of August, 1751; and her brother, John Chrysostom Wolfgang Amadeus, the subject of this biography, on the 27th of January, 1756.

As his family increased Leopold Mozart was obliged to devote every hour that he could spare from his laborious official duties, to tuition on the violin and clavier; and being soon in high esteem for the pupils he had formed, his circumstances so far improved as to enable him in the year of Wolfgang's birth to publish at his own expense a work of considerable importance in the theory and practice of music, entitled " An Attempt towards a Fundamental System for the Violin." [1] This performance gradually extended his reputation as an artist and as

[1] *Versuch einer gründlichen Violinschule, mit vier Kupfertafeln, etc. versehen.*—AUGSBURG.

a methodical, sound, and intelligent instructor, throughout the whole continent; and it may be undoubtedly considered, next to the education of his own son, as the greatest benefit he ever conferred upon the art. The selection of examples and the system of fingering laid down in this violin school were thought excellent; and though an approximation to that of Tartini was discovered in the general principles, it permitted much greater freedom in the management of the bow. The best violin players of Germany during the latter half of the eighteenth century formed themselves upon the principles inculcated in this work.

Even at this day the name of Mozart had emerged from obscurity and was mentioned by musicians with respect. In proof, it may be told that one of the earliest publications in musical literature, the critical letters on the art printed at Berlin, in 1759-60, which were successively addressed to the most distinguished men, such as Emanuel and Friedemann Bach, Kirnberger, Marpurg, Benda, etc., made its *coup d'essai* with Leopold Mozart. " Could we," said the writer, " in addressing our weekly musical dissertations to some man of eminent desert, make a fitter commencement than with yourself? "

Leopold Mozart possessed, in addition to his musical talent, a strong feeling for the sister arts, and no inconsiderable share of literary ability. One instance will suffice to portray his romantic and enthusiastic character. Having read some of the devotional verses of the Protestant poet Gellert with much pleasure, he addressed to him, though a stranger, a letter so full of feeling and elegance, that Gellert, delighted at the compliment, replied in the warmest terms of friendship and regard. They never met, however, for the poet was at this time an hypochondriacal invalid, and soon afterwards died.

Within the circle of his immediate acquaintance at Salzburg, the character ascribed to this musician was that of a satirical humorist. He exhibited a singular compound of qualities—a mixture of sense and superstition, of enthusiasm and caution, of benevolence and prejudice; but the impression left by his intercourse was on the whole highly agreeable, and he lived not less admired for his talents than esteemed for his character.

The wonderful musical genius of his family came to light almost accidentally. When the girl had reached seven years of age she became her father's pupil on the clavier, at which her progress was great and uniform, and finally made her mistress

of the highest reputation that any female performer had ever
acquired on a keyed instrument. Her brother, at this time
three years old, was a constant attendant on her lessons, and
already showed, by his fondness for striking thirds, and pleasing
his ear by the discovery of other harmonious intervals, a lively
interest in music. At four he could always retain in memory
the brilliant solos in the concertos which he heard; and now
his father began, half in sport, to give him lessons. The musical
faculty appears to have been intuitive in him, for in learning to
play he learned to compose at the same time:—his own nature
discovering to him some important secrets in melody, rhythm,
symmetry, and the art of setting a bass. To learn a minuet he
required half-an-hour; for a longer piece, an hour; and having
once mastered them, he played them with perfect neatness and
in exact time. His progress was so great, that at four years of
age, or earlier, he composed little pieces which his father wrote
down for him.

In teaching his children Leopold Mozart at first employed
manuscript lessons written by himself in a book appropriated
to that purpose; composition or the transcribing of music was
perpetually going forward in his house; and thus the little boy,
with the love of imitation natural at his age, was led to make
his first essays in holding the pen—those of a composer. The
book in which the father wrote the infantine productions of his
boy was preserved by the sister as a precious relic to the end of
her life; and though it would be gratifying to see his *first*
composition as the source of a mighty stream of genius, some
uncertainty exists as to its precise identity. However, the specimen here given was undoubtedly composed in his fourth year.

During 1760 and the two following years, he was continually
exercising himself in this manner,[1] and acquired great experience
in design and modulation; and now the father, no longer in
doubt respecting the precocious genius of his son, resolved to
bring both him and his sister to the Bavarian court at Munich,
whither he carried them in January 1762.

The boy was always extremely animated and intelligent.
Before he applied himself to music he entered into the usual
pastimes of childhood with such interest, that over a pleasant
game he would forget everything, even his meals; but afterwards he lost much of his relish for these recreations, or liked

[1] A characteristic selection from these compositions will be introduced
at the end of the work.

them only in proportion as they were mixed with music. One of the great favourites of Wolfgang, and his especial playmate, was Andreas Schachtner, the principal trumpeter in the archbishop's band; a man of cultivated mind and considerable

talent in poetry, the intimate friend of the family. Whenever the playthings were removed from one chamber to another, if this companion were with him, it must be done to music; and he who carried nothing must play or sing a march. Such was the ascendancy that the art had gained.

His disposition was characterised by an extreme sensibility and tenderness, insomuch that he would ask those about him ten times a day whether they loved him, and if they jestingly answered in. the negative, his eyes would fill with tears.

The first studies in arithmetic were pursued by little Wolfgang with such ardour, as for a time to supplant even music in his affections. The walls, the chairs, the tables, and even the floor were now covered with figures; and his predilection for this branch of science, with the reputation of expertness in it which he now acquired, were preserved by him throughout life.

His desire of knowledge was great on all subjects; but in music he astonished his teacher, not so much by an avidity of information, as by the impossibility of telling him anything which he did not know before. This was a mystery which Leopold Mozart contemplated in silent amazement. Had he merely shown the same excellent disposition for music as his sister, merely made the same rapid progress on the clavier, there would have been little to astonish even in an age when infant musical education, now so well understood and appreciated, was in a great degree experimental; but to see this child so early display the ambition, and even the science of the composer, was truly wonderful. The genius thus revealed in various incidents, partly comic and partly pathetic, raised in the paternal heart feelings of devout gratitude, and in every friend of the family the warmest interest and sympathy.

One day as Leopold Mozart, accompanied by a friend, had just returned home from church, he found little Wolfgang very busy with pen and ink. " What are you doing there? " said his father. " Writing a concerto for the clavier," replied the boy. " The first part is just finished." " It must be something very fine, I dare say—let us look at it." " No, no," said Wolfgang, " it is not ready yet." The father however took up the paper, and he and his friend began at first to laugh heartily over his gallimatias of notes, which was so blotted as to be scarcely legible; for the little composer had continually thrust his pen to the bottom of the ink-stand, and as often wiped away with the palm of his hand the blot thus brought up, intent solely upon committing his thoughts to writing. But as the father examined the composition more attentively, his gaze became riveted to the page, and tears of joy and wonder began to roll down his cheeks, for there were ideas in this music far beyond the years of his son. " See," said he, smiling to his friend, " how regularly and correctly written it is; though no use can be made of it, for it is so immensely difficult, nobody could play it." " It is a concerto," returned little Wolfgang, " and must be practised before it can be performed. It ought to go in this way." He then began to play it, but was unable to accomplish more than give a notion of his design. This concerto was written with a full score of accompaniments, and even *trumpets and drums*.[1]

What the ideas of a child of six years old could have been respecting the combination and employment of instruments may be dismissed from the imagination for another wonder, which is, however, rather a matter of fact than of conjecture; namely, that at this age Mozart knew the effect of sounds as represented by notes, and had overcome the difficulty of composing unaided by an instrument. But having commenced composition without recourse to the clavier, his power in mental music constantly increased, and he soon imagined effects, of which the original type existed only in his own brain.

Leopold Mozart had now for some time declined all engagements as a teacher of music at Salzburg, the better to superintend the education of his children. Of the journey which the father, son, and daughter made to Munich, in January 1762, no further intelligence has transpired than that they remained three weeks; that Wolfgang performed a concerto in the presence of the elector, and together with his sister excited lively admiration.

From this successful opening tour the children returned to Salzburg, to pursue their music with renewed spirit; and the boy began at this time to make acquaintance with the violin,[2]

[1] So says Nissen; but the trumpets and drums are probably a biographical flourish, designed to embellish a story that needed no addition of the marvellous. The scores of Mozart, which have been preserved from his tenth year, show that he wrote for use, and not for ostentation; his wind instruments being seldom more than oboes, bassoons, and horns; such, in fact, as the orchestras of the day readily supplied.

[2] Nissen and other biographers of Mozart state that he brought this violin from Vienna, at the close of 1762, and first began to practise it by stealth. There is improbability on the face of this story; but it is distinctly disproved by a letter of Leopold Mozart's, written on the road to

somebody having presented him with a little instrument adapted to his size and age. New faculties and fresh sources of wonder were now disclosed.

Before he had received any regular lessons, his father was one day visited by a violinist named Wenzl, an excellent performer, for the purpose of trying over some new trios of his composition. Schachtner the trumpeter, who tenderly loved the little musician, has related the anecdote connected with this performance. " The father," he says, " took the bass part on the viola, Wenzl played the first violin, I the second. Little Wolfgang entreated that he might play the second violin; his father, however, would not hear of it, for as he had had no instruction, it was impossible that he could do anything to the purpose. The child replied, that to play a second violin part it was not necessary to have been taught; but the father, somewhat impatiently, bid him go away and not disturb us. At this he began to cry bitterly, and carried his little fiddle away, but I begged that he might come back and play with me. The father at last consented. ' Well, then, you may play with Herr Schachtner, but remember, so softly that nobody can hear you, or I must immediately send you away.' We played, and the little Mozart with me, but I soon remarked to my astonishment that I was completely super-fluous. I silently laid my violin aside and looked at the father, who could not suppress his tears. Wolfgang played the whole of the six trios through with precision and neatness; and our applause at the end so emboldened him, that he fancied he could play the first violin. For amusement we encouraged him to try, and laughed heartily at his manner of getting over the difficulties of this part, with incorrect and ludicrous fingering indeed but still in such a manner that he never stuck fast."

On the 19th of September 1762, the whole family set out for Vienna. The letters during their tour are addressed to M. Hagenauer, at Salzburg, an Italian merchant, in whose house they lived, occupying the second floor, the ground floor being the warehouse—incidents in the picture of their home, which are introduced merely to help the imagination to a feeling of the locality in which the childhood of Mozart was principally passed. We must content ourselves with a few notes on the road.

The Bishop of Linz was so fascinated by the children, that he detained them five whole days at Passau; by which they lost

Vienna, where he describes the boy softening the custom-house officer by a minuet on the violin.

money. Concerts, however, replaced it, and now for a glimpse of the little musicians in the simple but picturesque language of the father.

" The children are in good spirits, and everywhere just as if at home. The boy is frank and confiding to every one, but particularly to officers, whom he seems to have known all his life. My children are the admiration of every one, the boy especially. Counts Herbenstein and Schlick, the principal personages of this place, will make a great noise about us at Vienna, and in all probability our affairs will prosper, God only preserving us, as hitherto, in health. I request you to have four masses offered for us at Maria-Plain [1] as soon as possible."

On the 16th of October he writes from Vienna:

" We left Linz on the Feast of the Holy St. Francis, and arrived at Matthausen. The following Tuesday we reached Ips, where two Minorites and a Benedictine, who had been our companions on the water, said mass, between which our Wolferl [2] rattled about on the organ, and played so well, that the Franciscan fathers who were entertaining some guests at dinner, quitted the table, and together with their company hastened into the choir, when their astonishment was inexpressible. At night we were at Stein, and arrived here on Wednesday. Our business with the revenue officers was short, and from the principal search we were entirely absolved. For this we had to thank our Mr. Wolferl, who made friends with the *douanier*, showed him his clavier, and played him a minuet on his little violin." . . .

Here follows a long list of counts, chancellors, and bishops, at whose houses they " conversed with the first ministers and ladies. Everywhere," writes the father, " the ladies are in love with my boy. By this time we are the common talk in all places." At the opera he overhears the Archduke Leopold speaking about his son with some one in another box, and con-

---

[1] A celebrated shrine lying at a short distance from Salzburg. Leopold Mozart and his correspondents, Hagenauer and his wife, were genuine inhabitants of a monastic city, steady believers in the efficacy of vows, the mediation of saints, and every other article of Catholic devotion. Such traits of simplicity and religion in the letters of a man, now plunging into the vortex of fashionable life, are highly characteristic, and well display the school of morals and manners in which Mozart was educated.

[2] The household diminutive of Wolfgang, in Germany, where *erl* seems to be the common termination of all the names used in the " little language " of affection.

ceives from this a favourable omen of his introduction to the emperor, concerning which he had been in some doubt. Mozart's first appearance at the Austrian court is thus described:

" At present I have not time to say more than that we were so graciously received by both their majesties, that my relation would be held for a fable. Wolferl sprang into the lap of the empress, took her round the neck, and kissed her very heartily. We were there from three to six o'clock, and the emperor himself came into the ante-chamber to fetch me in to hear the child play on the violin. Yesterday, Theresa's day, the empress sent us, through her private treasurer, who drove up in state before the door of our dwelling, two robes, one for the boy, the other for the girl. The private treasurer always fetches them to court." . . .

Meantime the father receives letters questioning him as to the extent of his absence from Salzburg. Such inquiries disquieted all his journeys. His replies intimate that he sees no probability of reaching home before Advent; but his mind is too much engrossed with his children to dwell much on that subject, although it gives him no little uneasiness.

" To-day we were at the French ambassador's, and to-morrow we shall go to Count Harrach's. We are everywhere fetched and sent back in the carriages of the nobility. We have agreed to be present from six to nine o'clock at a grand concert, in which all the greatest artists of Vienna will exhibit. Not to be too late, we are engaged four, five, even eight days in advance, as was the case with the Postmaster-general, Count Paar, on Monday. On one occasion we were at a place from half-past two till near four o'clock; then Count Hardegg sent his carriage for us, which took us full gallop to the house of a lady, where we stayed till half-past five; afterwards, we were with Count Kauniz till near nine.
" Would you like to know how Wolferl's dress looks? It is of a lily colour, of the finest cloth, with a waistcoat of the same, the coat, etc., with double broad gold borders. It was made for the Archduke Maximilian. Nannerl's dress is the court costume of an archduchess. It is of white brocaded taffeta, with all sorts of ornaments." . . .

But in the midst of all these triumphs, suddenly comes a reverse:

... "Happiness and glass, how brittle are ye! I had lready been thinking that we had been for a whole fortnight ut too happy, when it pleased God to send us a little cross, and ve thank His infinite goodness that it is now over. On the 21st, t seven in the evening, we were with the empress, on which ccasion Wolferl was not himself, and soon after exhibited a ort of scarlet eruption. Pray get read three holy masses to .oretto, and three to the holy Francis de Paula."

.   .   .   .

His next letter is in better spirits:

"My little boy's danger, and my trouble, are now, thank iod! past. We paid our good physician with music yesterday. iome of the nobility have sent to us, in the meanwhile, to iquire after Wolferl, and to congratulate him on his *fête* day. That was, however, all."

The father expected presents. The nobility, however, who reatly dreaded small-pox, and every kind of eruptive disease, vere too much occupied by their fears, and the family passed our weeks in profitless seclusion. At the end of this time they vere again in public, and at court. The rest of the triumphs of he little Wolfgang consist in verses from "one Puffendorf;" hoe buckles from the Countess Theresa Lodron; and "nods nd wreathed smiles" from the empress. The Countess .eopold Kinsky even puts off on his account a party she was to iave given to Field-Marshal Daun—a marvellous great man, vho had a coat for every day in the year.

Characteristic traits remain to be added to the history of this ourney. The Emperor Francis took much pleasure in diverting iimself with the little magician, as he was wont to call Mozart, nd put his address to the test in a variety of ways; among ithers, by covering the keys with a handkerchief, and desiring iim to play with one finger. Such tasks as this taught the boy oon to distinguish between his hearers, and not to throw away iis best music upon those who did not appreciate it. He had he feeling of an artist; and in order to make him do his best t was necessary sometimes to deceive him, by telling him that his or that hearer was a profound connoisseur; his performance vas then full of fire and self-concentration, but in other cases he ilayed only trifles—dances and the like.

As he was one day about to commence a concerto, with the imperor seated near him at the clavier, on looking round he saw himself surrounded by court personages only. " Is M. Wagenseil here? " he inquired of the emperor. " He ought to be here; he understands the thing." Wagenseil was sent for, and the emperor having given up to him his place at the clavier, " I am going to play one of your concertos," said little Mozart, " will you turn over for me? "

It must be confessed that he was but an indifferent courtier. The princes of the imperial family cultivated music, and one of them (afterwards the Emperor Joseph) happening to exhibit a solo on the violin when the Mozarts were in attendance in the ante-room, heard the little critic exclaiming, " Ah! that was out of tune," and then again, " *Bravo !* " The honest, undisguised truths which the prince heard on this occasion he never forgot, nor ever recurred to them without good-humoured laughter.

The following anecdote relates also to this visit. As the two archduchesses were one day leading the boy between them to the empress, being unused to the highly polished floor, his foot slipped and he fell. One of them took no notice of the accident, but the other, Marie Antoinette, afterwards the unfortunate Queen of France, lifted him up and consoled him. He said to her, " You are very kind, I will marry you." She related this to her mother, who asked Wolfgang how he came to form such a resolution. " From gratitude," he replied, " she was so good; but her sister gave herself no concern about me."

At the beginning of the year 1763 the family were again at Salzburg, preparing for a journey of much greater extent in the summer. The delicate organisation of the young magician was shown at this time in an invincible horror of the sound of the trumpet. He could not bear that instrument when blown by itself, and was alarmed to see it even handled. His father, thinking to remove this childish fear, though, one must needs think, in this instance with less than his usual prudence, desired that it should be blown before him, notwithstanding all his entreaties to the contrary. At the first blast he turned pale and sank to the ground, and serious consequences might have ensued had the experiment been persisted in.

His ear was indeed exquisitely fine, of which the following is a proof. He had, on a certain occasion, played the violin of his friend Schachtner, which was so great a favourite with him on account of its soft, smooth tone, that his usual name for it was " the butter fiddle." Some days afterwards, Schachtner, on entering the house, found the boy amusing himself with his own little violin. "What have you done with your butter fiddle?" said he, and continued to play; but on a sudden he stopped, pondered awhile, and then added, "If you have not altered the tuning of your violin since I last played upon it, it is half a quarter of a tone flatter than mine here." At this unusual exactitude of ear and memory there was at first a laugh, but the father thought proper to have the violin sent for and examined, and the result proved that the boy was perfectly correct.

The wonder that his talents created, and the applause that he received, had no ill effects; he remained a simple and affectionate child, free from vanity, dutiful to his parents, who governed him rather by looks than words, and so obliging that how long soever he might have played, he was always ready to return to the instrument without a murmur, if his father desired it. He carried his obedience so far, that he would not accept presents, still less venture to eat anything offered him by friends without permission. The only point on which it was necessary to be peremptory with him was his music; for even at these years he would wholly forget himself in the pursuit of his ideas, and would often have sat playing, to the injury of his health, had he not been driven from the clavier.

Before he went to rest at night a little solemnity took place, which could not, on any occasion, be omitted. He had composed a tune, which was regularly sung by himself at this time, standing in a chair, while his father, standing near him, sang the second. The words were merely: *oragna figata fa marina gamina fa.*

Between the singing, and after it, he would kiss his father on the tip of the nose; and having thus expressed his childish affection, go quietly and contentedly to bed. This custom was observed till he had passed his ninth year. For his father and instructor, who appeared in every point of view in a light that commanded respect, he cherished sentiments of veneration, and one of his most ordinary sayings was, " God first, and then papa." [1] It was an odd fancy of his at this time, that when his father became old, he would have him preserved in a glass case, the better to contemplate and admire him.

The children having made great progress in music, the family, including the mother, set out on a new expedition on the 9th of June 1763. Wolfgang was now in his eighth year, and during this journey he played the clavier, the organ, and the violin; he sang, played, and composed extempore, played and transposed at sight, accompanied from score, improvised on a given bass, and was able, in fact, to answer every challenge. I thus group his performances in order to enable the reader to form an immediate estimate of the versatility of his powers.

The little party no sooner arrive at Wasserburg in Bavaria, than with the enthusiasm of musicians they immediately make their way to the organ in the cathedral. The incident as related in one of the father's letters, is full of interest.

" To amuse ourselves I explained the pedals to Wolfgang. He began immediately *stante pede* to try them, pushed the stool back, and preluded standing and treading the bass, and really as if he had practised many months. Every one was astonished; this is a new gift of God, which many only attain after much labour."

We next find them at Munich, from whence the father writes, on the 21st of June 1763.

. . . " Arrived on the 12th, and on the following day we drove to Nymphenburg. The Prince of Zweibrücken who made our acquaintance at Vienna, saw us from the palace window walking in the garden and beckoned to us. After he had conversed with us for some time, he inquired if the elector knew that we were here. Upon our replying in the negative he sent one of the gentlemen near him, to ask the elector if he would not like to hear the children, and a command was shortly sent to us to attend the concert at eight o'clock. Wolferl acquitted himself as usual.[2] On the next day we went to Prince Clement. The only difficulty now is to contrive how to free ourselves from this place, as people are kept waiting for their money so long

---

[1] *Nach Gott kömmt gleich der Papa.*
[2] He played a concerto on the violin, and made the cadences extempore.

here that they are at last glad to get what they have expended. On the 18th the elector dined in the city; we were present, and he, his sister, and the Prince Zweibrücken conversed with us during the whole entertainment. I permitted the boy to say that we should set out on the morrow. The elector twice expressed his regret at not having heard the girl; on the second occasion I replied that a couple of days would be of no consequence. I should not be detained by the prince, but he is waiting to see what the elector gives. Personally, I cannot complain of the elector, who is most gracious; he said to me yesterday, ' We are old acquaintances, it must be nineteen years since we first met.' But apostles themselves must first think of their own affairs and of the purse.

" P.S. We are at last furnished forth. The elector has sent us a hundred, and the prince seventy-five florins "

The next letter, dated Ludwigsburg, July 11, 1763, describes a profitless stay at Augsburg, and a tedious journey in search of the reigning duke, from whom it was difficult to gain either an audience, payment, or dismissal. The state in which Jomelli lived at Stuttgard with a great revenue, carriages and horses, while maintaining a houseful of his countrymen, forms an interesting feature of it. But intrigue is attributed to him, and great prejudice against the Germans.[1] At this place Leopold Mozart falls in with Nardini:

" I have heard a violin player named Nardini, who in beauty, equality, and purity of tone, and in a certain singing taste is not to be surpassed. He, however, plays no difficulties."

They shortly afterwards arrive at Schwetzingen, the summer residence of the court.

[1] The character here given of Jomelli seems to be the result of hasty and ill-founded suspicion. Metastasio describes him in a letter to Farinelli, dated November 1749, as of a spherical figure, gentle disposition, with an engaging countenance, pleasing manners, and excellent morals, " I have found in him all the harmony of Hasse, with all the grace, expression, and invention of Vinci." And in another letter: " If ever you should see him, you will be attached to him." When Leopold Mozart was at Naples, in 1770, he found occasion to change his opinion, and was quite won over by his kindness. The fate of Jomelli shows the sensibility of his nature. He had lived twenty years, with splendid reputation, in the service of the Duke of Wurtemburg, where he imbibed the German taste for harmony. On his return to Naples, he wrote two operas, which were thought heavy, and so ill received by his countrymen on this account, that vexation broke his heart. He composed his famous *Miserere*, and died.

B

" The Prince of Zweibrücken introduced us. Yesterday a concert was given on our account; it was the second since May, and lasted from five o'clock till nine. I had the pleasure to hear, besides good singers of both sexes, the admirable *flauto traverso*, Wendling.[1] The orchestra is incontestably the best in Germany, composed entirely of young people of good character —who are neither drinkers nor dicers—nor yet clownish persons; their conduct is as estimable as their talent. My children have set all Schwetzingen in commotion."

Passing through Heidelberg, their first visit, as usual, was to the organ.

" After walking about Heidelberg, our Wolfang tried the organ in the Heil. Geist Kirche, and played so admirably, that his name was ordered by the dean of the city to be inscribed on the organ as an eternal remembrance." [2]

The Elector of Mayence was ill: the family therefore gave one concert at the Roman King, and drove off to Frankfort.

" Our first concert here was on the 18th. All in astonishment as usual. Wolfgangerl in extraordinary spirits.

" One morning during the journey, Wolfgang on awaking began to cry. I asked him what was the matter. He said he was so sorry that he could not see his friends Hagenauer, Wenzl, Spitzeder, Reible, Leitgeb, Vogt, Cajetan, Nazerl, and the rest.[3] At Mayence, Nannerl was presented with an English hat, and a set of bottles for the toilet (worth four ducats); here again with a snuff-box, etc., and Wolfgang also with a snuff-box of porcelain.

" Indeed we are obliged to travel *noblement*, not only for the preservation of our health, but for the credit of our court; and

[1] Wendling afterwards became one of the most generous and enthusiastic of the friends of young Mozart, who took an opportunity of bringing his talents, and those of his daughters, conspicuously before the public, in the opera of " Idomeneo." The German flute, now in the infancy of its mechanism, was called the *flauto traverso*, to distinguish it from the *flute à bec*, which was held longitudinally. The length of the concerts in the middle of the last century, while the scope of instrumental music was yet limited, may be a subject of some surprise. In Germany they ordinarily lasted four hours—in Italy often five.

[2] Organ, inscription and all, are now gone. Several years ago the organ was sold for the use of some obscure church in the country.

[3] Chiefly names of musicians belonging to the chapel of Salzburg. As the common characteristic of childhood is readily to forget the associations of home amidst the excitement of strange scenes, this unusual trait of affection will not escape notice.

as we have no intercourse but with persons of rank and distinction, we are treated with great politeness and attention.

. . . " At Bonn we found no elector, but at Aix-la-Chapelle there was the Princess Amelia, sister of the King of Prussia. She has, however, no money. If the kisses that she gave my children, especially to Master Wolfgang, had been louis d'ors, we should have been well off ;—but neither host nor postmaster will take kisses for current coin."

He then describes the bad prospects for his expenses to Paris :

" My children have, indeed, had various costly presents, which I do not intend to turn into money. Wolfgang, for example, two magnificent swords; one from the Archbishop of Mechlin, Count Frankenburg, the other from General Count Ferraris. The girl has received a present of Flemish lace from the archbishop, and all sorts of finery from others. Of snuff-boxes, etuis, and the like, we have enough to set up a shop. I suppose that a box full of our Peruvian treasures, has reached Salzburg by this time. But in money I am poor." . . .

These frequent references to money difficulties in the letters of the elder Mozart, in a correspondence which it must be borne in mind was strictly confidential, afford curious evidences of the state of society, and the absolute poverty of the nobility.

So far as Leopold Mozart's own feeling was concerned, his constant disappointments in this way, perplexed as they were by overwhelming personal kindnesses, had no other effect upon him than as they threatened from day to day to impede and embarrass his progress.

The family were favourably introduced at Paris, through the lady of the Bavarian ambassador, daughter of Count Arco, chamberlain to the Archbishop of Salzburg. They were lodged in her hotel; but it was a time of court mourning, which formidably increased their expenses and obstructed their receipts. In spite of the recurrence of these details, they are essential to impress the nature of the expedition, and the fortunes of the artists upon the reader.

A letter in Grimm and Diderot's correspondence enables us to follow our hero into the private society of Paris. Details of facts already familiar are omitted.

" The other day a lady asked him if he could accompany by ear an Italian cavatina which she knew by heart. The child began a bass which was at first not absolutely correct—it being impossible to accompany a song, the melody of which is unknown beforehand; however, no sooner was the performance at an end than he requested the lady to begin again, and now he not only played the melody with the right hand, but accompanied it with the bass without the least embarrassment; and this he did ten times, at each repetition altering the character of his accompaniment. He would have continued it twenty times had he not been stopped."

The account of the reception of the family by the French court at Versailles is wanting in the correspondence. This void has been partly supplied by Mozart's sister, who remembered that Madame de Pompadour had her brother placed upon a table, and upon his advancing to salute her, she turned away: upon which he said, rather angrily: "Who is this that will not kiss me? The empress kissed me."

The little boy played before the Royal Family at Versailles; and gave an organ performance in the chapel there, which was attended by the whole court. His organ playing was more highly esteemed at this period than even his performance on the clavier. Two grand concerts were also given before the public at large, and the Mozarts became much in fashion;—their portraits were elegantly engraved, poems were written upon them, and they were everywhere treated with distinction. Here too, Wolfgang published his first works: two sets of sonatas for the clavier with an accompaniment for the violin—the one dedicated to Madame Victoire, the king's second daughter; the other to the Countess Tessé.

Wolfgang received in acknowledgment a gold snuff-box from the countess, while the Princess Carignan, with oriental gusto and elegance, presented him with a silver standish and silver pens. "The people are all crazy about my children," writes the father. The satirical humour of Leopold Mozart is well displayed in a letter addressed to Madame Hagenauer, dated Paris, February 1, 1764. He regrets the odious ugly embellishments and excessive painting of the French ladies, and continues:

"As for their religion—the miracles of the French female saints, I assure you, are not scarce, the greatest are performed by those who are neither maids, wives, nor widows—and are all worked by the living body. Suffice it to say, that it costs some trouble here to discover who is the mistress of the house;

every one lives according to his or her fancy, and if there is
not a special mercy of God, it will one day fare with the state of
France as of old with the kingdom of Persia." . . .

A picture of the etiquette of the court of Versailles with the
triumph of natural emotion over lifeless forms and ceremonies
is introduced:

" I may observe that it is not the custom here to kiss the
hands of the royal family; or to molest them when they are
au passage as they call it (that is when they traverse the royal
apartments and gallery in their way to church), by presenting
any petition or speaking to them; nor when the king or any of
the royal family passes is there any bowing, or kneeling, or
other testimony of respect than that of standing perfectly erect
and motionless. In this posture the king and his family pass
close before one, and you may imagine what sort of impression
must have been made upon a people so wedded to the formalities
of their court as the French, when I tell you that the king's
daughter, both in the apartments and in the public *passage*,
as soon as she saw my children stopped, drew near them, and
not only gave them her hand to kiss, but kissed them and
received numberless kisses in return. The same may be said of
Madame the Dauphiness.

" But what most astonished the spectators was, that at the
public dinner, *au grand couvert*, on New Year's evening, *we alone
had the way cleared for us to the royal table*,[1] where Master Wolf-
gangus had the honour to stand near the queen, to converse
with and amuse her constantly—now and then eating something
which she gave him from the table, or kissing her hand. The
queen speaks as good German as we do; but as the king knows
nothing of it, the queen interprets all that our heroic Wolfgang
says."

On Christmas Day they went to the chapel of Versailles, and
attended matins and three masses. The music is thus described:—

" I heard there music that was both bad and good. Everything performed by single voices, which was intended to pass as
an air, was vapid, cold, and miserable; in a word, French; the
choruses, however, were all good, indeed excellent. I went
daily with my little man into the royal gallery, at the king's

[1] The Swiss Guard marched before them. How astounding to the
faculties of poor Madame Hagenauer must have been this grandeur; but,
in reality, in the history of events, what a trifle!

mass, to hear the choir in motets, which are always executed. The king's mass is at one o'clock, except he goes hunting, and then it takes place at ten o'clock; and the queen's at half-past twelve."

The next topic is the difficulty of their movements in Paris, often made in three sedan-chairs, when the weather was bad; and the expense of which, combined with a court mourning, was serious. As usual, the court delayed to pay them, and their affairs, in German phrase, travelled " by the snail post." Leopold Mozart is now discursive on French manners:

" Pomp and splendour are still extravagantly admired and pursued by the French, consequently, no one is rich but the farmers; the gentry are overwhelmed with debts. The greatest riches are possessed by some hundred persons, among whom are several bankers and *fermiers généraux*, and their money is chiefly spent on Lucretias, *who, however, do not stab themselves.*"

Now for the fashions of the day:

" The ladies wear their clothes trimmed with fur in summer as well as winter; they wear fur round their necks, fur in their hair instead of flowers, and on their arms instead of bands, etc., etc. The most laughable thing is to see a sword band (which is here the fashion) ornamented with a fur border. That must be a capital method to prevent the sword from freezing."

He then comments on the selfish and unnatural practice of deserting their new-born children, which prevailed among the Parisians, and gives a dreadful picture of its effects:

" But observe the wretched consequences (of committing children to the nursing of peasants). You will scarcely find any place so abounding in miserable and mutilated objects. Scarcely have you been two minutes in a church, or walked through a couple of streets, than you are beset by some blind, lame, deformed, or half-putrifying beggar; or you see some one lying in the street, whose hand when he was a child was devoured by a pig; or another, who, at the same time of life, fell into the fire while his nurse and her husband were at work in the fields, and had half his arm burnt off; besides a crowd of others whom I could not from disgust ever look at in passing.

" Now to turn from the horrible to the charming, and first to that which has charmed a king. You would like, would you not, to know what sort of looking person Madame de Pompadour is? She must have been very handsome, for she is still an elegant person. Her figure is imposing; she is large and plump, but well proportioned; her complexion fair, with some resemblance in her eyes to the empress. Her apartments towards the garden at Versailles are like a paradise, and she has a magnificent hotel just built in the *Faubourg St. Honoré* at Paris. In the room where the harpsichord was, which was gilt and beautifully ornamented and painted, we observed her portrait and the king's, both of the size of life.

"There is constant war here on the subject of French and Italian music. French music, the whole of it put together, is not worth a straw; but desperate attempts are now making to introduce something better, and as the French are beginning to give way, I hope that in ten or fifteen years there will be no such thing as French taste. The engraver has now in hand four sonatas by Mr. Wolfgang Mozart. Imagine the noise these sonatas will make in the world, when people read on the title page that they are the work of a child seven years old, and one who, if unbelievers demand a proof, which has happened ere now, is in condition to set the bass, or the second violin part, to any minuet that may be laid before him, without troubling the clavier. You will in time hear how excellent these sonatas are; an *Andante* in one of them is of especial taste. I may tell you that God daily works new wonders in this child. On our return he will, please God, be able to do good service in the court music. He now accompanies at all public concerts. He transposes *prima vista* the airs he accompanies, and everywhere plays off at sight whatever pieces may be placed before him, whether Italian or French. My girl plays the most difficult pieces by Schoberth and Eckard that are yet known; among these the most difficult are by Eckard, which she executes with incredible clearness; indeed, in such a manner, that the envious Schoberth cannot conceal his jealousy, which has occasioned much merriment."

The concerts of the children were given at the theatre *de M. Felix, rue et porte St. Honoré.* This was a little theatre in the house of a man of fortune where the nobility got up private amateur performances. Madame de Clermont, who resided there, procured them the favour; she was, however, assisted dy the Duke de Chartres, etc., leave for two concerts being bir ctly opposed to the privileges of the opera.

Here we have a character of Grimm, very different from that drawn by Rousseau in the *Confessions* yet not altogether inconsistent with its veracity:

" This Mr. Grimm, the most particular friend that I have here, a man of learning and of great benevolence, is secretary to the Duke of Orleans. My letters were all useless, whether of the French ambassador at Vienna, or the Austrian ambassador at Paris, or the recommendation from the minister at Brussels— even from Prince Conti, the Duchess d'Aguillon, and others, of whom I could compose a litany. The single Mr. Grimm, to whom I had a letter from a merchant's wife at Frankfort, did everything. He mentioned us at court, and provided for our first concert, towards which he sold 320 tickets, and consequently paid me 80 *louis d'ors*. He gave us also our wax lights. . .

" M. de Mechel, an engraver, is now hard at work on our portraits, which have been very well painted by M. von Carmontelle, an amateur. Wolfgang is playing the clavier, I behind his chair the violin. Nannerl leans with one arm on the clavier, and holds in the other hand music as if singing." . . .

Having succeeded well at Paris, the family set out for England, by way of Calais, on the 10th of April 1764, and remained there till the middle of the following year. They lodged in London at the house of a Mr. Williamson in Frith Street, Soho. Both the children were heard by their majesties on the 27th of the same month, and again in the month following, when the boy played on the king's organ with similar approbation to that he had already received at Versailles.

The public performances of the young musicians consisted principally of double concertos on two claviers; the boy also sang airs with the greatest feeling. Both in Paris and London it was usual to place before him various difficult pieces by Bach, Handel, Paradies, etc., which he played off, not only at sight and with perfect neatness, but in their exact time and style. It is related of John Christian Bach, music master to the queen, that he took little Mozart between his knees and played a few bars, which the boy continued; and that thus changing and playing by turns, they performed an entire sonata admirably, and as if by one pair of hands. Mozart ever retained the greatest regard for this Bach and his works.

The account of their first appearance at the English court is dated London, May 28, 1764.

. . . " On the 27th of April, five days after our arrival, we were with their majesties from six to nine o'clock. The present we received on leaving the royal apartments was twenty-four guineas only, but the condescension of both the exalted personages is indescribable. Such were their friendly manners, that we could not believe ourselves in the presence of the king and queen of England. . . . What we have here experienced surpasses everything. A week afterwards, we were walking in St. James's Park when the king and queen came driving by, and although we were all differently dressed, they knew and saluted us; the king, in particular, threw open the carriage window, put out his head, and laughing, greeted us with head and hands—particularly our Master Wolfgang. . . .

" On the 19th of May we were again with their majesties from six o'clock to ten. Nobody was present but the two princes, the brother of the king and the brother of the queen. Twenty-four guineas again on going away.

" We are going to take what they call a benefit on the 5th of June, though the usual concert season is now over, and as the expenses will be forty guineas we cannot hope to get much. *Basta !* We shall do well enough, if through God's blessing we all keep well, and particularly our intrepid Wolfgang.

" The king placed before him pieces by Wagenseil, Bach, Abel, and Handel, all of which he played off. He played on the king's organ in such a manner that his hearers preferred him on the organ to the clavier. He then accompanied the queen in an air, and a performer on the *flauto traverso* in a *solo*. At last he took up the bass part of one of Handel's airs that by chance lay in the way, and upon the mere bass performed a melody so beautiful that it astonished everybody. In a word, what he was on leaving Salzburg is but the shadow of what he is at present; he surpasses all that you can imagine.

" He is now sitting at the clavier playing Bach's trio, and desires to be remembered to you; and not a day passes in which he does not speak of Salzburg, and of our friends and companions, at least thirty times. His head is at present full of an opera which he wishes to have performed by his young Salzburg acquaintance, and I am often obliged to reckon up the young people who are to compose his orchestra."

The concert of the family on the 5th of June was most fashionably patronised, and very profitable, though the father was alarmed at the extraordinary expense of an English orchestra. He records with due honour to the profession that " Most of the musicians would take nothing." Another concert was given at Ranelagh on behalf of a public charity. " I have permitted Wolfgangerl," says the father, " to play the British patriot and perform on organ concerto on this occasion. *Observe, this is the way to gain the love of the English.*" Of the former of these concerts he observes:

" I can send you no more particulars than you will find in the papers. It is sufficient to say that my girl is esteemed the first female performer in Europe, though only twelve years old, and that the high and mighty Wolfgang, though only eight, possesses the acquirements of a man of forty. In short, those only who see and hear can believe; and even you in Salzburg know nothing about him, he is so changed."

The father was evidently not prepared for the progress to which he bore testimony; his son had left Salzburg a prodigy of address and feeling in musical performance, but in the course of a few months he had overrun a great part of the field of high musical composition; he wrote for the orchestra with effect, and had intuitively acquired a power which in others is the result of long experience, foresight, and calculation. He was now about to commence symphonist and we shall see how he began. The cause was in a measure accidental.

Returning from a concert at Lord Thanet's, Leopold Mozart caught a severe cold which terminated in quinsy, and brought him to the brink of the grave. As every instrument was silent while he lay in this state, the boy, in order to employ himself, wrote a symphony, which was his first attempt of that kind. His sister sat near him copying while he was at work, and he said to her, "Remind me that I give the horns something good to do."

The symphony commences in this spirited manner:

The score consists of two violins, tenor and bass, two oboes, and two horns.

We detect the ardent nature of the boy, and his decisive mode of workmanship, in a curious postscript at the beginning of the next year. " The symphonies at all concerts are by Wolfgang." He must, therefore, have written others, which are lost.

The family now removed to Chelsea, and resided in the house of a Mr. Randall, in Five Field Row. The father being recovered orders twenty-two masses, and undertakes the conversion of " one Sipruntini, the son of a Dutch Jew," a great violoncello player. How he sped is not known, but he desires to acquire the character of a missionary. Towards the close of 1764 appeared a third set of sonatas, dedicated to Queen Charlotte,[1] for which she sent fifty guineas. The dedications of these works, written for the composer with all the affectation and exaggerated compliment that belong to the *vieille cour,* would give a bad impression of the artless child, had not the Hon. Daines Barrington painted him to the life in a couple of sentences: " Whilst playing to me," he writes, " a favourite cat came in, on which he left his harpsichord, nor could we bring him back for a considerable time. He would also sometimes run about the room with a stick between his legs by way of horse." These are certainly not the diversions of a man, and yet, despite them, the infantine voice and childish countenance, it is curious that he suspected the father of imposition with regard to his son's age. Mr. Barrington made his visit to the Mozarts the subject of a long paper in the *Philosophical Transactions;* he went expressly to puzzle the boy, but found it beyond his power. The child played his score of a new duet, and sang a part in it at sight; he also sang two extemporary dramatic airs on words selected by himself with the felicity of genius, *Affetto* and *Perfido,* conjuring up those inspirations of tenderness and reproach on the mere mention of a friend's name, the great singer, Manzuoli. Still, the Hon. Mr. Barrington having fortified himself by the opinions of sundry musicians, retained his doubts, and applied, through the Bavarian envoy, Count Haslang, for a certificate of the boy's birth, which, when obtained, fully vindicated the honour of the father, and left the son in full possession of his reputation as a musical prodigy. Young as he was, he even at this time exercised a permanent influence on English music. The first introduction of clavier

[1] Published by Bremner, in the Strand.

duets (pieces for four hands) is ascribed to him. Among the
trophies of his achievements in England, the father preserved
an official letter from the British Museum, acknowledging an
anthem, and other MS. compositions, the performances of his
" very ingenious son."   However, as time wore on, the family
began to feel the usual influences of declining novelty.   The
receipts of their concerts gradually diminished, while an outlay
of £300, which their first year in London had cost, did not tempt
them to try a second.   The father conceals the real causes of
his dissatisfaction under a sudden censoriousness on the subject
of English manners, to which it is surprising he did not earlier
give vent.   He had rejected some proposal, and lost money.
He continues:

" But what does it signify to talk much of a matter that I
resolved upon, after deep consideration, and many sleepless
nights, especially as it is now over, and I am determined not
to bring up my children in so dangerous a place as London,
where people for the most part have no religion, and there are
scarcely any but bad examples before the eyes. You would be
astonished to see how children are brought up here, to say
nothing of religion."

Their departure from England is announced in a letter from
the Hague, dated September 17, 1765.

" The Dutch ambassador in London had several times recommended us to go to the Prince of Orange at the Hague, but
preached to deaf ears. However, on the very day of our
departure, he visited our lodgings, and finding us gone, followed
us post haste, conjuring us to go to the Hague, as the Princess
von Weilburg, sister of the Prince of Orange, had a vehement
desire to see this child.   I complied the more readily as nothing
must be refused to a lady in her delicate state."

This was probably an excuse for his going to Holland, intended
to be communicated to the authorities at home.   At Lille,
Wolfgang performed on the great new organ belonging to the
Bernhardine fathers, and at Antwerp on the organ in the
cathedral.   They had not been many weeks at the Hague before
the daughter was seized with so alarming an illness that it was
thought necessary to administer to her, as a dying person, the
last offices of the church. The good father prepared her to
resign herself to the divine will:

" Had any one heard the discourses which I and my wife and daughter had, and how we convinced her of the vanity of the world, and of the blessed deaths of children—Wolfgang in the meantime in another chamber amusing himself with his music—assuredly they could not have listened with dry eyes."

The following varies the monotony of a sick chamber by a truthful and characteristic touch.

" At last the Princess von W. sent the celebrated old Professor Schwenkel to us, who treated the disorder in a new manner. My daughter, who lay in a state between sleeping and waking, and was a little delirious, would sometimes in her doze begin to talk in one language, sometimes in another, which notwithstanding all our trouble made us now and then laugh a little. This also somewhat counteracted Wolfgang's melancholy."

The continuation of this letter illustrates the practical value of religion and its heavenly influence in the hour of sickness. But now for the superstition of this sensible man. He opens his prayer-book at a lucky spot, and conceives it to be a direct assurance from Heaven that his daughter will recover, which he ultimately does. Of course this was owing to the masses and invocations which he had ordered. He next expresses a kind wish to gratify his daughter in a peculiar fancy:

" My daughter," he writes, " had been thinking much of the pious Crescentia, and would gladly have a mass said in her honour. However, as we do not feel authorised to do this, until our church has decided something in relation to that holy personage, I leave it to your wife to discuss the matter with some of the Franciscan fathers in consistory, and to make such an arrangement, that my daughter may be satisfied, and the ordinances of God, and of our church, not violated."

Fresh misfortunes awaited the family in Holland where Wolfgang now fell ill, and with difficulty struggled through an inflammatory fever which greatly reduced him for several weeks. The kind sympathy of the court was not wanting on his occasion—for the father speaks of friends who shared their affliction, but whose names he would not mention lest it should be attributed to vanity. It is curious to observe how his Catholic prejudices rub off upon the road. At Augsburg, when he had just left home, he attributed the failure of his concert to the coldness of the Lutherans, but journeying to Paris he made the acquaintance of two Saxon advocates of that persuasion whom he furnished with letters to Salzburg, describing them as " the most delightful people," and *though they were Lutherans* different from any Lutherans that he had ever known. Now in Holland he finds the reformers absolutely " wise and pious.' It must be told that, notwithstanding a general prohibition of concerts in Lent, he was allowed to give two—because the miraculous gifts of the child redounded " to the honour and glory of God." Herein, perhaps, we may find a key to his modified opinions.

On recovering from the severe illness just mentioned, the young musician wrote a symphony and a *Quodlibet*[1] for the installation festival of the Prince of Orange; he next composed a set of six sonatas (the fourth during this journey) for the clavier and violin, which he dedicated to the Princess of Nassau-Weilburg, besides sundry airs and variations. What an evidence of application at a time when study and practice were so often interrupted by visits and performances! But this was not all; in March 1766 (probably for some solemnity in Lent) he produced an oratorio for two soprani and a tenor.[2]

The excitement of fancy in which he lived during the tour is well displayed in an anecdote preserved by his sister. He imagined himself a king; and that the population of his dominions were good and happy children. The idea pleased him so much that the servant who travelled with them — happening to draw a little—had to make a chart of this Utopia while the boy dictated to him the names of its cities, towns, and villages.

While the young composer was thus revelling in the visions of his own creation, the happiness of his father was alloyed with many anxieties. He was now returning home in considerable uncertainty respecting his reception by the archbishop, his leave of absence having long since expired. The tour in which he had engaged, though not altogether unprofitable in a pecuniary point of view, had still been less so than the great patronage which the family received, and the sensation they

---

[1] The title is " Galimathias Musicum." It is composed for the orchestra with a part for the harpsichord obligato. All the instruments have solos in turn, and the whole is wound up by a fugue on the national Dutch air " Prince William," which is described by the father as " sung, whistled and piped by everybody in Holland."

[2] The instrumental score is for four-stringed instruments, oboes, bassoons and horns. The date and superscription of the MS. are in the hand-writing of Leopold Mozart.

universally created, might have led them to expect. The profusion of the age in dress, and the necessity of keeping up a
certain style, caused a formidable deduction from their means;
while every now and then illness not only made further inroads
on their resources, but threatened in some fatal moment to
wreck all their hopes. At every step disquieting apprehension
went hand in hand with pleasure, and the more the parents
were convinced of the treasure of genius contained in that
mysterious casket—the brain of their son—the more their fears
for him augmented. To the natural gifts and affectionate
docility of his children, Leopold Mozart was indebted for being
no longer in the obscure station of a music-master at Salzburg,
but in a sphere better adapted to his disposition and talents—
travelling, and mixing in society which displayed the world
under its most interesting aspects of character and manners;
and if we would accurately picture to ourselves the state of his
mind, it is only necessary to consider how suddenly a death in
the little family might reduce him to his original condition—
to retrace the old path, and to contrast amid the miserable
realities of age, solitude, and poverty, the glorious achievements
of the time present. How far this was fulfilled the sequel will
show.

Meanwhile, the children, unconscious of the cares of which
they were the object, were cheerful and happy. Left much to
themselves in their recreations and amusements, with nothing to
divert them from each other's society, they seem to have lived
in a little world of their own, with a strong mutual necessity for
each other, and souls as harmonious as their own music. How
happy must the girl have been! What an enthusiastic admirer
of her brother, and how willing to have her smaller musical
capacity amplified and extended by the overflowings of his!

From the end of 1765 to May in the year following we have
no particular account of their movements. They are then discovered still in Holland, in good health and flourishing condition.
The father is rejoiced at being able to transmit his *Violin
School* to Salzburg, translated into Dutch, and published in
a handsome form.

" The publisher," he writes, " a bookseller in Haarlem, came
to me and presented the book in a most respectful manner. He
was accompanied by the organist, who invited our Wolfgang,
to play on the celebrated great organ at Haarlem, which he did

on the following morning. This organ is a magnificent work of sixty-eight stops, all of metal, as wood could not withstand the dampness of the climate."

Though urged to return direct to Salzburg, he was in no hurry to comply. After revisiting their old friend, the Archbishop of Mechlin, the family returned to Paris, whither Fame went before them. Even Leopold Mozart, so long second to his son, began to show the love of distinction. We find him positively charmed by receiving a visit from the Crown Prince of Brunswick, "a most agreeable, handsome, and friendly gentleman," who on entering says, "Are you the author of the *Violin School?*" It was at this time in Paris, that Wolfgang made his first essay in church music;—the Kyrie of a mass for four voices and four-stringed instruments. The melody of this composition has many traces of his peculiar suavity and grace.

The rest of the journey, though protracted to the end of the year, was a mere holiday excursion. We trace the travellers from Dijon to Lyons, thence into Switzerland, taking Winterthurm, Schaffhausen and Donauschingen on their return. The principal events of the whole time consist in joyful visits and invitations, and pathetic adieus. But at length they are on the road home, and the father revolves the plan of the future education of his children, not without a certain misgiving of events that may disconcert all his plans. Speaking of their progress, he writes:

"Every moment that I lose is lost for ever, and if I formerly knew how valuable time is to youth, I know it more now. You are aware that my children are used to work; should they learn to make excuses that any one, in the house for instance, hindered their occupation, and become accustomed to idle hours, my whole building would fall to the ground. Custom is an iron path. . . . But who knows what sort of reception we shall get on our arrival? Perhaps such an one that we shall be glad to pack up our knapsacks and set off again."

He had, in fact, become so fascinated with the pleasure of travelling, that we can scarcely consider this alternative, even in the gipsying style proposed, as very distressing.

PART II

HIS BOYHOOD

THE prophetic apprehensions of Leopold Mozart had a partial accomplishment, and before we establish the family again in the quiet of Salzburg, which was towards the close of the year 1766, it may be necessary to explain the " misgivings " which attended his return. These relate entirely to his serf-like position at the court of his prince. He feared that he had been educating musicians whose services would be appropriated without any acknowledgment; and though he escaped this during the life of the reigning archbishop, the course of a few years showed that his prognostics were not ill-founded.

As no one better appreciated his son's genius than Leopold Mozart, the silent gratitude and modesty with which he witnessed its gradual expansion, marks his good taste and feeling. Indeed, he was by this time so accustomed to his son's exploits, that far from expressing exultation at them, he only incidentally alluded to them in his correspondence. To what severe trials the invention and address of the boy were perpetually exposed, must, therefore, be learned from other pens; and when it is considered that any one failure would have involved irretrievable disgrace, his laurels will be deemed fairly and honourably won.

" I have seen him," says a writer from Paris,[1] " engage in contests of an hour-and-a-half's duration, with musicians who exerted themselves to the utmost, and even perspired great drops to acquit themselves with credit in an affair that cost their opponent no fatigue. He has routed and put to silence organists, who were thought very skilful in London. His playing with Bach is known—he did the same thing here with M. Raupach, a fine *extempore* player, formerly settled at St. Petersburg. He is in other respects one of the most amiable creatures that can be conceived—in all that he does or says, there is spirituality and feeling adorned by the peculiar grace and gentleness of childhood."

[1] Probably Grimm. The letter is dated 1766.

C

It is remarkable that the most doughty opponent with whom
he engaged on this journey, and chiefly in extemporaneou
fugue-playing, was a boy of his own age, named Bachmann, who
afterwards became a monk, and was never known more. Though
inaccessible to flattery, a sensitiveness to anything like dis
respectful treatment, was characteristic of his boyhood, as i
well shown in the following anecdote preserved by his sister.

" The family were one day visited, on their return from thi
tour, by a pompous gentleman, who was in some difficulty how
to address Wolfgang—whether in the respectful or familia
style.[1] At last he thought fit to steer a middle course. ' And
so *we* have been in France and England, and have been at court
and have done ourselves great honour.' The little hero, jealous
of his dignity, replied, ' Yet I never remember to have seen you
anywhere but at Salzburg.' "

There was now an interval of some months of comparative
repose, in which Mozart practised the works of Emanual Bach
Handel, and Eberlin, and studied the scores of Hasse, Handel
and the old Italian masters. He began, also, to receive some
honour in his own city—he was introduced to the especial notice
of the archbishop,[2] and employed by the university to write
music to a Latin comedy there enacted, called " Apollo and
Hyacinth." He wrote, in addition, an Easter cantata on the
subject of the Passion, a symphony, and four concertos for the
clavier. These last were probably composed in the prospect o
a journey to Vienna, which was undertaken by the whole family
on the 11th of September 1767.

One incident worth notice occurs on this journey. At the
monastery of Mölk the party went over the building withou
being known, but on touching the organ the organist immediately
discovered Wolfgang by his play. A royal marriage was on the
tapis at Vienna, but before a month had elapsed the breaking ou
of the small-pox, which carried off the bride of the King o
Naples, disconcerted all the plans of the travellers, and com

[1] In the third person plural, or the second person singular, by which th
Germans distinguish their more worshipful or familiar acquaintance.
[2] The Hon. Daines Barrington, who made frequent inquiries concernin
him after he left England, was informed, in the summer of 1768, that th
archbishop, not believing such masterly compositions could be genuine
had him confined for a week with music paper and the words of an oratorio
which he set within that time. The oratorio " La Betulia liberata," in tw
parts, is of the date referred to, but whether or not produced in the manne
described, is doubtful.

pelled their instant flight to Olmütz. There Wolfgang sickened,
and the father in his distress gratefully commemorates the kind
offices of a good Samaritan, Count Podstatsky, who, from the
mere impulse of benevolence, took a whole family with a child
in this condition into his house!

The time at Olmütz passed somewhat heavily, as the boy
lay blind nine days, and during the course of several weeks it
was necessary to be careful of his eyes. One of the friends who
visited him daily was the archbishop's chaplain, Hay (afterwards
Bishop of Königsgräz), an adept in all games with cards, and
under his instructions Wolfgang soon became a skilful competitor
in that art. A fencing master who came to the house was also
laid under contribution, and amused him by some lessons in
fencing. He entered with more than the usual vivacity of his
age upon any new exercise which demanded corporeal activity,
quickness of eye, and certainty of hand. If this exercise had
any heroic colouring, and were associated with ideas of manli-
ness and courage, so much the more pleasing was it to his
youthful imagination. Thus fencing and horsemanship were
as much in the ascendant with him now as billiards and dancing
at a future day. On the 29th of November the father writes
from Olmütz:

" *Iterum, iterumque Te Deum laudamus.*

" My daughter has got safely through the small-pox. I pray
you let a mass to Loretto be said."

Early in this year the boy composed a German operetta
called " Bastien und Bastienne," which was performed in a
private theatre, in the garden of Dr. Mesmer, a friend of the
family, who resided in the suburbs of Vienna.[1]

[1] It is in one act only, and has this pleasing introduction, which reminds
one of the " Sinfonia Eroica."

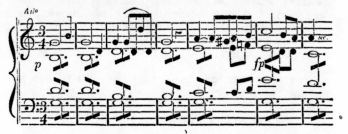

Hitherto admiration and sympathy had attended Mozart in his progress through Europe; but the scene was now to change. The attention which his genius for composition and his splendid clavier playing excited among the great, alarmed the musicians of Vienna for the stability of their reputation, and united them against him as their common enemy. This outbreak of envy towards a boy of twelve years of age is an unparalleled tribute to talent; but the testimony which is extorted at the expense of evil passions is scarcely worth what it costs. Truth and simplicity should be the basis of character in all who make ideal beauty the object of their lives, and the artist who wants these is no better than a money-changer in the Temple.

The favour which the Mozarts enjoyed at the Court of Vienna, of which the following is a picture, may account for the irritation that existed:

"You cannot possibly imagine," writes the father, "with what affability and goodness the empress conversed with my wife, partly respecting the children's small-pox, and partly upon our arduous journey; now and then patting her cheek or pressing her hands; the emperor, meanwhile, talking with Wolfgang upon music and other matters, or saying something that called up many a blush upon the face of Nannerl."

A boy of twelve, armed with four new concertos, and who demolished every difficulty that could be placed before him, was to be suppressed by stratagem. It were desirable that the crooked policy of the Viennese musicians, as described by the father, belonged only to history:

"The plan of operation adopted by these gentry (clavier players and composers) is to avoid every opportunity of seeing us, and of inquiring into the scientific attainments of Wolfgang. For why? In order that in the many instances in which they are asked, whether they have heard the boy, and what they think of him, they may answer—that they have not heard him; that it is impossible; that it is all quackery and harlequinade; that it is got up beforehand; that he had already learned the things put before him; that it is ridiculous to believe he composes.

"Now you understand why they shun us. For whoever has seen and heard, cannot thus speak without the risk of losing his character.

"I laid a trap for one of this sort of people. I had persuaded some one quietly to give us intelligence when he would be present, and our friend was to bring this person an extraordinarily difficult concerto, which could be placed before Wolfgangerl. We came together, and he had the opportunity of hearing his concerto played by Wolfgang, as if he knew it by heart. The astonishment of this composer and clavier player, and the expressions of admiration he used confirmed all that I have stated above. He ended by saying, 'I can say no less as an honest man, than that *this boy is the greatest man in the world;* it could not have been believed.'"

These cabals were not all—the family spent much money without any prospect of regaining it, accidents of various kinds prevented their giving concerts, and some of their noble friends were shy of the small-pox. In this state of affairs, it became desirable to retrieve their fortunes at a stroke; and the production of an opera, by enlisting the public on their side, offered the readiest means of putting their professional enemies to silence. The emperor had given the first idea of this work, and Leopold Mozart eagerly seized upon it, anxious to submit the genius of his son to the severest test. He had, however, a very low opinion of the public taste of Vienna; which has undergone little change during a century, and promised at the time alluded to but small success for music dependent on its own intrinsic merit. This is his character of it:

" That the Viennese in general have no taste for serious and sensible things, indeed, have no notion of them is well known; and their theatre, in which nothing prevails but childish trash, such as dances, devils, ghosts, witches, Jack-puddings, and harlequinades, proves it. One may see a gentleman, even one decorated with an order, clapping his hands and laughing himself out of breath at some harlequin's trick, or silly joke,[1] who during the most moving and beautiful situation, or the most eloquent dialogue, will talk so loud with a lady that his more sober neighbours can hardly catch a word."

The title of the libretto selected by Mozart for his opera was *La finta semplice,* and to the choice of an *opera buffa* the composer was probably determined rather by the means of the company than his own inclinations. There were no other singers at that time in Vienna; and, will it be believed that with such a

[1] The writer seems to be of opinion, with Dr. Johnson, that the measure of a man's mind is to be taken from his mirth.

set they even attempted Gluck's " Alceste! " The history of
this boyish work is one of managerial duplicity which though
common enough to those connected with theatres has peculiar
interest in reference to Mozart, and a moral for ill-used dramatic
genius in general. Hardly had the subject been proposed to
him than the work was completed; the next step seemed to be
to bring it out; but no—delays, excuses, evaded promises,
purposely confused rehearsals, and every other stratagem that
malice could suggest were put in operation to suppress it, till
at length it was as wholly ruined as if it had been committed to
the flames; for being written with a view to a particular company, it was unavailable for any other. The father, a man quite
ignorant of the strategy of theatres, was slow to conceive the
extent of secret animosity of which his son was the object; but
when he saw this, and the utter shamelessness and absence of
principle with which theatrical proceedings were conducted, his
indignation was unbounded, and the occasion certainly justified
it. " The whole hell of music," he writes, " has bestirred itself
to prevent the talent of a child from being known." It was
not merely the expense of a long stay in Vienna, undertaken on
the strength of this opera, which vexed him, but the plausibility
which its suppression would give to the voice of slander, and
the injury which might accrue therefrom both abroad and at
home. Once engaged in this odious business, however, he sees
with great acuteness the drift of his enemies whose object it was
to suppress the genius of his son till a few years had made it " fall
into the ordinary course of events." What added to his vexation was that his noble friends would not believe in the existence
of any cabal against the boy. In the midst of this dispute he
learns from Salzburg that his salary is suspended and even his
situation is in some danger, he is requested to return, but
refuses, and is determined to assert the honour of his son at
all hazards. He adroitly makes common cause with the archbishop:

" The honour of our gracious prince is also concerned. His
highness does not retain cheats, mountebanks, and liars in his
service and give them his gracious permission to travel into
foreign parts, like conjurers throwing dust into the eyes of
people, no; but like respectable men who travel for the credit of
their prince and fatherland, to acquaint the world what a
miracle it has pleased God to work in Salzburg."

He wished to conclude this opera successfully and go to Italy, foreseeing what *might* happen and what in fact *did* happen in spite of all the fame his son had acquired in boyhood.

" Or should I perhaps set myself down at Salzburg sighing for better fortune until Wolfgang is grown up, and see myself and children led by the nose till I am an old man and unable to undertake a journey, and Wolfgang is of an age and growth that have diminished the wonder at his performances.   But if my boy makes the first step in Vienna through his opera, ought he not to pursue so fair and open a path with increased diligence? "

· Wearied with promises, Leopold Mozart at length obtained an audience of the emperor and stated his grievances.   An examination was instituted into the whole affair, and the manager Affligio commanded to reply.   The history of the entire transaction is comprised in the following letter:

" After many of the nobility of this place had convinced themselves of the extraordinary talent of my son by the concurrence of foreign testimony with personal examination and proof, it was generally admitted that it would be one of the most remarkable events of either ancient or modern times were a boy of twelve years old to compose an opera and direct its performance himself.   This opinion was confirmed by an article written at Paris, in which the learned writer, after a detailed examination of the genius of my son, affirms that there is no doubt of this boy's competency to produce an opera at twelve years old.   Every one thought that in so famous a matter, a German ought to give his own country the preference; such was the unanimous opinion, and I followed it.

" The Dutch ambassador, Count von Degenfeld, to whom the ability of the boy was long since known in Holland, was the first who made the proposal to the manager Affligio; the singer Carattoli was the second; and the agreement with the manager was concluded at the house of the court physician, Laugier, in the presence of the young Baron von Swieten, and the two singers Carattoli and Caribaldi.   The whole party thought, the two singers especially expressing themselves with vehemence, that even middling music, from so young a boy, would be from its rarity wonderful; but that to see the child at the clavier, directing the orchestra, would draw the whole city to the theatre.   My son accordingly began to write.

" As soon as the first act was ready, I requested Carattoli

himself, in order to make sure, to come and hear it, and give
his opinion upon it. He came, and his astonishment was so
great that he returned the next day, bringing Caribaldi with
him. Caribaldi not less surprised, in a day or two brought
Poggi to me. Both applauded so loudly that upon my repeated
question whether they thought it good, whether he ought to
proceed, they showed some anger at the want of confidence, and
exclaimed frequently with emotion, *Cosa! Come! Questo è
un portento. Questa opera andrà alle stelle. Cuna meraviglia.
Non dubiti, che scrivi avanti!* with a multitude of the like
expressions. Carattoli said the same things to me in his own
chamber.

" Encouraged by the applause of the singers, I permitted my
son to continue the work, taking care, however, to make an
agreement for payment with the manager, through the Physician
Laugier. This was done, and Affligio, promised 100 ducats;
but to shorten my expensive stay in Vienna, I stipulated that
the opera should be performed before the emperor's journey
to Hungary. Some alterations, however, which the poet had
to make in the text retarded the composition, and Affligio
undertook to perform the work on the return of his majesty.

" The opera had now been ready some weeks, the copyists
were at work; the first, and shortly afterwards the second act,
were distributed. Meantime, my son on various occasions at
the house of the nobility, had been obliged to perform airs and
even the whole finale of the first act on the clavier; of which at
the house of Prince Kaunitz, Affligio was an eye and ear witness.

" The rehearsals were now about to begin; when—who could
have expected it? But from this time the persecutions of my
son commenced.

" It is of rare occurrence, indeed, that an opera goes well on
the first rehearsal, and without requiring alteration in any part.
For this reason it is usual to employ the clavier alone at the
commencement; and not to rehearse with the full orchestra, till
the singers have well studied their parts, particularly the finales.
Yet, here, quite a different course was adopted. The parts
had not been sufficiently studied; the singers had no rehearsals
at the clavier, and the finales had not been practised together;
and yet, they chose to rehearse the finale of the first act, with
the full orchestra, in order to give the work from the first a confused and unfavourable appearance. No one present could
call it a rehearsal without blushing. I will say no more of the

unkind behaviour of those whom their conscience accuses on this occasion. May God forgive them!

"When the rehearsal was over, Affligio said to me, that the music was good, but here and there a little too high, which would render some alterations necessary,—I could talk them over with the singers; and as his majesty would be back in twelve days, he would perform the opera in four, or at most, in six weeks without detaining me a day longer—and then there would be time to get everything in order; that he was a man of his word, and would keep his promises strictly, that alterations in operas were nothing new, other operas wanted them continually.

"The alterations required by the singers were accordingly made, and two new airs inserted in the first act; but during this time 'La Caschina' was performed at the theatre.

"The period appointed was now over, when I heard that Affligio had distributed the parts of another opera. A report was in circulation that Affligio would not perform the opera, and that he had even said the singers could not sing it: these, who had just before not only called it good, but extolled it to the skies.

"As a counterpoise to this scandal, I made my son play his opera through at the young Baron von Swieten's, in the presence of Count von Spork, the Duke of Braganza and other connoisseurs. The whole party were astonished at the pretext of Affligio and the singers; and they all with much emotion unanimously declared that so unchristian, false, and wicked an allegation was incomprehensible; that the opera surpassed many Italian operas; [1] that instead of encouraging so heavenly a talent, there was a cabal in the background, the object of which evidently was to prevent an innocent boy from obtaining his deserved honour and success.

"I went forthwith to the *Impressario* to learn the real truth. He told me that he had never been adverse to the performance of the opera; but he must be excused for looking to his own interest; doubts of the success of the opera had been hinted to him; he had therefore put the 'Caschina' and 'Buona figliuola' in rehearsal, but would immediately afterwards perform the boy's opera; and should it not succeed, he would at least be prepared with two other operas. I reminded him of my long stay, and of the inconvenience of a longer one. He replied, 'What does it signify? A week more or less—we shall then take you in hand.' The matter rested thus. The airs of

[1] The testimony of Hasse may be added to the above.

Carattoli were altered, and everything was done to satisfy
Caribaldi, Poggi, and Laschi, each of whom assured me in
particular that he had nothing to object to. Affligio was now
solely responsible. The four weeks flew by; and the copyist
told me he had received no orders to write out the altered airs;
and as at the last rehearsal of the 'Buona figliuola,' I perceived that Affligio was about to give another opera the preference, I spoke to him on the subject. Hereupon he directed
the copyist, in my presence and that of the poet Coltellini, to have
everything ready in twelve days, that the opera might be
rehearsed with the orchestra in a fortnight.

"But the enemies of the poor child, whoever they are, have
again prevented it. The same day the copyist was ordered to
cease writing; and two days afterwards, I learned that Affligio
had resolved not to bring the boy's opera on the stage. To be
certain, I went to him, and received for answer, that he had
consulted the singers who allowed that the opera was an incomparable work, but not dramatic; and for that reason, could not
be performed by them.

"This was incomprehensible to me. For how could the
singers unblushingly depreciate what they had previously
applauded with such enthusiasm; a work to which they had
themselves encouraged the boy, and represented as excellent to
Affligio? I replied, that he could not expect that the boy should
have the great trouble of writing an opera for nothing. I
reminded him of his contract; and gave him to understand
that he had detained us four months, and led us into an expense
of more than 160 ducats. I told him of my lost time, and
assured him that I should expect not only the 100 ducats for which
he had agreed with the Physician Laugier, but my expenses on
his account. To this my just demand, he returned an unin-
telligible answer, which discovered his embarrassment, and with
which he, I scarcely know how, endeavoured to break off the
whole affair, till at last he quitted me with the most scandalous
expressions, that if I wished to caricature the boy, he would
not object to the opera's being piped, fiddled, and laughed at.
Coltellini heard the whole.

"Such was the reward of my son for his great trouble in
writing an opera, the original score of which contains 558 pages;
to say nothing of lost time and expenses. And what becomes
of that which after all lies nearest my heart, namely the fame
and honour of my son, since I dare not venture to press for the

performance of the opera, having been given to understand clearly enough, that all possible pains would be taken to spoil it; that it would be said the composition is not fit to sing, or that it is not dramatic, or that it is not well composed to the words, or lastly that he did not write it himself; with a world of other absurd and contradictory stuff, which upon a close examination of the musical powers of my child (for his own honour most ardently desired by me), would vanish like smoke, to the shame of the envious and detracting slanderers—and convince every one that its sole object is to extinguish and render unfortunate an innocent being to whom God has granted extraordinary talent which other nations have applauded and encouraged, and this, in the metropolis of his own German Fatherland." [1]

Nothing discouraged by this lost labour and the falsehood to which he had been sacrificed, the young composer, in little more than a month, was ready with three works, a solemn mass, an offertorium, and a "Trumpet concerto for a Boy." These pieces were so much applauded, as to compensate in some measure for his previous ill fortune.

"The 'Mass,' etc., by Wolfgang, which was performed on the feast of the Conception, in the presence of the court, himself beating time (writes his father), has in some measure recovered for us that ground which we had lost through the wickedness of our enemies and opponents."

The commencement of this mass, which is here inserted, will be esteemed an interesting record of the occasion, and of Mozart's style of counterpoint at twelve years of age.

---

[1] I will merely add to this account of " La Finta semplice," that being at Offenbach in 1842, for the purpose of looking over the MSS. of Mozart, in the possession of M. André, I saw this monume t of youthful genius. The

On the return of the family to Salzburg, Wolfgang pursued his studies in the higher departments of composition, and improved his acquaintance with the Italian language. Nearly the whole of the year 1769 was passed in this quiet manner. It appears from the court calendar of his native city, that he was now appointed concert-master in the musical establishment of the archbishop, a place of little honour and less profit; but which, nevertheless, he would not hold as a mere sinecure. He began, therefore, to produce frequent masses, and the principal era of his numerous compositions of that class, extends from this time to the year 1778, when he was twenty-two years of ago. The disadvantages under which he wrote his masses will be hereafter seen in a letter addressed by him to the Padre Martini, in which he explains the causes of the inequalities apparent in those pieces.

The father, who was ill at ease in Salzburg, and hoped to settle elsewhere, the more willingly withdrew himself from the duties of composition, in the hope that his son, benefiting by the opportunities of practice thus thrown in his way, might the better enable him to accomplish his design. The attainment of this, however, was remote and uncertain.

In December, 1769, the father and son set off for Italy, and remained from home till March 1771. This was a complete holiday tour, and was entered upon in the most congenial spirit by both the travellers. Leopold Mozart, now freed from the carking cares of money, appears in his true character, as a man of taste, charmed with the attractive objects which presented themselves on all sides; and Wolfgang, delighted with the

notation is bold, and differs much from the delicate music-writing of the composer's maturity. It would befit our idea of Handel.

novelty of the scene, and the general sympathy with his art, is the most mercurial of companions. We have an interesting picture of Italian enthusiasm in a letter from Verona:

" Next day we went to the organ in the principal church, and though only six or eight persons knew our intention, we found the whole city in the church, and some stout fellows were obliged to precede us to clear the way to the choir, and we had then to wait more than half a quarter of an hour, to reach the organ, as every one was anxious to be the next."

On another occasion of this kind at a monastery, the crowd was so great that the monks were obliged to conduct them to the organ by a private passage. Their first concert over, the nobility vied with each other in showing them attentions, and they were *fêted* in turn by the Marchese Carlotti, Conti Carlo Emily, Marchese Spolverini, Marchese Dionysis S. Fermo, etc. A private gentleman, Signor Luggiati, also employed a painter on the portrait of Wolfgang. The kindness of this reception had probably its influence on the following light-hearted communication of the boy with his sister, the historical interest of which is agreeably heightened by the playful mixture of languages and the characteristic drollery of the manner.

" VERONA, *7 Gennajo* 1770.

" DEAREST SISTER,—A letter of a span's length I have received after long waiting for an answer in vain.

" The German Clown now ceases, and the Italian begins. *Lei è piu franca nella lingua Italiana di quel che mi ho imaginato. Lei mi dica la cagione, perchè Lei non fà nella commedia che anno giocato i Cavalieri. Adesso sentiamo sempre una opera titolata : Il Ruggiero. Oronte, il padre di Bradamante, è un principe (fà il Signor Afferi) bravo cantante, un baritono, ma* [1] forced when he pipes up into his falsetto, yet not so much so as Tibaldi at Vienna. *Bradamante, innamorata di Ruggiero (ma* intended to be the wife of Leone, but won't have him) *fà una povera Baronessa, che ho avuto una gran disgrazia, ma non sò la quale recita* [2] under a feigned name but the name I don't know; *ha*

[1] " You are more at home in the Italian language than I had imagined. You must tell me the reason why you did not play in the comedy which the *Cavalieri* acted. Now we hear nothing but an opera entitled ' Il Ruggiero.' Oronte, the father of Bradamante, is a prince (played by Signor Afferi), a clever singer, a baritone, but forced, etc."
[2] " Bradamante, in love with Ruggiero, etc., is played by a poor baroness, who has had a great misfortune, but I don't know what—"

una voce passabile e la statura non sarrebbe male, ma distuona come il diavolo. Ruggiero, un ricco principe innamorato di Bradamante, è un Musico ; canta un poco Manzuolisch ed a una bellissima voce forte ed è già vecchio ; ha 55 anni ed a una [1] voluble throat. Leone, who is to marry Bradamante *ricchississimo è,*[2] but whether rich or not off the theatre, I cannot say. *La moglie di Afferi che ha una bellissima voce, ma è tanto sussuro nel teatro che non si sente niente. Irene fa una sorella di Lolli del gran Violinista che habbiamo sentito a Vienna, a una* rugged *voce e canta sempre* about a quarter of a note too *hardi o troppo a buon ora. Ganno fa un signore che non so come si chiama ; è la prima volta che lui recita.*[3] Between each act there is a ballet. There is a capital dancer who calls himself Monsieur Roessler. He is a German, and dances admirably. When we were the last time (but not quite the last time) at the opera, M. Roessler came to us in our *Palco* (as we have the box of M. Carlotti free, having the key thereto) and talked with us. *Apropos,* everybody is in the *Maschera* at present, and it is extremely convenient that any one who wears a mask is privileged from taking it off if any one salutes him; and the name is never mentioned, but it is always *Servitore umilissimo, Signora Maschera. Cospetto di Bacco* there's for you. The strangest is that we go to bed at half-past seven o'clock. *Se Lei indovinasse questo, io dirò certamente che Lei sia la madre di tutti gli indovini.*[4] Kiss mamma's hand for me, and thee I kiss a thousand times, assuring thee that I will ever remain—Thy faithful brother,

> "*Portez vous bien et aimez moi toujours.*"

The winter was very cold, and the journey expensive, and as the receipts of their concerts consisted " chiefly in admiration

---

[1] " She has a tolerable voice, and not a bad figure; but sings horribly out of tune. Ruggiero, a rich prince, in love with Bradamante, is a *Musico*, sings a little in the style of Manzuoli, and has a beautiful and powerful voice, but is already old—he is fifty-five, and possesses a—"

[2] " Is very rich."

[3] " Afferi's wife has a most beautiful voice, but it is such a whisper in the theatre that one hears nothing. Irene is played by a sister of Lolli, the great violin player we heard at Vienna; she has a rugged voice, and always sings about a quarter of a note too sharp. Ganno is played by a gentleman whose name I don't know—it is the first time he has performed."

[4] " If you should guess this, I shall certainly say that you are the queen of all guessers."

---

[1] The singers alluded to in these letters, under the name of *Musica Uomo,* etc., are of the race of *male* soprani, now fortunately extinct.

and bravos," [1] they might have found some difficulty in proceeding had they not been aided from time to time by the hospitality of the monasteries. There Wolfgang generally rejoiced at night in a well-warmed bed. The fresh air in travelling, and the open fires of Italy, produced a visible effect upon his health. His complexion is described as being of a reddish brown about the nose and mouth, " like the emperor's." In this favourable condition he absolutely intoxicated his Italian hearers; the poets, we are told, made verses upon him, " as if for a wager," and the father excused himself for not sending the journals containing accounts of his performances to Salzburg with the words, " you know what takes place on such occasions, you have seen it often enough." On arriving at Mantua a concert was given by the Philharmonic Society, which was in reality a public trial of his powers. The programme containing the particulars merits preservation as a musical curiosity.[2]

At Milan, the people crowded to the concerts of the " *giovenetto ammirabile*," and the same shouting, clapping, and noise of bravo upon bravo, prevailed. How little these applauses spoiled the natural character of the boy may be observed in a letter to his sister, dated January 26, 1770:

" I am exceedingly pleased that you so much enjoyed the sledge-drive of which you write to me, and wish you a thousand opportunities for such pleasure, that you may lead a right happy and cheerful life. But one thing troubles me, which is, that you permit poor Herr von Mölk to be so eternally sighing

---

[1] This was the general answer to all inquiries from home respecting their gains.

[2] Series of compositions performed at a public concert of the Philharmonic Society of Mantua, on the evening of January 16, 1770, on occasion of the presence of the extraordinary young musician, Signor Amadeo Mozart.— 1. A Symphony of the Composition of Sign. Amadeo.—2. A Concerto for the Harpsichord, presented to him, and executed by him at sight.— 3. Air by a Professor.—4. Sonata for the Harpsichord performed at sight, introducing variations of his own invention; and lastly, the whole repeated in a different key to that in which it was written.—5. Violin Concerto by a Professor.—6. Air sung and composed extempore by the said Signor Amadeo, on words not previously seen by him, accompanied by himself on the Harpsichord.—7. A second Sonata for the Harpsichord, performed extempore by the same on a subject proposed by the leader.—8. Air by a Professor.—9. Concerto for the Oboe by a Professor.—10. Fugue for the Harpsichord, on a given theme, executed extempore by Signor Amadeo, and brought to a perfect termination according to the rules of counterpoint.—11. Symphony, in which he will improvise a part for the Harpsichord from a single violin part placed before him.—12. Duet by Professors. —13. Trio, in which Signor Amadeo will perform a part extempore on the Violin.—14. Final Symphony, the composition of the above.

and grieving, and would not go out with him in the sledge, that he might have the pleasure of upsetting you.[1] How many clean pocket-handkerchiefs will your cruelty have cost him? . . .

" Of news, I know nothing, except that Gellert, the Leipsic poet, is dead, and since his death, has written no more poetry. Before I began this letter, I had just finished. an air from Demetrio, which begins thus: *Misera tu non sei*, etc.[2] . . ."

He next gives an account of the operas at Mantua and Verona:

" The opera at Mantua was beautiful—it was ' Demetrio.' The *prima donna* sings well, but quietly; and if you did not see her acting, but merely singing, you would fancy that she did not sing, for she cannot get her mouth open, and moans out everything, which is, however, no new thing to hear. The *seconda donna*, has a presence like a grenadier, and a strong voice; she really does not sing amiss, considering that it is her first appearance on the stage. *Il primo uomo, il musico* is named Caseli; he sings beautifully, but has an uneven voice. *Il secondo uomo* is old, and me he pleases not. The tenor's name is Ottini; he does not sing badly.

" I forget the name of the second tenor, who is still young, but not remarkable. *Primo ballerino*, good; *prima ballerina*, good; and, it is said, not ugly; but I have not seen her near. A *grotesco* is there, who leaps well; but does not compose as I do; that is, as the pigs grunt. The orchestra is not bad.

" There is a good orchestra at Cremona, and the first violin is named Spagnoletta. The *prima donna* tolerable, but old, I believe, as the hills—sings not so well as she acts, and is wife to a violin-player in the orchestra, named Maschi. The opera is ' La Clemenza di Tito.'[3] *Seconda donna*, young and pretty on the stage, but nothing out of the way. *Primo uomo, musico*, Cicognani, pretty voice, and beautiful *cantabile*. The two other *musici*, young and passable. The tenor's name is ·*Non lo so*, he has an agreeable appearance, and is much like the king at Vienna. *Ballerino primo*, good; and a most horrid dog. A girl-dancer was there, who did not dance badly, and who is not

---

[1] The gallantries of the sledge are well known. The lady sits wrapped in furs, while her inamorato drives her with speed equal to the wings of love himself; though sometimes a little at the risk of both her neck and his own.

[2] Hence the flurry and animal spirits of these volatile letters and postscripts, which were mostly written as recreations in the intervals of serious composition.

[3] The same subject was afterwards selected by himself.

ugly either on or off the stage, which is saying much for a *capo d'opera*. The rest as usual.

" I cannot write you much about the opera at Milan, as we did not go; we were told that the piece was not successful. *Primo uomo*, Aprile, sings well,—has a beautiful even voice. We heard him in a church at a festival. Madame Piccinelli, of Paris, who sang at our concert, plays at the opera. Herr Pick, who danced at Vienna, is now dancing here. The opera is called " Didone abbandonata,' and will not run long. Signor Piccini, who is to write the next opera, is here. I have heard that it is to be called ' Cesare in Egitto.'

            " WOLFGANG DE MOZART,
    " Elder von Hochenthal, Freund des Zahlhausens."

The influence of Count Firmian, a constant friend of the Mozarts, procured Wolfgang the engagement to compose an opera for the ensuing Christmas. As no dramatic work of his was known in Milan, he was obliged to produce several airs and recitatives on the spot, in proof of his competency, which were sung at the house of Count Firmian. His engagements made him extremely careful of his health.

" Wolfgang," writes the father, " will never injure himself by eating or drinking. He will not touch anything which he thinks unwholesome, and eats many days little or nothing. He is still plump and well, and in excellent spirits the whole day."

Both the travellers delighted in the noble church music of Italy; they were frequently in the cathedrals and noticed, at a requiem performed on the old Marquis Litta, that the *Dies iræ* was three quarters of an hour long! Their evening amusements were more lively, and they engaged with great alacrity in the festivities of the carnival. The father writes:

" The tailor was here just now with the cloaks, etc., that we have been obliged to have made. As I looked in the glass when we were trying them on, methought ' here am I, going to play the fool in my old age.' [1] They become Wolfgang incomparably, and my comfort in the midst of such silly expenses is, that the things will serve for other purposes, and may be, at least, used as foot-cloths, etc."

The young composer responded heartily to his sister's account of the carnival at Salzburg:

[1] He was now fifty-one years of age, and evidently well pleased with the folly.

                                           D

" *Cara sorella mia*,—I am quite pleased to hear that you have so much enjoyed yourself. You may, perhaps, think that I have not enjoyed myself, but indeed the number of times is not to be told. We have been, I believe, at least six or seven times to the opera, and then afterwards to the *feste di ballo*, which begin, as at Vienna, after the opera, with this difference, that there is more order in the dancing at Vienna. We have also seen the *facchinata* and *chiccherata*. The former is a masquerade, which is amusing to see; the people dress as *facchini*, or domestic servants. There was a *barca* full of people, and many went on foot. There were four or six sets of trumpets and drums, and some bands of fiddles and other instruments. The *chiccherata* is likewise a masquerade. The Milanese call *chiccherata* such as we term *petits maîtres*, or coxcombs, and all takes place on horseback, which is amusing. I am as much rejoiced to hear that Herr von Aman is now going on better, as I was concerned to hear of his misfortune. What masque had Madame Rosa? What Herr von Mölk and Herr Schidenofen? Pray write me word, if you know, and it will give me great pleasure.[1]

" Kiss mamma's hand for me 1000000000000 times. Compliments to all good friends."

Between Milan and Bologna the boy was inspired by a beautiful adagio, and on arriving at his inn he committed to paper an entire composition. This, his first quartet for stringed instruments, is dated " Lodi, seven in the evening." At Parma they fell in with Signora Guari, the celebrated *Bastardella*, who sang three airs to them.

" I could not," writes the father, " have conceived it possible, to sing to C in *altissimo*, if my ears had not convinced me of the fact. The passages which Wolfgang has written were in her air, and these she sang somewhat softer than the deeper notes, but as beautifully as an octave pipe in an organ. In short, the trills and all were just made as Wolfgang has written them;

[1] These recollections of home, amidst the dissipation of the life he was now leading, afford touching proofs of the sincerity of his attachments. His postscripts are full of suggestions, even where despatched in a line. " I am distracted with business, and cannot possibly write more to-day." Or when he sends a message to a friend:—" Tell the child-man, Urserl, that I thought I had returned all the songs; should I, however, absorbed in high and weighty considerations, have brought them with me to Italy, I will not fail, if I find them, to say so in a letter. *Addio*, children, farewell. I kiss mamma's hand a thousand times, and send thee a hundred busses or smacks on thy wondrous little horse-face. *Per fare il fine*, I am thine, etc."

they are note for note the same. Besides this, she has good
alto notes, as low as G. She is not handsome nor yet ugly, but
has at times a wild look in the eyes, like people who are subject to
convulsions, and she is lame in one foot. Her conduct formerly
was good; she has, consequently, a good name and reputation."

Wolfgang also speaks of this extraordinary singer:

"We heard her delightfully at her own house. She has a
beautiful voice, a rapid execution, and an inconceivable compass upwards. She sang the following notes and passages in
my presence."

At Bologna he visited Farinelli,[1] and astonished Padre Martini, "the idol of the Italians," by his skill in extempore fugue. He came off with the same honours at Florence, where the Marquis of Ligneville, the most rigorous contrapuntist in all Italy, gave him various abstruse subjects for fugues, and heard them scientifically treated and played off "as one swallows a morsel of bread." The father was delighted, and the correspondence displays his excellent spirits. Here is an escapade at the end of one of his letters:

"My friends must excuse my not writing to them. *Komm-abit aliquando Zeitus bequemus schreibendi. Nunc Kopffus meus semper vollus est multis gedankibus.*" [2]

In the midst of the most constant activity and exertion, the boy attempts to persuade his sister that he is utterly abandoned to indolence:

"O thou pattern of diligence—I have been such an idle fellow myself for a long time, that I thought there would be no harm in my setting to work for a little while. Every post-day, when the German letters come, the dinner tastes much better. Pray write to me who sings at the oratorio; also what the oratorio is called; also, whether you like the minuets of Haydn, and whether they are better than the first.[3] That Herr von Aman is again well delights me from the bottom of my heart; tell him to take care of himself, and to keep quiet. Pray tell him so." . . . .

Arriving at Rome in the Holy Week, they hurried to the Sistine Chapel, to hear the "Miserere" at matins, and approached the pope, who was waiting on the poor at table, so nearly as to be quite close to him. The scene is graphically described by the father, and represents the young musician in a situation of some difficulty, but rescuing himself with the happiest self-possession.

"Our handsome dress, the German language, and the freedom with which I desired my servant to tell the Swiss Guard to

---

[1] This celebrated singer now lived retired in the vicinity of Bologna, in the possession of a princely revenue, from which it is thought he afforded Padre Martini the means of forming his magnificent library.

[2] "A convenient time for writing will come; but at present my head is fully occupied."

[3] This probably refers to Michael Haydn, brother of the great composer.

make way, soon helped us through every difficulty. Some took Wolfgang for a German nobleman, others for a prince, and the servant did not undeceive them. I was taken for his tutor. In this manner we proceeded to the table of the cardinals. There it happened that Wolfgang placed himself between the chairs of two cardinals, one of whom, Cardinal Pallavicini, beckoned to him and said: ' Will you have the goodness to tell me in confidence who you are?' Wolfgang told him. The cardinal replied with the greatest astonishment: ' What, are you that famous boy of whom so much has been written to me?' Upon this Wolfgang rejoined: ' Are you not Cardinal Pallavicini?' The cardinal said ' Yes, why do you ask?' Wolfgang then observed, ' that we had letters to his eminence, and desired to wait upon him.' Upon hearing this the cardinal expressed the greatest pleasure, complimented Wolfgang on his Italian, and added: ' *Ick kan auk ein benig deutsch sprekken.*' At our departure Wolfgang kissed his hand, and the cardinal taking his baret from his head made him a very polite compliment.

" You are aware that the celebrated ' Miserere' of this place is in such high esteem that the musicians of the chapel are forbidden, under pain of excommunication, to take any part of it away, to copy it themselves, or through another person. However, *we have it already.* . . . Meantime, we will not entrust this mystery to strange hands: *ut non incurremus mediate vel immediate in censuram ecclesiæ.*" [1]

The difficulty of putting down in notes the music performed by a double choir, abounding in imitation and traditional effects, of which one of the chief is characterised by the absence of a perceptible rhythm, is scarcely conceivable. Hence the wonder at the unexampled *theft* of the " Miserere " of Allegri. Mozart accomplished his task in two visits to the Sistine Chapel. He drew out a sketch on the first hearing, and attended the performance a second time on Good Friday, having his MS. in his hat for correction and completion. It was soon known at Rome that the " Miserere " had been taken down, and he was obliged to produce what he had written at a large musical party where the *Musico* Christoferi, who had sung in it, confirmed its correct-

[1] The same letter which contains the news of this scientific exploit incloses also a country dance (!) by Wolfgang, with his directions as to the manner of performance. It was, probably, a little offering to the court during his absence.

ness. The generous Italians were so much delighted that they forgot to call upon the pope to excommunicate the culprit.

From Rome the father sends this anecdote:

"At Florence we found a young Englishman, pupil of the celebrated Nardini. This boy, who plays exquisitely, and who is just of Wolfgang's size and age, met us at the house of the poetess Signora Corilla. The two boys performed by turns the whole evening, amidst continual embracings. The other day the little Englishman, a most charming boy, brought his violin to us and played the whole afternoon. Wolfgang accompanied him also on the violin. The following day we dined with Mr. Gavard, treasurer to the grand duke, and the two boys played the whole afternoon, not, however, as boys, but as men. Little Thomas accompanied us home, and cried bitterly on learning that we were going to set off the next day. But perceiving that our journey was fixed for noon, he came to us by nine in the morning, and presented Wolfgang, among many embraces, with a poem which he had got Signora Corilla to write for him the night before. He then accompanied our coach to the city gates. I wish you could have witnessed this scene." [1]

In the comparative solitude of Rome, the young composer recurs to his home recreations in a characteristic manner. He thus writes to his sister, " Pray look for the art of arithmetic which you copied out for me, and which I have lost. Copy it again with other examples of sums—and send it to me here." He then alludes to his opera, and hopes that Manzuoli and De Amicis (prima donna) may be engaged in it, adding, " We should then have two good friends and acquaintances before us." He was disappointed, however, in both.

The Mozarts found a charming hostess at Rome, the wife of one of the pope's couriers, who would receive nothing for their entertainment, and provided amusement for her guests into the bargain.

" Immmediately after dinner," writes Wolfgang, " we play at

[1] This boy was the unfortunate but highly gifted Thomas Linley, who was drowned about his twenty-first year while amusing himself with some companions on the water in the park of the Duke of Ancaster. Mozart never forgot him; and when in after life he met English society at Vienna, the first person he mentioned was Linley. The late Rev. Ozias Linley, of Dulwich College, possessed a letter written by Mozart to his brother Thomas in Italian, and esteemed this document, in the handwriting of the composer f " Don Giovanni," beyond all price.

potch,[1] a game I have learnt here; when I come I will teach it to you."

On the 8th of May, they set out for Naples in the company of four Augustine monks, and enjoyed the hospitality of several convents. At Capua, they stopped to see a lady take the veil, and to hear a " Salve Regina " and symphonies performed by four coach-loads of musicians, whom they met coming thither for that purpose. On the day of their arrival at Naples they visited their London acquaintance, the English ambassador, Hamilton. Lady Hamilton [2] is described by the father as a very agreeable person, " who performs on the clavier with unusual expression. She was much alarmed at having to play before Wolfgang." Shortly afterwards, we find the young composer getting a headache over his book of arithmetic. He praises the bass which his sister has put to a minuet of Haydn, and suddenly inquires after a bird he left at home:

" Pray write to me, how is Mr. Canary? Does he sing still? Does he pipe still? Do you know why I think of the canary? Because there is one in the front room here, which makes a G♯ like ours. *Apropos*, Herr Johannes will have received the letter of congratulation we sent him; but if not, I must have already communicated the contents to him at Salzburg. Our new clothes came home yesterday, and we were beautiful as angels. Remember me to Nandl, and tell her to pray for me lustily."

The letter concludes with this message, turbulent in high spirits, to his sister:

" Go constantly to the Mirabella [3] in the Litanies, and listen to the ' Regina Cœli ' or the ' Salve Regina,' and then sleep soundly without bad dreams. Make my elaborate compliments to Herr von Schidenhofen *tralaliera—tralaliera*—and tell him to learn the Repeat Minuet on the clavier in such a manner that he do not forget it. And tell him to *do* it soon, that he may *do* me the pleasure of *doing* him an accompaniment. And *do* make my compliments to all other good friends, male and

---

[1] Mozart's ear was readily caught by the sound of ludicrous words. Hence a cleverness in comical rhymes which he afterwards exhibited in long letters to his friends.

[2] The famous Lady Hamilton.

[3] A summer palace of the Archbishop of Salzburg's, celebrated for its magnificent orangery.

female, and *do* take care of yourself, and *do* not die—that you may *do* me another letter, and I *do* one to you, and so we continue to *do* till we are *done* for;—still I am he that will *do*, till there is nothing more to be *done*.   Meantime I *do* remain,   W. M."

Their concert at Naples was highly successful. Jomelli invited them to his house, and Ciccio di Majo, whose church music is praised by the young composer as most beautiful, " was extremely polite."[1]   In the midst of a sonata, which he played at the *Conservatorio alla pietà* there arose a disturbance among the audience, from a notion that the brilliancy and rapidity of his left hand were owing to some magical properties in a ring he wore.   On the cause being explained to him he laid aside the enchanted circle; but the music was not found less extraordinary. The Mozarts were in the highest fashion, as will now be seen:

" All the carriages on the public drive of an evening carry flambeaux, which make a kind of illumination.   As we go daily, having the carriage of a nobleman always at our service, we have also our two flambeaux; the nobleman's servant carries one, and our servant the other.   Her majesty the queen always salutes us on the promenade in a particularly kind manner.   We were present at the great ball given on Easter Sunday by the French ambassador, in honour of the marriage of the Dauphin."

Their mornings were spent in a more intellectual manner— they visited all the curiosities of the neighbourhood, the baths of Nero, the grotto of the Cumean Sybil, Lago d'Averno, etc., and the boy concludes one of the letters in triumph, " I have now had a sail on the Mediterranean sea."   The amazing exaltation of his spirits is shown in a whimsical letter to his sister, expressed as usual in a mixture of languages—but the German on this occasion is an extraordinary patois.

" C.S.M.—Vesuvius is smoking furiously to-day.   *Potz Blitz und ka nent aini.   Haid homa gfresa beym Herr Doll.   Dos is a deutscha compositör und a brawa mo.*[2]   I shall now begin to write my life.   Alle 9 ore, qualche volta anche alle diece mi sveglio, e poi andiamo fuor di casa, e poi pranziamo da un trattore, e

[1] On their way home, after this journey, intelligence reached them of the deaths of Ciccio di Majo and of Caratolli, the singer, who had treated them with such duplicity at Vienna.   Jomelli died about the same time.

[2] A piece of fun; if it means anything, it may be translated—" Dined to-day with Mr. Doll, a German composer, and a worthy man."

dopo pranzo scriviamo, e poi sortiamo, e indi ceniamo, ma che
cosa? Al giorno di grasso un mezzo pollo ovvero un piccolo
boccone d'arrosto; al giorno di magro, un piccolo pesce; e di
poi andiamo a dormire.[1] Est-ce que vous avez compris?

"*Redma dafir soisburgarisch, don as is gschaida. Wir sand
Gottlob gesund da Voda und i.*[2] I hope that you and mamma
are also well. Naples and Rome are the realms of sleep. *A
scheni Schrift! Net wor?*[3] Write to me, and don't be so idle.
Altrimente avrete qualche bastonate da me. Quel plaisir! Je
te casserai la tête. I am so rejoiced at the portraits, and *i bi
torios, wias da gleich sieht; wons ma gfoin, so los i mi un den
Vodan a so macha. Mädli, las Da saga wo bist dan gwesa he?*[4]
The opera here is by Jomelli—it is beautiful—but the style is
too elevated as well as too antique for the theatre. De Amicis
sings incomparably, as likewise Aprile, who sang at Milan. The
dances are miserably pompous. The theatre is beautiful. The
king has the coarse Neapolitan manners, and when he is at the
opera always stands on a stool in order to look a little taller
than the queen. The queen is handsome and affable, for she
has greeted me at least six times on the Mole (that is a public
drive) in the friendliest manner.

"P.S. I kiss mamma's hand."

The father describes their return to Rome after a journey,
in which they had been twenty-five hours without sleep:

"As soon as we had eaten a little rice and a couple of eggs,
I placed Wolfgang on a chair. He began immediately to snore
and slept so soundly, that I undressed him completely, and put
him to bed, without his giving the least symptom of waking.
Although sometimes lifted from the chair and set down again,
he kept snoring on, and at last finished by being laid in bed fast
asleep. When he awoke at nine in the morning he could not
imagine how he had got to bed."

[1] " At nine o'clock, sometimes even at ten, I awake, and then we go out,
and then we dine at an ordinary; and after dinner we write, and then we
walk out, and afterwards sup. On a flesh day, half a chicken, or a little
morsel of roast meat; on a fast day, a little fish, and then we go to sleep."
[2] " You may call this vulgar, but it is witty. We are well, thank God,
both my father and I."
[3] " Beautiful writing, is it not? "
[4] " I am curious whether it is like. (The mother and daughter had been
painted in miniature.) If it please me, I will have myself and my father
done too. The girl wants to know where you have been, eh? "

In answer to an inquiry from home, as to their proceedings and receipts at Naples, the father replies:

" Have we played to the King of Naples? Nothing less I assure you—and received for it the bows which the queen made us in every place in which she saw us. The queen is unable to do anything of herself—and what sort of a person the king is, it will be better to tell you than to write." [1]

At Rome Leopold Mozart was surprised to hear his son addressed as *Signore Cavaliere*, and thought it a joke. However, he soon writes:

" What I told you about the cross of an order in my last is perfectly true. It is the same that Gluck has, and the precept runs thus—*te creamus auratæ militiæ equitem*. He will have to wear a beautiful gold cross. We are to have an audience of the pope to-morrow on this business."

Whatever the occupation during their tour, however much pressed for time they might be, letters were always interchanged on the *fête* days of any of the separated members of the family. [2] On the day after the postscript above, while they were at Bologna, came the libretto of the opera for Milan, not selected from Metastasio as the boy had recommended, but the work of a Turin poet. It was called " Mitridate, Re di Ponto," and had been produced at Turin by some other composer three years before. The prima donna was to be Antonia Bernasconi. Mozart's manner of bringing out the operas which he wrote for theatres at a distance, was to send the recitative first, and postpone the airs until acquainted with the powers of the singers; disliking the chance of having to do his work twice over. It was a saying of his, that he prided himself on suiting a singer with an air, as a tailor would fit him with a coat. The libretto

---

[1] Let Mrs. Piozzi's account of the manners of this eccentric monarch supply the omission:—" He shoots at the birds, dances with the girls, eats macaroni, and helps himself to it with his fingers, and rows against the watermen in the bay, till one of them burst out bleeding at the nose last week, with his uncourtly efforts to outdo the king." . . . He sometimes also sold fish in the market.—*Journey through Italy*, vol. ii.

[2] Here is a pleasant specimen:—" I wish that God may always give you good health, and let you live a hundred years to come, and not die till you are a thousand. I hope that you will learn to know me better in future, and then you may judge of me as you please. Time does not allow me to write much. The pen too is not worth a pin, nor more is he who guides it. The name of the opera which I have to compose at Milan is not as yet known."

was received in July, and the opera was to be brought out at
Christmas—a long interval for so rapid a composer; for the
present, therefore, the work may be considered as almost dismissed from his mind, though we shall notice its influence on
him as the time approaches. During the earlier part of their
stay at Bologna, the father was confined at an inn from the
effects of an accident on the road; and this procured for the son
a certain freedom in his movements which seems to have been
welcome.

" I have had the honour," he writes, " of going alone to the
churches about six times, and of viewing the magnificent ceremonies. Meanwhile, I have already composed four Italian
symphonies, besides airs, of which five or six are ready, and likewise a motet.

" Does Herr Tölpel come often? Does he still honour you
with his entertaining discourse? And Herr Karl von Vogt,
does he still do himself the pleasure of listening to your intolerable voice? Herr von Schidenhofen must assist you
diligently in writing minuets, or he shall not have a single bit of
sugar." . . .

Wolfgang is described as having grown taller and stronger in
every limb on this journey; but his singing voice with which he
used to recall the pathetic style of Manzuoli, was utterly gone.
' He can neither get high nor low," writes his father, " and has
not five pure notes, which much annoys him, as he cannot sing
his own airs, though often desirous of doing so." Both the
travellers enjoyed themselves at the country seat of Field-
Marshal Palavicini. Here Wolfgang amused himself with rural
diversions and met a Dominican friar, a reputed saint, who
excited his wonder by uniting with that character an enormous
capacity for eating. But music was not forgotten, nor the
Padre Martini, who lived in the town. While the father daily
visited the padre to discourse on the history of the art,[1] the

---

[1] The good friar was engaged on his *Storia della Musica*, the preliminary
chapters of which exhibit a curious arrangement. His work proceeds in
his order:—1. Of music from the creation of Adam to the deluge.
2. From the deluge to the time of Moses. 3. From the birth of that
Hebrew lawgiver to his death. 4. From the death of Moses to the reign
of David, etc. He enters upon a plan of this sort, after owning that
sufficient monuments and descriptions are wanting to exhibit the state of
music in the early ages of the world. Great disorder reigned in his apartments, where, according to Dr. Burney, he had collected 17,000 books and
MSS., but seats were not easily to be found.

boy's thoughts were occupied with the ancient church music
of Italy, and he produced a " Miserere " for men's voices in that
severe style for which Bologna had long been famous. His
election as member of the Philharmonic Society occasions a
graphic letter.

" The Philharmonic Society of Bologna, have unanimously
elected Wolfgang one of their body, and presented him with the
patent of *Accademico*. The usual preliminaries and trial of
skill, however, took place. He was obliged to present himself
at four o'clock in the afternoon, on the 9th of October, in the
hall of the academy. There the *Princeps Academiæ*, and the
two censors, who are experienced Kapellmeisters, gave him, in
the presence of all the members, an Antiphona from the Anti
phonarium, which he was to set in four parts, in a chamber
adjoining, into which he was conducted by the beadle, and the
door locked. As soon as he was ready, his composition was
examined by the censors, the Kapellmeisters, and composers
who then voted with black and white balls. The balls being
all white, he was called in. On his entrance he was welcomed
by a general congratulation and clapping of hands, the *princeps*
having acquainted him, in the name of the society, with his
election. Meantime, I and a companion were locked up in a
room on the other side of the hall of the academical library
Every one wondered at the rapidity with which he was ready
for many consume three hours over an Antiphona of three lines
You must know that the task is not an easy one;—many things
being inadmissible into this kind of composition, as he had been
forewarned. He had finished in little more than half-an-hour
The beadle brought the patent home to us.[1] There are among
other words:—*Testamur Dominum W. A. M. inter academia
nostræ magistros compositores adscriptum fuisse, etc.*"

Towards the beginning of November, Wolfgang was at Milan
working upon his opera; during the intervals of composition he
amused himself by acquiring the finger language, to converse
with a dumb lad who lived in the same house. In one of his
letters home, he calls himself as great a gossip as ever; but we
will take the father's account of him, and contrast it with the
levity of his own self-description. The woes of Mitridate
affected his spirits.

[1] This document has been preserved, together with the exercise per
formed, and both will be found in an Appendix.

" If our kind friends would, as they did the other day, put a
:tle merriment into their letters, they would do a good work,
r Wolfgang is now busy with serious matters, and is become
' grave, that I am quite pleased when at times anything
ieerful and pleasant falls in his way."

As the opera proceeded there were, however, real causes of
:xation. Bernasconi, the prima donna, distrusting the powers
: the boy to compose the airs for her, requested to see what
ie was to sing, which was instantly acceded to. The *cantatrice*
ade trial of a piece, and was charmed with it. Mozart then,
:qued at the want of confidence in his youth which she had
chibited, presented to her another, and then a third, leaving
ernasconi quite confounded at the sight of so rare a talent,
id so rich an imagination, at years so tender. Shortly after-
ards some enemy called on her with the words of the libretto,
:t to different music, and endeavoured to persuade her not to
ng any of the airs composed by Wolfgang.

" She absolutely refused this wicked person, being quite
verjoyed at the airs the young *maestro* had written for her,
i which he consulted her own wish and inclination, and so is
.aestro Lampugnani, who rehearses with her, and hardly knows
ow to extol Wolfgang's genius sufficiently."

These storms over, the opera was put into rehearsal:

" The first instrumental rehearsal took place on the 12th,
ut with sixteen performers only, in order to see that everything
 correctly written. On the 17th, the first rehearsal with the
ill orchestra will take place. This orchestra [1] consists of
)urteen first, and as many second violins, two claviers, six
ouble basses, two violoncellos, two bassoons, six violas, two
boes, and two *flaute traversi*, which, when there are no flutes,
lay with four oboes, four corni di caccia, and two trumpets, in
ll sixty performers. . . . Previously to the rehearsal with the
ttle orchestra, there were not wanting persons who endeavoured,
y satirical speeches, to prejudice the composition, as some-
iing juvenile and miserable, and who prophesied, so to speak,
ie utter impossibility that so young a boy, and a German, could
rite an Italian opera; and although they acknowledged him

---

[1] In the enumeration of this band, we revert so far to the antiquity of the
rt, and see the point at which Mozart commenced reformer of the dramatic
:chestra.

to be a great performer, they could not believe that he had tl
necessary insight into the *chiaro ed oscuro* of the theatre.   Froi
the evening of the first little rehearsal, all these people are struc
dumb, and have not a syllable more to say. . . ,   On S
Stephen's day, about an hour after *Ave Maria*, you may pictui
to yourself *Maestro Don Amadeo* at the clavier in the orchestri
and myself in a box as a spectator and listener.   Imagine hin
and wish him success, and pray a couple of Paternosters for thi
purpose."

The first night went off triumphantly; there was a hurricar
of applause, with cries of *Evviva il Maestro, Evviva il Maestrin*
"Mithridates" was performed twenty times consecutivel}
an extraordinary thing, as the first opera of the season rarel
attracted; and this success so well satisfied the manager thi
he immediately entered into an agreement with the boy 1
compose the first opera for the year 1773.   The Italians, wl
called Hasse *Il Sassone*, and Galuppi *Buranello*, named your
Mozart *Il Cavalieri filarmonico*.   It was shortly discovered thi
the airs surreptitiously carried to Bernasconi were compose
by the Abbé Gasparini, of Turin, and conscious that envy wi
still at work, the father took care to have the attestation of tl
orchestra that his son's music was " clear, intelligible, and eas
to play."

Before they left Milan, in February 1771, Wolfgang wi
elected member of the Philharmonic Academy of Verona, tl
diploma of which was transmitted to them.   They pursued the
road homewards, by way of Venice, in great spirits, stopping ;
Brescia, to hear the *opera buffa*, where they remembered to ha\
seen the former manager, Crosa, wandering about the streets (
Milan in rags, and with a long beard, begging.   " Such," exclain
the father, " is the reward of dishonesty."   On the way 1
Venice they heard something which appeared to them incredib
in Italy, above all places in the world, a duet in pure fifths; sur
by a poor man and woman in the street, without missing a not
They had never heard anything like this in Germany.   /
Venice they received perpetual invitations, and Leopold Moza
hus describes their gay life:

" Not only does the secretary of a nobleman fetch us in
gondola and attend us back, but the nobleman himself, and
the highest rank too (such as Cornaro, Grimani, Moncenig
Dolfin, and Valier), frequently accompanies us home."

At Padua they paid a visit to Padre Valotti, and Wolfgang
played on the fine organ in the incomparable church, San
Giustino. Thus closed their adventures in Italy for the
present.

On their arrival at home towards the end of March 1771,
they found a letter from their friend, Count Firmian, inviting
young Mozart, in the name of the Empress Maria Theresa, to
compose a grand dramatic serenata in honour of the nuptials
of the Archduke Ferdinand, which were to be celebrated at
Milan in the autumn. The Nestor of musicians, Hasse, was to
write an opera for the same occasion; youth and age would thus
meet in competition, but it was a generous and friendly one.
Mozart's work was an *azione teatrale*, with airs and choruses,
and entitled " Ascanio in Alba." In the interim, the composer
had some months at his disposal, which he occupied by writing
a litany, a *regina cœli*, several symphonies, etc.

The tour in Italy had opened great prospects to Mozart; for
in a country which was pre-eminently the seat of excellence in
the fine arts, and where to excite admiration was proportionably
difficult, his progress had been a perpetual ovation. Under
these circumstances, his genius was in a state of peculiar exaltation; for sympathy, it is to be observed, was the atmosphere
of his artistic existence, and he could neither play nor compose
to his own satisfaction, without the consciousness of being
enjoyed and appreciated. But the stamp of his great individuality as a dramatic musician was not as yet visible.

The superiority of his church to his opera music at this age,
shows of what he was capable when able to pursue without
restraint the dictates of his feeling and science. To this cause
we owe many noble works of the former class, which are still
sought out and enjoyed. But in the theatre he wrote for
success; and success which depends upon the multifarious tastes
of such an audience can only be insured by very gradual
deviations from tradition, especially during the youth of the
composer.

On arriving at Milan in August, the father and son were
graciously received by the royal bride. She no sooner saw
them, than she hastened towards them, drew off her glove,
and with extended hand began speaking to them at a distance
before they could address her. The work, however, for which
they came, was in suspense—the poetry did not arrive till the
beginning of September, and even then had to be returned for

alterations; so that the young maestro had to despatch the tw
parts of this performance, together with the ballet connectin
them, in little more than a fortnight. On the 25th of th
month, Wolfgang writes: " There are two more airs to compose
and then I am ready." We may see him at work in the follow
ing extract from one of his father's letters:

" Manzuoli often visits us, and Tibaldi comes almost ever
day about eleven o'clock, and remains sitting at the table wher
Wolfgang is composing till near one.[1]

" Every body is exceedingly polite and full of respect fo
Wolfgang. We have no trouble; the singers not only bein
celebrated in their profession, but good-hearted and sensibl
people. The serenata is, in fact, a little opera; and even a
opera itself is not longer as it regards the music." . . .

Everything proceeded fortunately during the rehearsals, a
which Hasse and the Mozarts met with the greatest cordialit
The opera and serenata were produced on the 17th of Octobe
and of the effect of the two the father gives the news:

" The serenata pleases wonderfully. Cavaliers and othe
people continually stop us in the street to offer their congratula
tions. In short, *I am sorry ;* for Wolfgang's serenata has s
knocked Hasse's opera on the head, that it is indescribable."

The archduke and his bride were not among the least gratified
they not only frequently inclined their heads from their bo
and applauded the maestro, but encored two airs sung b
Manzuoli and Gerelli.

While the serenata was running its successful career, Wol
gang produced a piece of instrumental harmony in eight part
which must have been a curiosity to the Italians.

The history of his compositions shows, that far from bein
exhausted, he was rather stimulated by production; and it i
remarkable that minor works never fell from his pen in suc
profusion as when he had just been engaged in some grea
undertaking. Amidst these occupations, their holidays com
menced. They went to dine with Hasse at Count Firmian'
and visited the celebrated soprano, Gabrielli, in order to mak
the acquaintance of all the famous singers. The compose

[1] A habit of composing among visitors and friends grew much upon him
and in writing " Don Giovanni " and the " Zauberflöte," we see him n
in the least distracted by the buzz and talking of a crowd.

fisliwetschek,[1] a favourite with both the Mozarts on account
f his talents and honourable character, also visited them.

It was on the occasion of hearing the rehearsal of " Ascanio in
.lba," that Hasse said publicly and with truth, " This boy will
hrow us all into the shade." Such a testimony from the rival of
Iandel and Porpora, and from one who had long been surnamed
the divine," is too remarkable to be forgotten. It was the
ıst memorial of the acquaintance of Hasse and Mozart.[2]

In the spring of the year 1772, a new archbishop, Hieronymus,
f the princely family Colloredo, was elected to the government
f Salzburg; and this event, which took place on the 14th of
[arch in that year, was celebrated by the serenata " Il Sogno
i Scipione," the poetry by Metastasio, the music by Mozart.
ome description of this tyrant of the family, who had the
reatest influence on the future fortunes of the composer,
annot be avoided. In figure he was tall and commanding;
ıuch devoted to horses and field sports, and fond of being
ırrounded by a brilliant assemblage of ladies. He had not
ıe least taste for music, and was long before he could be brought
) perceive that there was anything extraordinary in his young
ɔncert-master. When it is added that with his singular

[1] This composer, surnamed by the Italians *Il Boemo*, wrote about thirty
ɔeras and several oratorios, and was much patronised by the celebrated
abrielli, who liked to sing in them. Despite her patronage, however, he
said to have been found by the Mozarts in an indigent condition, the
:ofits of dramatic composition being at this time chiefly engrossed by the
ɔpyist. He died at Rome in his forty-fourth year, and was buried with
agnificent obsequies by a young Englishman, his pupil. How little
:cuniary advantage attended success in operatic composition may be seen
his Italian career as well as in Mozart's.

[2] Young Mozart's postscripts to his father's letters during this absence
'e characterised as usual by irrepressible vivacity and boyish drollery.
ι one he says, with something of the grotesqueness of Rabelais, " You
ay hope, think, believe, be of opinion, fortify yourself in the notion,
ıagine, picture to yourself and live in confidence, that we are well; but
can tell you so for certain." In another he gives us a glimpse of what
as probably his first love-fancy,—thus, writing to his sister: " What you
ıve promised me (you know beforehand what that is—O dear love!) be
ithful to—I pray thee." His sister was his confidante, and the subject
frequently alluded to in mysterious passages and broken hints of the
ırrespondence. In a subsequent note he transmits a message, in which
e lady's name is probably revealed: " Tell Mademoiselle von Molk that
look forward with pleasure to my return to Salzburg, hoping to receive
st such another present for the minuets as I had at the last concert.
ιe *will know what that is*." In the midst of all this flutter of sensations
ıd hard work, he continued to practise the language of signs until he
·mpletely mastered it, for the sake of holding intercourse with the dumb
ıy. " My chief amusement," he says, " is to make signs with the dumb
ɉ, which I do in perfection."

E

qualifications as an ecclesiastic, he combined *hauteur* ar
moroseness of manner, the relation of the parties may easily l
conceived; and although their acquaintance seems to ha·
begun favourably, their good understanding was of short duratio

The composer evidently took some pains to make a goc
impression on his new lord, for he now produced in successic
seven symphonies for the orchestra,[1] several divertimentos fi
instruments, etc.

The intercourse of the princes of Germany with the musicia1
of their household, appears to have been at this time remarkab
for anything rather than the *suaviter in modo*.   When o
Prince Antony Esterhazy recognised the genius of " the Moor
as he used to call Haydn, on account of his swarthy complexio
he is said to have received him into his establishment with the
words—" Go and dress yourself like a professor; do not let n
see you any more in this trim; you cut a pitiful figure."   Suc
was somewhat the style of the new archbishop.

But this subject may be dismissed for the present.   Amo1
the numerous compositions of the productive year 1772, l
church music exhibits a litany, which being well known, may l
instantly referred to in proof of Mozart's powers at sixtee
The grand fugue " Pignus futuræ gloriæ," still one of the mc
celebrated pieces at our musical festivals, forms part of tl
composition, which was written during the same month
" Il Sogno di Scipione," for some solemnity at which the princ
bishop presided in his ecclesiastical capacity.

In October, Mozart, accompanied by his father, set off f
Milan, to fulfil his engagement for the carnival opera of t:
new year, " Lucio Silla."   He was to receive for his labo
130 gigliati, and was provided with furnished apartments duri:
his stay.   In bringing out this work, the mismanagement "
the blessed theatrical people, who," as the father writes, " del:
everything to the last," was eminently conspicuous.   Aft
the recitative had been, as usual, forwarded from Salzbu1
the author of the libretto sent it to Vienna to be revised l
Metastasio, who not only made great alterations and improv
ments, but added an entire scene in the second act.   Tl

---

[1] These passing notices of the labours of Mozart's youth in particul
years, are not to be understood as embracing *all* that he wrote. I
certainty's sake, I have confined myself to the mention of those co:
positions which are dated by himself, omitting to reckon a great num1
of which the date, though probable, is undecided.   The wind-instrumei
of these symphonies are oboes and horns only.

bliged Wolfgang to re-write a considerable portion of the
ecitative. The non-arrival of principal singers occasioned
ther delays, and, at the end of the first week in December,
here were still fourteen pieces to write. The composer found
orrespondence difficult, and observes, " My thoughts are now
o intent upon my opera, that I am in danger of writing you an
ntire air instead of a letter." [1]

Another accident was the illness of the tenor, Cardoni, which
bliged them to seek a substitute at Turin and Bologna, who
hould have been a good singer, a good actor, and a person of
ome consideration, to represent " Lucio Silla " with a chance of
ccess. Signora de Amicis, the prima donna, was their kind
riend, and exerted herself much in their behalf; young Mozart
aving taken great pains to please her, and embellished her
rincipal air with new and peculiar passages of extraordinary
ifficulty. In the midst of the last rehearsals, which were
aborious, the music without ballet occupying four hours, they
vere present for three successive evenings at grand parties given
y Count Firmian, at which music went forward from five
'clock till eleven.

" Wolfgang," writes the father, " played every evening; but
n the third day he had to play immediately on the entrance
f their royal highnesses, and by their own desire. Both of
heir royal highnesses conversed with us for a long while."

It is a somewhat touching incident, that in the midst of all
his hurry and occupation, the two musicians found time to
ttend the cathedral to say prayers for the recovery of a sick
riend—their landlord, Hagenauer. At length the opera was
erformed, though not without troublesome and disagreeable
ccidents at the outset. The first was the delay of three hours
n commencing. Instead of beginning at the usual time, the
urtain rose at eight, and did not descend till two in the morning.
he composition which survived this ordeal must have possessed
xtraordinary fascination.

The scene in the theatre was one of unparalleled excitement.

" The archduke having five letters of compliments and good
ishes on the new year to write after dinner, with his own hand,

---

[1] He expresses nearly the same image of absorption, when he is com-
osing the third act of " Idomeneo." He writes to his father: " I am
ow so busy with the third act that it would be no great wonder if I were
o turn into a third act myself! "

to the emperor, empress, etc., come late; for you are to knc
that he writes very slowly.   Picture to yourself the whole theat
crammed full at half-past five o'clock, and the singers, both m‹
and women, on this the first evening, full of alarm at having
exhibit before so exalted an audience: and then think of the
frightened singers remaining in their terror, and the orchest
and the whole audience, of whom many were compelled to stan
waiting in the hot theatre, for three mortal hours before tl
piece began.   Secondly, you are to be informed that the tenc
who is a cathedral singer at Lodi, who was engaged one we‹
only before the performance, for want of a better, had nev
played in so large a theatre, and had even only twice in h
life been a *primo tenore* at Lodi.   This person being require
during the first air of the *prima donna* to make some demoı
stration of anger towards her, so exaggerated the demands ‹
the situation, that it seemed as if he were about to give her
box on the ear, or to knock her nose off with his fist, and at th
the audience began to laugh.   Signora de Amicis, in the heat ‹
her singing, not knowing why the public laughed, was surprise‹
and being unaware of the ridiculous cause, did not sing well tl
first evening, and an additional reason for this may be found :
a feeling of jealousy that the *primo uomo*, immediately on h
appearance on the scene should be applauded by the arc]
duchess.   This, however, was only the trick of a *musico;* for I
had contrived to have it represented to the archduchess that I
would be unable to sing from fear, in order to secure immedia·
applause and encouragement from the court.   But to conso
De Amicis she was sent for the next day to court, and had a
audience of both their royal highnesses for an hour."

The opera ran altogether between twenty and thirty night
at the end of which the composer, by his father's accoun
appears in very high spirits.   "Wolfgang is well, and whi
I am writing this, is making caprioles about the room."   " Tl
boy is father to the man;" such was Mozart in the intervals ‹
excessive application even to the last months of his life.[1]

"Lucio Silla " is the third Italian opera in three acts thε

---

[1] Postscripts as usual garnished the letters of the father, of which taI
a specimen, showing how Wolfgang, with that wonderful universalit
which distinguished him, was making playful acquisitions in other dire‹
tions, during the eventful crisis of " Lucio Silla."   " I have learned a ne
game here," he informs his sister, " which is called ' *Mercante in fiera.*'   ﾉ
soon as I get home we will play it.   I have also learned from a lady a ne
language, which is easy to speak, and troublesome to write, but useful."

ars witness to the unexampled diligence of his boyhood.
ith this composition, which shows him to have been still so
bmissive to the classical authorities of the age and country,
 to venture no innovations on the usual design or instru-
entation of the operas in fashion, his connection with Italy
ased. Germany was in future to be the theatre of his
ertions; but could either the father or his son have glanced
ı this page in their destiny, and have foreseen that they would
ver revisit Italy, their home journey to Salzburg would have
en as full of anxious foreboding as it was at present rich in
ıpe. Nothing would have given more pleasure to Leopold
ozart than to have established himself, or at least his son, at
orence; and during his present absence he even feigns a slight
ness to stay a little longer, in the hope of effecting his purpose.
Meantime, as the fame of the son increased, the pecuniary
sources of the family had become gradually impaired; for the
te tours of Mozart and his father had been far from productive.
veral indications of their straitened means are found in the
ters of the Italian tour, and in some which they afterwards
ote from Vienna; but they suffered these inconveniences
thout repining, thinking that a day might change the whole
pect of their affairs, and that such a genius as Wolfgang
ssessed, could never, in commercial phrase, " be brought
to the market " without commanding the means of ample
bsistence and comfort for the family.

PART III

HIS YOUTH

IT was with a design, of which the immediate object is unknowi that Leopold Mozart carried his son to Vienna, in the mont of July 1773. During their stay of somewhat more than tw months, Wolfgang composed among other music, six quarte for violins, tenor, and bass;—but the expedition itself seems 1 have been uninfluential on their future course of life, and merel to have afforded a temporary suspense to the monotony (existence at Salzburg, for which the elder Mozart had no acquired a great distaste; finding even in that isolated spo where primitive manners and good morals might easily hav been expected, plenty of room for the workings of envy and otho evil passions. In reviewing the numerous instrumental con positions of Mozart's youth we are struck with the effort 1 made to master his ideas. The quartet and symphony pro ductions of this period show many beautiful thoughts not yo turned to due account, but which he resumed and more full developed in subsequent compositions. Thus his memory i after life became a perfect storehouse of melodies and subjec that had long been floating in his imagination, and whic exquisite tact and judgment enabled him instantly to appl: We find this particularly in his operas and symphonies. Wii his quartet compositions of this period he was afterwards fa from satisfied; and when, about 1781, he made the acquaintano of Joseph Haydn at Vienna, he meekly acknowledged his ow inferiority in that department, and rejoiced to declare th publicly in behalf of his friend. Surely there is no mo beautiful aspect of the soul of Mozart than his passion for trui and his entire unselfishness.

In travelling with his father each seemed as a matter course to fall into a regular train of action; while one wa engrossed with the mechanical operations and plans of tl journey the other was wholly immersed in composition (recreations. Such a spiritual existence as this, from which 1

was afterwards cruelly awakened to the practical hardships of
life, at least ushered in his manhood. At Vienna we find him
at a concert in Mesmer's garden, playing on a new instrument,
the harmonica.[1] The rapidity with which he masters it is unnoticed by his father, who longs to possess one, but fears the
expense. His principal diversion at this time seems to have
been in exchanging pages of doggerel rhyme with a certain
M. Heffner, who held an appointment in the cathedral of
Salzburg.[2]

Of the various compositions on which he employed himself
during the remainder of the year in Salzburg, the most interest-
ng is his first quintet for two violins, two tenors, and violoncello,
a species of combination peculiar to himself, in which he afterwards carried the richness of chamber-music to perfection.
That his thoughts were continually bent upon extending the
effects of instrumental harmony, and that he had prepared himself for the revolution which he accomplished in the orchestra
by such exercises in combination as no other musician ever
made, will satisfactorily appear on consulting the MSS., which
are the record of his life from this time till his journey to Paris
in 1777. These works will be noticed in their place, as they are
blended with circumstances of the composer's personal history
which cannot be anticipated.

In December 1774, he went to Munich to write the *opera
buffa* for the carnival. This work, " La finta Giardiniera," first
manifested some of his most remarkable peculiarities as a
dramatic musician, and it is of great interest on that account.
Its melodies are imbued with elegance and tenderness, and the
whole may be considered as demonstrating an immense advance
in his art. His father was again his companion on this expedition, which was the last they ever made together. The
composer describes the effect of his opera in a letter to his
mother, January 14, 1775.

" My opera was brought out yesterday, and had, thank God!

[1] The sister of the celebrated Cecilia Davis had brought this instrument
into notice at Vienna. Mozart wrote a quintet, in which he combined it
with stringed instruments, in the last year of his life.
[2] These nonsense-verses may remind the reader of Canning's song on the
' University of Göttingen." He advises his correspondent to write better
verses, and continues:
" Sonst komm'
ich meiner Lebtag zu Salzburg nicht mehr in Dom;
denn ich bin gar *capax* zu gehen nach Constant-
inople, die doch allen Leuten ist bekannt "

such success that I cannot possibly describe to mamma the noise and commotion. In the first place the theatre was crammed so full that many persons were obliged to return home. At the close of every air there was a terrible noise with clapping and shouting ' Viva Maestro.' The electoress and the widowed lady, who were close to me, said ' Bravo.' The interval between the opera and the commencement of the ballet was entirely filled up with clapping and crying ' Bravo ' —now ceasing, and now commencing again, and so on. I and my father afterwards went into a room through which the whole court pass, and where I kissed the hands of the elector, the electoress, and others of the nobility, who were all very gracious. His Highness the Bishop of Chiemsee sent to me early this morning with congratulations on my success. ·

" With regard to our return, it will not be immediate—and mamma must not desire it, for she knows that we must have breathing time. We shall get home soon enough for—(*here something is erased*). But one true and necessary cause is that the opera will be performed again on Friday, and I must be present, or nobody would know it again, for they manage quite curiously here. A thousand little kisses to Bimberl."

The archbishop was at Munich, and though he did not hear the opera, its praises resounded in his ears on all sides. We see him in the following extract.

" Picture to yourself the embarrassment of his highness our lord and master, on hearing the praises of the opera from the electoral family and all the nobility of the court, and receiving their solemn congratulations thereon. He was, indeed, so embarrassed as to be unable to make any reply except by shaking his head and shrugging his shoulders."

Mozart was well pleased on this occasion to enjoy the companionship and sympathy of his sister, who was specially sent for from Salzburg to hear the opera. Her brother recommends her to be careful of taking cold on the journey in a clatter of ludicrous rhymes on one wo d; and seems altogether in the highest spirits, though again in the state of an " ingenious inamorato." [1] Her father's chief care is to place her in a

[1] Mademoiselle Molk is not now in his thoughts, but Mademoiselle Mīzerl, concerning whom we have the following: " My compliments to Roxalana, who is to drink tea with the Sultan this evening. Say to Mademoiselle Mizerl everything you can think of—she is not to doubt my love—I have

suitable house, where there is a staid mistress and a pianoforte. At all times the musician and the most circumspect of men, he provides against her losing anything even by this holiday excursion. She is to practise the sonatas of Paradies and Bach, and the concerto of Lucchesi. As a parting testimony to the excellence of " La finta Giardiniera " may be added that of the orchestra, who declared that " they had never heard a more attractive composition—the airs being all beautiful without exception." [1]

The present journey, likewise, gave occasion to two grand masses, an offertorium, and a vespers *de Dominica* for the chapel of the elector. Some of the finest of Mozart's church music originated at Munich, which assumed to be the seat of supreme authority in this branch of the art, for here Orlando di Lasso, the great Kapellmeister of St. John de Lateran at Rome, passed the last twenty years of his life at the head of an unrivalled choir, and here his motets were magnificently preserved on vellum. At Munich also lived Steffani the admired of Handel, who had relinquished the musical direction of St. Mark's at Venice, for appointments at that place. Surrounded by the traditions of such great masters, and writing for an excellent band and choir, it is not surprising that he was excited to unusual excellence.

On the 7th of March 1775, the father and son returned to Salzburg, where the court was soon enlivened by a visit from the Archduke Maximilian; and Mozart, being desired to celebrate the occasion by a serenata, produced " Il Re Pastore," in two acts, a work which was much admired.

He was now domesticated at Salzburg for nearly three years, an epoch of great interest in his personal history, as the misfortunes and disappointments of his future career, which form an almost incredible romance of real life, were chiefly prepared by circumstances evolved during this period.

It had been foretold by Grimm that monarchs would dispute

her constantly before my eyes in that charming déshabille." These oriental raptures commonly evaporate in a joke. In a postscript to his mother, written during the journey, he signs himself " thy attached, Franz Nazenblut," and dates Milan, May 5, 1756.

[1] The original scores of the eight extensive dramatic works, which we have noticed in their order, beginning with " Apollo and Hyacinth," and ending with " La finta Giardiniera " (of which the first act is lost), are still in the collection of M. André. Of these records of Mozart's youth not a note is known in England, though they are full of curiosity and interest. A multitude of his instrumental compositions, alike unknown, would certainly be well received in the present dearth of natural and spontaneous musical invention.

the possession of Mozart, and after the composition of " Don Giovanni," Haydn said that they would do so were they of his mind. But the public could not wonder at Mozart the man, as they had done at Mozart the child; and thus the general antici-pations of his future success, founded on the miracles of his infancy, were doomed, like Grimm's more glowing prediction, to be falsified by the event; for this great genius, whom all the world now acknowledges, neither achieved prosperity for himself, nor became an object for the generous strife of kings.

Salzburg was the first place in which he found his labours treated as of slight importance. His ready pen, at nineteen years of age, tested in numerous compositions for the church, the theatre, and the chamber; his brilliant performance on the clavier, organ-playing on festivals of the church, and most expressive violin-playing, may be thought to have been of some value to the archbishop, as he did not scruple to avail himself freely of the young man's services: but his munificence will excite surprise: all that Mozart received from him at this time being a nominal salary of about £1 1s. English *per annum*

This trifling acknowledgment (*spott-geld*) was what he had at first received when entered as a child on the establishment of the former prince, but now that he was fulfilling the double services of a most efficient composer and performer, it seemed high time to place him on a new footing; nevertheless, it was overlooked. Still he wrote on; determined to deserve, whether he obtained or not.

Among a multitude of compositions that he wrote for the archbishop's concerts, in 1775, are five concertos for the violin, which he probably performed himself.[1] His gentle disposition made him easily comply with any proposal to augment pleasure, however out of his usual course. During the following year, 1776, he seems to have made his last great effort to awaken the arch-bishop to some sense of his desert, and a due generosity of acknowledgment, by producing masses, litanies, serenades, divertimentos for instruments, clavier concertos, etc., too numerous for detail. But in vain; and what aggravated the injury of this monstrous appropriation of labour was, that the father, whose household economy was now somewhat pinched, on applying for permission to remedy these circumstances by a

[1] An act of complaisance; for violin-playing formed no part of his duty as concert-master. It will be observed that his father, on recalling him from Paris to Salzburg, in 1778, states expressly that he will *not* be expected to play the violin at court.

tour, was refused. From that hour Wolfgang threw by his
pen in disgust—at least as far as it concerned voluntary
labour.

Whatever the heart-burnings that such tyranny created, the
father not wishing to proceed to extremes with his prince, or
thinking it safe for the whole family to seek their fortunes elsewhere, concealed his feelings while he matured such a plan as in
the present posture of their affairs seemed most prudent. It
was determined that Wolfgang should resign his situation in the
household of the archbishop, and accompanied by his mother
proceed on a tour in quest of an appointment in the service of
some foreign prince, on obtaining which, his father and sister
could easily quit Salzburg, and establish themselves with him.
So feasible did this project seem, that Leopold Mozart did not
hesitate to incur some debts for the sake of carrying it into
execution.

But it is worth while to notice in this place the peculiar
direction of Mozart's studies in composition during the interval
now spent at Salzburg, where even the imperfection of the
orchestras seems to have exercised his invention—insomuch
that it is difficult to conceive any instruments, however hetero-
geneous, from which he would not have drawn effects. Here
he sometimes wrote masses without any *viola* part, and mostly
with incomplete wind instruments. The church service at
Salzburg requiring an instrumental piece called the " Epistle
sonata," he produced for that purpose many compositions of
which no model existed. Of this kind are many sonatas for
the organ and two violins; for the organ, two violins, and two
trumpets, or for the same instruments with the addition of
violoncello and bass, oboes and drums.[1]

Meanwhile, his pen was always at the disposal of his friends.
Mademoiselle Elizabeth Heffner, the sister of his rhyming
correspondent, was married in July 1776, and Mozart honoured
the occasion by a nuptial march for the full orchestra. The
Countess Lodron and her two daughters, who are said to have

[1] His divertimentos for wind-instruments display combinations at that
day quite as uncommon. Among them we find—ten pieces for two flutes,
three trumpets in C, two trumpets in D, and four drums; a divertimento
for the same instruments; several sestets for two oboes, two horns, and
two bassoons; pieces for the same instruments, with the addition of
clarionets and *corni inglesi* (tenor oboes); and last, though not least, an
adagio for two clarionets and three *corni di bassetti* (tenor clarionets).
These were the gradations by which Mozart's scores became eventually so
distinguished for the management and effect of the wind-instruments.

possessed incomparable talents on the clavier, received from him, during the same year, a triple concerto [1] for their favourite instrument. There was no style of music, however unusual the design or combination, in which he could not succeed; nor was there any sort of performer whom he could not please; so that never were the prospects of a young musician of such hopeful augury.

In September 1776, he transmitted a motet of his composition to the Padre Martini. This work was written at Munich, immediately after "La finta Giardiniera;" the elector having desired to hear some contrapuntal scientifically-treated composition by young Mozart. He was, therefore, obliged to prepare it in haste, for performance at the offertory on the following Sunday. The interesting facts narrated in this letter have been before alluded to; we have now only to invite attention to its modesty, earnestness, and just view of the artist's mission. Having described the origin of the work, he exclaims:

"Dear Padre,—I earnestly intreat you to give me your unreserved opinion thereupon. We live in this world to be continually advancing, and in science and the fine arts more especially, by interchanging views and communicating sentiments one to another, to be always learning something fresh.

"How often do I wish that I lived nearer to you, to have the advantage of your conversation and sympathy. I live in a country in which music has as yet had but little success. We still possess many fine players, and, more especially, scientific and tasteful composers, notwithstanding those who have already left us.

"With regard to the theatre, it is badly off in point of singers. We have no *musici*, and are not likely to have any, because they insist on being well paid, and liberality is not one of our failings. Meantime, I occupy myself in writing for the chamber and the church. There are two other contrapuntists here, namely, Michael Haydn and Cajetan Adlgasser. My father is Kapellmeister at the Metropolitan Church, and, therefore, I have the opportunity of writing for it as often as I like. But as he has already passed thirty-six years of his life in the service of this court, and knows that the archbishop has an antipathy to

[1] Sebastian Bach had already written concertos for three claviers; but that species of composition, which required the handling of a great master, had not penetrated into Southern Germany until the same idea struck Mozart.

the sight of old people, he at present troubles himself but little
with musical performances, and devotes himself to the literature
of the art as his favourite pursuit.

" Our church music differs exceedingly from that of Italy;
the more so, as a mass with *Kyrie, Gloria, Credo,* the epistle
sonata, the offertorium or motetto, *Sanctus,* and *Agnus Dei,*
must not last longer than three quarters of an hour at most,
even on the greatest festivals, when the prince himself officiates
at the mass. ˙A particular study is necessary for this kind of
composition, a mass having to be scored with all the instruments of the orchestra, and even with military trumpets!
Indeed? Yes, dear padre. Oh, how glad I should be to tell
you many things which I have to say."

In his reply, the Padre Martini approves the composition,
re-echoes all that Mozart has said respecting music, and begs
him to persevere! The benevolence of the good father had
made such a strong impression on the minds of the family that,
in commencing any new step in life, their first thought was to
turn to him as to their friend and counsellor. Some notion of
the extent of his musical influence throughout Italy and Catholic
Germany may be gathered from the fact, that the father who
had procured from him a written recommendation of his son,
prized it more highly than the diplomas of the academies of
either Bologna or Verona. The padre, however, does not appear
to have realised the hopes his friendship inspired.

From the excessive industry which characterised the twenty-
first year of Mozart's life, there is little doubt but that he was
often meditating on the advances of the " subtle thief of youth; "
though now less anxious to convince himself that he deserved,
than to have his deserts handsomely acknowledged. In the
autumn of 1776, he made several dramatic sketches. One of
them, composed for Signor Palmini, a buffo singer, shows somewhat of the happy comic style which he afterwards developed
in " Figaro." He describes this air as *in tempo commodo d' un
gran ciarlone ;* and gives the great chatterer, who is a military
man, a *capitano,* such a ludicrous clatter of triplets on one note,
with a syllable to each, as must have overpowered even the wife
whom he addresses. In such varied styles did he entertain the
court of Salzburg, where his talents were never undervalued till
he sought to be remunerated for them. Then however he was
told, in no measured terms, that his productions were worthless,,

and that he ought to go to a conservatorio in Italy to learn how to compose!

In September 1777, Mozart was prepared to accompany his mother on the projected tour, to offer his services to the first prince who would accept them. The correspondence of this period presents a kind of autobiography, in which there is much of that kind of truth which is said to be " stranger than fiction," and which, in some of its phases, can with difficulty be associated with so fascinating a talent. But if the history of the great musician's first practical acquaintance with life raise indignation at the dulness of the age that could refuse shelter and patronage to one as modest in his demands as he was rare in his powers, it is at least consoling to see the triumph of genius over circumstances. Mozart may be seen unworthily treated; he may occasionally appear in a pathetic aspect; but he is never humiliated, nor dispossessed of the bright reward of his own conscious superiority. And it may be here remarked, that even the vulgar distresses, which form but too prominent a part in the adventures of genius, acquire, through the softening influence of time, somewhat of the colouring of romance.

The mother and son left Salzburg on the 23rd of September 1777. The correspondence of this tour occupies a period of about sixteen months; and they had scarcely left home when it began. The following letter from the father, dated only two days after their departure, in reply to one he had already received, found them at Munich, the first place at which they stayed. It will remind the reader of a striking observation— " When I am reading a book, whether bad or good, it seems to be alive and talking to me; "[1] and, certainly, the nearest approach to this vitality is found in letters that are the genuine product of passion and situation.

" I received my dear Wolfgang's letter to-day, at noon, with the greatest joy; and M. Bullinger, who is now with me, and desires to be remembered, has also read it and laughed heartily over it. I am quite pleased to find that you are well; I am myself, thank God! much better. When you were gone, I went upstairs exceedingly faint and depressed, and threw myself upon a chair. I had taken some pains to keep out of the way at our separation, not to embitter the farewell; and in this hurry of mind I forgot to give my son the paternal blessing.

---

[1] In the commonplaces of Swift and Pope.

I ran to the window and sent it after both of you, but did not see you go out of the city gate; and you must have already passed, as I had been sitting a long time unconscious of anything. Nannerl wept so passionately that I was obliged to do everything in my power to console her.

" So passed such a melancholy day as I never thought in all my life to have experienced.

" I requested M. Glatz, of Augsburg, to call upon me early to-day, and we were both of opinion that you ought to put up at the Lamb, at Augsburg, in the street of the Holy Cross. The chambers there are neat and pretty, the dinners cost only thirty kreutzers a head, and it is an inn much frequented by people of the first consequence, English, French, etc. You will be quite close there to the Church of the Holy Cross, and also to my brother, Francis Aloys, who lives in the Jesuit's-street. You must have nothing to say to M. Albert, for it is very dear at the Three Moors, they charge very high for rooms, and every meal costs from forty-five to forty-eight kreutzers.

" In case you go to Augsburg, Wolfgang must immediately visit Stein, the organ builder. M. Stein, who has not seen him since he was seven years old, will hardly known him again. He might say that he was from Innsprück, and had commissions to look over instruments. M. Glatz tells me that M. Stein, M. Bioley, and M. Fingerl, will be able together to get up an excellent concert. You must also visit M. Christoph von Zabuesnig, who wrote the beautiful German poem on you at Salzburg, he is a merchant and a literary man; and through him something handsome and serviceable may, perhaps, be got into the *Augsburg Journal*. The merchant Gasser is he who packed and sent my books, free of expense, to Franckfort, and returned me the money. You must call on him, and thank him in my name; it is a favour which he has it in his power to show me at any time. My brother, or his daughter, can easily introduce you to *his grace* M. von Langenmantel, the chief magistrate, to whom you are to make my very respectful compliments. Mamma knows how intimately we have been acquainted. We travelled to Salzburg together, and M. von Heffner's father was with us.

" When you go to any court, you must not wear your cross; but you may wear it every day at Augsburg, it will create observation and respect there, and, in fact, in any place where there is no governing prince. If you choose to visit the convents of the Holy Cross and St. Ulrich, you can do so, and try their organs. M. Stein will, probably, take you to his organ at the Barefooted Friars. M. Hilber's son is in the convent at St. Ulrich. There is some organist and composer at Augsburg, that they make a great noise about, but I have forgotten his name.

"You will do well when you are staying anywhere, to get the servant always to put the boot-tree into the boots. The package of music can always be sent beforehand, and remain in the luggage warehouse; but you ought to buy a great oil-cloth, and have it well wrapped round the old one to make all secure.

"Should you leave Munich without being able to give me intelligence of it, you must put up a bill at the post-office with the following directions: 'If letters should arrive addressed—à Mr. Wolfgang Amadé Mozart, *Maître de Musique*, the same are to be forwarded to the host of the Lamb, in the street of the Holy Cross.'

"The breeches belonging to the iron-grey coat have been left behind. If I find no other opportunity of sending them, I shall give them, together with the Andretterinn music, some country-dances, and the *adagio* and rondos composed by Brunetti,[1] and anything else that may come to hand, to the messenger, who, if he should not find you, as he will probably not arrive before noon on Monday, can leave them with my brother at Augsburg.

"The service lasted till a quarter to eleven, and an *Agnus Dei* of Haydn's was again performed, as Rust was not ready.[2] The sonata was by Wolfgang. Don't forget to ask for letters at Munich, from the Prince von Chiemsee, for example. Count Seinsheim can also furnish you with recommendations to Wurzburg, the bishop is his father's brother."

This letter is promptly acknowledged by an account of their safe arrival, on the afternoon of the 24th, and their going to the custom-house, accompanied by a grenadier with a fixed bayonet. They meet two old acquaintances, Signor Consoli and M. Albert, and after a long spell at the clavier they all go to supper. The next day, Wolfgang calls on Count Seau, but

[1] Brunetti was a solo violin-player attached to the household of the archbishop. Several of Mozart's sonatas for piano and violin were written for performance with him.
[2] This characteristic incident must not be overlooked. On the very first Sunday of Mozart's absence, a composer for the cathedral is *not ready* with his work. That, we may be sure, had never been a complaint against him.

he is gone out into the country to hunt, and has taken Bernard, the master of the chorus, with him. Patience!

" There is a certain Professor Huber here, perhaps you may remember him better than I do. He tells me that he both saw and heard me at the young M. von Mesmer's, the last time that we were at Vienna. He is of about the middle size, pale, with whitish grey hair, and in features, not much unlike the under riding master. His situation is that of vice-intendant of the theatre, and it obliges him to read through every play presented for performance; to improve, to add to, to alter, or to refuse it. He comes to Albert's every evening, and often talks with me.

" To-day is the 26th. On Friday I again called on Count Seau, at half-past eight in the morning. It happened that as I entered the house, Madame N., the actress, was just coming out, and she asked me, ' Do you wish to see the count? ' ' Yes.' ' He is at present in his garden, and there is no knowing when he will come out of it.' I asked where his garden was. ' Oh,' said she, ' I want to speak to him, too, and we will go together.' We had scarcely reached the gate before we met the count, at some twelve paces distant. He knew me instantly, and addressed me by name. He was very courteous, and seemed well acquainted with everything that had happened to me. We ascended the garden steps slowly and quite alone, during which time I briefly explained my business. He told me that I ought to go directly to the elector and request an audience of his highness. But should I not be able to obtain that, I ought to put the matter into writing. I begged him to keep what I had told him secret, which he promised me. On my saying to him that a real composer might here be lost, he replied, ' That I am well aware of.' " [1]

He next goes to the Bishop of Chiemsee, who promises to speak to the electoress on his behalf. His friend, Herr Albert, also speaks to Count Schönborn, and his wife (sister to the archbishop), who are passing through the town; and they are

[1] That a pretender might succeed and prosper is illustrated by an anecdote which he gives us in this very letter:—" M. Johannes Krönner has been appointed vice-concert-master, and that through a rude speech. Two symphonies of his composition (*Dio mené liberi*) had been performed; the elector said to him, ' Did you really compose that? ' ' Yes, your highness.' ' Who taught you? ' ' A schoolmaster in Switzerland. People think a great deal of composition; but this schoolmaster taught me more than all our composers here put together could have done.' "

F

incredulous on hearing of his paltry allowance at Salzburg.[1] In reply to all these minute particulars of "hope deferred," his father writes to exhort him to persevere, telling him how to proceed, to write a few things gratis for the theatre, and to ascertain the elector's taste, and adapt himself to it. He encloses his two *Diplomata*, and an attestation from Padre Martini,[2] and adds, "It will create great astonishment when it is known that you have been a *maestro di capella* in these academies for seven years."

But the difficulties still increase, although the son, in the following letter, evidently prefers all this disappointment, with its dim prospect of success in the distance, to the drudgery and obscurity of Salzburg.

"I was with Prince Zeil to-day, who said to me very politely, ' I fear that we shall not be able to accomplish much here. I spoke privately to the elector when I dined with him at Nymphenburg. He replied that it was too early as yet—he ought to travel in Italy and get fame. I deny him nothing—but at present it is too early.' There we are! Most of these great gentlemen have such a horrible mania for Italy.

"The Bishop of Chiemsee also conversed privately with the electoress on the subject. She shrugged her shoulders, and said that she would do all that she could, but was very doubtful. Count Seau inquired of the bishop, who related to him everything that had passed. 'Are you not aware that Mozart has not so much at home, but that he might remain here with a little assistance?' The bishop replied that he did not know it, but was doubtful. However, Mozart could be spoken with on the subject. This was the reason why Count Seau was so absorbed and thoughtful on the following day. I like to be here—and I and many of my friends are of opinion that if I could stay here a year or two and earn a reputation by my compositions, that I should rather be solicited by the court than have to solicit.

"To-day the 30th, after talking with Wotschika, I went to court by nine o'clock. I found everybody in hunting uniform.

---

[1] He ends with an expression of disgust at the mode of life in Salzburg. "I am always," he says, " in my best humour, and feel as light as a feather, *since I have left all that chicanery behind me.*" . . .

[2] In this document the padre testifies to Mozart's compositions in various styles, and says that, at fourteen years of age, he tried him with a multitude of subjects *extempore* on the harpsichord, and that he executed them all with great skill and perfect art.

When the elector approached me, I said, 'Will your highness
be pleased to permit me to lay myself and my services humbly
at your feet?' The elector answered more than once, 'Yes,
my dear child; but there is no vacancy at present.'

" M. Wotschika advises me to let the elector see me
frequently."

The father now begins to suspect that secret enemies are at
work, and to distrust Munich. He advises him to continue his
journey, pointing out places, such as Mannheim, Trier, Mayence,
where the mania for Italy does not extend. He tells him that
there are no Italians at all in the service of the little Protestant
princes, and concludes with a hint that he is beginning to be
missed at Salzburg.[1]

The next letter from the son, in which he makes a proposal
for his future life, his art uppermost in his thoughts, is full of
interest. How characteristic the touch about people who
sneeze, talk, or take snuff, while music is going on.

" MUNICH, *October* 2, 1777.

" I played to Count Salern and the countess, for two days
together, a great many things out of my head. You cannot
imagine how delighted the count was; and he understands
music, for he always says *bravo* in those places where other
cavaliers take a pinch of snuff, or begin to sneeze, or to hem, or
commence a conversation. I told him that I only wished the
elector had been present, that he might have heard; he knows
nothing about me, he does not know what I can do. I would
put it to the proof; he might collect all the composers in Munich,
and add to them others from Italy, France, Germany, England,
or Spain. I would write with any of them. I told him my
Italian adventures, and requested that if I happened at any time
to be the subject of discourse, he would allude to them. He
said, ' My power is but small, but what I can do, I will with all
my heart.'

" It is his opinion, that if I could manage to remain here, the
business would be accomplished as a thing of course. And

---

[1] The steward of the household was a great friend of Mozart's, and had
just bought four horses, and was longing for Wolfgang's return that he
might see them, for he had acquired the taste for horses, which prevailed
at Salzburg, from the example of the archbishop, who kept no less than
two hundred in his stables. This archbishop, who was too haughty to do
justice to Mozart's genius, nevertheless felt the void which his absence left
in the concerts.

were I entirely alone it would not be so absolutely impossible; for I should get 300 florins, at least, from Count Seau, and my board would be of little consequence, as I am perpetually invited out, and if not Albert is delighted to have me to dinner. I eat but little, drink water, and finish with some fruit and a small glass of wine. I would, provided my friends saw no objection, make an engagement with Count Seau to produce four German operas every year, partly *buffe*, partly *serie*. I should then have a night or benefit for myself, which is at present the custom, and this would produce me at least 500 florins, which, with my salary, would be 800, if not more, for Reiner, an actor and singer, took on his night 200 florins; and I am a great favourite here, and how much more so should I become if it were in my power to elevate the national lyric stage of Germany? And that I should certainly do, for on hearing the German melo-drama, I felt a violent inclination to write.[1]

"The *prima donna* here is a native of this place, named Keiserin. She is the daughter of the cook of a certain Bavarian nobleman, and a very pleasant girl on the stage; but I have never seen her nearer. When I heard her it was her third appearance. She has a beautiful voice—neither strong nor weak, but very pure and good in the intonation. Her singing master is Valesi, and you soon discover by her performance that he knows both how to sing and how to teach singing. When she sustains a note for a couple of bars, I have been delighted to observe how beautifully she makes the *crescendo* and *decrescendo*. Her shake is at present but slow, but that I like, for it will be so much the purer and clearer when she quickens it. Besides, it is easier to do fast. The people are exceedingly pleased with her, and I with them. Mamma was in the parterre; she went at half-past four to get a place, but I not till half-past six as I am well known and free of the house, and can go into the boxes when I will. I was in the box of the Brancas. As I looked at the Keiserin through my glass she sometimes drew a tear from me; and I often called *brava ! bravissima !* when I remembered that it was but her third attempt on the stage.

"The piece is called 'Das Fischermädchen,' and is a very good adaptation, with music by Piccini. They have no original

[1] True self-appreciation. It was only for him to compose, and the German lyric stage *must* be elevated. How the "Don Giovanni," "Zauberflöte," "Figaro," etc., rise up to confirm the truth of this prediction, and to heighten the interest of a moment at which it was unaccomplished!

pieces as yet; but they now wish to give a German *opera seria,* and it is suggested that I compose it. Professor Huber, whom I before mentioned to you, is one of the persons who express this desire.

"Baron Rumling said to me a short time ago, ' The theatre is my delight; good actors and actresses, a good company of singers, and such a capital composer as yourself.' That is, indeed, but talk; and people sometimes say more than they mean; but he certainly never spoke to me so before.

"At eight o'clock this morning I went to Count Seau. I explained myself briefly, and said, ' I merely call to give your excellency a clear view of myself and my affairs. I have been reproachfully told to travel in Italy. It is well known that I have spent sixteen months in Italy, and have written three operas. What happened to me there besides, you will see by these papers.' I then put the diplomata into his hands, and observed, ' I only show these to your excellency, in order that if you hear any unjust observations on me, you may be able to take my part with confidence.' He asked me if I intended to go to France. I said that I intended to remain in Germany. He, however, understood at Munich, and laughing with pleasure replied, ' So, you intend to stay here.' ' No,' I returned, ' I should have been very glad, and to confess the truth, if I had only had for that purpose some small allowance from the elector, it would have been a pleasure to me to devote my pen to the service of your excellency, and without the least motive of interest.' At these words he pulled off his night-cap to me."

To all this the father, desirous for his fame as well as his profit, answers that he must not throw himself away.

. . . "That you could support yourself alone at Munich is no doubt true; but what honour would there be in that? How the archbishop would laugh! You can do that in any place, not at Munich only. But one must not make oneself so little, or throw oneself away at that rate. There is no need as yet."

This advice appears to have awakened the pride or the reason of the young composer, who soon afterwards sets out for Augsburg, where he meets some pleasant adventures, which he relates with wonderful dramatic gusto, but is still as far from attaining the object of his journey as ever. He writes from Augsburg on the 14th of October 1777.

"We left Munich on the 11th, at noon, and reached this place safely by nine o'clock in the evening. We propose, at present, to continue our journey on Friday, that is the day after to-morrow; for, to convince you of the generosity of Messieurs the Augsburgers, I assure you I never visited a place in which I was so overwhelmed with compliments. My first visit was to his worship, the magistrate. I was conducted thither by M. Vetter, an excellent and amiable man, and a citizen of the highest respectability, who had, however, the honour to sit cooling his heels in the hall like a footman, until the arch-magistrate released me. I did not forget, at the commencement of our interview, to present the respectful compliments of my father. He remembered everything very graciously, and inquired of me, ' How has the gentleman been? ' ' Exceedingly well, thank God,' I replied, ' and you—I trust that you have been in good health.' His politeness increased upon this, and he said, ' they,' and I said, ' Your Grace,' as indeed I had done from the beginning. I had then to mount up with him to his son-in-law, who lives on the second floor, and meanwhile M. Vetter had the honour to sit waiting on a stair in the hall. I was obliged forcibly to restrain myself, or I should have taken the liberty to allude to this. In these apartments I was detained for three quarters of an hour, playing on a good clavichord of Stein's, in the presence of his son, his young wife, and an old lady. I played fantasias, and afterwards whatever music they had, *prima vista;* among the rest, some very pretty pieces by one Edelmann. They were all excessively polite, and so was I, it being a rule of mine to use people in their own way. Happening to mention that I should call on Stein after dinner, the young gentleman immediately volunteered to conduct me thither. I thanked him for his kindness, and promised to call at two o'clock in the afternoon. I went, and we set off together in company with the brother-in-law, who, in appearance, perfectly resembles a student. Although I had requested them not to let it be known who I was, M. von Langenmantel was still so imprudent as to say to Stein, ' I have here the honour of presenting to you a virtuoso on the clavier,' and he smiled. I immediately protested against this, declaring that I was nothing more than an unworthy pupil of M. Sigl, at Munich, from whom I was charged with many thousand compliments. Stein shook his head doubtfully, and at length said, ' Perhaps I have the honour of seeing Mr. Mozart? ' ' Oh, no,' said I, ' my name is Trazom.[1] I have brought a letter to you.' He took the letter, and was about to open it instantly, but I did not leave him time. 'What! will you stay to read the letter now?' said I. 'Pray open the door of your warehouse, and let us see your pianofortes, for I am most anxious to try them.' He opened the door, saying, 'Well, let it be as it may, I cannot think that I am deceived.'

"I ran immediately to one of the three pianofortes that stood in the room, and while I was playing he could scarcely get the letter open from his anxiety to ascertain the truth. He read the signature only. 'Oh!' cried he, and embraced me over-joyed. I shall shortly give you some account of his instruments."

In this scene, so graphically depicted, and in that frequent recurrence of dialogue and situation, which, in all his letters, makes such a striking contrast to the narrative style of general correspondence, Mozart's destination for the theatre is clearly indicated.

His next letter from Augsburg enters into a minute criticism upon Stein's pianofortes, showing how thoroughly he under-stood the secrets of their workmanship. Pianofortes were just at that time coming into use, and those of Stein, one of the chief musical mechanics and improvers of keyed-instruments in the last century, were amongst the earliest and best specimens. He charged 300 florins for his best instruments. Mozart was not satisfied with playing on the pianos; he resolved to try the organ, to the infinite surprise of the maker.

"When I told Herr Stein that I should like to play upon his organ, for that the organ was my passion, he was much surprised, and said, 'What! can such a man as you—such a pianist, like to play on an instrument that has no softness, no expression, no *piano* or *forte*, but where everything goes on alike?' 'That is all of no consequence, the organ is still in my eyes and ears the king of instruments.' 'Well—at any rate;' and so we set off together. I soon found by his talk, that he did not expect me to do much upon the organ; he thought that I should merely play it like the clavier. He told me that he had taken Chobert, on his own request, to the organ, and added, 'I began to regret it, as Chobert told everybody, and the church was tolerably full; for though I knew that the man possessed

[1] An anagram formed by the inversion of the letters of his name. What ready whim there was in this!

spirit, fire, and rapidity of finger, I also knew that such qualities were of no great use on the organ. However, when he commenced, I soon altered my opinion.' I made no other reply than, ' What, do you think Herr Stein that I shall *run about* upon your organ? Ah, that must be treated in an entirely different manner.' When we reached the choir, I began to prelude; he smiled; then came a fugue: 'I can now believe,' said he, 'that you like to play the organ, since you play in that manner.' "

His " name-day " being now arrived, his father writes to him, exhorting him to fulfil all the duties of a good Christian. The passage is illustrative of the kind of letters which used to pass on such occasions between the members of a family; a pious custom, but liable to degenerate at last, from systematic repetition, into mere formality.

" You know me. I am no pedant, no monk, or sham saint; but one request you cannot refuse me, and this is, that you will take such care of your soul as not to let the dying hour of your father be embittered by the heavy self-reproach that he had neglected anything necessary to your eternal salvation. Farewell! Be prudent; be happy! Cherish and respect your mother, who has now but too much trouble in her old age; and love me as I do you—that is as your truly anxious and careful father."

During Mozart's stay at Augsburg, he visited the convent of the Holy Cross. This introduces us to new characters, and fresh scenes and criticisms. The sketch of Stein's daughter is a perfect bit of caricature.

" The dean, a pleasant cheerful man, is named Zeschinger: he is a relation of Eberlin's, and knows you quite well. At night, at supper-time, I played the Strasburg violin concerto. *It went like oil.* Every one praised the pure round tone. They then brought a little clavichord, on which I preluded and played variations by Fischer. Then some one whispered the dean to get me to play in the organ style. I requested him to give me a subject; but as he did not comply, one of the monks gave me one. I played upon it in a jocose style, and in the middle (the fugue was in G minor), I began in the major, but still playfully and in the same *tempo ;* then came the subject reversed; and, at last, the thought struck me of giving a sportive character to the theme of the fugue. I did not stop long considering, but did it at once, and it went as accurately as if cut out with a razor.

" The dean was quite beside himself with pleasure. ' Well,'
said he, ' I could never have believed what I have just heard;
though the bishop, indeed, told me that he had never in his
life heard any one touch the organ in such a connected, solemn
style.' The bishop had heard me some days before, when the
dean was not present. At length some one produced a fugued
sonata for me to play. ' Gentlemen,' said I, ' this is too much;
I must confess that this sonata is not to be played so very
easily.' ' Yes, that I will believe,' cried my great friend the
dean, ' as if that were possible!—there is and there can be
nothing too difficult.' ' However,' said I, ' I will just try it.'
Then I heard the dean behind my back calling me names—' O
you *Erzschufte !* ' ' O you *Spitzbube !* '[1] I played till eleven
o'clock, and was at last absolutely bombarded with subjects for
fugues, and Stein has just put before me a new sonata by Becché.

" *Apropos* of Stein's little girl: whoever can see and hear her
play without laughing, must be like her father—*of stone.*[2] She
does not place herself in the middle of the instrument, but
towards the treble notes, for more convenience in moving about
and making grimaces. The eyes are distorted; when a passage
comes twice over, it is played twice as slowly the second time;
if three times, still slower. When she has a passage to execute,
she lifts her arm into the air, and if it requires any particular
emphasis, it is done with the arm and not with the finger, and
that in the heaviest and worst possible manner. The most
delightful of all, however, is that when a passage occurs which
ought to flow on as smoothly as oil, and of course requires that
the fingers should be changed, she gives herself no concern on
that point, but at the proper time lifts up her hand, and begins
again quite at her ease; through which one is in frequent
expectation of a false note, and a very curious effect is produced.[3]
I merely write this to give my father some notion of clavier-
playing and teaching, which he may at a future time turn to
account.[4]

[1] Appellations that, like " *conjuror* " and " *rogue*," portray the intoxicat-
ing effect of the performance, and the interest and affection which the
artist excited personally. Whoever has witnessed the enthusiasm which
even minor musical genius sometimes creates in the social circle, will easily
feel the vivacity and truth of this description.
[2] A pun upon the name of Stein, which means stone.
[3] The little girl, whose playing is here so ludicrously described by Mozart,
was afterwards married to the celebrated pianoforte-maker, Streicher, of
Vienna, and became the protecting friend and kind monitress of Beethoven.
[4] These criticisms upon the mechanism of performance are invaluable,
and show Mozart's great mastery of the subject. In a subsequent letter

"M. Stein is absolutely besotted in his daughter. She is a
present eight years and a half old, and learns everything by
memory. She might become clever; she possesses talent; bu
on this plan she will never acquire rapidity, because she pursue
the very best method to make the hand heavy. The mos
necessary, the most difficult, and principal thing in music
namely, the *time*, she will never acquire, if she is accustomed
from infancy to play out of time. I have talked with Stein fo
two hours together on this subject, and have already made a
convert of him. He now asks my advice in everything. He
has been besotted with Becché;[1] but he now sees and hears tha
I play more than Becché; that I make no grimaces, and ye
play so expressively that no one has yet used his pianofortes
so well, and that I am always accurate in the time. They al
wonder at that. They cannot comprehend the manner of keep
ing the left hand independent in the *tempo rubato* of an adagio
for they are accustomed to let the left hand follow the right. Coun
Wolfegg, and others who are great admirers of Becché, have
just said publicly at the concert, that I put Becché on the shelf
The count walked up and down the concert-room, declaring
that he had never heard anything like it in his life. He said to
me, 'I must tell you that I never heard you play as you have
done to-day; and I shall say the same thing to your father
when I see him at Salzburg.'

"What do you think came next after the symphony? The
concerto for three claviers.[2] M. Demler plays the first, I the
second, and M. Stein the third. Then I played alone the las
sonata in D for Durnitz, then my concerto in B, then again alone

from Mannheim, he exposes with like minuteness the vile performance o
the Abbé Vogler. "His mechanism," he says, "is wretched; the lef
thumb is just like the late Adlgasser's, and he plays all the runs of th
right hand downward with his first finger and thumb."

[1] A celebrated clavierist of the day settled at Mannheim.

[2] Dedicated to the Countess Lodron and her daughters. It commence
in this manner, and may carry the reader back to the Augsburg concert:

strict fugue in C minor; then a magnificent sonata in C major,
nd with a rondo out of my head made an end. There was a
rodigious hubbub and noise. Stein did nothing but make
ɩces and grimaces of astonishment; and Demler laughed con-
nually. This last is quite a curious man; when anything
leases him, he laughs immoderately. He almost began to
ꞷear at me.

"The concert brought ninety florins, without deducting
ⅹpenses. Including two ducats that we took in the room, we
ave altogether made 100 florins. The expenses are not more
ɩan sixteen florins thirty kreutzers, as I had the room free of
ɔst; and the greatest part of those who assisted have, I
elieve, given their services.

"I kiss your hand, and thank you dutifully for the wish on
ꞁy name-day. Be under no apprehensions for me; I have God
lways before my eyes; I know his power; I fear his anger;
ut I also know his love, his compassion and mercy to his
reatures; and that he never forsakes those who serve him.
have entirely resigned myself to his will, and in the conscious-
ess of doing so, live contented and happy. I shall certainly
o my best to live carefully according to the advice and instruc-
ɩon that you have had the goodness to give me."

The travellers quitted Augsburg, and went through Donau-
ꞟörth and Nördlingen as far as Hochenaltheim, the residence
f the Prince of Wallerstein. After staying there for a couple
f days, they pursued their journey to Mannheim, which they
ƨached on the 30th of October. On the following day, Mozart
ꞟent to a rehearsal, and could hardly preserve his gravity, the
eople stared at him in such a fashion. Some who knew him
y reputation, were civil and respectful; but for the rest—
they think," says he, "because I am little and young, that
othing great or old can be in me;—*but they shall soon see.*" [1]

He had now reached the residence of another German elector,
ꞟhich was the seat of no small pretension in musical matters.
'he orchestra of the prince's chapel at Mannheim, formed by
he elder Stamitz, had the reputation of being the best in
ꞁermany; and the musicians who pass in review, in the course

[1] In Bayle's anecdotes of men of learning, we find the same sentiment
ⅹpressed in a repartee. On Baldus (another little man) entering an
ssembly, they exclaimed "*Minuit præsentia famam,*" to which he in-
ꞁantly replied, "*Augebit cœtera virtus.*" The promptness of this was
ꞁuch applauded.

of the following letters, were mostly more or less celebrate
By some of them, who admired without fearing the genius
young Mozart, he was received with open arms; but by othei
secretly intrigued against; and after being kept in suspense l
specious behaviour, and delusive hopes, for more than fo·
months, he finally lost his expectations of an engagement, pri
cipally, as it is believed, through the machinations of the Abl
Vogler, the second Kapellmeister, a man whose high admiratic
of Mozart was accompanied by envy as profound, and who fe
the instability of his footing in the presence of such a rivε
Detesting the unworthy arts by which charlatans impose upɩ
the favour of the great, it is to be feared that the composer w
not sufficiently cautious in his relations with the party wl
disliked Vogler, and that some of his shrewd and sarcast
criticisms may have taken wind, and reached the ears of tl
favourite. But of this the correspondence will afford ε
opportunity to judge.

"This is my second letter from Mannheim. I go every dε
to Cannabich's, and my mother accompanied me to-day. Ca·
nabich [1] is quite a different man from what he used to be; tl
whole orchestra agree in this opinion. He is exceedingly parti
to me. He has a daughter who plays the clavier very prettil
and in order to win his friendship entirely, I am now at work ɩ
a sonata for her. When I had completed the first allegro aɪ
the andante, I took it to the house and played it. You cann
imagine how pleased they are with it. Some of the orchest
were present, namely, young Danner the horn-player, Lang, aɪ
the oboist Ramm, who plays excellently, and has a fine pu
tone. I have made him a present of a concerto for the obc
which was copied in a room at Cannabich's. The man is out
his wits with pleasure. I played the concerto to him to-day ɩ
the pianoforte at Cannabich's; and *though it was known to be miɪ*
it pleased very much. Nobody says that it is a bad compositio·
because the people don't happen to understand it. They shou
inquire of the archbishop, and he would be sure to put them
the right way.[1]

"I played all my six sonatas at Cannabich's to-day. Kape
meister Holzbauer afterwards took me to Count Savioli, t·

[1] Cannabich was a violin player, educated by the elder Stamitz, a
leader of the Mannheim orchestra. It was afterwards his good fortune
lead the opera of "Idomeneo" on its first production. He was a dabb
in composition, having studied under Jomelli.
A sneer at the court of Salzburg.

perintendent of the music, with whom I found Cannabich.
olzbauer told the count in Italian, that I was very desirous of
e favour of playing before the elector, as I had been here
teen years ago at seven years of age; but now I was grown
ler and bigger, and in my art likewise. 'Yes, indeed,' said
e count, ' that is the—' What do I know whom he takes me
r? Cannabich then began to speak. I appeared as if I heard
thing and entered into conversation with those about me. I
served, however, that he spoke of me in a very serious and
rnest manner. The count then said to me, ' I hear that you
ay tolerably well on the clavier; ' to which I replied by a bow."

He gives an account of the orchestra, which was powerful
d good; but adds, that he would hardly trust a mass of his
be produced here:

" Merely because, under present circumstances, it is neces-
ry to write principally for the instruments, it being utterly
possible to conceive anything more wretched than the vocal
partment. Six soprani, six alti, six tenori, and six bassi, to
enty violins and twelve basses, stand just in the proportion
o to 1."

Of Vogler, who had just then been appointed, he says, that
: was a musical jester, a fellow who imagines great things and
ecutes little; and that he was detested by the whole orchestra.
e is pleased, however, with a mass by Holzbauer:

" On Sunday I heard a mass by Holzbauer,[1] which though
ritten six-and-twenty years ago, is still exceedingly good.
e writes very well; has a good church style; makes an effective
sposition of the voices and instruments; and his fugues are
cellent."

Sensible as he was that the brevity of the movements, and
at the style which he had adopted in his own masses,[2] in
ference to the taste of the archbishop, might unfit those
orks for general use, he refrained only from exhibiting himself

[1] Holzbauer, here commended by Mozart, was a native of Vienna, and
e of many successful musicians who in youth prosecuted the art under
fficulties. He learned the elements of music of the choir boys at St.
ephen's, and composition by the perusal of the " Gradus ad Parnassum "
Fux. He married a singer, and made the tour of Italy with success.
is compositions are voluminous; he wrote more than 180 symphonies for
e orchestra. He was now sixty-six years old.
[2] Amongst the last things he composed before he left Salzburg were the
asses known in the English editions as Nos. 2 and 4.

as a church composer at Mannheim, through apprehension of
the impotence of the choir. This appears a sufficient refutation of
the charge reiterated against him by the Italians of a preferenc
of instruments to the human voice.

In contemplating the splendid fragments contained in th
masses—which after all afford at once the truest and mos
accessible evidence of the character of Mozart's powers befor
the composition of " Idomeneo "—events, in their day ap
parently the most perverse, may be seen to have conspired i
favour of the musician. Had the Prince of Salzburg patronise
the *ancient* ecclesiastical style, which in Mozart's time, an
probably by the composer himself, was thought to be the onl
proper method of writing for the church, what could hav
accrued from his labours but fresh reams of counterpoint?—
an art, which however tastefully managed, could develop no nev
principle, having been thoroughly understood and exemplifie
by Italians and Germans from the commencement of th
century.

But thrown upon his own resources for the style and forr
of his masses, he seized upon every occasion that could b
gained for the general advantage of the art. Thus accompani
ment and modulation proceeded to the great improvement c
dramatic music; towards which many of the masses may b
considered as preliminary studies. The " Crucifixus," whic
is generally treated dramatically, often displays chromati
harmony, wrought up to the highest pitch of the awful sublime
while the " Benedictus " exhibits those sweet cadences an
" dying falls " which afterwards became so conspicuous i
Mozart's operas. Nor were the interesting problems of counter
point disregarded, as the frequent canons and brief fugues c
those works evince.

They had been now upwards of a month at Mannheim, an
the young composer has at last an audience, by appointment
with the electoress, to whom he is introduced by Count Saviol
She remembers his former visit—fourteen years before—but n
longer recognises his person. His reception puts him into hig
spirits.

The son continues:

" The whole court are highly pleased with me. Durin
both the times in which I played at the concert, the prince an
princess came and placed themselves close to me at the clavie

fter the concert Cannabich contrived that I could speak to the
bility.   As I kissed the elector's hand, he said, 'I believe
is now fifteen years since you were here.'   'Yes, your high-
ss, it is fifteen years since I had that honour.'   'You play
comparably.'   When I kissed the hand of the princess, she
id, '*Monsieur, je vous assure, on ne peut pas jouer mieux.*'"

Great hopes grow out of the affability of the elector, who
nverses with him in the friendliest manner:

"He said, 'I hear that you have written an opera for Munich.'
Yes, your highness.   I commend myself to your gracious
:otection; it is my great desire to write an opera here; and
beg that you will not quite forget me.   I can do something
erman too, thank God.'—'That may be easily managed,' he
:plied.
"The elector has one son and three daughters, the eldest of
hom and the young count play the clavier.   He inquired my
)inion confidentially respecting his children; and I answered
ith sincerity, but without prejudice to the master.   Cannabich
;reed with me.   The elector, in leaving us, thanked me very
)litely."

In the evening he goes to the flute-player, Wendling, and is
ι such an admirable humour, that he does nothing but play
it of his head.   Everybody about him is thrown into ecstacies.
fterwards to the children of the elector, "where," says he,
my heart was in my playing."   He tells us, too, that the
ector sat close to him all the time, and "remained perfectly
ill."   He is overwhelmed with caresses and marks of favour on
l sides.

"I had to go yesterday with Cannabich to Count Savioli to
:tch my present, which was, as I had imagined it would be,
)thing in money, but a handsome gold watch.   I would rather
ιve had ten carolins than the watch, although with its chain
ιd devices estimated at twenty carolins, for on a journey money
necessary.   I have now, with your permission, five watches;
ιd I have a great mind to have another watch-pocket made in
l my clothes, in order that when I visit noblemen, I may wear
vo watches (as is now the fashion), and at least prevent any of
ιem from presenting me with another watch." [1]

[1] Notwithstanding this, he was presented with another watch, to his
.ortification, a few days afterwards.

Let us now turn from these pleasant incidents to a sketc
of the Abbé Vogler in the best manner of this admirable painte
of character.

"Vogler's history is short. He came here in miserabl
plight, exhibited on the clavier, and composed a ballet. Hi
condition excited pity, and the elector sent him to Italy. Aftei
wards, on visiting Bologna, the elector inquired of the Padr
Valotti respecting Vogler—' O alterra, questo è un grand uomo,
etc. He then asked Padre Martini—' Alterra, è buono, ma
poco a poco, quando sarà un poco più vecchio, più sodo, si farà
si farà. Ma bisogna che si lengi molto."

"Vogler on his return became a priest, and was immediatel
appointed court chaplain. He has composed a ' Miserere
which everyone tells me is perfectly intolerable to listen to–
the harmony being all wrong. He found that it was not muc
relished, and went to the elector to complain that the orchestra
from spite to him, played badly on purpose; in short, he s
managed matters (engaging also in some serviceable intrigue
with women), that he has been appointed vice-Kapellmeistei
He is a fool, who fancies that there can exist nothing better c
more perfect than himself. He is hated by the whole orchestra
He has often brought Holzbauer into trouble. His book wi
better teach arithmetic than composition. He gives out tha
he will make a composer in three weeks, and a singer in si
months; but the products of his system have not yet made thei
appearance. He contemns the great masters, and spoke to m
himself of Bach with great disrespect. Bach composed tw
operas here, of which the first pleased more than the seconc
As the title of the last mentioned was ' Lucio Silla,' the sam
which I had composed at Milan, I felt curious to see it. Holz
bauer had told me that Vogler possessed it, and I asked him t
lend it me. ' Willingly,' said he, ' I will send it you to-morrov
But you will not find any master-strokes of genius in it.' ,
few days afterwards on our meeting, he said to me very satir
cally, ' Well, you have now seen something beautiful. Have yo
gained any ideas from it? One air is very pretty—how do th
words go? ' he inquired of somebody near him. ' Of which air?
' Why, of that abominable air of Bach's [1]—let me see—Oh, ye:

[1] The Bach for whom Mozart on several occasions in the correspondenc
expresses great affection, was John Christian, the eleventh son of Sebastia
Bach. He composed many beautiful opera airs; but his instrument:
music, which enjoyed reputation in its own day, from being easy to execut
is now forgotten.

Pupille Amate," which he was certainly drunk when he wrote!'
really thought that I must have taken him by the nose. I,
owever, made as though I had heard nothing, and went away
ithout saying a word. He has already outlived his favour at
ourt."

Dismissing Vogler to oblivion, he gives us a little adventure
i the chapel, " where," says he, " I played the organ for amuse-
ient. He came in during the *Kyrie*, waited till it was over, and
hen the priest gave out the *Gloria*, made a cadence. It was so
ifferent from anything they had ever heard that everybody
tared, and even Holzbauer broke out into an exclamation."

" The people laughed a good deal, when they heard me
lways accompany the *Pizzicato* on the keys. I was in my best
umour. There is always a voluntary here in the place of the
Benedictus, so I took a phrase from the *Sanctus* and fugued
pon it. There they all stood making faces. After the *Ite
iissa est*, I played a fugue."

How fertile in the " smiles and tears " which make up the sum
f human life are these youthful adventures! When he speaks
f playing and being in his " best humour," the imagination is
xcited to the utmost to conceive the beautiful things he did;
hile he, in the midst of all the mental concentration and
bstraction of a fugue, was still sufficiently master of himself to
bserve the grotesque admiration that prevailed around him.
The conceited Mannheim musicians who, as he writes, stared
t him " so absurdly " on account of his insignificant figure,
.ow stared more than ever; and we may well picture to our-
elves the commotion in the orchestra of the electoral chapel,
hen, after mass had begun, the slight form of this extraordinary
outh was discovered, proceeding among the desks of the
ıusicians to a place at the organ. How far the wonders there
xecuted surpassed expectation, this record of the looks and
rimaces of his auditory sufficiently avouches.
The next noticeable incident is a mass of Vogler, upon which
re have a valuable criticism.

" Yesterday, that is, Wednesday the 19th, was again a gala
ay. I attended the service, at which was produced a bran new
ıass by Vogler, which had been rehearsed only the day before
esterday in the afternoon. I stayed, however, no longer than

G

the end of the *Kyrie*. Such music I never before heard in m
life; for not only is the harmony frequently wrong, but he goe
into keys as if he would tear one in by the hair of the head; no
in an artist-like manner, or in any way that would repay th
trouble, but plump and without preparation. Upon the conduc
of the ideas, I will not attempt to speak; I will merely say, tha
it is quite impossible that any mass by Vogler can satisfy
composer worthy of the name. For though one should discove
an idea that is *not bad*, that idea does not remain long in
negative condition, but soon becomes—beautiful? Heave:
save the mark!—it becomes bad—exceeding bad; and this i
two or three different ways. The thought has scarcely had tim
to appear before something else comes and destroys it; or i
does not close so naturally as to remain good; or it is no
brought in in the right place; or it is spoiled by the injudiciou
employment of the accompanying instruments. Such i
Vogler's composition."

This summary of the principal methods by which the effec
of good ideas in a composition may be destroyed, is to be recom
mended to the thoughtful student as matter for deep considera
tion. The lesson is Mozart's.

There is another happy morsel of criticism upon the pei
formance of M. Fränzl, who is well known to the classica
players of the present day:

"I like his playing much. You know that I am no grea
amateur of difficulties.[1] He, indeed, plays difficulties, but i
such a manner that nobody is aware of them; it seems as
one could immediately do the same thing, which is the highe:
merit of execution. He possesses a very beautiful round ton
and not a note is missed in his performance; you hear ever
thing, and nicely marked too. He has also a beautiful *stacca*
in a bow both up and down, and such double shakes as his
never before heard. In a word, if no absolute sorcerer, he
certainly a very solid fiddler."

This passage shows what progress had been made in th
bravura style of violin-playing in the latter half of the la:

[1] Upon this point I venture to quote here a passage from an article c
Mozart, which I wrote many years ago:—" The great masters, howev
they might differ in their mode, were unanimous in making *expression* tl
perfection of their art; and if we could have a manual of their sentiment
we should certainly find an accordant opinion upon the uses of executic
both in singing and playing."—*Foreign Quarterly Review*, vol. iv.

century, and raises a natural surprise that " double shakes and
a beautiful *staccato* in a bow "—the most striking acquirements
of great players in our own time—should be found in a violinist
of that early date.

It is now evident that the young Mozart was anxious to
remain at Mannheim—his reason for which will presently peep
out: and he tries to show in his letters to his father, that there
are projects worth cultivating before him.   He has already two
pupils who pay him a louis d'or a month, and he hopes and
strains through all channels of interest for the children of the
elector—his " arch-pupils " that are to be.   The Count Savioli
promises to speak for him from day to day—but one day there is
hunting, and another is a gala; and at length he determines to
take a bold step in the matter himself:

" To confess the truth, on going away I felt a little suspicious,
and resolved, therefore, to take my six easiest variations on
Fischer's minuet, which I had already written for the purpose, to
the young count, in order to have the opportunity of speaking
personally to the elector.   You can scarcely imagine the delight
of the governess on my going in.   I was very politely received,
and on my taking out the variations, and saying that they were
for the count, ' Oh, that is excellent,' she replied, ' and have
you not something also for the countess ? '   ' Not yet,' said I,
but if I remain here long enough to write anything, it will give
me great pleasure.'   ' By the by, I am delighted to hear that you
remain here for the winter.'   ' I—I know nothing at all about
t.'   ' I am astonished.   That is very curious; for the elector
just said to me: *Apropos*, Mozart stays here for the winter.'
If he said so, he has said it who can command it; for certainly
t would be impossible for me to stop without the assistance of
he elector.'   I then related the whole story to her.   We agreed
hat I had better come on the morrow (that is to-day) at four
o'clock, and bring something for the countess; she undertook
o speak to the elector before I should arrive, and I should then
ee him myself.   I went to-day, but he was not to be seen."

He now begins to think that he shall stay the whole winter,
as he is a favourite with the elector, and something must turn
up; and so hoping for better news, he sends his sister the sonata
he had composed for Mademoiselle Cannabich.[1]

[1] Concerning this sonata, the following criticism by the father is con-
ained in a letter of December 11, 1777:—" The sonata is distinguished,

At last, after many disappointments, he is so fortunate as to find himself in the actual presence of the elector:

"On Monday, I had the good fortune, after attending the children morning and afternoon for three days, to find the elector: It was, indeed, so late, that we had given him up, and expected to have had our trouble for nothing, when we saw him coming. The governess immediately placed the countess at the clavier, and I sat by giving her a lesson; and in this position the elector found us on entering. We rose up, but he desired us to continue our employment. When she had done playing, the governess observed that I had written a beautiful rondo. I played it, and he was very much pleased, 'But,' said he, 'do you think she will be able to learn it?' 'Oh yes, I only wish that I were so fortunate as to teach it to her.' He smiled and said, 'I should like it very much, but would it not spoil her to have a second master?' 'Oh, no; that depends merely upon whether he is a bad or a good one. I hope that your highness has confidence in me, that you will rely upon my ——.' 'Oh, certainly,' he replied. Upon this, the governess said, 'Mr. Mozart here has composed some variations on Fischer's minuet for the young count.' I played these also, and they pleased much. He now began to play with the countess; and I to make my acknowledgments for the present. At last, he said, 'I must consider of it; how long can you stay?' 'As long as it may please your highness to command. I have no engagement at all, and am entirely at the disposal of your highness.' This was all that passed. I went again this morning, and heard that the elector again said, 'Mozart stays here for the winter.' We have now proceeded so far that I *must* wait."

Next day Savioli tells him that he had spoken to the elector, but could bring him to no determination. Upon this Mozart complains of his indecision, that it had entailed great expenses on him, and hoped the elector would give him some work. "Work," says the ardent composer, "is my pleasure." The count promises to speak again next day, and he does speak, and gets an answer at last—and such an answer! Mozart meets him:

"I went up to him, and on seeing me, he shrugged his

It has somewhat of the mannered and peculiar taste of Mannheim; but not sufficient to injure your own good style." The power of assimilating all music to himself was wonderful; here he wrote in the Mannheim taste, and at Paris in the French taste, but still he was always Mozart.

shoulders. 'What,' said I, 'no answer still?' 'I am very sorry,' said he, ' but, alas! it is all in vain.' '*Eh bien,*' replied I, ' the elector, however, might have told me so a little sooner.' ' Yes,' he returned, ' and he would not have made up his mind now, if I had not represented to him how long you had been detained here, and how your money was being swallowed up at an hotel.' ' That is what most annoys me,' said I, ' for it is not handsome. But for the rest, I am exceedingly obliged to you, Herr Count, and I request that you will thank the elector in my name for his gracious, though rather tardy, intelligence, and assure him that he would have had no cause to repent if he had engaged me.' ' Oh,' returned he, ' of that I am more convinced than you perhaps imagine.' When I told Wendling of this decision, he turned quite red, and said with passion, ' We must find a way. You must stay here at least two months, till we can go to Paris together.'

"The other day, on going as usual to dine with Wendling, he said to me, ' Our Indian (so he calls a Dutch gentleman who lives here upon his fortune, an amateur of the fine arts in general, and a great friend and admirer of mine), our Indian is a capital fellow. He will give you 200 florins if you will write for him three little short and easy concertos, and a couple of quartets for the flute. You will get two pupils, at least, through Cannabich who will pay well. You can write a set of duets for the clavier and violin, and engrave them by subscription. You can always eat here morning and evening, and lodge with the advocate Seravius; so all that will cost you nothing.'

" I shall have enough to do in two months with three concertos, two quartets, and four or six duets for clavier and violin, besides a new grand mass which I intend to compose and present to the elector." [1]

This terrible frustration of his hopes, in spite of the energy of resolution with which it is borne, and the generous offers of the musicians to atone for the neglect of the court, makes a deep impression on the mind of the father, who now writes to his son a letter, no less remarkable for tenderness and affection than for sagacity and good sense:

. . . " I must now address you very seriously. You know for how many years together they have been trying our patience

[1] The twelfth mass of Mozart is a work of which the origin is obscure; but I am inclined to think, from the extensiveness of its plan and the fulness of its instrumentation, that it was composed at this time.

at Salzburg, and how frequently both you and I have desired to
get away. You will remember, too, the arguments which I
used, and which prevented our *all* giving up Salzburg at once.
They are now put to the test; great expenses on a journey, and
few, or at least very slow, receipts to meet them—what would
this be to encounter with a whole family? To have suffered
you to go by yourself, and to leave the thousand things that are
necessary to be looked after on a journey to your care; you
who were unaccustomed to do without assistance; little acquainted with the various kinds of money, and totally ignorant
of that of foreign parts; without the least notion of packing,
etc.; for you to have travelled under such circumstances, was,
at that time, impossible. I often represented to you, that even
if you should stay at Salzburg for a couple of years over your
twentieth, you would lose nothing, for in that time you would
have an opportunity of looking into some other branches of useful science, and of enlarging your mind by the perusal of good
books in different languages, as well as of practising the languages
themselves. I further represented to you, that a young man,
though he should have fallen from heaven, and was enabled to
see far, far beyond all living masters, would still never get the
reputation he deserved, age being essential to that; and while
a man is under twenty, the envious, the malicious, and the
persecuting, find the materials of their trade in youth itself,
and an easy argument to prove out of few years, small experience. Can you doubt that something of this sort has been at
work with the elector respecting the teaching of his children?
Moreover, I am as little a friend to servility of conduct as yourself, and you may remember what I wrote about Munich, that
you were not to *throw yourself away ;* and all these endeavours
to be able to stay by the aid of a little society of ten persons are,
in my opinion, *too crawling.* You have, however, been thus
induced, through the persuasions of good-hearted and well-
meaning friends, but these are straw fires that quickly burn
out, and end in smoke. That I now wish you an appointment
is true—but such an appointment only as you might get at
Mannheim, or Munich, or some other place, where you would
not be refused an occasional tour; but on my account no
appointment *per decretum* for life. If you had such a place for a
couple of years only, it would not prevent your travelling into
France and Italy. You yourself know well enough that it is
through years, and through titles, such as composer to an elector,

hat consequence and respect are obtained. And it was my
pinion with respect to Munich, that there was no meanness or
ervility in seeking a temporary engagement there, because that
ilone would afford the opportunity of displaying the extent of
rour knowledge and ability; there being so many people about
:ourts who are always ready to prevent this, and time and
pportunity being essential to it.

" No one has worked more against Wolfgang than Vogler.
: said this long ago to M. Bullinger and Nannerl."

Distressing as all these unrealised expectations must have
een under ordinary circumstances, to one so conscious of his
genius and so impatient for opportunity as Mozart, he appears
:o have borne them with wonderful equanimity. He every now
ind then even breaks out into a fit of mirth and exultation.
Once he tells us that he went into the Lutheran church and played
:or an hour and a half in such a way on the organ—" it came
:ight from the heart." Here, in truth, lay the secret that
:ascinated him all the time to Mannheim, and which sustained
1im in the midst of all reverses. It was during this visit to
Mannheim that he first fell seriously in love. The lady was a
Mademoiselle Weber, fifteen years of age, and a great singer.
But I must let him prepare the way for the avowal of this
oassion to his father in his own manner—full of that lover-like
evasion and ingenuity which unconsciously betrays itself.

" On Wednesday next I go for a few days to the Princess of
Orange, at Kirchheim-Poland; they gave me so good an account
of her here, that I at last resolved to go. A Dutch officer, with
whom I am intimate, was terribly scolded by her for not bringing me with him, when he went to pay his congratulations to
her on the new year. I shall get at least eight louis d'or by this
journey; for the Princess, being an extraordinary amateur of
singing, I have had four airs copied for her; and as she possesses
an elegant orchestra, and gives concerts daily, I intend also to
present her with a symphony. The copying of the airs will be no
great expense, as a certain M. Weber, who will accompany me,
has written them.

" This Weber has a daughter who possesses a pure and beautiful voice, sings admirably, and is just fifteen years of age. She
has nothing to study but the action to be the *prima donna* on
any stage. The father is a thoroughly honest German, who has
brought up his children well, and this is the cause why the girl

is pursued here. He has six children (five girls and a boy) and has been obliged to support a wife and family for fourteen years on an income of 200 florins, which, now that he has provided the elector with a very accomplished singer, is doubled She sings my air for *De Amicis*,[1] with its terrible passages admirably, and will also sing this at Kirchheim-Poland.

" Now for something else."

And so he runs off, to divert attention from the grand secret to an account of a dinner-party at the house where he lives where there were fifteen guests, the young lady of the house undertaking to play, in the evening, a concerto he had taught her. Vogler, who was determined to make his acquaintance calls upon him, and is one of the party. The description of the evening is highly amusing. Vogler sends home for his two claviers that were tuned to one another, and his " tedious ' engraved sonatas, which poor Mozart had to play through.

" You are to know that, before dinner, he had scrambled through my concerto (the same which the young lady of the house plays) *prima vista*. The first movement went *prestissimo*, the andante *allegro*, and the rondo again *prestissimo* He played the bass, for the most part, differently from that written, and often changed both harmony and melody entirely As for his rapidity, it surpasses everything; neither eyes or hands can follow it. But what kind of sight-playing is that? Hearers—I mean those who are worthy of the name—can only say that they have *seen* music and clavier playing; they hear think, and feel as little during it as the performer himself. You may easily suppose how insupportable it was, as I was in no condition to say, ' Much too fast.' Besides, it is much easier to play a thing quickly than slowly; because, in the former case, many notes may be dropped out of a passage, and not missed; but is that desirable? In rapid execution the performer may change the right and the left hands without its being noticed; but is that good? And in what does the art of playing at sight consist? Certainly in this: in playing a piece in the exact time in which it should go, and in giving to all the notes, passages, etc., their appropriate expression, so that a listener might imagine that he who played it had himself composed it."

While Mozart remained in this unsettled condition at Mann-

[1] A celebrated bravura air in " Lucio Silla."

heim, not absolutely neglecting the object of his journey, but still, in the spirit of youth, giving himself up to the adventures of the time, and appearing less solicitous for success than might have been expected, his father, whose entire thoughts were bent upon the expedition, was in a state of great anxiety. Recollecting that the good offices of the Padre Martini might be valuable at this juncture, he addressed a letter to him, in which he carefully recapitulated all the circumstances, and besought his intercession; but, it is to be feared, without producing any useful result.

Mozart's short excursion from Mannheim to the Princess of Weilburg's, at Kirchheim-Poland, in company with his young mistress and her father, was one of the most delightful events of his youth. He was now supremely happy, and not in the least desirous of going further in the pursuit of fortune. The princess was a most unusual amateur of music, and both played and sang admirably. During a stay of eight days, he played twelve times at court, and once, by desire, performed before her on the organ in the Lutheran church. He presented four symphonies of his composition to her, and, on taking leave, received a gratuity of seven louis d'or.

Meantime his father had been persuading him to continue his journey to Paris; but though the streets of that capital had been paved with gold, there was here " metal more attractive." He was dismayed at the prospect of the teaching in which he expected to be employed at Paris, and now that he felt the stirrings of the divinity within, disliked to sacrifice his genius to a mechanical occupation, however well paid. His fears on this head were groundless; but the evils that awaited him at Paris were, unfortunately, not imaginary. The views which he entertained of his onward journey will be gathered from a passage in one of his letters.

" I am a composer, and the son of a Kapellmeister, and I cannot consent to bury in teaching the talent for composition which God has so richly bestowed upon me. I may say so without pride, for I feel it now more than formerly. My head is full of projects in dramatic composition: French operas rather than German, and Italian rather than either."

To this gusty and passionate repudiation of the drudgery of teaching, so natural in the circumstances, the cautious and thoughtful father transmits the following answer—a letter so wise and precious in its kind as to challenge universal admiration. This letter is dated from Salzburg, on the 16th of February 1778.

"Your letter of the 7th, with the accompanying French air, came safely to hand. To see something again by my dear Wolfgang, so excellent in its kind, made me breathe more freely. Every one is right in conjecturing that your compositions will generally please at Paris, and you know, as well as I, how well able you are to imitate any kind of taste in composition. With regard to *lesson-giving* in Paris, there is nothing to be alarmed at. In the first place, people will not be so ready to turn off their masters and send for you; and, secondly, no one will apply, nor will you accept of any one, unless it may be a lady, who already plays well, desirous to acquire style from you, and this work must be well paid for. Such ladies as these will take infinite pains to procure subscribers to your compositions. Besides, the ladies command everything at Paris; they are, in general, great amateurs of the clavier, and there are many who play excellently. These must be your mark, together with composition; for, by publishing pieces for the clavier, violin quartets, symphonies, collections of French songs with clavier accompaniment, such as you sent me, and, lastly, by operas, you may make both money and fame. What impediment is there? But you are for having everything succeed on the instant, before people have had time to see you, or to hear what you can do. Peruse the great catalogue of our former acquaintances at Paris; they are all, or for the most part, persons of the highest consequence in that city. They will be all anxious to see you again, and if only half-a-dozen of them patronise you—indeed, one of the chief would be sufficient—you may have everything your own way.

"I enclose two unsealed letters of recommendation, which you must be careful of, and present to M. Joseph Felix Arbaur, the great jeweller at Paris. Mr. Mayer is the first commissioner with whom Count Wolfegg lodged. The duplicate letters, in which everything is put down circumstantially with respect to apartments, etc., have been sent off to-day, and these are only to show that you are the party for whom the application is made

"This being in all probability the last letter that you will receive from me at Mannheim, I address it to you alone. How deeply the wider separation which is about to take place between us affects me, you may partly conceive, though not

feel it in the same degree with which it oppresses my heart.
If you reflect seriously on what I have undergone with you
two children in your tender years, you will not accuse me of
timidity, but, on the contrary, do me the justice to own that
I am, and ever have been, a man with the heart to venture
everything, though indeed I always employed the greatest cir-
cumspection and precaution.   Against accidents it is impossible
to provide, for God only sees into futurity.   Up to this time we
cannot be said to have been either successful or unsuccessful;
but, God be thanked, we have steered between the two.   Everything has been attempted for your success, and through you for
our own.   We have at least endeavoured to settle you in some
appointment on a secure footing; though fate has hitherto de-
creed that we should fail in our object.   This last step of ours,
however, makes my spirit sink within me.   You may see as
clearly as the sun at noonday that, through it, the future condition of your aged parents, and of your affectionately attached
sister, entirely depends upon you.   From the time of your birth,
and indeed earlier, ever since my marriage, I have found it a
hard task to support a wife, and, by degrees, a family of seven
children, two relatives by marriage, and the mother, on a
certain income of twenty-five florins a month; out of this to
pay for maintenance and the expenses of childbed, deaths, and
sicknesses; which expenses, when you reflect upon them, will
convince you that I not only never devoted a kreutzer to my
own private pleasure, but that I could never, in spite of all my
contrivances and care, have managed to live free from debt
without the especial favour of God; and yet I never was in debt
till now.   I devoted all my time to you two, in the hope and
indeed reliance upon your care in return; that you would procure for me a peaceful old age, in which I might render account
to God for the education of my children, and, without any other
concern than the salvation of my soul, quietly await death.
But Providence has so ordered, that I must now afresh commence the ungrateful task of lesson-giving, and in a place, too,
where this dreary labour is so ill paid, that it will not support
one from one end of the year to the other; and yet it is to be
thought a matter of rejoicing if, after talking oneself into a
consumption, something or other is got by it.

"I am far, my dear Wolfgang, from having the least mistrust
in you;—on the contrary, on your filial love I place all confidence
and every hope.   Everything now depends upon fortunate

circumstances, and the exercise of that sound understanding which you certainly possess, if you will listen to it; the former are uncontrollable—but that you will always take counsel of your understanding I hope and pray. You are now going into a new world, and must not think it prejudice in me to account Paris so dangerous a place; *au contraire*, my own experience gives me no cause to think it dangerous. But my former and your present circumstances are as wide asunder as heaven and earth. We were in the house of an ambassador, and on the second occasion in a private dwelling; I was a staid man and you were children; I avoided all acquaintance, and particularly shunned familiarity with people of our profession; you may remember that I did the same in Italy. I formed the acquaintance and sought the friendship of people of condition only, and among these, merely with people of a certain age, and not with youths, however high their rank. In order to preserve my liberty, I seldom invited any one to visit me at home, but held it more prudent to make visits abroad. For if I should not like a person, or have work or engagements, I can stay away but if, on the other hand, people come to me, and prove disagreeable, I know not how to get rid of them; and a person not otherwise unpleasant may sometimes hinder needful occupation

"You are now a young man of twenty-two years of age here is none of that seriousness of years which may dissuade a youth, let his condition be what it may—an adventurer, a libertine, a deceiver—be he old or young, from courting your acquaintance, and drawing you into his society and his plans One may fall into this danger unawares, and then not know how to recede. Of the other sex I can hardly speak to you, for there the greatest reserve and prudence are necessary, Nature herself being our enemy; but whoever does not employ all his prudence and reserve in his intercourse, will with difficulty extricate himself from the labyrinth—*a misfortune that usually ends in death*. How blindly, through inconsiderate jests, flattery and play, one may fall into errors at which the returning reason is ashamed, you may perhaps have already a little experienced and it is not my intention to reproach you. I am persuaded that you do not only consider me as your father, but as your truest and most faithful friend, and that you know and see that our happiness or unhappiness—nay, more, my long life or speedy death is, under God, so to speak, in your hands. If I know you aright I have nothing but pleasure to expect in you, which thought must console me in your absence for the paternal pleasure of seeing, hearing, and embracing you. Lead the life of a good Catholic Christian; love and fear God; pray to him with devotion and sincerity, and let your conduct be such, that should I never see you more, the hour of my death may be free from apprehension. From my heart I bless you, and remain, till death, your faithful father, and most sincere friend.

"LEOPOLD MOZART."

This letter, enforced by the mortifying failure of his hopes, determined the future course of the son. Paris was now his great object, and he writes in full anticipation of the successes that were to crown his efforts there. The activity into which his mind had been thrown during his visit to Mannheim, was a healthy preparation for greater labours; for, as the elector would not employ his pen, he gave the benefit of his prolific leisure to his friends and their friends. The instrumental performers crowded around him, especially those on wind instruments; they attached themselves to him enthusiastically; and what with writing concertos, putting accompaniments, composing sonatas, etc., his hands were never idle.[1] It is worth noting as an illustrative trait, that he preferred to associate with orchestral performers, and even with amateurs who " played prettily on the clavier," rather than with composers: probably for this very sufficient reason, that the former understood and acknowledged his genius, while the latter treated him with suspicion and disingenuousness.

One of the chief delights he looked forward to at Paris was the prospect of writing something for the *concert spirituel*, where the orchestra was admirable, and where choruses (which he took great pleasure in composing) could be ably performed. He inferred that the French held the chorus in high estimation,

---

[1] He composed, amongst other things, an air for the celebrated tenor Raff, offering to alter it in any way to suit him, or to compose a fresh one. But Raff thought it beautiful, and only begged him to shorten it; for Raff was advanced in life, and was not " in condition to hold out so long." Mozart instantly complied, observing that " cutting away was easy at all times, but making additions, not so easy: " and with such completeness did he treat his subjects, leaving nothing at least to be added, however he might retrench his luxuriance. On another occasion he selected, *for practice*, words which had already been set by Bach (John Christian—the English Bach, as he was called); " because," says he, " I know Bach's air so well, and like it so much, that it is always running in my head, and I wished to see whether in spite of this I could not compose an air upon the same words, which should not in the least resemble that of Bach. You may see, in fact, that there is not the least resemblance."

from having been accustomed to Gluck's compositions in that way, and from the only objection which the Parisians raised against Piccini's opera of "Roland," being that the choruses were too thin and weak, and the music of too monotonous a character. "Rely upon me," he writes to his father, "I shall strain every nerve to do honour to the name of Mozart, and I have no fears for the event."

As the opera of "Roland" is a work of some historical interest; having been the cause of those furious dissensions between the Gluckists and the Piccinists, which threw the whole of Paris into a state of agitation in 1777, the year before Mozart's arrival in that capital; a glance at its origin, and the feuds it produced, will be of interest in this place.

Gluck, who at sixty years of age had entered upon a new career of the most brilliant order, and had already produced at Paris four of those works with which his fame is principally associated,[1] was sojourning at Vienna, and just commencing "Roland," when the news reached him that the directors of the opera had engaged Piccini to treat the same subject. He immediately threw what he had written into the fire—or so at least he informed his friend, the *bailli du Rollet*, in a letter which was published in *l'Année Litteraire*. This impetuous and disdainful style of proceeding was quite characteristic of Gluck, and its announcement served as the signal for war. It will be seen by the letter itself, which has now become valuable to the history of the art, that the writer had profited by his intimacy with the brilliant society collected at the suppers then in fashion, and had learned to deal out a sarcasm pretty handsomely.[2]

This letter served the double purpose of mortifying his enemy, Marmontel, and of winning over to his side the French musicians, who were taken by an equivocal compliment to their national vanity, at the expense of Italy. That Gluck foresaw the danger of a revulsion towards the Italian taste on the theatre of his fame and fortune, where he had hitherto enjoyed an absolute sway; and that he looked upon Piccini as no contemptible rival;

[1] "Iphigenia in Aulis," "Orfeo," "Alceste," and "Armida."
[2] In this letter, he says that he is not at all the man for rivalry; that Piccini would have a great advantage over him, with novelty at his side, and having nothing to do but to follow the route he (Gluck) had struck out. "I will not speak on the subject of patronage," he observes; "I am quite sure that a certain politician of my acquaintance (Carraccioli) will give dinners and suppers to three-fourths of Paris for the sake of making proselytes, and that Marmontel *qui sait si bien faire des contes, contera* throughout the kingdom the exclusive merit of M. Piccini."

is evident. Two formidable parties immediately started up. Suard and the Abbé Arnaud headed the Gluckists; while Marmontel, La Harpe, Ginguené, and even the cold D'Alembert himself, sided with the Piccinists. The journals were crowded daily with epigrams and *bon-mots*, and all Paris, including persons of the highest rank, and even ladies of distinction, took part in the tumult. But the dispute becoming tedious at last, was finally settled by an appeal to Marie-Antoinette, who having been the pupil of Gluck, declared herself resolutely in his favour.

The triumph of Gluck led to still higher success than any he had yet achieved. The theatre could not contain the crowds that came to the general rehearsal of his operas, the first that were made public in France, and at which the spectators were entertained not less by the eccentricities of the composer, and his singular sallies of humour, than by the composition. It was the custom of Gluck, in superintending a rehearsal, to put off his great-coat and wig and indue a night-cap; but when the music was concluded, and he was ready to resume his apparel, noblemen of the first rank, and even princes, thought themselves honoured in assisting him. Still the music of this great master had no very strong present influence in ameliorating the taste of the French. The declamatory and impassioned style of his operas led the uncultivated performers, too frequently, to mistake ear-piercing shrieks and cries for expressive singing— and the composer himself was honoured with the soubriquet of *Grand Hurleur*.[1]

Such was vocal music at Paris when Mozart and his mother arrived there, on the 23rd of March 1778; and the instrumental was not in a much more favourable condition.

Mozart is scarcely settled in Paris, when he is deep in a " Miserere " for Passion-week, to contain three choruses, a fugue, and a duet, and to be instrumented for a large orchestra. He is afterwards engaged on two concertos, and an opera for the French theatre, in two acts, the subject to be " Alexandre and Roxane." The first chorus of the " Miserere," he tells us, was pronounced to be charming and effective by Gossec, the well-known French composer. " Gossec," says he, " is a good friend of mine, and a very dry person."

---

[1] This style prevailed in Paris even so lately as 1797. " The principal singers," says Kelly, speaking of the " Iphigenia," " made a shriek louder than I thought any human beings capable of producing." What the delicate organs of Mozart suffered from these declamatory inflictions, will be best imagined from his own description of French singing.

In the midst of these avocations he is beset with invitations. He constantly dines at the house of M. Le Gros, the director of the concert, and is asked almost daily by Noverre and Madame D'Epinay. But his great friend is Baron Grimm.[1]

"Baron Grimm and myself often vent our indignation at the state of music here, that is to say, between ourselves; but in public it is always ' *bravo! bravissimo!* ' and clapping till the fingers burn. What most displeases me is, that the French gentlemen have only so far improved their taste as to be able to *endure* good things; but as for any perception that their music is bad—Heaven help them!—and the singing— *oimè!* "

Upon this question of French taste he received much excellent advice from his father, who counselled him to consult it in the opera, for the sake of applause and good pay, as well as notices in the newspapers, " which," adds he, " at all times I could wish, *if only to vex the archbishop.*"   The vision of this unsympathising archbishop was always casting its shadow upon them even in their brightest moments!

Through the influence of Baron Grimm, Mozart has the honour of an interview with the Duchesse de Bourbon. But he was not yet accustomed to the elegant indifference of the fashionable *salon,* and he writes in the humour that may be anticipated from such a reception.

"On my arrival I was ushered into a great room without any fire, and as cold as ice; and there I had to wait for half an hour until the duchess came. At length she appeared, and very politely requested me to excuse the clavier, as not one in the house was in order, but said she would be very glad to hear me play. I replied that I should be most happy to play something, but that at present it was impossible, as I could not

---

[1] His father had strongly recommended him to the friendship of Baron Grimm, advising him to cultivate his favour by a perfectly childlike confidence. " The mode of life in Paris," he goes on, " is very different from that of Germany, and the manner of expressing oneself politely in French —to recommend oneself—to seek protection, etc., has a decided peculiarity, so much so, that Baron von Grimm formerly instructed me in it, and inquired of me what I would say, and how express myself." But Paris had undergone a woful change in the interval—(what changes have passed over it since, the reader need not be reminded of)—" Paris is altogether a different place from what it was," writes Wolfgang Mozart in reply; " the French have no longer the *politesse* which distinguished them fifteen years since; their manners approach rudeness, and their arrogance is abominable."

el my fingers from cold, and I requested that she would have
he goodness to let me go into a room in which there was a
re. '*O oui, monsieur, vous avez raison,*' was the answer.
he then sat down and began to draw, in company with several
entlemen, who all made a circle round a large table. This
isted for an hour, during which time I had the honour to be
1 attendance. The windows and doors were open; and my
ands were not merely as cold as ice, but my feet and body too,
nd my head began to ache. There was *altum silentium,* and
really could not tell what would come of all this cold, headache,
nd tediousness. I frequently thought, ' were it not for Mr.
irimm, I would this instant go away;' however, to shorten
iy story, I at last played on the wretched, miserable piano.
Vhat most annoyed me was, that madame and all the gentle-
ien pursued their drawing without a moment's cessation, and
onsequently I was obliged to play to the walls, chairs, and
ables. Such a combination of vexatious circumstances quite
vercame my patience, and after going through one half of
he ' Fischer ' variations, I rose up. There were a great many
loges. I however said, and it was perfectly true, that I could
lo myself no credit with this clavier, and that I should prefer
electing another day when there would be a better one. But
he duchess would not let me off; and I was obliged to wait
nother half-hour, for the duke; meantime she came and took
ier place beside me, and listened to me very attentively, and I
oon forgot the cold and the headache, and, in spite of the
vretched clavier, played as I am accustomed to play when in
ood-humour. Put me down to the best clavier in Europe,
iut with people for hearers who either do not, or will not, under-
tand, and I should lose all pleasure in playing. I gave Mr.
irimm a full relation of everything."

In Paris, as it had been everywhere else, some crooked destiny
vas at work to render all his labours fruitless. The hard work
ie bestowed on his choruses was in vain. They performed only
wo of them, and those not the best, so that he was hardly
ecognised; but there was great applause, and, although he
hought nothing of Parisian applause, he was satisfied. He
ries to extract hope out of everything.

" With respect to the *Sinfonia Concertante,* he says, there
s again an *imbroglio,* and I am compelled to suspect something
iehind the curtain—for I have my enemies here also—and

H

where indeed have I been without them? That is, however, a
favourable sign."

Le Gros hurried him grievously in the composition of the
symphony, then let it lie for several days without getting it
copied, and finally set it aside altogether, with one excuse or
another about time. The musicians were enraged at the dis
appointment, which Mozart attributed to the machinations of
one Cambini, an Italian maestro, to whom he had inadvertently
given offence.[1]

His father had advised him to go out as much as he could
and cultivate the acquaintance of influential people. But there
was a difficulty in the way which he had not calculated upon.
Thus writes the son upon these points:

"You advise me to visit a great deal, in order to make new
acquaintances, or to revive the old ones. That is, however
impossible. The distance is too great, and the ways too miry
to go on foot; the muddy state of Paris being indescribable
and to take a coach, one may soon drive away four or five
livres, and all in vain, for the people merely pay you compli
ments, and then it is over. They ask me to come on this or
that day—I play, and then they say, ' *O c'est un prodige, c'est
inconcevable, c'est etonnant ;* ' and then ' *à Dieu.*' "

All this, however, might have been endured, so far as mere
superciliousness and hauteur to the professional musician were
involved, if these people had possessed any real feeling or love
for music; but it was their total want of all taste, their utter
viciousness, that rendered them hateful to Mozart. He was
ready to make any sacrifice for his family, but longed to escape
from the artificial and heartless Parisians.

"If I were in a place where people had ears to hear, hearts to
feel, and some small degree of perception and taste, I should
laugh heartily over all these things—but really, as it regards
music, I am living among mere brute beasts. How can it be
otherwise? It is the same in all their passions, and, indeed, in

---

[1] The circumstance is thus described by Mozart in one of his letters:-
" It was at the house of Le Gros that I innocently displeased him. He had
written quartets, of which I heard some at Mannheim that are very pretty,
and I praised them to him, and played him the commencement of one; but
Ritter, Ram, and Punto, who were present, would not permit me to stop
they compelled me to go on, and what I did not know I was obliged to
invent. I did so, and Cambini was quite beside himself, and could not
forbear saying, ' *Questa é una gran testa !* ' But he did not like it."

very transaction of life; no place in the world is like Paris. Do
ot think that I exaggerate when I speak thus of the state of
ıusic here—ask any one except a native Frenchman, and if he
e fit to answer the question, he will tell you the same. I must
ndure out of love to you—but I shall thank God Almighty if
 leave this place with my healthful natural taste. It is my
onstant prayer that I may be enabled to establish myself, that
 may do honour to the German nation, and make fame and
ıoney, and so be the means of helping you out of your present
arrow circumstances, and of our all living together once more,
heerfully and happily." [1]

These objections, urged with so much earnestness, produced
nother letter of sober admonition from his father, who warns
im again and again of the danger of a precipitate judgment,
nd the necessity of perseverance. He touches in detail upon
very point.

"That one takes a hundred walks for nothing in Paris—I
now by experience, as I believe I have told you. That the
'rench pay in compliments is likewise not unknown to me.
.nd that you will find your enemies wherever you go is quite
ndeniable—for such is the case with every person of great
ılent. All those who are at present in repute at Paris, and
ɛated in nests, will not like to be driven from those nests;
ıey must be apprehensive of having that consequence lowered
ɔ which their interest is attached. It is not merely the jealousy
f Cambini that you have awakened, but that of Stamitz, Piccini,
nd others. Is Piccini at Paris still? Is not Gretry jealous?
Vendling told you that music had altered—but I was in-
redulous. Instrumental music had indeed improved some
ime ago—but vocal music will not change in a great hurry.
ιut, in any case, let not envy discourage you, or put you out

[1] His opinion of the French popular taste is expressed in a similar spirit
l through. He had no objection to make an effort to secure success in
ıeir own way, but he thought that way contemptible. In a letter of a
.ter date, speaking of his new symphony, he says, he cannot tell whether
'will please or not; and, to confess the truth, that he does not much care:
-" For whom will it displease? As for the discerning Frenchmen, who
ıay be present, I should certainly desire to give them pleasure; but for
ıe jolterheads, I don't see that it will be any great misfortune not to please
ıem. Yet I still hope that the asses will find something in it to like; and
ıen I have not forgotten the *premier coup d'archet*, which is sufficient.
he cattle here make a very important matter of that. But for my part,
see no great difference; they begin here much in the same manner as in
:her places. This, however, is for a laugh." . . .

of countenance—it is the same everywhere. Remember Italy
—your first opera, your third opera, ' D'Ettore,' the intrigue
about ' De Amicis; ' etc.—but one must beat one's way through
everything. If you and your mother have sufficient to live
upon at present, we must await a favourable turn of affairs in
Germany. You tell me that you are to write an opera, take
my advice, then, and recollect that your reputation will entirely
depend *on your first production.*"

To take infinite pains in studying the popular taste—to
make sketches and play them over—to consult friends—to
write things that should be easy for amateurs—and never to
write hastily—are the items of the sage counsel which he receives
from his father. That Mozart would willingly have adapted
himself to any course likely to open a channel for legitimate
exertion, is evident from the occupation to which he now applied
himself. He assures his father that he has work enough to
carry him through the winter, and no less than three pupils
and that he might have more but cannot take them on account
of the distance. One of these pupils is a duke's daughter; and
the picture of Mozart trying to teach this lady composition—
genius drudging at no genius—will show how laboriously,and with
what self-suppression he worked for the bare means of existence

" Among these pupils one is daughter of the Duc de Guines
with whom I am in high favour, and I give her two hours
instruction in composition daily, for which I am very liberally
paid. He plays the flute incomparably, and she magnificently
on the harp. She possesses much talent and cleverness, and
in particular, a very remarkable memory, which enables her
to play all her pieces, of which there are at least two hundred
without book. She is doubtful whether she has genius for
composition—particularly with respect to thoughts or ideas
her father (who, between ourselves, is a little too much in love
with her) affirms that she certainly has ideas, and that nothing
but modesty and a want of confidence in herself prevent their
appearing. We shall now see. If she really have no ideas, and
I must say I have as yet seen no indication of them, it will
be all in vain, for God knows I can give her none. It is not
her father's intention to make any very great composer of her
' I do not wish her,' he says, ' to write any operas, airs, con
certos, or symphonies, but merely grand sonatas for her instru
ment, as I do for mine.'

"I gave her the fourth lesson to-day, and as far as the rules
of composition go, am tolerably satisfied with her; she put the
bass to the first minuet which I placed before her, very correctly.
We now commenced writing in three parts. She tried it, and
fatigued herself in attempts, but it was impossible to help her;
nor can we move on a step further, for it is too early, and in
science one must advance by the proper gradations. If she had
genius—but alas! there is none—she has no thoughts—nothing
comes. I have tried her in every imaginable way; among
others it occurred to me to place a very simple minuet before
her, to see whether she could make a variation upon it. That
was all to no purpose. Now, thought I, she does not know how
to begin, so I varied the first bar for her, and told her to continue
the variation pursuing that idea; and at length she got through
tolerably well. I next requested her to begin something herself
—the first part only—a melody; but after a quarter of an hour's
cogitation nothing came. I then wrote four bars of a minuet
and said, ' What a stupid fellow I am! I have begun a minuet
and cannot finish the first part of it. Have the goodness to do
it for me.' She distrusted her ability, but at last, with much
labour, something came to light. I rejoiced that we got something at last. She had now to complete the entire minuet, that
is to say, the melody only. On going away I recommended her
to alter my four bars for something of her own; to make another
beginning even if she retained the same harmony, and only
altered the melody. I shall see to-morrow how she has
succeeded." [1]

How admirably all this is described—with what freshness
and gusto!

The opera is his solace through all this slavery. " There is
no doubt," he exclaims, " of its being accepted, for Noverre
wrote it." Noverre is about to compose a ballet, too, for

[1] Upon this account of the duke's daughter, Leopold Mozart makes some
shrewd remarks. After advising his son to keep in favour with the duke,
because he has great power at court, where festivities may shortly be
expected on the approaching accouchement of the queen, he goes on:—
' You write that you have to-day given mademoiselle, the duke's daughter,
her fourth lesson—and are for having her compose already;—do you
suppose that every one has a genius like yours? It will come by degrees:
she has a good memory. *Eh bien !* let her steal—or more politely, appropriate—but nothing can be done at first, till courage comes. You have
adopted a good method with variations—only pursue it. And should
Moniseur le Duc hear some little thing composed by his daughter, he will
be beside himself with pleasure."

which he is to supply the music; and, of course, there is n
doubt about that. But there is doubt about everything tha
depends on the caprice of theatres, and neither opera nor balle
were ever produced.[1]

Yet there are always friends about him—especially instru
mentalists—under the worst circumstances. Rudolph, th
horn-player, offers him the place of organist at Versailles, witl
a salary of 2000 livres, and permission to go where he likes fo
six months of the year. But he sets about calculating, an
discovers that these 2000 livres would make only 333 dollar
and two livres, which in Germany would be something, but i
nothing in Paris: a dollar goes so frightfully in Paris! Witl
his invariable prudence, the father desires him to weigh al
circumstances carefully before he declines this offer.

"Consider," he observes, "that you leave half a year dis
engaged for another service; that it is, probably, an engage
ment for life, sick or well; that you can resign at any time
that you are at court, consequently daily under the eye of th
king and queen, and so much the nearer to fortune; that on :
vacancy you may become one of the Kapellmeisters; that yoi
may, in time, become instructor on the clavier to the roya
family which would be very lucrative; that nothing woul
prevent you from writing for the theatre or the *concert spirituel*
or from publishing music, and dedicating it to your patron
among the great, Versailles being the summer residence o
many ministers; that Versailles is itself a little city, or at leas
is inhabited by so many persons of distinction that pupils ca
never be wanting; and, lastly, that it would be the most certai
way of obtaining the patronage of the queen, and becomin
popular. Read this to Baron Grimm, and hear his opinion." [2]

---

[1] In reference to the subject of operatic composition, as it was the
cultivated in Paris—or rather as it was neglected—he says elsewhere:–
" With regard to the opera, the case stands thus: it is exceedingly difficul
to meet with a good poem. The old *libretti*, which are the best, have nc
been adapted to the modern taste; and the new are good for nothing;—fc
the poetry, the only thing in which it is possible that the French can hav
any pride, becomes worse and worse daily; and that, at least, ought t
be good, as they do not understand music."

[2] The minuteness with which Leopold Mozart stores up and answers a
the points in his son's letter, cannot fail to attract attention. It was
matter that cost him some trouble and arrangement, which he describe
to his son in this way:—" I should forget a hundred things that I wish t
write to you about, if I were not to make brief memoranda on a sheet (
paper, which I especially reserve for that purpose. When anything strik
me which it is desirable to communicate to you, I note it down in a fe

Notwithstanding all these arguments, however, Mozart declined the offer, and was sustained in his refusal by the sanction of Baron Grimm. In fact, he never had any serious thoughts of accepting it from the first. " Whoever enters the royal service," he says, in a subsequent letter, " is forgotten at Paris, and then—organist! A good appointment would be very acceptable to me, but nothing under Kapellmeister, and well paid."

During Mozart's absence at Paris, the Archbishop of Salzburg began to be sensible—though more from the representations of foreigners who visited his court, than from his own judgment—that he had made a great mistake in losing Mozart. He felt that he could not be replaced; and proceeded accordingly, with diplomatic artifice, to pave the way for his return; which circumstances soon rendered as desirable to Leopold Mozart as to the archbishop, though neither of them liked to confess as much; both appeared to act from any motives rather than the true ones. Towards the end of June, the father gives an account to his son of the stratagem which was put into motion to entrap him.

" On Trinity Sunday, at the conclusion of the Litany in the afternoon, Count Starnberg asked me, at the priest's house, whether I could not call upon him on the following morning, as he had something to say to me. I went, and found no one with him but his brother, a major in the imperial service, who is staying with him and endeavouring to cure himself here of the alarm which Prussian powder and ball have given him. He told me that an organist had been recommended to him, but that he did not like to enter into the business without knowing whether he was a good one; he wished, therefore, to inquire whether I knew him; his name, he told me, was *Mandl*, or something like it, but he was not quite certain. *Oh, thou awkward devil !* thought I; here has a commission been sent to Vienna to look out for and recommend some person, and the name, etc., of the client is forgotten! It was not intended that I should perceive this introduction to be a mere decoy to lead me to talk about my son, but I—not one word. I said that I had not the honour words; and when I write to you, I take this sheet of paper, and first extract the novelties, then read your last letter through, and reply to it. You might do the same. I strike my pen through such memoranda as are the subject of my letter, and reserve those which are left for the next occasion. And you, my dear wife, must put the lines closer together in writing;—you see how I do it."

of knowing this person, and that I would never venture to
recommend anybody to the prince, for that it would be exceed
ingly difficult to find such an one as would suit him in ever
respect. ' Yes,' said he, ' and I shall myself decline recommend
ing any one, for it is much too difficult a task. Your son ough
to be here now (Bravo! well said, thought I); what a pity tha
such a man is not a great minister of state and ambassador!' To
this I replied that we would speak on the subject candidly an
without reserve; and I then asked him whether every possibl
means had not been employed absolutely to drive him fron
Salzburg? I began from the beginning and suppressed nothin
of all that had happened to us; at which his brother was quit
astonished, and he himself totally unable to deny the truth o
the statement. We next proceeded to speak of the whole musica
establishment, on which I declared my candid opinion, and h
assented, acknowledged it perfectly true, and at last told hi
brother, that of all the foreigners who visited the court o
Salzburg, young Mozart alone had been the general object o
admiration. He wanted to persuade me to write to my son
but I told him that I could not do so, that it would be a vai
effort, that my son would ridicule such a proposal; moreovei
that I must in that case inform him of the salary that he was t
expect; for, as to such a stipend as Adlgasser's, he would mos
probably take no notice of it if offered. Indeed, were his highnes
to resolve upon allowing him fifty florins a month, it was doubtfu
whether he would accept it. We then left the house altogethe
and they went to the riding school, whither I accompanie
them, still conversing on the same subject,—I adhering to wha
I had at first advanced, and he assuring me that he was entirel
in the interest of my son.

" You are to know that the prince can get no good organis
who is at the same time a good performer on the claviei
He now says, though merely in confidential talk among hi
favourites, that Becché is a charlatan and a mountebank, an
that Mozart far surpasses everybody; and he would muc
rather have some one whom he knows, than pay a high pric
for another of whom he knows nothing. He is unable to offe
any one a small stipend, by annexing the hope of an increase
income from teaching, the pupils being few; and those tha
there are I have, with the reputation, moreover, that no one i
able to teach more judiciously. Herein lies the difficulty. Bu
I am not writing all this with the idea of persuading you, m

dear Wolfgang, to return to Salzburg; for I do not place the slightest reliance on the word of the archbishop, and I have not spoken to the countess, but have rather avoided every occasion of coming in contact with her, as she might easily construe the least sentence from me into solicitation and compliance. If anything comes of this, they must propose very favourable and advantageous conditions, which is scarcely probable. We will, however, await them, and make a vow against nothing, except having our noses bitten off."

How this crafty negotiation might have terminated it is needless to inquire; for the issue was unhappily precipitated and determined by the most melancholy event that had yet befallen the family—the death of Mozart's mother, who expired at Paris, July the 3rd, 1778, after a fortnight's illness. In these trying circumstances he acted with a tenderness, fortitude, and discretion highly honourable to his character; and which prove that he could summon all the qualities which become a man at such a crisis, however helpless and abstracted in the common concerns of life. On the night of her decease, he wrote to his father's confidential friend, the Abbé Bullinger, the letter following:

" PARIS, *July 3rd*, 1778.

" MY DEAR FRIEND,—Sympathise with me on this the most wretched and melancholy day of my life. I write at two o'clock in the morning to inform you that my mother—my dearest mother—is no more! God has called her to himself, I saw clearly that nothing could save her, and resigned myself entirely to the will of God; he gave, and he can take away. Picture to yourself the state of alarm, care, and anxiety in which I have been kept for the last fortnight. She died without being conscious of anything—her life went out like a taper. Three days ago she confessed, received the sacrament and extreme unction; but since that time she has been constantly delirious and rambling, until this afternoon at twenty-one minutes after five, when she was seized with convulsions, and immediately lost all perception and feeling. I pressed her hand and spoke to her; but she neither saw me, heard me, nor seemed in the least sensible; and in this state she lay for five hours, namely, till twenty-one minutes past ten, when she departed, no one being present but myself, M. Haine, a good friend of ours whom my father knows, and the nurse.

"I cannot at present write you the whole particulars of the illness; but my belief is that she was to die—that it was the will of God. Let me now beg the friendly service of you, to prepare my poor father by gentle degrees for the melancholy tidings. I wrote to him by the same post, but told him no more than that she was very ill, and I now await his answer, by which I shall be guided. May God support and strengthen him! Oh, my friend! through the especial grace of God I have been enabled to endure the whole with fortitude and resignation, and have long since been consoled under this great loss. In her extremity I prayed for two things: a blessed dying hour for my mother and courage and strength for myself; and the gracious God heard my prayer, and richly bestowed those blessings upon me. Pray therefore, dear friend, support my father. Say what you can to him, in order that when he knows the worst, he may not feel it too bitterly. I commend my sister also to you from the bottom of my heart. Call on both of them soon, but say no word of the death—only prepare them. You can do and say what you will; but let me be so far at ease as to have no new misfortune to expect. Comfort my dear father and my dear sister, and pray send me a speedy answer. Adieu. I remain your much obliged and grateful servant,

"WOLFGANG AMADEUS MOZART.

"Rue du gros chenet, vis-à-vis celle du croissant,
  à l'hôtel des quatre fils Aimont.

("For yourself alone.")

On the same day, with a fortitude far beyond his years, he addressed his father, to prepare him gradually for the terrible news he had commissioned his friend to break to him.

"PARIS, *July 3rd*, 1778.

"The cause of my having left your letter of the 11th of June so long unanswered is, that I have very unpleasant and melancholy intelligence to communicate. My dear mother is very ill. At the beginning of her illness she was, as usual, bled, and this seemed to relieve and do her good; but in a few days she began to complain of sudden chills and heats, which were accompanied by headache and diarrhœa. We began now to use the remedy that we employ at home—the antispasmodic powder. We wished that we had brought the black, but had it not, and could not get it here, where even its name *pulvis epilepticus* is unknown. But as she got worse continually, spoke with difficulty, and so far lost her hearing, that it was necessary to call out in speaking to her, Baron Grimm sent us his physician. She is still very weak, and is also feverish and delirious. They want to give me hope; but I have not much. I have been long already—for days and nights together—between hope and fear; but I have now entirely resigned myself to the will of God, and I hope that you and my dear sister will do the like. What are the means then to give us calm and peace, in a degree, if not absolutely? I am resigned, let the end be what it may, because I know that God, who, however mysteriously he may proceed to human eyes, ordains everything for the best, so wills it; and I am not easily persuaded out of the belief that neither physician nor any other man, neither misfortune nor accident, can either take or give life, but God alone, though these are the means which he mostly employs; but even these not always. We see people constantly sinking and dying around us; but I do not say, on that account, that my mother must and will die, or that we have lost all hope. She may recover if it be the will of God. I, however, find consolation in these reflections, after praying to God as earnestly as I am able for my dear mother's health and life; they strengthen, encourage, and console me, and you must needs think I require them. Let us now change the subject, and quit these melancholy thoughts. Let us hope, if not much, and put our trust in God, consoling ourselves with the reflection that everything is well ordered which the Almighty orders, and that he best knows what is essential to our temporal happiness and our eternal salvation."

He then, to divert attention from this distressing subject, describes the reception of the symphony he had written for the opening of the *concert spirituel;* which was huddled through so disgracefully at the rehearsals, that he declares he had determined, if it went so badly in public, he would certainly go into the orchestra, take the violin out of the hand of the leader, and direct it himself; an ebullition of anger so unlike his habitual gentleness, that it must be referred to the agony of mind he was then suffering, in consequence of the dangerous illness of his mother.[1]

[1] These forebodings were happily disappointed in the sequel. The symphony had great success. The audience were captivated, particularly by a p ssage in the middle of the first allegro; and no less by the andante and the last allegro. The description of the closing part is very curious:—

To this letter Leopold Mozart, believing when he sat down to write it that his beloved wife was yet living, wrote the following profoundly pathetic answer.

"SALZBURG, *July 13th,* 1778.

"MY DEAR WIFE AND MY DEAR SON,—Not to be wanting on your name-day, my dear wife, I write under the present date secure that the letter must reach its destination some days beforehand. I wish you all manner of happiness, and pray Almighty God to preserve you from this day, for many years not only in health, but in as much content as is possible on the changeable theatre of this world. I am fully convinced how necessary the society of your husband and your daughter is to your real happiness. God will dispose everything for the best according to the conclusions of his unsearchable wisdom and most holy providence. Could you have believed, a year ago, that you would spend your next name-day in Paris? But, improbable as it might have appeared to many at that time (if not to ourselves) it is just as possible that we may, by God's help, find ourselves all together again before we expected it; for this is what lies most at my heart—the separation from you—to be at such a distance and *to live at such a distance.* In other respects we are all well, thank God! We kiss you and Wolfgang a thousand times and beg you, of all things, to be careful for the preservation of your health.

"The foregoing was written yesterday, the 12th. To-day the 13th, that is to say, just now, at a little before ten o'clock in the morning, your melancholy letter arrived. The impression it made upon us you may imagine. We have so wept together as scarcely to be able to read the letter—and your sister! Great and merciful God! thy most holy will be done! My dear son, notwithstanding all possible submission to the

"As I had observed that all the last allegros here, as well as the first began with all the instruments together, and generally *unisono,* I commenced this with the two violins only, *piano,* for eight bars—which was immediately succeeded by a *forte;* the audience consequently, as I had anticipated, began to hush down every noise during the *piano,* and then to hear the *forte* and to clap their hands were one and the same thing. Immediately that the symphony was over, I went quite pleased into the Palais Royal—took some refreshment—*prayed the Rosenkranz that I had vowed, and then went home.*" He, who had only just before been in a mood to rush upon the leader and dispossess him of his instrument before the public! This symphony was the first ever produced for a grand orchestra and is a fine work, but scarcely at all known. Imagine a time when the *forte* of a symphony was accompanied by *clapping,* and the instrumental art improving amidst the chaotic noises of a Christmas pantomime!

divine will, you will find it but human and natural that my
tears should almost prevent my writing. What am I to conclude? Scarcely otherwise than that, even now while I write
this, she is dead—or else she must be better—for yours is dated
on the 3rd, and it is now the 13th. You say that the bleeding
did her good; but that some days afterwards she complained of
cold and heat. Your last letter was on the 12th of June, and
then she wrote, ' yesterday I was bled '—and wherefore on a
Saturday and a fast-day? Perhaps she ate meat. She certainly
delayed the bleeding too long, I say so because I know her, and
remember her way of putting off from one day to the next; and
this would naturally happen in a strange place, where one must
commence inquiries for a surgeon. The thing is now done,
however, and cannot be altered. I place the most perfect
reliance on your filial affection, that you have taken every
earthly care of your excellent mother, and, if God spares her to
us, will continue to do so—for that excellent mother—the apple
of whose eye you were—who loved you beyond measure—was
so proud of you—and who (as I know better than you) lived
wholly for you. But should all our hopes be vain! Should
we have lost her; Great God! then you will want friends—
trustworthy friends—for not only will you have funeral expenses,
etc., to meet, but a great many expenses of another kind, with
which you are totally unacquainted, in which a foreigner is
easily overreached and taken in, and if he have not judicious
advice, is led into unnecessary outlay and half ruined:—but it
is impossible that you can understand these things. Should
this misfortune have happened, request Baron von Grimm to
permit you to place your mother's things in his charge, to prevent
your having so much to attend to; or else lock everything
securely; for as you are frequently from home for the whole
day, your apartments may be broken into and robbed. God
grant that all these precautions may be needless; but herein
you recognise your father. My dear wife!—my dear son!
As she was ill a few days after the bleeding, she must have
been ill from the 16th or 17th of June. She waited too long;
she expected that by keeping herself quiet in bed, by diet, and
other simple remedies, she would soon be better. I know how
it is in such cases; one hopes and delays from one day to the
next; but, my dear Wolfgang, diarrhœa, with fever, requires
instant medical advice, to know whether the fever may be
removed or must be left, since cooling remedies increase the

relaxation, and if that is stopped at an improper time, the *materia peccans* occasions inflammation.

" I congratulate you on having had such success with your symphony at the *concert spirituel.* I can fancy all your apprehensions and uneasiness—but your resolution of running into the orchestra, if it had not gone well, was but the momentary suggestion of passion. God forbid! You must control such impulses as these, they are exaggerated; such a step would have cost you your life, which no man of sense would risk for a symphony. An affront like this, a public affront too, would be revenged sword in hand, not by a Frenchman merely, but by any other man who calls himself a man of honour.

" I wrote her my felicitations at the commencement of this letter, and Nannerl intended to conclude it with hers; but she is unable, as you may easily suppose, to write a single word, for the news comes just now when she was going to write, and every letter that she attempts to form, sends a gush of tears into her eyes. Do you, her dear brother, supply her place—if, as we hope and trust, it is still to be supplied.

" But no! you can no longer do it! she is gone! You take too much pains to comfort me, and that is never so anxiously done, unless the loss of all earthly hope, or the event itself, naturally force one to it. I write this at half-past three o'clock in the afternoon. I now know that my dear wife is in Heaven! I write it with weeping eyes, but with entire submission to the divine will.

" M. Bullinger found us, as every one else did, in deep affliction; I handed him your letter without saying a word; he dissembled very well, and having read it, inquired what I thought about it. I said, that I firmly believed my dear wife was no more. He almost feared the same thing, he told me— and then like a true friend entered upon consolatory topics, and said to me everything that I had before said to myself. We finished our conversation, and our friends gradually left us with much concern; M. Bullinger, however, remained behind, and when we were alone, asked me whether I believed that there was any ground for hope after such a description of the illness as had been given. I replied, that I not merely believed her dead by this time—but that she was already so on the very day that the letter was written; that I had resigned myself to the will of God, and must remember that I have two children, who I hoped would love me, as I lived solely and entirely for them; indeed, that I felt so certain, as to have taken some pains to write to, and remind you of the consequences, etc. Upon this he said, ' Yes, she is dead,' and in that instant the scales fell from my eyes; for the suddenness of the accident had prevented my perceiving, what I else should have suspected, as soon as I had read your letter—namely, how probable it was that you had privately communicated the real truth to M. Bullinger. In fact, your letter stupified me—it at first was such a blow as to render me incapable of reflection. I have now no more to say. Do not be anxious on my account, I shall bear my sorrow like a man. Remember what a tenderly loving mother you have had—now you will be able to appreciate all her care—as in your mature years, after my death, you will mine, with a constantly increasing affection. If you love me, as I doubt not but you do, take care of your health—on your life hangs mine, and the future support of your affectionate sister. How incomprehensibly bitter a thing it is, when death rends asunder a happy marriage—can only be known by experience. Write me the whole particulars—perhaps she lost too little blood? It is most certain, however, that she relied too much on herself, and that the physician was called in too late—meanwhile the inflammation *in intestinis* had gained ground. *Take care of your health,* and let us not be altogether miserable! Nannerl as yet knows nothing of Bullinger's letter, but I have so prepared her, that she already believes she has lost her dear mother. Write to me soon—and everything—when she was buried—and where. Great God! that I should have to look for the grave of my dear wife in Paris!' "

The bereaved son, alone in the great crowd of Paris, but bearing his new and trying position with Christian resignation, after the lapse of a few days communicates in full the sad event to his father and sister.

" PARIS, ce 9 Juillet, 1778.

" MONSIEUR, MON TRÈS CHER PÈRE,—I hope that you are now prepared to receive with firmness some intelligence of a very melancholy and distressing character; indeed, my last letter, of the 3rd, will not have encouraged you to expect anything very favourable. On the evening of the same day (the 3rd), at twenty-one minutes after ten at night, my mother fell happily asleep in God, and was already experiencing the joys of heaven at the very moment that I wrote to you. All was over—I wrote to you in the night, and I trust that you and my sister will pardon this slight but very necessary artifice;—for when, after all the distress that I had suffered, I turned my thoughts towards you, I could not possibly persuade myself to surprise you all at once with the dreadful and fatal news. Now, however, I hope that you have both prepared yourselves to hear the worst; and after giving way to the reasonable and natural impulses of your grief, to submit yourselves at last to the will of God, and to adore his inscrutable, unfathomable, and all-wise providence.

.   .   .   .

" I write this in the house of Madame d'Epinay and M. Baron de Grimm, with whom I am now staying, and where I have a pretty little room with a pleasant prospect, and am, as far as circumstances will permit, happy. It would be a great additional comfort were I to hear that my dear father and sister had resigned themselves with fortitude and submission to the will of God; trusting him entirely, in the full conviction that everything is ordered for our good. Dear father — be comforted! Dearest sister—be comforted!—you know not the kind intentions of your brother towards you; because hitherto they have not been in his power to fulfil.

" I hope that you will both be careful of your health. Remember that you have still a son—a brother—who will exert himself to the utmost for your happiness, well knowing what sacrifices you are both ready to make for him, and that when the time shall come, neither of you will oppose the fulfilment of his honourable wishes.[1] Oh! then we will lead a life as peaceful and happy as is attainable in this world; and at length, in God's time, meet all together again in the enjoyment of that object for which we were created.

" With regard to Noverre's ballet, I never mentioned more than the probability of his composing a new one. He has just been in want of half a ballet, to which I have written the music: that is to say, six pieces were by other hands; these consisted of miserable French tunes merely—the rest, namely, the symphony and country dances (about twelve pieces in all) were by me. This ballet has been played four times already, with great applause. I now resolutely refuse to do anything without stipulating the terms beforehand; for what I have just done was out of friendship to Noverre. I have conversed with

[1] He here alludes to his union with Aloysia Weber, to which he turns as the source of consolation for the future nearest to his thoughts.

Piccini [1] at the *concert spirituel*. When we meet by accident he is very polite, and I also; but I give myself no trouble to cultivate an acquaintance with him, nor with any other composers; they understand their affairs, and I mine, which is enough. If I should be engaged to write an opera, I shall have plenty of annoyance; but that would not be worth mentioning, as I am used to it, were it not for the confounded French language, which is so detestable for music! How wretched it is; the German is divine in comparison; and then the singers—indeed it is a shame to call them so, for they don't sing, but shriek and howl with all their might, through the throat and nose.

"I am to compose a French oratorio for the *concert spirituel*, against the next Lent. I am in wonderful favour with M. le Gros, the director."

Much, however, as M. le Gros was delighted with the symphony, which he called his *best*, he thought the andante too full of modulation and too long; and Mozart, although he held a totally different opinion, composed another, to pamper him with a fresh proof of his inexhaustible genius. In his succeeding letters he desires to have mass said at Maria Plain and at Loretto, as he had done at Paris; and presents his sister on her name-day with a little prelude he had composed for her. The playfulness and readiness with which he struck into new paths is surprising. "This is not a prelude," he writes, "merely to go from one key to another, but a capriccio to try a piano; and especially adapted for that purpose." His imagination was practical in the smallest details, as well as universal.

The apprehensions of Leopold Mozart at this juncture were not to be concealed. He saw in his son's residence at Paris, under his present circumstances, a thousand nameless risks, and in his anxiety to rescue him from the evils he dreaded, he appealed to his old friend, the Padre Martini, to intercede on his behalf.

But the Padre was not a very active friend, and, although he entertained great admiration for Mozart, he did nothing to promote his interests. The only alternative that presented itself to Leopold Mozart was the immediate return of his son to

---

[1] This celebrated musician survived both his old antagonist Gluck, and Mozart. He returned to Paris after the revolution; but music being much neglected, was compelled to live in poverty and seclusion. Shortly before his death he presented to the First Consul the following memorial: "*Piccini is starving.*" This appeal did not remain unnoticed, even in that time of fierce contention; and some small provision was made for him.

Salzburg. He could no longer bear the separation, and he ha‹
been preparing the way by interviews with the countess, wh‹
was very anxious that Wolfgang should once more enter th‹
archbishop's service. A vacancy having occurred by th‹
death of Lolli, it was proposed that his salary should be be
stowed upon Leopold, who had petitioned for an increase
" after many years of diligent and irreproachable service,'
and that Adlgasser's salary should be given to Wolfgang
making altogether 1000 florins per annum. The father announce
this proposal to his son, and urges him to accept it. The stres
he lays upon these beggarly terms is affecting, as it shows tha
the family, notwithstanding their long servitude at Salzburg
and the applause they had won from crowned heads, courtiers
and popular assemblies, had still a hard struggle.

" If this takes place we can rely for a certainty on 115 *florin*
a month at least, and as it is at present on more than 120 *florin*
a month of certain income; *without reckoning what I get by th*
sale of my violin school which produces at least fifty florins a year
or what your sister earns for herself, who has now ten florins ‹
month certain, out of which she clothes herself, as she instruct
the two little daughters of the countess, daily, but I the elde‹
two. In this account, also, no reckoning is taken of what yoı
might make for yourself by private engagements. For thougl
we must not count upon much of that sort here, yet you knov
that from time to time you have taken something; and even iı
this manner we are better off than in another place where it i‹
twice as dear: and we cannot so exactly rely upon the money
Here at least we are supported."

The only difficulty he apprehends in the way of this arrange
ment, by which they were to be kept like caged birds, beatinç
their wings in vain against the bars, and singing for the pleasurı
of others, is the archbishop's miserable parsimony. He trie‹
to reconcile his son to the proposal, should it be carried out, bȝ
reminding him that he must be celebrated before he can hopı
to command fortune; that there is plenty of time before him
that Gluck is probably sixty, and that it is not more than si›
or seven and twenty years since he first began to be talkeç
about;—arguments which might probably have weighed littlı
with his correspondent, had they not been strengthened bȝ
hopes of a still more interesting kind.

In the next letter, he tells him that, to his great surprise, thı

archbishop has not only consented to the terms, by which the
son was to be concert master, with a salary of 500 florins, but
politely expressed his regret that he could not do more; and
that whenever he wished to write an opera, he might have leave
to go; making, at the same time, a mean excuse for denying
them the journey of the year before, by saying, "that he could
not endure the wandering about on such begging expeditions."
This insulting phrase his highness thought fit to apply to the
honourable tour of an artist. But the attraction that seems
to have determined the movements of Wolfgang transpires in
a casual sentence of this letter. The fame of Mademoiselle
Weber's singing had reached Salzburg, and there was some
prospect of an opera there, at which she was to assist by invitation of the court, and to live with the Mozarts, whose lodgings
are, fortunately, capacious enough for her reception.

"The prince and the whole court are wonderfully taken with
Mademoiselle Weber, and are absolutely determined to hear her;
she will, therefore, reside with us. Her father appears to me
to have no head; I will manage the matter better for them, if
they will follow my advice.

"People are always asking me here, why we two single people
live in such great lodgings, for which we must pay so dear.
But I have always thought, either *I go away* or *you come*, and
in either case, it must be better; we have a stable, too, belonging to the house, and I can keep a horse. If I like to buy a
little chaise, or *Würstl*, I can give the great carriage in exchange.
My next will tell you when to set off."

The next and last letter from Salzburg contains advice for
the journey. The prudent father recommends his son to see
the elector, if possible, on his way through Munich, and to say
that he had accepted the appointment at Salzburg out of filial
regard. "Here," says Leopold, "you may add some 200 or
300 florins, and say your appointment is 700 or 800 florins as
concert master;"—a little device that may be pardoned in consideration of the straits to which they were driven in making
head against the favourites of fortune. The chance of writing
an opera for Munich is pointed out. "For," he observes,
'Schweitzer and Holzbauer will not write every year, and even
should Michl write, he will soon be *out-Michled*." The archbishop, it seems, had yielded up every point to render his
position easy and agreeable. "*You are not to play the violin*

at court," the father adds, " but to preside at the clavier, with
the entire power of direction, while the absolute control of the
prince's music, and the inspection of the chapel-house, are
confided to me."

With these prospects, such as they were, before him, Wolf
gang Mozart quitted Paris on the 26th of September 1778.

The complete failure of this expedition on one ground after
another, the uncertainty of procuring even a bare subsistence
far less of such an appointment as he had a right to expect
must, it will be supposed, have opened the eyes of both the
father and son to the startling truth, that genius may be too
great (as well as too small) for success.   And yet it is probable
that in the change of events produced during the last few
months, neither of them dwelt much on the ill omens of their
first experiment; the father being engrossed with the cares
incident to his promotion at Salzburg, and the son full of the
expectation of meeting Mademoiselle Weber under the paternal
roof.

Had Mozart remained at Paris, and worked his way (for the
various pleasing and elegant things he wrote there were not
without their influence even on the French taste of that time)
it would have been much to his personal advantage.[1]   His
industry and genius, everywhere conspicuous, would have been
gradually appreciated and rewarded in France; but destiny
had more congenial work in store for him than that of reforming
and ameliorating French music; work in which the taste of
Europe at large was concerned.

In the last letter received by Mozart previously to his
departure from Paris, his father advised that he should not
omit the opportunity of again offering his services to the elector
at Munich. An alteration had occurred which gave some
likelihood of success to an application at this juncture; it was
that the electorates of Mannheim and Munich were now united
and that the fine orchestra at Mannheim, among whom Mozart
enumerated many friends and admirers, was consequently
removed to Munich, as, in future, the principal residence of the
government.   The only effect, however, which this had upon
the composer was to bring together the choice band who executed

---

[1] This visit to Paris gave rise to a symphony in D for the *concert spirituel*
commonly called the French symphony to the *sinfonia concertante*, to two
quartets for the flute, a concerto for the harp and flute, six sonatas for the
clavier, etc., besides the greater part of a ballet which he wrote for Noverre
and several pieces of church music in lieu of Holzbauer.

his " Idomeneo," consisting of the picked men of the two orchestras, and to make his sojourn at Munich during the composition of that opera the more agreeable, by surrounding him with his old associates.

His journey to Salzburg occupied more than three months, a lingering one for a young man in his situation; but capable of satisfactory explanation.

Towards the end of October, he was at Strasburg, giving concerts, of which we have the following humorous account. The first concert was by subscription, for concert giving was at that time a more miserable business there than even at Salzburg.

" I played entirely alone, and took no music with me, to be sure of losing none. In brief—I made *three louis d'or ;* but the chief thing was the *bravo* and *bravissimo,* which resounded on all sides; and I must inform you, that Prince Max, of Zweibrücken, honoured the room by his presence. That every one was pleased, I need hardly say.

" When this was over I wished to take my leave, but was persuaded to wait till the next Saturday, and give a grand concert at the theatre—in which *my receipts were the same,* to the amazement, the shame, and disgrace of Strasburg. The manager, Mr. Villeneuve, gives the worst character to the inhabitants of this truly abominable city; I have, indeed, made it little more—but the expenses of the orchestra, which was very bad, but very dear; the lights, the printing, and the numerous attendants at the entrances, caused a very heavy deduction. However, the applauding and clapping tormented my ears as much as if the theatre had been full. Every one present loudly and publicly complained of the negligence of their town's folk— and I frankly told them, that if I could rationally have expected to meet so meagre an audience, I should much rather have given the concert *gratis,* for the mere pleasure of seeing the theatre filled; indeed, I should have preferred to do so; for, upon my honour, nothing is more melancholy than to see a grand enter- ainment of eighty covers, and only three persons to dinner— and then it was so cold! I, however, soon warmed myself, and to show messieurs, the Strasburgers, that I did not take the thing to heart, I played a good deal for my own amusement [1]— a concerto more than I promised—and, at last, for a long time,

[1] Handel exhibited kindred sentiments on similar occasions, when he found thin attendance at his oratorios; he is said to have comforted himself with the observation:—" Never mind—the music will sound the better! "

out of my head. That is now over—and I have, at least, won honour and reputation."

.During all this time dramatic music was gradually gaining the ascendency in his imagination; and as he felt the increase of his powers in that department, he prepared to abandon models and authorities, and to give a new aspect to the lyric stage. The eagerness and enthusiasm with which he devotes himself to this subject are characteristically portrayed in a letter to his father, dated

" MANNHEIM, *November 12th,* 1778.

" I reached this place safely on the 6th, and gave all my kind friends a very agreeable surprise. I may, perhaps, make forty louis d'or here; but shall be obliged to stay six weeks, or, at longest, two months. Seiler's company, which is known to you by reputation, is now at Mannheim. M. von Dallberg is the director of it; and he will not let me off till I have written a duodrama for him. To confess the truth, I did not long hesitate in complying, for this is a sort of drama that I have always been wishing to compose. I forget whether I wrote you any description of this kind of piece when I was here the first time; having, on that occasion, twice witnessed the perform-ance of one with the greatest pleasure. Nothing, in fact, ever so much surprised me; for I had always fancied that no effect could thus be produced. You are aware that nothing is sung, but that declamation is substituted for singing. The music is like that to an accompanied recitative, having now and then between its phrases a sentence spoken, which produces the most magnificent effect. The one I saw was ' Medea,' by Benda; but there is another by the same, ' Ariadne in Naxos,' both of them truly excellent. You know that of all the Lutheran Kapellmeisters, Benda has ever been my favourite; and in these works I take such delight that I always carry them about with me. Fancy my happiness in now having that to compose for which I have constantly been longing. I will tell you an opinion of mine—that the greater part of the recitatives in operas should be treated in this manner, and only sung *when the words are well adapted to musical expression.* They have established here an amateur musical society like that at Paris. M. Franzl is the leader, and I am just now writing, on that account, a double concerto, for clavier and violin." [1]

[1] This concerto was never completed. It proceeded somewhat beyond a hundred bars, and then the multiplicity of avocations, with which he

The duodrama here alluded to is "Semiramis," which, it is to be feared, has been irrecoverably lost. He wrote it without pay, out of regard for M. von Gemmingen, the author of the libretto, and for his own pleasure.

From Mannheim he proceeded by way of Kaysersheim; instead of Stuttgard, as he originally intended; changing his course in consequence of travelling in company with the bishop of that place, who was much gratified with his society. On Christmas day he reached Munich, from whence he wrote abrupt notes, simply indicating that he had seen the electress, presented her with his sonatas, and had a gracious reception, and that he had contrived to have her informed of his intention to set off in a few days, in order that he might be speedily furnished forth.

The flurry of these brief notes, and his sudden willingness, after lingering so long upon the road, to return homewards, may be easily accounted for. He had no sooner reached Munich, than he hastened to the house of the Webers, who were settled there with the rest of the Mannheim musicians.

The father of the young Aloysia had witnessed Mozart's attachment to his daughter with peculiar satisfaction, believing that the union of such a composer and such a singer could not but be prosperous; and Leopold Mozart, from his readiness in informing his son, as an additional motive for him to leave Paris, that Mademoiselle Weber was engaged to sing at the concerts of the archbishop, appears to have been thoroughly cognisant of the relation in which the parties mutually stood. However, none of these expectations were to be fulfilled, for an old and sufficient reason: the inconstancy of womankind.

As Mozart entered the apartment of his mistress, he found her with altered inclinations; she seemed scarcely to know him from whom she had parted as lovers part — with tears. Some eye-witness of the scene has rendered it graphic, by recollections of the personal appearance of the composer, who was now in mourning for his mother, and dressed after the Parisian fashion, in a red coat with black buttons. Perceiving the change that had taken place, he immediately sat down to the clavier, and sang aloud, " *Ich lass das Mädel gern, das mich nicht will,*" expressing his readiness to resign a girl who did not

was surrounded during the few weeks of his stay, was thrown aside. This fragment, which will be found in the catalogue of his unfinished pieces, is described by the Abbé Stadler as promising a work of greater beauty in its kind than any he had yet produced.

love him, either in an extempore composition, or in a song ver
happily selected. He now turned his attentions towards he
younger sister, Constance; and, during the time that the famil
of the Webers spent at Salzburg, in 1779 (in the course of whicl
the elder made her first appearance on the stage of the Municl
Opera), found many opportunities to cultivate the good opinio
of one who better understood him, and was more fitted t
partake his fortunes. From this time Constance Weber becam
his pupil in pianoforte playing, and he instructed her witl
pleasure. Their acquaintance was renewed at Vienna, ripenec
into a mutual attachment, and ended, as we shall see by anc
by, in marriage.[1]

Whether his father had any reason to suspect the turn whicl
this affair had taken, or that he had merely lost patience at th
long time which this journey from Paris had consumed, must b
left to speculation; but finding that his son had fixed no specifi
time for leaving Munich, he wrote to him on the 11th of Januar
1779, commanding his immediate return in more decisive term
than he had ever before employed.

"You will have perceived from the letter which I sent on th
7th to M. Becke, which contained a message to M. Gschwende
and one to yourself, that it is my desire that you prepare to se
off in company with M. Gschwender according to my reques
to him in that letter. I desire that you embrace this oppor
tunity without fail, and as he departs earlier than Madam
Robinnig, that you make all necessary arrangements for tha
purpose, if you do not wish to give me very serious offence.
hope, however, that from the instructions contained in m
letter of the 7th, you have so ordered your affairs as to hav
nothing to detain you; that you can send the superfluity of you
luggage by the diligence on the 13th, and set off with M
Gschwender, for that is a favour which he certainly canno
refuse. The present from the electress cannot possibly detai
you: for as the sonatas were presented on the 7th, everythin

[1] Aloysia Weber eventually married a tragedian, named Lange; a unioi
which proved so unfortunate that it was the town talk of Vienna. He
greatest success as a *prima donna* on the theatres of the continent, a
Hamburg, Amsterdam, etc., took place after Mozart's death; and to thi
success his admirable compositions for her mainly conduced. Conversin
on the subject of her youthful rejection of Mozart some years since a
Vienna with a friend of the author's, Madame Lange observed that sh
knew nothing of the greatness of his genius—she saw him only as *a littl
man.* Her subsequent regrets in some measure atoned for the levity witl
which she treated him.

with ordinary attention must be ready in a week. There can
be no excuse; you have seen the opera; consequently have
done all that you wished."

That Mozart expected little from the new scheme of life laid
down for him at Salzburg, or the terms conceded to him by the
archbishop; and that he loitered on the road in the vague hope
that something might turn up to give a new direction to his
future plans; is clear enough. But matters had now undergone an unexpected change, sufficient to determine him at least
for the present; and he rejoined his father about the middle
of January 1779.

PART IV

HIS MANHOOD

THE Court Calendar of Salzburg for 1779, and the year following, records the name of Mozart as court and cathedral organist. Thus, after having rejected with contempt the offer made to him at Versailles, we find him holding a similar appointment in a place of far less consideration under the authority of that archbishop who had been throughout, in some sort, his evil genius. Nor had time diminished the force of this malignant influence, or soothed the sense of animosity at either side. A short connection with Salzburg and its affairs re-opened all the old wounds.

Soon after his return, he renewed his acquaintance with the family of the Webers, the eldest daughter of which, as has been mentioned, was now singing at the concerts of the archbishop, and formed his first particular intimacy with her sister Constance, his future wife. His opportunities of enjoying this pleasant intercourse could not, however, have lasted more than a few months, as the family soon left to attend the *début* of Aloysia Weber on the stage at Munich, and were afterwards travelling in various parts of Germany.

The first work of importance he now produced at Salzburg was a mass,[1] which, judging from the style of the composition, was designed for a high festival of the church, and the date renders it probable that it was produced at the Cathedral on Easter Sunday. This elevated and truly admirable composition announces the great career of Mozart as symphonist and dramatic musician. He seems to have seized the occasion to gratify and astonish the whole music-corps of the city, and not even to have forgotten the archbishop, who liked a pompous style and to hear the trumpets. The soprano solo was doubtless intended for the Weber; and we may conceive the emotions

---

[1] No. 1 of the English edition of the Masses. To the original score, as generally known to our musicians, Mozart added an appendix, containing accompaniments for two horns and three trombones. The date of the work is March 23, 1779.

)f the other composers and artists at the energetic and fiery
Credo. What an advance in his genius within a few months!
Some of the symphonies he produced for the court this year
appear by their beginnings to be well worth knowing. In
others he probably pleased himself less; for in August we find
him engaged in a third symphony, which, from its singular plan
and abundant solos, must have been destined rather to surprise
and amuse, than to develop the higher qualities of instrumental
music.[1]

Indeed it would seem that he was soon thrall to the court
taste, and compelled to produce once more under restrictions
that must have been deeply mortifying; for how could this
mighty and impassioned genius condescend to purposes of mere
amusement, or suspend its nobler speculations and projects to
become the puppet of triflers? To increase his dissatisfaction,
he had the almost undivided task of producing novelties for the
court of Salzburg, Michael Haydn and every other composer on
the establishment being seldom called upon for anything while
young Mozart was at hand.

The hours which he was enabled to devote to meditation and
self-improvement were principally employed on the musical
drama, and the transformation of style and independence of
models which have been justly thought to characterise
' Idomeneo," and to stamp it with the maturity of the master,
were now in active progress. That the opera of " Zaïde,"
though the MS. is without date, was the preparatory step to
' Idomeneo," and a study in dramatic composition made at this
period, seems collaterally proved by facts; as well as borne
out by its internal evidences of prodigal invention—of the
exuberant mind rejoicing and luxuriating in its new creations,
and scarcely knowing when or where to stop. Soliloquies,

---

[1] The existence of this curiosity among the symphonies of Mozart is so
imperfectly known to the musical public, that some description of its plan
may not be unwelcome. It consists of *eight* movements. The trio to the
first minuet has *obligato* parts for a flute and bassoon, both which have
concerto passages. The fourth movement is a concertante, in which all
the wind instruments, including the trumpet, are *obligato* in turn, and have
each a cadence. The fifth movement is a rondo, in which the two flutes
and the two oboes are *obligati*. To this succeeds an *andantino* in the form
of an entr'acte, and then a second minuet, followed by two trios, of which
the second has an obligato posthorn! The score of this production, which
has been partially published, discovers so few traces of Mozart worthy of
the epoch of " Zaïde," " Idomeneo," and the grand mass in C, that it is
with difficulty referred to the same period, notwithstanding the date and
autograph of the composer.

interrupted at times by strains of music responsive to the situation or passion, in the manner of recitative, form a feature of "Zaïde;" and it is plain, from the minute description of this kind of composition given by Mozart, in letters to his father, that he had never employed his pen upon it, until, on returning from Paris, the accidental hearing of Benda's "Ariadne in Naxos" inflamed his ambition, by discovering new truths and fresh modes of expression in his art. Again, there is a connection between the opera of "Zaïde" and that of "Die Entführung aus dem Serail," produced by him a few years afterwards at Vienna, which shows that the former could not have been long dismissed from his mind.[1] The dramatic business is similar in both; and it is remarkable, that the theme of the last quartet in "Zaïde" is introduced as a middle phrase in one of the most beautiful songs in "Die Entführung."[2] Among the inducements to leave Paris, enumerated by his father, some slight musical dramatic performances to take place at Salzburg form one. This certainly furnishes a conjecture as to the origin of "Zaïde."

To account for the sudden perfection of that most important branch of the lyric drama, accompanied recitative, as exhibited in "Idomeneo," would be difficult, were no intervening studies to be found. But putting "Semiramis" out of the question, the melodramatic part of "Zaïde" alone, viewed in connection with certain letters of Mozart, which exhibit the close observer of dramatic propriety in action and declamation, may easily suggest what improvements such a master of instrumental music would bring to the previous attempts of Benda and Gluck. Every onward step of the composer throughout his youth shows his respect for antiquity; and progress, so well calculated, naturally became solid and assured. Mozart was the same man even in the sudden transition to "Idomeneo:" he only saw with more vivacity what was to be done, and the extent of his power to accomplish it. Since this time the lyric drama has seen many innovators, whose career only proves that

[1] M. Fétis conjectures that "Zaïde" was the opera for which Mozart entered into treaty with a Venetian manager in 1773; a treaty, by the way, which never reached completion. But the original German libretto, omitting all consideration of the maturity of the style of the music, is decisive against its having been written for Venice at the period supposed. See *Biog. Univ. des Musiciens*. Art. Mozart.

[2] The passage in question appears in the pathetic air, in G Minor, "Taurigkeit ward mir zum loose." It is first recognised as a symphony, though in altered notation $\frac{2}{4}$ instead of $\frac{4}{4}$.

originality, to have permanent influence, must not be the growth of wayward impulse, or the sudden ambition of notoriety —but of calm and deliberate mental power.

Towards the winter of 1780, Mozart received from the Elector of Bavaria an engagement to compose the *opera seria* for the ensuing carnival. " Idomeneo," the subject selected for this occasion, is an echo of the Greek drama; and the libretto was arranged so as to produce the greatest effects of the grand opera, through the colouring of heroical times, scenes, situations, and the classical mythology.[1] The author of the text of this work was the Abbate Varesco, a resident at Salzburg, and friend of his father. Having wrung from the archbishop his slow consent to profit by the joyful opportunity of distinction now offered, he engaged in the work, and completed it with a rapidity which, considering its extent, beauty, and classical purity of style, is truly amazing. He quitted Salzburg on the 6th of November 1780; but few, if any, of the important parts of the music could have been written at this time, as he was not yet aware who were to be the singers. They proved in the event a motley set, from whom no great effects of combination were to be elicited. Among them were Raff, the septagenarian tenor; Del Prato, a broken-down *musico*, who had never before appeared on the stage; and the two daughters of Wendling, the flute player. On the other hand, there was a chorus; and an orchestra— perhaps the most extraordinary in Europe—abounding in artists of the highest talent as solo players. If therefore compelled to shun concerted music for the principal vocalists, he could freely follow the bent of his fancy with respect to the instruments; and of this privilege he memorably availed himself.

There is nothing which gives a more lively idea of Mozart, of the glowing animation and spirituality of his nature, than " Idomeneo," [2] written in the bloom of his life, at five and twenty

[1] The story of this opera is a new version of Jephthah's " Rash Vow." Idomeneo, a king of Crete, in danger of perishing in a storm at sea, propitiates the angry Neptune, by promising to sacrifice to him the first object he may meet, if permitted to land. It is his son Idamante. Endeavouring to escape, the victim is stopped by prodigious appearances, and the wretched father, and the despairing mistress, Ilia, are moving towards the sacrifice when they are interrupted by the oracle, which deposes Idomeneo, and places Idamante and Ilia on the throne of Crete.

[2] The author of the lives of *Haydn and Mozart*, in a note upon " Idomeneo," p. 370, asserts that the composer was at this time deeply enamoured of Mademoiselle Constance Weber, and that his attachment to her " supplied him with the subjects of the impassioned airs which his work required." The whole note is erroneous, and properly refers to the composition of a subsequent opera, " Die Entführung aus dem Serail."

years of age. Youthful fire and invention were never so happily tempered with consummate experience. To conceive the enthusiasm manifested at Munich, we are to think of its musical condition: of artists who had brought tone and facility of execution upon their instruments to great perfection, but to whom the mind that animates the mass was wanting: who could not ordinarily get beyond such music as that of Holz-bauer, and a routine of novelties that left the art where they found it. In " Idomeneo " they were awakened by the magic touch of genius to a new life in their art;—they found themselves discoursing in an unheard and rapturous language, and the effect upon them was one of intoxication and enchantment. Even Mozart himself may have been somewhat surprised at what he had here accomplished, though he had put his utmost force into a work produced with eagerness and exaltation of fancy, and with the enjoyment of his labours in no very distant prospect.

His letter, with intelligence of his arrival at Munich, is dated November 9. After giving a few hours to the joyful greetings of the friends by whom he was here surrounded, he begins his preparations for the opera. He describes our old acquaintance, Count Seau, of Munich, as now thoroughly intimate with the Mannheim orchestra, or in his own characteristic phrase, they are " like melted wax." His first business with the count con-cerned the libretto, which was to be printed at Munich, and still wanted alterations and abbreviations of the recitative. These matters arranged, we may observe him in every stage of the progress of his opera, until its final production, sustain-ing some new duty. He is composer, teacher of the singers, the orchestra, and the chorus; he plans the action and the stage effects; he speculates upon the desires and tastes of his audience; and exhibits perfect confidence in his judgment on the lyric drama. But he is in nothing more instructive than as the critic of a libretto.

" I have now a request to the Abbate. I wish to have the air of Ilia in the second scene of the second act somewhat altered, to suit a particular purpose, *Se il Padre perdei, in te lo ritrovo :*— this strophe could not be better. But it is followed by what always appeared to me in an air unnatural—namely, the speak-ing *aside*. In dialogue such things are proper enough, a little sentence—*aside*, is quickly delivered; but in an air in which the words have to be repeated, it produces a bad effect. Were, however, this not the case, my object in this place requires a purely flowing natural air, in which, not being so much tied to the words, I could easily wander at will; for we have settled here to have an *aria andantino* concerted with four obligato wind instruments—Flauto, oboe, corno, and fagotto, and this I request to have as soon as possible.[1] The beginning may remain if he pleases—for it is charming.

"Now for a vexation. I certainly have not the honour of knowing the hero Del Prato, but according to the accounts I receive of him, Ceccarelli [2] is almost better; for he is often quite out of breath in the middle of an air, and moreover *never yet appeared on the stage ;* and Raff is a statue. Just fancy now the scene in the first act.

"As good news, I have to inform you that Mademoiselle Dorothea Wendling is with her *scena—contentissima,* and made me play it to her three times successively."

The libretto arrived piecemeal from Salzburg, with the father's warmest sympathy in the undertaking. Leopold Mozart seems desirous to gratify Count Seau by attributing the corrections rather to his criticisms, than the suggestions of his son. That he hoped much from this first opportunity of the exhibition of his son's genius by the famous Munich and Mannheim orchestra, aware of the surprise which it would occasion, and the honour he would gain, is evident. His letter concludes:

"What you write concerning the singers is melancholy: the main interest must be thrown consequently into the composition itself. That I am as delighted as a child at the idea of the admirable orchestra, you may easily suppose. I wish that I may soon be able to join you."

The first week passes without any particular application to the composition of the opera. Mozart dines with his friends Cannabich, Quaglio, and Legrand, the ballet master, and they converse over the project at their ease. He speaks of having been introduced by Cannabich into the family of a Countess

[1] The air, in E flat, " Se il Padre perdei," is here referred to. It is, I believe, the first specimen in the musical drama of an air concerted with wind instruments. We may imagine the pleasure he had in writing it to gratify four particular friends, and especially the warm-hearted and enthusiastic Wendling.

[2] An Italian singer—a *musico*—belonging to the household of the Archbishop of Salzburg.

Baumgarten, who proves a most valuable connection; and he
attributes what appear to be his present favourable prospects to
her influence.

But he has time to think of other matters besides his opera
Not content with what he had formerly written at Munich
for the Church, he is desirous that the latest productions of his
pen in that style should be known, and hopes to recommend
himself through them to the patronage of the court.

" Be so good as to send me the scores of the two masses that
I have with me, and the mass in B major likewise." . . .

We see the humour of the master, and his conscious power
in a slight touch, characteristic of the commonplace church
music of the period: he writes,

" I have just heard a mass, by one Grua; of this sort of thing
one might easily compose half a dozen a day."

But his mode of working at his opera is particularly instructive
Having omitted the second duet, he assigns as a reason:

" If you consider the scene, you will observe that an air, or duet
renders it feeble and cold, as well as very tiresome to the other
actors who must be standing by at this place; the magnani-
mous contest also beween Ilia and Idamante would be too
prolonged, and consequently lose all its interest."

Another task, which demanded the nicest dexterity, was to
adapt his airs to the powers of the singers. In performing this
we see that he was obliging and kind-hearted:

" Another alteration must now be made, for which Raff is to
blame. He is, however, in the right, and were it otherwise, one
must do something to please his gray hairs."

Raff, though enjoying a sort of " latter spring " of life, had
a feeble tone, and, as has been already observed, was unable
to sustain notes of any length. His airs were therefore to be so
constructed as to allow him breathing time,—to exhibit what
he could yet do in the bravura style, and even here and there
in the cadence; while the orchestra was to confer a dignity on
the composition which was totally beyond the ability of the
singer. We shall see how compassionately Mozart helped him
over his difficulties: not neglecting, however, to turn what was
inevitable to the profit of the opera:

" In the last scene of the second act, Idomeneo (Raff) has an
.ir, or rather a sort of cavatina, between the choruses; it will
ιe better to substitute for this a mere recitative, between which
he orchestra can be effectively employed. For in this scene,
ι̇hich, on account of the action and grouping, we have planned
ιith *Legrand*, will be the most beautiful of the opera, there
ιill be such noise and confusion on the stage, that an air would
ιake but an indifferent figure; besides, it is to thunder, *and
ι̇at will never be heard if Raff sings*. A recitative between
he choruses will be decidedly better. Lisetta Wendling has
epeatedly sung her two airs through, and is much pleased with
hem. I have it from a third hand, that both the Wendlings,
)orothea and Lisetta, have highly praised their songs. Raff
ι my excellent attached friend. I shall, however, have to teach
ι̇y *molto amato castrato del Prato* the whole opera through,
ι s he has no notion of studying an air worthy the name, and
ιas an unequal voice.

" I had almost forgotten my best news. Last Sunday after
ervice, Count Seau presented me *en passant* to the Elector,
ι̇ho kindly said to me, ' I am glad to see you here once more.'
ιnd on my answering, that I would use my best exertions for
he satisfaction of his highness, he tapped me on the shoulder
ιnd said—' Oh, I have not the least doubt that the whole will
ιo off perfectly well.' "

From another passage in Mozart's correspondence we gather
. more accurate idea of the talents of Signor del Prato. His
inging is described as being like that of the best of the boys
ι̇ho from time to time present themselves as candidates for
dmission into the cathedral choir at Salzburg! It surely
equired all the skill of the composer to manage such materials.

In the meantime, Schickaneder,[1] the manager of a theatre
t Vienna, had been to Salzburg, and being desirous of a certain
ιong by Mozart, had engaged the father to write to his son at
ſunich to compose it. This work he despatches at once,
ιcarcely missing the time on " Idomeneo." He sends home the
ir with these words:

" Be under no apprehension, dearest father, about my opera,
ι s I trust it will have complete success. There may be some
light cabal, but it will in all probability only prove matter of

---

[1] This manager afterwards appears in Mozart's history in a very un-
ιvourable light.

K

laughter; as I have not only all the most distinguished and powerful families of the nobility in my interest, but all the principal musicians, Cannabich especially."

His first idea was to treat the scene in which the oracle speaks, at some length; youthful enthusiasm naturally inducing him to protract a fine situation. But he afterwards altered his plan on critical grounds.

" Tell me—do you not think the discourse of the subterranean voice too long? Consider it rightly. Imagine the theatre; the voice must be terrible—it must raise a shudder in the audience who are to think it real; but how can such an effect be produced, when through its long speaking the hearers are more and more convinced of its unreality? If the ghost in 'Hamlet' spoke less, the effect would be heightened. This part may be easily shortened, and with gain rather than with loss." [1]

He then quits the wide fields of imagination, to descend to the minutiæ of the practical; or perhaps it might be better said, that his genius, comprehending the entire domain of art, found even in trivial mechanical details means to excite the imagination. Desiring to produce the effect of a distant march, he writes:

" I now require for the march in the second act, which is first heard in the distance, some *sordini* for trumpets and horns, of which there are none here. Send me some by the next diligence, that I may get others made from them."

It is curious that the mutes which soften the tone of brass instruments were not possessed at this time by the first orchestra in Germany, though they were familiar to Mozart and the Salzburg musicians. We detect in this slight circumstance, the effect which the master mind of the composer had upon the musical improvement of his native city. Before the end of the month, the first rehearsal took place with all the wind instruments, but only six violins—one lady and gentleman being the audience. He anticipated the effect of his music, and went to

---

[1] In fact, thus it stands in the score, though the original scene is also given with its majestic modulations and solemn chorus of brass instruments. Having concentrated, in a very brief passage, all that was necessary to the immediate effect upon the audience, he cut off at once what might have better pleased him as a musician.

he rehearsal, he tells his father, as much at his ease as if he
ıad been invited to a feast.[1] The first impression produced by
" Idomeneo " merits preservation. Count Seinsheim, one of
he two listeners, said, " I assure you, that though I expected
ıuch from you, this I really did not expect." Now for the
ıusicians:

" On reaching home with Cannabich after the rehearsal—for
here was still much to settle and talk over with the count—
Iadame Cannabich met me at the door and embraced me with
.elight at my success; and then Ramm (oboe) and Lange
horn) came in half crazy. Ramm, whom, if you knew him, you
ʋould call a true German, his face does in such a manner ex-
ıress everything that he thinks — said to me, ' I must own
hat I never yet heard any music that made such an impres-
ion upon me, and I assure you that I have thought of your
ather fifty times at least, and of the delight that he will have
ı hearing this opera.' But enough of this.

" My cough has become somewhat worse at the rehearsal.
Vhen fame and honour are the stake, one easily overheats
neself in playing for them, however coolly one may at first
et to work. Raff called upon me again yesterday, to hear his
ir in the second act. He is as much enamoured of his song
s a young and ardent man of his lady-love, for he sings it
efore he goes to sleep at night, and the first thing when he
wakes in the morning. He told Baron Vieregg, the principal
querry—' Hitherto I have been always obliged to alter the
arts written for me—the recitatives as well as the airs; but
ow everything remains as it was written—there is not a single
ote out of my compass.' "

In addition to the favourable report of the opera which
,eopold Mozart received from his son, its fame reached him
ıdirectly through certain musicians of the Salzburg orchestra
ʋho corresponded with their brethren of Munich. " I cannot
ıppose," he writes, " that these are compliments, for I know
our work, and am perfectly convinced that, if properly per-
ırmed, it must have its effect." Becke had written that the
ıusic brought tears into his eyes, and the general opinion was,
ıat it was the most beautiful music ever heard. But the father

[1] Mozart seems to have a fondness for this image as representing the
ıjoyment attending a good musical performance, and the first hearing of
fine composition in particular. We may recollect he uses it at the
trasburg concert, " a grand entertainment of eighty covers."

wished a splendid success, and tenders a little impracticable advice on the occasion.

" Consider that for every dozen real connoisseurs, there are a hunderd wholly ignorant—therefore do not overlook the *popular* in your style of composition, and forget to tickle the long ears." To this the composer replies, " Don't be apprehensive respecting the pleasure of the crowd; there will be music for all sorts of people in my opera, but *nothing for long ears*."

The next inquiry from Salzburg concerns the score—" Will it not be copied? You must be careful on this point. For such payment as you receive the score cannot be given up." Mozart replies with frankness, " Concerning my property in the score there was no need for mystery, so I opened the matter at once to the count, and find that it was always the practice at Mannheim, where a composer was well paid, to return the original work to him."

This inquiry respecting a matter of business touches a jarring string; he recalls his existence at Salzburg, and breaks out with warmth:

" How goes on the archbishop? Next Monday I shall have been absent from Salzburg six weeks. You know, my dear father, that it is only my love to you that keeps me at Salzburg —for, by Heaven! if it rested with me, I would have torn up my appointment and relinquished my situation before I came away. I assure you, upon my honour, that though I have no dislike to Salzburg itself—its prince and proud nobility become daily more and more insupportable to me; and I shall, therefore, look forward with pleasure to a letter which may inform me that my services are no longer required. The distinguished patronage I have here would well supply both my present and future wants, to say nothing of what might accrue by deaths, for which nobody can wait—and yet these are no disadvantage to an unemployed man.

" Come to Munich soon and hear my opera, and then tell if I have cause to be unhappy when I think of Salzburg; for you know how difficult it was to get away this time, and that, unless upon some great occasion, a journey cannot be thought of. It is enough to make one cry to think upon the subject. But out of love to you anything in the world." . . .

The rehearsals went on with energy during the whole month of December; and when the second act was ready, the performers removed from a small apartment at Count Seau's to a large one in the palace, where the elector was to be a listener *incognito*, in a chamber adjoining, and they were, as the musicians phrased it, to rehearse for life and death. Mozart was, as usual, long beforehand with the copyist and musicians, and he gives us the following picture of his feelings on the completion of an opera.

" It is a pleasant thing, though, is it not?—when one, at last, comes to the end of a long and laborious work, and quits it with fame and reputation: as is almost my case, for there remain now only three airs and the final chorus in the last act, the overture and the ballet—*et adieu partie !* "

The musicians at Salzburg were meanwhile collecting in little knots to enjoy the news of Mozart's success, which indeed formed the general subject of conversation throughout the city. Michael Haydn, Brunetti, Hafeneder, and others, had listened with great pleasure to the account of the opera sent by M. Esser, a solo violin player, who was now on a tour, and had followed Mozart to Munich. In confirmation of this opinion, came another letter to Fiala,[1] describing the storm chorus in the second act as of so powerful an effect, that " no one could hear it in the greatest heat of summer without feeling cold as ice." [2]

Leopold Mozart receives these accounts as favourable omens of the success of the third act, and he less fears any falling off in the interest of the work in that part, as the greatest situations occur there. He doubts not but it will be—*Finis coronat opus.* At the same time he sends some advice, which exhibits his sagacity both as a musician and man of the world.

" Endeavour only to keep the orchestra in good humour, and by flattery and praises to incline them to serve you; as I know your way of writing—that it requires the most unusual attention from every instrument; and it is really no joke when the attention and diligence of an orchestra are thus kept upon the stretch during three hours at least. Everyone, nay even the most

---

[1] Fiala was one of the most celebrated oboe players of the eighteenth century. Being in his youth unable to procure a living by the instrument he had selected, he entered the service of a Saxon nobleman, in which situation he perfected his execution, and then set out on his travels. He at length engaged in the orchestra of the Archbishop of Salzburg, where he was much admired. He was still living in 1811.

[2] The chorus in D minor, *Corriamo, fuggiamo.*

wretched tenor player himself, has a lively pleasure in being complimented *tete-à-tete*, and will, in consequence, become so much the more zealous and attentive; and such a civility costs you no more than a word or two. However, all this you know as well as I, and I now only mention it because the rehearsals do not always afford an opportunity for it, and then it is forgotten —while as soon as the opera is on the stage, you will want the friendship and zeal of the entire orchestra. It is then that the attention of every individual player must be exerted to the utmost.

"You know that one cannot expect all to be our friends. A doubt—an *if*, or a *but*, must sometimes be intermixed. It was doubted whether the second act would prove as original and excellent as the first. Now that doubt is removed, there will be some few more who will be doubting about the third act. But I will wager my head that there will be some who doubt this: *whether, when the work is brought upon the stage, the music will have as much effect as it had in the chamber rehearsals?* For this reason, the entire zeal and goodwill of the orchestra is necessary."

The musicians lost no interest in the progress of the third act. Recitative rehearsals were held at Wendling's, where the trouble Mozart had to get Del Prato through the quartet *Andrò ramingo* was very great; six times in succession this piece was tried, before it would go even tolerably. These difficulties were followed by others during the stage rehearsals; in which the composer's wishes were frequently opposed, notwithstanding the responsibility attached to his arduous work. He met these embarrassments in a characteristic manner.

"Among various minor disputes," he writes, "in which I have been obliged to engage, I have had a violent altercation with Count Seau, respecting the trombones—I call it violent, because I was obliged to lose my temper before I could carry my point." [1]

Towards the middle of January 1781, "Idomeneo" was quite ready; still Mozart was glad at its postponement for one

[1] This passage affords a curious illustration of the composer's general equanimity and mildness of manner. To be angry on this occasion was a duty which he owed to his art. It may be well to compare this, and a few ebullitions of the like kind, on the subject of music dispersed here and there in the course of his life, with the testimony of his sister-in-law, Sophie, as to his general tone and temper in domestic intercourse. She had never seen him angry.

or two weeks, for the sake of more careful rehearsals. Expectation of the first night was wrought to the highest pitch. The composer had not only brought the third act of his work to the climax desired by his father and himself; but, in addition to his other labour, had composed the divertissement, which occupied the place of a ballet, the more readily that the music might be entirely by one master. He had hoped that the first performance would take place upon his birthday, by which time his father and sister would have arrived from Salzburg to partake his pleasure; but in this he was disappointed. The elector fixed the 29th of January, on which occasion the accustomed audience of the Munich opera was increased by a concourse of people from Salzburg, desirous of hearing the wonderful composition of their townsman. Each successive representation received immense applause, and the triumph of the composer was complete.

With this work, the most important in its influence on music, Mozart crowned his twenty-fifth year.[1] The score is still a picture to the musician. It exhibits consummate knowledge of the theatre, displayed in an opera of the first magnitude and complexity; which unites to a great orchestra the effects of a double chorus on the stage and behind the scenes; and introduces marches, processions, and dances, to various accompaniments in the orchestra, behind the scenes, or under the stage. This model opera, in which Mozart rises on the wing from one beauty to another through long acts, was completed, as we have seen, within a few weeks, and ever since has defied the scrutiny of musicians to detect in it the slightest negligence of style.

The impassioned melancholy which pervades the music in the first air of Ilia; in the meeting of the father and the son, when the consequences of the vow are evident; and in the scene between Ilia and Idamante in the third act, when they are contending which shall die; is still entirely unscathed by

---

[1] M. Fétis considers " Idomeneo " as the basis of all the music of our day. After remarking on the new disposal of the instruments of a grand orchestra in the overture to " Idomeneo," he proceeds thus: " To prove that all these inventions really belong to Mozart, it is only necessary to recollect, that in 1780, when ' Idomeneo ' was composed, Haydn had neither written his six symphonies for the Duke of Wurtemburg, nor those for the Loge Olympique, which are of the date of 1784, nor the ' Seven last Words,' nor, lastly, his twelve symphonies for Salomon's concerts, which did not see the day till 1792. In these last works alone the illustrious symphonist employed all the resources of the orchestra previously to writing the ' Creation.' " From an essay entitled " Mozart, ses Œuvres, son Influence on l'Art et les Artistes."

time.[1] Expression is wonderfully heightened throughout these scenes by peculiar accents of the instruments, by the doubling and thickening of the parts as the situation warms, and a magnificent effect of harmony, which musicians call the "inverted pedal." The poetry of these mechanical means Mozart was the first to exemplify in effects which are still modern; and the only indications of an antique style, which "Idomeneo" bears, are in a few airs, in which, to gratify the singers, he permitted the accustomed cadence to remain. While solemnity is the perminent characteristic of "Idomeneo," the scenes of that opera have many changes admirably planned for relief and variety of character.

The chorus of mariners at the port of Sidon, "Placido è il mar," and the opening of the third act in the royal garden, where Ilia walks and introduces the beautiful air to the Zephyrs, have a calm and sweet expression, which contrasts beautifully with the portentous sounds and sights that have previously occupied attention.

While "Idomeneo" was running its prosperous course, the composer was in great spirits; and, probably thinking that his friends of the Munich orchestra had had in his opera enough of "passion's solemn tears," he changed their weeping to a laughing mood, by one touch of his wand—the canon, "O Du eselhafter Martin."[2] In this jovial production, he entirely postponed all pretension to the sublime, and seemed bent only on showing how effectively music and words might be combined for a laugh. Of the same date with these varied compositions is the Offertorium in D minor, "Misericordias Domini," profoundly ecclesiastical in its sytle, and uniting the severe school of ancient counterpoint with some of the effects of the day, as governed by his own turn of thought.

---

[1] These pieces are still the greatest attractions of classical performances. The great dramatic scene, the sixth of the third act; which comprises "O voto tremendo," the solemn march, the prayer of Idomeneo, and the responses of the Priest of Neptune, the parting of the lovers, and the voice of the oracle; produces all its original effect when heard from time to time in private.

[2] This address to the "foolish Martin" tells a tale of gay suppers at Munich, and of the excessive merriment which accompanied the run of "Idomeneo." The words and music are both by Mozart; but the former are in the original, so entirely in the style of Rabelais, and so adapted to the orgies of an orchestra, that when the canon itself was afterwards produced in public, a new version of words was attached. Compared with the convivial catches of Purcell's time, the offence of this canon is slight. It is, in fact, a harmless Monkish joke of questionable taste.

For the first time apparently, fully aware of the high destiny of his genius, and of its influence on the amount of human pleasure, he became more and more indifferent as to his own immediate interest, thinking that the favourable hour would come, and that the powerful of the earth could not remain for ever deaf and blind to his merit. Gladly would he have established himself for life with Cannabich, Wendling, and the rest of the old Mannheim orchestra in Munich; and the efforts he made to accomplish this object have been told. It is certain that Count Seau was authorised to express the readiness of the composer to enter the service of the Bavarian court; but the elector made no motion towards this object, and left the Archbishop of Salzburg in undisturbed possession of his organist. Again, it is doubtful whether he was truly served by the friend whom he trusted. Greater credulity is required to believe his long train of ill-success the effect of chance, than of the jealous alarm of men already in office, and fearful of their prerogative in the society of so gifted an associate.

The leave of absence granted by the archbishop was gradually extended from weeks to months; and, by an extraordinary stretch of indulgence, Mozart was permitted to remain at Munich till the middle of March 1781, when he was commanded to follow the Salzburg court to Vienna.

This removal to Vienna in the train of his highness, led to results which influenced the rest of his life, casting him upon a course of incredible labour, interrupted only by sudden gleams of pleasure too fierce and rare to be enjoyed with moderation.

In a letter dated March 17, 1781, the composer acquaints his father with his safe arrival in Vienna. The new circumstances in which he found himself placed were not likely to mitigate his ancient aversion to the arch-tyranny of the prelate, who now heaped indignities upon him of so offensive a description, that it cannot be surprising to find him resenting them, rashly perhaps, but with a sense of what was due to himself and his art which commands our respect.

" Yesterday, the 16th, by nine o'clock in the morning, I reached this place, God be thanked, safely and well. I write this in Mesmer's garden in the Landstrasse. Now about the archbishop. I have a delightful apartment in the same house in which he dwells. Brunetti and Ceccarelli lodge in another house. *Che distinzione !* My neighbour, Herr von Klein-

mayern, loads me with civilities, and is really a very charmin
person. Dinner was served at half-past eleven in the forenoor
which was for me unfortunately rather too early, and there sa
down to it—the two valets in attendance, the controller, Hei
Zetti, the confectioner, two cooks, Ceccarelli, Brunetti, and m
littleness. The two valets sat at the head of the table, and
had the honour to be placed at least above the cooks. No
methought I am again at Salzburg. During dinner there wa
a great deal of coarse silly joking; not with me, however, fc
I did not speak a word, unless absolutely obliged, and then
was always with the greatest seriousness. So when I ha
finished dinner, I went my way. There is no table in th
evening, but each has three ducats—with which you know or
may do a great deal! Our excellent archbishop glorifies hin
self with his people, receives their services, and pays ther
nothing in return.

"Yesterday we had music at four o'clock, and there wei
about twenty persons of the highest rank present. Ceccarel
has already had to sing at Palfy's. We go to Prince Gallitzi
to-day, who was one of the party of yesterday. I shall no
wait to see whether I get anything: if not, I shall go at once t
the archbishop, and tell him without reserve, that if he will nc
allow me to earn anything he must pay me—for I cannot liv
upon my own money."

That he whose transcendent genius has asserted its empii
over the whole musical world, and who even at this time ha
put forth unmistakable evidences of his greatness, should t
put down to table with cooks and valets, is something to marv
over in this retrospect of Mozart's chequered existence. Bu
how admirably he bore himself in this situation, silent an
grave, and keeping aloof from the rude company, withou
offending their prejudices by the betrayal of his feelings. In h
next letter, dated a week later, he enters more at large upo
his mode of life.

"What you tell me concerning the archbishop's vanity i
possessing me may be true enough—but what is the use to me
One does not live by this. And then with what distinctio
am I treated? M. von Kleinmayern, Boenecke, and th
illustrious Count Arco have a table to themselves; now it woul
be some distinction if I were at this table—but not with th
valets, who, besides taking the head of the table, light th

lustres, open the doors, and attend in ante-rooms. And then if we go to a concert, Messieurs the Salzburgers have to wait until monsieur the valet has gone in and sends word to them by a footman that they may enter—as Brunetti himself told me. I thought to myself as I listened—'Only wait till I come.'

" The other day, in going to Prince Gallitzin's, I went alone on purpose; and on reaching the top of the stairs, there stood M. Angerbauer ready to tell the servant to conduct me in. I took no notice, however, either of the valet or the footman—but went straight through the apartments to the music room, the doors being all open—and so direct to the prince, and paid my respects to him, and then remained standing and conversing. I had quite forgotten Brunetti and Ceccarelli—who were out of sight, and stood leaning against the wall quite at the back of the orchestra—from which place they did not venture to advance a single step. I go this evening with M. von Klein-mayern to one of his friends—the Counsellor Braun, who every one tells me is a very great amateur of the clavier. I have already dined twice with the Countess Thun, and go there almost every day. The countess is one of the most charming, lovely women I ever knew in my life—and I am in great esteem with her.[1] I have also dined with Count Cobenzl.

" My principal object now is to introduce myself in some favourable manner to the emperor, for I am absolutely deter-mined that he shall know me. I should much like to play my opera through to him and some good fugues—for his taste lies in that direction. Oh, had I but known that we should have been at Vienna in Lent, I would have written a little oratorio, and performed it for my benefit at the theatre—as is the custom here. I might easily have written it beforehand, being acquainted with all the voices.

" How gladly would I give a public concert, but it would not be permitted, that I know for certain; for now, observe. You are aware that there is a society here which gives concerts for the benefit of the widows of musicians, and at which every-

---

[1] The Countess Thun was worthy of the enthusiasm with which Mozart alludes to her. This tasteful amateur and distinguished lady had been the pupil of Haydn, and her patronage had a powerful influence on his fortune; for, having by chance discovered that he was the composer of a sonata of great merit, she immediately appointed him her instructor on the piano-forte and in singing, though up to that hour he had been living in a garret, and enduring extreme privations. From this time his circumstances improved. The countess, it may be added, was one of the chief favourites of the Emperor Joseph.

body connected with music plays *gratis*. The orchestra is 18 strong, and no artist possessed of any benevolence or sympath with the unfortunate, refuses to play if asked by this society for such conduct recommends him equally to the emperor an the public at large. Starzer was employed to invite me, and instantly agreed; though I said it depended on the good wi of my prince of which I could not doubt, the performance bein gratuitous, and for a charitable and in some sort religiou object. He would not consent, however, and the whole of th nobility here have taken it very ill of him. I am only sorry o this account; I should not have played a concerto, but as th emperor would be in the proscenium box, I should have prelude quite alone, then played a fugue and the variations (*Je sui Lindor*). Whenever I have done that in public I have alway received the greatest applause; it succeeds invariably, ever one finding something to his taste. Countess Thun would hav lent me her beautiful pianoforte by Stein for this purpose."

Notwithstanding the ungracious selfishness of the arch bishop, Mozart played at the concert after all. The nobilit teased his highness into it, and compelled him to consen Instead of being proud of the distinctions won by his servan he was churlish of them, and could not bear Mozart to do an thing on his own account, or for the gratification or advantag of others. The applause at the concert, to use Mozart's word "was without end;" but what pleased the player best was th remarkable silence, and the occasional bravos which burst ou in the midst of his performance. This was especially gratifyin in a place where there were so many excellent clavier player and Mozart could now have easily made money by giving concert, the ladies themselves having offered to dispose (tickets for him, but the archbishop would not allow it. "H prefers," says the oppressed musician, "that his people shoul lose than gain." Yet, in spite of his tyranny, Mozart got a pupi the Countess Rombeck, and played at a concert at old Princ Colloredo's, for which he was presented with five ducats. Bu the struggle was rapidly drawing to a close. Every day thre up some new incident to show how completely the archbisho stood in the way of Mozart's progress.

"We had a concert to-day at which three pieces, new on of course, of my composition were performed—namely, a rond to a concerto for Brunetti, a sonata for myself with accompan

ient for a violin, which I composed between eleven and twelve
ast night; but in order to be ready, wrote out only the violin
art for Brunetti, and retained my own in my head; and a rondo
or Ceccarelli, which was encored—and for all this work I get
.othing. What makes me half desperate is, that I was invited
o Countess Thun's on the evening of our concert, but could not
o; and who do you think was there? The emperor. Adam-
erger and Weigl were also there; and each had fifty ducats.
Vhat an opportunity!"

It was clear this could not last. Either Mozart must
urrender up his honest ambition in the low servitude of a
eggarly office, or assert his intellectual independence at all
azards. Such a man could not hesitate long in the choice
f the alternative. March and April passed over in a sort of
onflict, sometimes on the verge of open war, and always point-
ig to ultimate separation. At length, after enduring much
idignity, Mozart requests his dismissal. In a letter dated the
2th of May, he relates the whole history of this curious quarrel.

"My last letter will have informed you that I requested my
lismissal from the service of the prince on the 9th of May, and
.t his own desire; for in the two audiences which I had pre-
iously had, he said to me, 'Take yourself off, if you don't
hoose to remain in my service.' What wonder then, if, after my
nduring such appellations as *fellow, careless fellow*, and the like,
.nd worse, he should be taken at his word in 'Take yourself off.'

"On the day following, I gave Count Arco a petition to
resent to his highness, together with my travelling expenses,
vhich consisted of fifteen florins forty kreutzers for the diligence,
.nd two ducats for food, etc. He, however, would accept neither,
.nd assured me that I could not resign without the consent of
ny father. 'That is your duty,' said he. I told him immedi-
.tely that I knew my duty to my father as well as he, and that
t would give me much concern to have to learn it at this time
.f day. 'Well, then,' he replied, 'if he is satisfied, you may
equest your dismissal;' but if not, 'you may also request it.'
1 pretty distinction! As for the edifying discourse that passed
ietween the archbishop and me in three audiences, together
vith what this beautiful man of God has lately said to me
new, it had so powerful an effect upon my frame, that being
.t the opera in the evening, I was obliged to leave in the middle
f the first act, and return home to lie down; for I was quite

feverish, trembled in every limb, and rolled about the streets like a drunken man. The following day, which was yesterday, I was obliged to pass at home, and the entire forenoon in bed. Your supposition that I shall get into ill odour with the nobility and the emperor, is quite unfounded; for the archbishop is hated here, and, above all, by the emperor; and it is the very reason of his ill-humour that the emperor did not invite him to Luxemburg.

" I will now just inform you what was the principal ground of offence. I knew not that I was a valet in attendance, and that ruined me. I ought to have lounged away a couple of hours every morning in the ante-chamber; indeed, I had often been told that I ought to show myself, but could never recollect that this was a part of my duty, and therefore contented myself with coming when the archbishop sent for me. As far as this, I have spoken as though we were in the presence of the archbishop; I now speak to you alone, my dearest father. Of all the injustice that I have endured from the archbishop from the beginning of his reign till now, of his incessant insults, and of all the impertinence and the affronting speeches that he has uttered to my face, as well as of the incontrovertible right that I have to leave him,—nothing need be said here, for nothing can be said that can bring their truth into question.

" I will merely mention what my inducements to leave are, all consideration of offence and dissatisfaction apart. I have the highest and most valuable connection here that can be; I am treated with the greatest favour and distinction in families of the first rank, and paid into the bargain; and shall I sacrifice all this for 400 florins [1] in Salzburg without encouragement? What would be the end of it? Nothing, certainly, but that either I must die of mortification, or be again compelled to quit. It is unnecessary to say more: you are yourself aware how the matter stands. But this I will add—my history is known throughout the whole city of Vienna; and I am advised by the whole of the nobility not to suffer myself to be led about any longer." . . .

This is written with candour and modesty. The motives on both sides were obvious enough, nor does it appear that, outraged as he was, Mozart, throughout the whole of this painful and unequal contest, ever offered any personal offence to his

[1] This looks as if the original income of 500 florins had been reduced.

nperious lord. Separation was now inevitable, and it took
lace without delay; though not before the steward of·the
rchbishop, Count Arco, had endeavoured, by every representa-
ion in his power, to dissuade the composer from the step he
leditated. It is easy to conceive how the little interludes of
buse in which the worthy prelate indulged—nobly thinking,
hat after feeding his retainers he was privileged to kick them—
lay have been softened to, or even forgotten by, the subject of
hem, while he had a home to retire to, and could impart the
auses of his vexation to a father and sister. But on this
is first journey in the suite of his prince his position was
ntirely changed, and humiliating beyond endurance. Sources
f annoyance opened to him in every possible way. His meals
'ith the principal servants of the establishment; his apartment
-a less distinguished one than others had in the same retinue;
le new duties required of him; all helped to show that the
omposer of " Idomeneo "—the author of a revolution in
ramatic music—had established no higher claim to respect
l the opinion of the archbishop than his own valets and cooks.[1]
t is too much to suppose that this nobleman was fully aware
f the qualities of his concert-master; his notions of Mozart
ere formed upon the opinions of others; and thinking himself
cured by the poverty of his dependent, he hoped to live on,
ratifying his spleen and lordly will by quietly and *comfortably*
lsulting the gifted man who had condescended to eat his bread.
But even had no rupture been produced from these causes,
must have ensued from the fact that the whole of the highest
bility of Vienna were spectators of the dishonourable circum-
ances and treatment of the composer.
The step, however, of resigning a pension, and of throwing
lmself entirely upon the public for fame and support, was a
.ore important one than his sanguine imagination and excite-
ent of feeling permitted him at the time to contemplate,

[1] The patronage of genius at this time is a curiosity in the history of the
ts. It is further exemplified in a youthful adventure of Rousseau.
riving at Paris in 1741, with his play of " Narcissus," a project for
nplifying the reading of music, and fifteen louis in his pocket, as his
tire dependence, he is invited to dinner by some great ladies, who at
st intend to turn him over to their housekeeper, but correct themselves.
e says of Madame de Beuzenval: " Elle avoit peu d'idée des égards qu'on
it aux talents. Elle me jugeoit même en cette occasion sur mon maintien
us que sur mon équipage, qui, quoique très simple, etoit fort propre, et
annoncoit point du tout un homme fait pour diner à l'office. J'en avois
blié le chemin depuis trop longtemps pour vouloir le rappendre."—
nfessions, tome ii.

How far his being an *unappointed* composer may have hastened the production of his immortal works, is open to question; but that his life was sacrificed in struggling against the difficultie in which he was thereby involved, is beyond a doubt.

In the absence of any immediate design of a new dramatic composition, and delighted at the effect which his public per formance on the pianoforte had created at Vienna, Mozar forgot all the fears he had expressed previously to his journey to Paris; thought no more that teaching would interfere with the higher vocation of his muse; and was content to become the fashionable performer, teacher, and pianoforte composer of the day. This mode of life for a time had its temptations and its success; and he hoped that he might still better assist his father at Vienna than at Salzburg, as he was at intervals able to remit to him sums of from ten to thirty ducats. But here commenced the precarious existence which the composer was for the future destined to lead. For, not only was the taste of Vienna then as now, proverbially variable and flippant — not only was concert-giving an uncertain speculation, and teaching an inconstant source of income—but in a man, who, like Mozart had, from time to time, strong impulses to write for the theatre it frequently happened that the order and regularity of his engagements were made to yield to the object which engrossed him; and that the profits of his time were sacrificed on the one hand, without any proportionate advantage on the other.

In his present temper, and with his elastic constitution Mozart was not easily discouraged. He was young, hopeful energetic; with a pen that never halted for ideas, and an activity in writing that defied fatigue. He had had small experience in those stern realities of life for which the artist has unfortunately but too soon to exchange the glowing visions of fancy. When reminded of the fickleness of the Viennese public he contented himself by replying, "The Viennese are certainly prone to change, but in the theatre only; and my peculiar art is too much admired to render me apprehensive of going out of fashion. Here certainly is found the true atmosphere of the pianoforte; and if I admit that the taste may change, it will be some years first."

The greatest advantage that the composer derived from his settlement in Vienna, was the facility of the journey to Prague in which city his works gradually acquired a high reputation and himself a circle of genial and discerning friends. Gerber

he author of the lexicon of music, supposes that this change
)f residence had great influence in refining and beautifying
Mozart's style of composition; and that in the secluded life of
Salzburg he might easily have encountered the fate of the great
Friedemann. Bach.[1] The modifying power of circumstances
ipon Mozart's style is, indeed, an interesting consideration.
Whatever of striking, new, or beautiful, he met with in the works
)f others, left its impression on him—and he often reproduced
:hese effects—not servilely, but mingling his own nature and
feeling with them, in a manner not less surprising than delight-
ul. This may be seen in the purposes to which he turned
iis acquaintance with Benda's monodrames in "Idomeneo;"
vith Gluck's operas in "Idomeneo;" and "Don Giovanni;"
ind lastly, with Sebastian Bach's choral motets in the "Zauber-
löte." Had the Princess Amalie of Prussia succeeded in per-
;uading Leopold Mozart to take his little boy to Berlin, where
ie would have heard the grand choral and organ compositions of
Sebastian Bach performed in the best style, it is impossible to
:onceive what results might have ensued; but we should think
:hat a nature so sensitive to the beauty of counterpoint, must
iave been affected even to the colouring of the whole future of
irtistic life.

It was during the first years of Mozart's establishment at
Vienna, while he was principally in esteem as a virtuoso on the
)ianoforte, and the wonder at his attainments was still fresh,
:hat he commenced acquaintance with the celebrated forty-
;ight preludes and fugues, *Das wohltempirirte Clavier* (the
vell-tempered clavier) of Sebastian Bach, a work which excited
iis enthusiastic admiration, and ever remained the favourite
'elaxation of his severer studies. Not content with simply play-
ng these fugues, he put several of them, as we have seen in a
MS. in his own handwriting, into score, designing to enjoy their
)eauty and symmetry through the medium of another sense.[2]

---

[1] William Friedemann, the eldest and most gifted son of John Sebastian
Bach. It was the misfortune of this fine organist and musician to survive
he taste for the school of music founded by his father—to see his com-
)ositions appreciated by a few connoisseurs only, and disregarded by the
)ublic at large. He was a man of innocent life; but his disposition was
)bstinate and sombre, and he was unable to adapt his style to circum-
;tances. During many years he depended for existence on the bounty of
riends, and died in extreme misery at Berlin, in 1784.

[2] The alacrity with which the great composer became a learner is charac-
eristic. Like Chaucer's student,
" Gladly wolde he lerne, and gladly teche."
The five fugues of Bach which Mozart preferred are the following, from

L

To the study of Bach and Handel, Mozart was scarcely less induced by his own secret inclination than by the sympathy of his friend, the Baron von Swieten, a member of the privy council, the superintendent of the royal library of music at Vienna, and an intelligent amateur to whom the art is indebted for the suggestion of many valuable undertakings in which both Mozart and Haydn have done themselves honour. The baron survived Mozart twelve years, but during a great part of his life he enjoyed the closest intimacy with both these composers.[1]

From the year 1781, for four or five successive years, scarcely any pianoforte player was thought of in Vienna but Mozart the third and fourth of which he certainly derived hints for the overture to the " Zauberflöte," and the finale to the " Jupiter Symphony."

The late Mr. Attwood, organist of St. Paul's, who was for a time Mozart pupil, remembered that this volume of fugues was always lying open on his pianoforte. He also remembered, that on entering the musician's apartment one morning, he found the floor strewed with sheets of a score, thrown down one by one as they were finished, and left to dry. It was in this way the overture to " Don Juan " was produced.

[1] Baron von Swieten used to have music performed in his house with a full orchestra. He suggested the " Creation " and " Seasons " to Haydn and patronised Beethoven, inducting him, as he had done Mozart, into the particular study of Bach.

ınd his engagements to play at the parties of the chief nobility were very numerous. He became considerably occupied in ;eaching; composed a variety of instrumental things—among ›thers a set of sonatas, which he published by subscription; and ed a life of great activity.[1]

The Emperor Joseph suggested many undertakings to Mozart, and completely won his regard by the affability and :ordiality of his demeanour towards him; but there is reason :o doubt whether his own preference was not, like that of his :ourt, decidedly in favour of the Italian musicians, who now, luring a long series of years, had been supreme in their art at Vienna. The anecdotes of this emperor, which have descended :o us in connection with the lives of the great men who have rendered his reign so memorable in the history of music, are certainly not of a kind to convey any high idea of his taste or perspicacity as an amateur. The full harmony of Mozart's ›rchestra oppressed the royal ears, educated as they had been ın the bald *partitions* of the Italians. With regard to this composer the emperor was as a puppet, moved by the wires of ›pposing factions; being wholly destitute of the judgment which would have poised him, and enabled him to decide for ˈimself. If the Prince de Cobentzel and the Countess Thun at ›ne time persuaded him that Mozart was a great musician, at ınother the friends of the Italian party gave him a different bias; and all the while he piqued himself on being superior to influences, and on exercising a strict impartiality. With much good nature in his manner towards Mozart, and a kind of ınstinct of his superiority—for he saw him perform feats of ȿkill which no other musician about the court would have dared to attempt—his friendship never extended to the purse; nor iid he think of attaching the composer to his service by any provision, until it seemed probable that absolute necessity would drive him from Vienna. The Emperor Joseph has had the credit of having thoroughly understood and appreciated Mozart; but what sort of patronage to an artist struggling with diffi- ːulties must that be which ends in a joke—a laugh—a miserable

[1] On the evening of his name-day, in 1781, he was serenaded in one of ˈis own compositions, a piece which he had composed for a family festival ›n Theresa's day, on which occasion it was performed at three different ›laces, for when the performers had finished at one place, they were .mmediately carried off to play at another. The principal reason for its ›roduction was to give M. von Strak a notion of his power. M. von Strak ˌas one of the principal pages to the emperor, and, as the reader will iiscover by and by, repaid Mozart's courtesy by neglect and indifference.

pension? Such will be found to have been the history of thei: connection.[1]

One of the greatest amusements of the emperor was to witnes: exhibitions and contests of skill. On Clementi's arrival a: Vienna there was a scene of this kind, which produced som< excitement at the palace. The Italians had now a champion and hoped that the vigorous execution and highly-finishec mechanism of Clementi might be successfully opposed to Mozart who was beating them out of the field in every department o: music, whether of composition or performance. Mozart himsel: showed that he did not despise the antagonist selected for him by doing that which he at other times entirely neglected— namely, practising. He is known to have exercised his finger: against this encounter; though, after it was over, it woulc appear to have dwelt very little on his mind; for, in the lettei in which he speaks of it to his father, he only alludes to it incidentally. He begins with an account of his mode of life and engagements. This is still 1781, in the month of December:

" Every morning at six o'clock I am attended by my *friseur*, and then I write till. ten. At ten o'clock I have a lesson to give at Madame von Trattner's, and at eleven at the Countess Rombeck's, and each pays me six ducats for twelve lessons.[2] If you can listen to the wretched story of my being hated by the whole court and nobility, pray write to M. von Strak, Countess Thun, Countess Rombeck, Baroness Waldstädter, M. von Sonnenfels, Madame von Trattner, or, in a word, to whom you will. Meantime, I may just inform you, that the emperor lately passed a grand eulogium on me at table, accompanied by the expression, ' *C'est un talent decidé !* ' and, moreover, the day before yesterday, the 24th, I played at court.

" A clavier-player, an Italian, named Clementi, has just arrived here. He, too, was in attendance. Yesterday I received fifty ducats for my playing. Now about this Clementi. He

[1] For the Emperor Joseph's character at large, the reader must be referred to the chronicles of the day. He is represented by Mrs. Piozzi as " a stranger upon principle to the joys of confidence and friendship," and as masking his cold-heartedness and insincerity under a flattering surface. He was also eccentric in his mode of life—dined off the meanest viands, and then in the evening, *at a party*, would exhibit considerable relish for " a dish of hot chocolate thickened with bread and cream." He might have been one of the nine kings in " Candide," who meet at a poor inn without enough among them to pay for a supper.

[2] Mozart's payment for lessons was consequently at the rate of five shillings English each! How incredible does it now appear that his genius could ever have been submitted to such indignity!

ossesses considerable execution, and when you have said this ou have said everything. He has a brilliant right hand, and his principal passages are thirds; but, in other respects, not a arthing's-worth of taste or feeling—a mere mechanic.

"The emperor, after we had complimented one another ufficiently, commanded that he should begin. 'La Santa Chiesa Catholica,' said the emperor, Clementi being a Roman. He preluded and played a sonata. The emperor then said to me, *Allons, d'rauf los!*'[1] I preluded and played variations. The princess royal then produced some sonatas by Paesiello, in a miserable manuscript of his own, from which I had to play an Allegro, and he an Andante and Rondo. We then each of us took a theme and played upon it on two pianofortes. Curiously enough, though I had borrowed for myself the pianoforte of Countess Thun, I only played upon it when I played alone, as he emperor so desired it. The other pianoforte was out of tune, and had three of its keys sticking down. 'It is of no consequence,' said the emperor. I see clearly enough that the emperor is aware of my attainments in the art and science of music, and wishes to do me justice in the eyes of foreigners. Besides, I know by a sure hand that he was well satisfied with me; for he was extremely gracious, conversed with me privately, and even talked of my marriage."

It was, probably, his desire to get his father's permission to marry, which made him dismiss Clementi in this cavalier manner; for it is certain that he spoke highly of him, and even with friendship, in his letter to his sister. But he may have thus underrated his rival, lest his father might become alarmed about his prospects, or the permanency of his favour at court.

His success as a pianoforte player among the fashionable world of Vienna, was now at its height; but dramatic composition could not long be banished from his thoughts. On the 31st of September of the same year in which he quitted the archbishop, he received the libretto of the opera "Die Entführung aus dem Serail," and with such delight, that during the first two days he wrote two airs for it, and the terzetto which closes the first act. The scheme of this opera, which was patronised by the Emperor Joseph, and intended to naturalise the Italian taste in dramatic music in Germany, by means of native singers and actors, had been mentioned to Mozart soon

[1] As if giving the word of command to an Austrian artilleryman—" Come, blaze away! "

after his arrival at Vienna; but, after working at the opera for
some time, he appears to have laid it aside in consequence of
court festivities and other hindrances to its production. In
fact it was not performed till the summer of the following
year, 1782.

A letter addressed to his father during the progress of this
work exhibits may pleasing traits of the composer. Independently of the interest with which this letter will be read
on account of its minute history of the composition of the opera
its critical acumen must excite surprise and admiration. Mozart
possessed a wonderful faculty of criticism, and was as profound
a judge of what was fitting in the poet as in the composer.

"VIENNA (date uncertain), 1781.

"The opera began with a monologue; so I requested M
Stephani to write an arietta, and then after Osmin's little song
instead of the two talking together, a duet. As we intend
the part of Osmin for M. Fischer who certainly possesses an
admirable bass voice (although the archbishop once told me that
he sung too low for a bass, and I have consequently advised
him to sing higher), it will be desirable to turn his voice to
account, the more especially as the singer is a great favourite
with the public here. In the original libretto, Osmin has but
one single little song, and nothing more to sing but in the
terzetto and finale. He will now have an air in the first, and
another in the second act. I gave the air quite complete to M
Stephani, having written the music long before he knew anything at all about it. You have only the beginning and the
end, which will certainly produce a good effect, a comical turn
being given to the rage of Osmin through the employment of
the Turkish music. In the execution of the air Fischer will
be enabled to show off his beautiful low tones. The *D'rum
beym barte des Propheten, etc.*, though in the same measure, is
in quick notes; and the audience will fancy, as the man's anger
goes on increasing, that this must be the end of the air; but
the *allegro assai*, in another time and key, will just then produce
an excellent effect; for as a man in such a towering passion
outsteps all the boundaries of order and moderation, and wholly
loses himself in the excess of his feelings, so also must the music
As, however, the passions, whether violent or otherwise, must
never be expressed to disgust—and music, even in the most
terrific situation, never give pain to the ear, but ever delight

it and remain music—I have chosen no very distant key to F the key of the air, though not the nearest related, D minor, yet the next in succession, A minor.

"With respect to Belmont's air in A major, *O wie ängstlich, O wie feurig*, etc., can you imagine how it is expressed?—the beating heart by the violins in octaves. This air is the favourite of every one who has heard it and my own too, and is expressly written for Adamberger's voice. One sees the trembling and the irresolution, the heaving of the swelling bosom which is expressed by a *crescendo ;* one hears the whispers and the sighs expressed by the first violins *con sordini*, with a flute in unison. The chorus of janizaries is everything that can be wished, being short and jovial, and just fit for the Viennese.

"Constanza's aria I have been obliged to sacrifice somewhat to Mademoiselle Cavalieri's powers of execution. I have endeavoured to express the words *Trennung war mein banges loos, und nun schwimmt mein aug' in thränen*, as well as the style of an Italian bravura air would permit. I have altered *hui* into *schnell*, thus: *Doch wie schnell schwand meine freude*, etc. I don't know what the opinion of our German poets may be— though perhaps unacquainted with the theatre in operatic matters, still methinks they might, at least, not suffer their people to talk as if to a parcel of swine.

"I will now speak of the terzetto which concludes the first act. Pedrillo has given out his master for an architect, in order to afford him an opportunity of meeting his Constanza in the garden. He is received into the service of the pacha; but Osmin, the overseer, who knows nothing of this, and is moreover a churlish fellow and arch enemy of all strangers, is impertinent, and rudely refuses his admission into the garden. The commencement is very short, and, as the text permitted, I have written mostly in three parts; then the major begins *pianissimo*, and must go very fast; and at the end there will be a great deal of noise, which is the principal thing belonging to the end of an act, where the more noise the better, and the shorter the better, that people may not cool in their clapping. The overture is short, and changes from *forte* to *piano* continually; at the *forte* the Turkish music always accompanies, and in this manner it modulates through the keys, so that I believe no one will go to sleep over it, though he should not have slept for a whole night before.

"I am now somewhat anxious. The first act has been ready

these three weeks, besides an air in the second act, and the
drunken duet, which consists of nothing more than my Turkish
tattoo; but I cannot proceed a step further, as the whole story
is being altered at my own request. At the beginnng of the
third act there is a charming quintet, or rather finale, with which
I should like to conclude the second act. To effect this a great
alteration will be necessary, indeed an entirely new intrigue,
at which Stephani is over head and ears at work.

" As for the text of the opera you are quite right in what
you observe upon Stephani's work in general; yet he has not
badly conceived the character of the stupid, surly, and malicious
Osmin. I am well aware that the versification is none of the
best, but it so luckily fell in with the musical ideas that were
wandering about in my head that it could not but please me;
and I would venture a wager that nothing will be missed at the
performance. Indeed I must praise some of the poetry of the
piece. Belmont's air, *O wie ängstlich*, etc., could scarcely be
better written for music. The *Huj* and *Kummer ruht in meinem
schoos* excepted (for Kummer[1] is not a peaceful sensation), the
air is not bad, particularly the first part, and I well know that in
an opera the poetry must be the obedient daughter of the music.
Why do the Italian comic operas please universally, notwithstanding their miserable libretti—even at Paris, of which I
myself was witness? Because the music is supreme, and everything is forgotten for it. So much the more, therefore, must
an opera please of which the plan is well contrived and the words
wholly written for the music, and not for the satisfaction of a
miserable rhyme, which in a theatrical representation only does
mischief; for the rhyming versifier introduces words, and even
whole verses, that put to flight or destroy the best ideas of the
composer. Verse is indeed indispensable to music, but rhyme, on
account of the rhyming, most injurious; the gentlemen who set
to work so pedantically continually go to the dogs, they and their
music together. It would be most desirable were a good composer, who understood the theatre, to be united with that true
phœnix—a judicious poet; such a pair would have no cause
to lament over the applause of ignorant admirers. Dramatic
poets appear to me to have as many mechanical tricks as
trumpeters; if we composers were to abide so firmly by our
rules (which formerly, when nothing better was known, were
good enough), we should produce as wretched music as they

[1] Grief.

vretched books. But now, methinks, it is time to have done.
have prated sufficiently."

The letters written by Mozart during the composition of
' Idomeneo," have already shown in a considerable degree the
habit of a critical judgment to which he had accustomed himself,
nd exercised on every drama in which he engaged. Indeed,
t is not a little interesting to observe him speculating on the
ffects of all the music he discovers, and endeavouring to put
ff his own nature and cultivated taste, to sympathise with the
eelings of the mass of his audience. But if the letter just given
ntroduce the reader to little that is new in these respects, it
mply portrays the high state of enthusiasm, and the sanguine,
hopeful frame of mind with regard to his prospects, in which the
omposer lived at this time. At the latter end of the year 1781
he could see this favourite opera, " Die Entführung," in such a
tate of forwardness that a week or two, at any time, would
erve to put the finishing hand to it; and, to crown the felicity
vhich he expected from his *début* as a dramatic composer
t Vienna, there was the prospect of his speedy union with
Constance Weber.

It is a strong argument of the virtuous nature of the young
Mozart, that he so early formed his ideal of earthly happiness in
. marriage of sympathy and affection. Even before he had
ttained his twentieth year, he had begun to adopt an old-
ashioned notion of this sort—probably encouraged by the
nfluences of home; and to this may be attributed the compara-
ive freedom from vice in which his youth passed; the more
urprising in one exposed to unusual temptations, whose employ-
nent it was to think and to feel voluptuously, and who had to
ursue the language of love in his music through all its gradations
nd varieties. How easy it would have been for a young man
f abilities and good nature, in an atmosphere of less attractive
issipation than that of the gay world of Paris, to form dangerous
ntimacies, to lose his self-respect—and become what by a
trange misnomer is called *à bonnes fortunes*, has been but too
requently and unhappily exemplified in the private life of
rtists.

The family of the Webers, to whom Mozart had become
ttached during his sojourn at Mannheim, was now transplanted
o Vienna; and whenever he could escape from his occupations in
ublic, and among the great, it was in their house that he sought

to unbosom himself of cares, and indulge his genial aspirations
His love for Constance Weber extended to her family, whom he
befriended in every possible way; ever paying them the attentions of a good son and brother. Even Aloysia Weber, who
had so treacherously broken her faith to him—but was now
justifying his high opinion of her talents in a most successfu
career as a dramatic singer throughout most of the lyric theatres
of Germany—could depend upon his kindness to compose for
her whenever she stood in need of a new scena. Constance
without the magnificent voice and brilliant execution of her
elder sister, was still a singer of very considerable powers [1] and
great taste. She possessed a real insight into the art, and was
a competent judge of most of that in which her future husband
excelled. The degree to which Mozart had educated the
musical taste of Constance Weber will best appear from a letter
of the 20th of April 1782, addressed to his sister:

" I herewith send you a prelude and a three-part fugue
. . . That this fugue has seen the light, you are indebted
to my Constance. Baron von Swieten, to whom I go every
Sunday, lends me the works of Handel and Sebastian Bach
after I have played them through to him, to take home with
me. As soon as Constance heard the fugues, she was quite in
love with them; she will now listen to nothing but fugues, and
to Handel and Bach only in that style. Hearing me at this
time frequently play fugues out of my head, she enquired
if I had never written any, and upon my answering ' No,
absolutely scolded me for having neglected the most beautiful
and scientific part of music; nor did she give me any rest till I
had written her a fugue. This is the origin of the one now
sent. I have purposely written *andante maestoso* above it, in
order that it may not be played fast; for if a fugue be not
played rather slowly, the entrance of the subjects loses in clearness and distinctness, and the effect is injured, if not destroyed

[1] The mass in C minor, which was afterwards incorporated in the
cantata " Davidde penitente," will sufficiently prove what has been here
advanced. This composition, which was intended by Mozart as a votive
offering for the recovery of his wife in her first confinement was produced
in August 1783, at St. Peter's church, Salzburg, during a visit of the
Mozarts, when the wife sang the solos. The " Et incarnatus," a soprano
solo, concerted with wind instruments, is most beautiful. Some unpublished *solfeggi* for a soprano voice, show that after his marriage he was still
cultivating her vocal talent. The MS. has two inscriptions. On one page
" *Per la mia cara Costanza :* " on another, " *Solfeggio per la mia cara
Consorte.*"

When I have time and opportunity I intend to write five others, and present them to Baron von Swieten, who possesses an immense treasure of good music, the quality of the works considered, though but a small one in point of number. Do not, therefore, I beg, let any one see it; but learn it by heart, and play it, which, with a fugue, is no such easy matter."

In a letter addressed a few days previously to his father, Mozart writes:

" Send me the six fugues by Handel. I go every Sunday, at twelve o'clock, to the Baron von Swieten, where nothing is played but Handel and Bach; and am now making a collection of the fugues of Bach—not only of Sebastian, but of Emanuel and Friedemann Bach; and, besides these, a collection of Handel's fugues, towards which I want these six. You have probably heard that the English Bach [1] is dead.—What a loss for the musical world! "

At this time Joseph Haydn was established as Kapellmeister in the service of Prince Nicholas Esterhazy, and enjoyed a very extensive reputation, which, indeed, the native energy of his genius, and the fortunate circumstances of his mature life, enabled him to earn with ease in a variety of compositions. He was frequently at Vienna, in the suite of his prince; and it was natural that Mozart, who had long lived on terms of mutual esteem with Michael Haydn, at Salzburg, should be predisposed to a regard for his brother;—but the simplicity, benevolence, and sincerity of Joseph Haydn's character, when united with the charming qualities of his genius, offered more than the materials for an ordinary friendship. The attachment of these two men remains accordingly one of the most honourable monuments of the virtuous love of art, that musical history can produce. Haydn was at this period about fifty years of age. His constant habit of writing five hours a day had accumulated in a series of years a large collection of quartets, pianoforte music, church music, and symphonies, most of which were greatly

[1] John Christian Bach, music-master to her majesty Queen Charlotte. The most celebrated sons of John Sebastian Bach were thus distinguished in Germany: William Friedemann was termed the Halle Bach; Charles Philip Emanuel, the Berlin Bach; John Christopher, the Buckeburger Bach; and John Christian, the English Bach. When it is considered that the patriarch of harmony, John Sebastian Bach, had a family of twenty children, all of whom were possessed more or less of musical talent, the necessity of this additional distinction will not be questioned.

admired for the spirit and elegance of their style, and the clearness and originality of their design.[1] Mozart at once saw and acknowledged the excellence of Haydn; and in his future intercourse with that master, took the part which the difference of their age, if not of their genius, rendered graceful—by deferring to his judgment with all the meekness of a learner. To Haydn he submitted many of his compositions before publication; delighting often to call him his master and model in quartet writing, which he now began to cultivate in earnest; and omitting no circumstance which could gratify the veteran musician in possessing such an admirer. Haydn on his part repaid all this devotion with becoming generosity. However conscious that, in the universality of musical power, his own genius must be placed at a disadvantage in comparison with that of his friend, he harboured no envious or unworthy sentiment; and death alone interrupted the kind relation in which each stood to the other.

At the musical parties which Mozart gave from time to time, when he had new compositions to try, and leisure to indulge his disposition for sociality, Haydn was a frequent guest, and no one more profoundly enjoyed the extraordinary beauty and perfection of Mozart's pianoforte playing. Years after, when those fingers, and the soul which animated them, were sought for in vain, a few touching words from Haydn spoke more feelingly to the imagination, in the description of that beauty, than the most laboured and minute criticism could have done. " Mozart's playing," said he, " I can never forget."

To conceive what it was that Haydn could not " forget," it would be vain to speak of the refinement and delicacy of style; the beautifully *speaking* expression which went to the heart; the evenness, neatness, and rapidity of both hands; or the force and character of the left hand (at that time something unusual); though all these were the undoubted characteristics of Mozart, they have also belonged to other fine players, and,

---

[1] The regularity of Haydn's life, though probably not unknown to the reader, deserves to be recalled in this place.   He rose at six o'clock, dressed himself with scrupulous neatness, and then sat down at a little table near his piano, to write till noon, which was his dinner time.   At two o'clock daily he attended the concert of his prince, which lasted for an hour and a half; and twice a week directed an opera, which took place in the evening. When there was no opera he superintended the rehearsal of some new piece or other, supped at seven o'clock, and then passed the rest of the evening with his friends, or in the society of Mademoiselle Boselli. Such was Haydn's existence at Esterhazy, or Eisenstadt.

herefore, to do justice to the idea of his artistical perfection
n the pianoforte, we must conceive the great composer inter-
reting his own nature. That must needs be fine playing where
he spirit of " Don Juan," " Figaro," etc., animates the keys.
The great effects which are said to have been produced by
Beethoven in his improvisation on the piano, and in an inferior
legree by Hummel, may be attributed to the same cause.
ndeed, in that performance which presents us with the clear
and well-defined ideas of the master, delivered in the heat of
conception, there is generally a charm which may be elsewhere
ought in vain.

The pianoforte compositions of Mozart of all kinds, sonatas,
variations, concertos, etc., began now to be in general request;
irst in Bohemia, and soon afterwards throughout Germany at
arge. The originality of style, and the exquisite melodies
vhich characterised these works, opened a new field in the art;
and, before a few years had elapsed, the whole musical world
vas in amazement at the dignity which pianoforte music had
attained through the contributions of this master.

In the spring of the year 1782, Mozart entered into a
peculation with " one Martin," who had received the emperor's
ermission to give twelve concerts in the Augarten, and four
grand serenades in the principal squares; the orchestra to be
composed of mere dilettanti, except the bassoons, trumpets,
and drums.

These Sunday garden fêtes in the spring and early summer
are peculiarly characteristic of life in Vienna, where the pleasures
of the promenade, and the enjoyment of the air and sunshine,
egularly succeed the observances of religion. In such a scene,
vhere all the beauty, rank, and talent of the capital are
requently assembled, the spirit of the season is irresistible.
And there is the music. An orchestra is erected in some green
valk among the trees; and the first sound is the signal to
uspend conversation, to sit down quietly, or to cluster round
he musicians. Mozart, who, like Rousseau, felt that one of the
nost delightful privileges of his art was that of " communicat-
ng emotions," was not less inclined to an experiment in open
air concerts, from his sympathy with the pleasurable at large,
han from that eager desire of new effects which continually
exercised and strengthened his invention. A style of instru-
nental music at once light and ariose—somewhat between the
ymphony and the dance, but calculated to give elegance and

tenderness of sentiment to the promenaders—was at any time
attractive to him, and among his easiest work. Her serenade
were not such as " the starved lover sings," but imbued with al
the genius of the south; in fact, when we consider the emotion
created by Mozart's instrumental music, and by the adaggio
of his symphonies in particular, the imagination of the autho:
may be compared to a Mahommedan paradise; for in no othe:
element can such refined voluptuousness and elegant repose be
conceived to originate.

The judgment with which this warm imagination wa:
tempered, was never more forcibly shown than when the
composer was writing *beneath* himself, in promenade or garder
music. No thought too good for the occasion found place
He was rich enough in ideas to spare his best on any occasion
and thus, at all times, preserved the unity and due correspondence of his style. His method of writing for wind instruments, with which the Bohemians (great practical musicians
were highly delighted, showed the most exact discrimination
whether the instrument were employed in the solo, the concerto
or in accompaniment, he treated it in a peculiar and appropriate
manner. Though only theoretically acquainted with the nature
and genius of these instruments, his intimacy with the performers made him quickly master of any advantage that could
be derived from an improvement in their mechanism.

The difficulties which had impeded the production of " Die
Entführung aus dem Serail " being now removed, that opera
was performed by royal command on the 12th of July 1782
The author of the drama, Bretzner, had conceived a plot that
presented many happy situations for stage effect, which Mozart
did not omit to turn to good account. Among the original
singers were Mademoiselle Cavalieri, Mademoiselle Tayber
and Messrs. Fischer, Adamberger, Dauer, and Walter. The
success which crowned this undertaking was of the most decisive
character; crowded houses every night, and the call for the
repetition of favourite pieces, attested the delight of the audience
and quite destroyed the hopes of those who intrigued against the
composer, and would have been willing spectators of his failure

The repertory of the German lyric stage was, at this time
miserably poor in comic operas. Some few attempts in that
style by Benda and Reichardt excepted, together with " The
Doctor and Apothecary," by Dittersdorf—ephemeral productions that now exist only in the chronicles of the historian

—there is absolutely nothing to deprive Mozart of the honour
f having struck out an entirely new path in this work.
Appearing after " Idomeneo," it could scarcely be believed to
ave proceeded from the same pen. There is not the least
orrespondence between the forms of the melody, the harmony
r modulation of the two works; and notwithstanding the
melancholy to which Mozart's genius was naturally disposed,
infavourable as it may be thought to variety of style, he
ierein showed triumphantly that music had no formulas for
iim, that new situations constantly suggested new thoughts,
md that to diversify his pieces in succession, from the air to the
:horus, was one of the most remarkable elements of his power.

Notwithstanding the defects of the singers who failed in
ieveral parts for want of rehearsals, and the perils that momen-
:arily threatened the reception of the piece on the first and
iecond nights, it produced on those two occasions no less than
t200 florins. The great popularity of the piece rendered it
iecessary to prepare it speedily for the garden orchestra, in
irder to anticipate others who would have taken it with im-
iunity. From a passage in a letter to his father, we see how
:ngrossed Mozart was at this period:

" I have now no slight task to get my opera arranged in
iarmony [1] by Sunday week, or another will be beforehand with
ne, and reap the profit; and, in addition to this, I have to
write a new symphony! How all this is to be done I know
iot. You cannot imagine the difficulty of arranging an opera
in harmony, to make it fit for wind instruments without sacri-
ficing any of the effect. I must borrow the night for this work,
and to you, dearest father, be it devoted. You may rely on
hearing from me every post-day. I shall write as fast as
possible, and as well as haste will permit.

" Count Zitchi has just sent to invite me to go with him to
Luxemberg, and call upon Prince Kaunitz. I must therefore
leave off to dress; for when indisposed to go abroad I am constantly in *déshabille*. The copyist has just sent me the rest of
the parts. Adieu! I kiss your hand 2000 times, and embrace
my sister with the truest affection."

Success was now carrying the imagination of the composer
into dreams of another kind. His heart longed for her who

[1] So the Germans term arrangements made for the wind instrument
bands that frequent the public gardens.

ought to participate in these triumphs, and in the following letter we have the first open request for his father's consent to his marriage.

" My opera was given yesterday with great applause, to the honour of every Nannerl in the kingdom,[1] and, notwithstanding the dreadful heat, the theatre was crammed to the ceiling. It is to be repeated on Friday next; though I have protested against this, for I do not like to have it whipped on at such a rate. The public, I can say with truth, are quite crazy about this opera; and it really is very pleasant to have gained such applause. I hope that you have received the original safely. Dear, good father, I must now beseech you by everything in life to give me your consent to marry my dear Constance. Do not suppose that the mere marriage is in my thoughts. Were that the case I would willingly wait; but I see that the state of my health and spirits now render it indispensable. My heart is ill at ease, my head distracted; and, in such a condition, how is it possible to think or work to any purpose? "

This was written on the 27th of July. On the 31st he urges his suit again:

" The theatre is crowded on every performance of my opera, which was played for the fourth time yesterday, and will be repeated on Friday. You write to me that the whole world is of opinion that my boasting and free speaking have made me enemies among the professors of music and other people. What sort of world? Probably the Salzburg world? For every one here has plenty of opportunities of seeing and hearing the exact contrary; and that shall be my reply. Meantime, you must have received my last letter, and I have not the least doubt that the next I get from you will contain your consent to my marriage. I gather from your letters that you neither can nor will offer any opposition; for Constance is a respectable, good girl, of worthy parents. I am now able to earn bread for her, and as we love one another and wish to be together, there can be no reason for delay."

The reply to these cogent arguments must have been speedy as well as favourable; for in a few days Mozart was happy in the possession of his bride. On the 4th of August 1782, the

---

[1] The 26th of July is St. Anne's Day. The recollection of this was of course intended by Mozart to gratify his sister.

marriage was celebrated at the house of the Baroness Wald-stetten; and the delight of the occasion was enhanced by a little triumph, for Madame Weber, making, at the last, some difficulty and show of unwillingness to part with her daughter, Mozart was obliged to carry her off by stratagem. This practical illustration of his own opera, " Die Entführung " (The Abduction), afforded a subject for much agreeable and good-humoured pleasantry to the friends of the composer. But the account of the marriage must be given in his own words. The letter is thrown off in the bounding and exulting spirit of an epithalamium.

" VIENNE, *ce 7 d'Aout*, 1782.

" MON TRÈS CHER PÈRE!—My dear Constance, now, thank God! my wife, was long ago informed by me of the whole state of my affairs, and of what I had to expect from you. Her friendship and love to me, however, were so great, that she joyfully and unhesitatingly confided her whole future life to my keeping, and joined her fate to mine. I kiss your hands, and thank you with all the tenderness that a son should feel towards a father, for the kind consent and the paternal blessing. My dear wife will write next post-day, to beg the blessing of her kind father-in-law, and the continuance of her beloved sister's friendship. No one was present at the ceremony except the mother and youngest sister, M. von Thorwart, M. Landrath von Zetto, and M. von Gilowsky.

" When we were joined together, my wife began to weep and I too—and indeed they *all* wept, even the priests themselves, at witnessing our emotion. Our whole marriage feast consisted in a supper given by the Baroness von Waldstetten; which was, in fact, rather princely than baronial. During supper I was surprised by a concert from sixteen wind instruments, who played my own compositions. My dear Constance now looks forward with pleasure to a visit to Salzburg, and I am sure that, when you see her, you will congratulate me on my happiness, if you are of my opinion, that a virtuous, well-disposed wife is a treasure to her husband.

" My opera was played again yesterday by desire of the Chevalier Gluck. Gluck has paid me many compliments upon it, and I am to dine with him to-morrow."

Of the nine years which this union lasted, one whole year and a half was consumed by the very serious illness of Madame Mozart, which scarcely permitted her during that period to

M

leave her bed; and in addition to this a young family grew
rapidly about her; so that whatever might have been the
happiness, doubtless great, enjoyed by the sympathetic pair,
it was chequered with unusual care and sorrow.   The con-
stitutional delicacy of his wife would have been a sufficient
misfortune in itself, had Mozart's pecuniary resources been
ample and assured; but with fluctuating and stinted means,
their family troubles acquired increased severity.   For a while,
indeed, everything prospered—but the scene soon altered; and
the married lovers were obliged to descend from their poetical
world of love and imagination into a more prosaic one;—to
listen to the clamour of creditors, whose demands they could
not satisfy, and to be sometimes cast upon extremities for the
supply of current wants.

It was probably in reference to these embarrassments that
the Emperor Joseph one day said to Mozart, " Why did you not
marry a rich wife? "   To which the composer, with that dignity
and self-reliance which characterise all his answers to the great,
immediately replied, " Sire, I trust that my genius will always
enable me to support the woman I love! " [1]

The occasional difficulties here alluded to, fortunately involve
no suspicion of a laxity of principle in either Mozart or the
partner of his fortunes.   Their youth and inexperience, their
education in the houses of artists, and the trust in good fortune
so natural to people in their condition, to whom hope is always
bountiful, may plead their excuse; but what will best satisfy
those who rightly think that genius cannot claim exemption
from moral obligations, nor, unaccompanied by integrity, be
fitly honoured, is the fact that every debt was in the end fully
paid.   This record is due to the high principles of honour evinced
by the widow of Mozart on the death of her husband, and affords
a proof of the existence of those sentiments in each, which both
had learned to reverence.

[1] An anecdote may here be told which will place the manners of the
Emperor Joseph in an amiable light, and show in what way he worked
upon the affections of Mozart.   Shortly after his marriage, as the composer
and his bride were walking in the Augarten, at Vienna, accompanied by a
dog, the lady, joking upon the attachment of her canine favourite, whom
she wished to astonish, said, " Pretend now to beat me."   As Mozart was
proceeding to obey her, the emperor stepped out of a neighbouring summer-
house, exclaiming, " What! what! only three months married, and
beating already."   Mozart explained the cause, at which the emperor
laughed; and then turned the conversation upon some pleasant passages
in their first acquaintance, during the lifetime of his father, which have
been before narrated.

The most striking fact in this career of alternate success and adversity, is the production in such profusion of the imperishable works of the composer under circumstances of depression, and frequently in opposition to the demands of nature for repose and relaxation.

The exact order of Mozart's productions during the first year and a half of his establishment at Vienna is more difficult to trace, than that of perhaps any period in his life. Amidst the hurry and distraction attendant upon a new scene of existence and the formation of new connections, the good practice of dating his compositions, which up to this time he had generally observed, may easily have fallen into disuse. Enough, however, may be ascertained to prove beyond controversy that this was the era of his matured strength in instrumental composition. To the garden concerts may be traced two serenades and a divertimento for wind instruments; of the former, one piece best known in the more select concert-rooms as a magnificent quintet in C minor,

Allegro.

was in its original form a serenade for two oboes, two clarionets, two horns, and two bassoons.[1]

It was in the month of July 1782, during the first success of "Die Entfhürung," that the symphony in D was produced.

Allegro con spirito.

How must the energy of such an opening have astonished the Vanhalls and the Stamitzs; but not to mention obscure or half-forgotten names, how must it have astonished even Haydn himself! The specimens of composition adduced will show what rank Mozart took among the musicians of Vienna almost immediately on his removal there; and the pre-eminence

---

[1] The weight and strength of the subject adapt it for completer effect in the shape of the otetto.

established by those works which are among the earliest of his writing now usually performed in concert-rooms, he not only preserved, but heightened to the end of his life; giving an impulse to orchestral and instrumental music in general, such as it had never yet received from the hand of any master.

The Italian opera composers residing at Vienna, among whom may be reckoned Salieri, Righini, Anfossi, Martini, etc.,[1] the last, indeed, a Spaniard by birth but by education an Italian, were anything but pleased at the prospect of having, from time to time, such an antagonist in the field of dramatic composition. Accustomed to the supremacy of their countrymen in all matters connected with the lyric drama, and enjoying, as it were, an ancient right of superiority on the stage of Vienna, they listened in jealous alarm to the excellence of the new master; and for the future omitted nothing which the spirit of intrigue could suggest to frustrate his expectations, and to destroy at once both his profit and his fame. Through their credit with the ladies of the court, and by this channel with the Emperor Joseph himself, they possessed unfortunately but too many means of obtaining their end. When Mozart heard from the mouth of the emperor, the remarkable criticism on his new opera, "Too many notes, my dear Mozart," and replied at once with frankness and independence, "There are just as many, please your majesty, as there should be," he was perfectly aware from what quarter that opinion had emanated. The most active and inveterate against Mozart of all the Italian *clique* was Salieri. This composer, whose talents were just sufficient to enable him to live in some estimation, was a creature of Gluck's. Salieri had been with that master in Paris, and to him Gluck had confided the libretto of his opera of the "Danaides,"[2] the work

---

[1] The real name of this composer was Vicenté Martin y Soler. He was a choir boy of the cathedral of Valencia, who becoming enamoured of an Italian singer, followed her into Italy, where *la faim le talonnant*, says his biographer, he turned composer. His melodies were highly popular, and Mozart himself introduced one from "La Cosa Rara," into the supper scene in the second finale of "Don Juan." In a conversation at Leipsic, in the year 1789, Mozart thus expressed himself concerning Martini. "Many of his things are really pretty—but in ten years' time no one will take any more notice of him." This prediction has been fully verified.

[2] Salieri imitated the style of Gluck in his opera, "Tarare," and other works, which are now, according to the usual fate of imitations, forgotten. As this composer has long been notorious for his animosity against Mozart, some personal description of him may not be unwelcome. The mother of the celebrated Signora Storace, who saw him repeatedly at Vienna, described him as a little man, with an animated countenance, and peculiarly fine eyes, and his appearance altogether reminded her strongly of Garrick.

with which he intended to close his own labours, when an attack
of apoplexy made him suddenly cease writing, and consult the
preservation of his health in retirement.

From this time, the year 1780, when Gluck was in the 68th
year of his age, he finally renounced the toils of public life, and
every new project of ambition, to pass the remainder of his days
at Vienna. Here he was more at home than in France; his
works were held in as much estimation, and were better performed;—in particular the operas which he had written at
Vienna, " Orfeo," " Alceste," and " Paris and Helen," maintained their hold on public favour, and were occasionally reproduced with great care. To a man of Gluck's peculiar turn of
mind, which united with genius and simplicity an egotism truly
splendid, this homage to his productions was in some sort a
necessary of existence. The possession of a large fortune, and
the honour of the most familiar intercourse with princes—in
fact, he had written an opera for the nuptials of the Emperor
Joseph, the principal characters of which were sustained by the
archduchesses of the imperial family—all these things, with
which an ordinary man might have been content, were nothing
unaccompanied by praise in its strongest form, which, when
not offered by others, he did not scruple to administer to himself.[1]
It has been truly remarked of Gluck and Handel that they,
among all the great musicians, were the two who most enjoyed
the art through the medium of their own productions. It may
suggest a ludicrous commentary on this fact, to know that
Handel had condemned Gluck. In the year 1745, Gluck was
engaged to write two operas in London, one of which, on the
subject of the fall of giants, was heard by Handel, who pronounced it detestable, and cared but little afterwards for the
productions of its author.

Notwithstanding this high authority against him, Gluck was
one of the great men who have established an era in the art;
and the credit of Handel's discernment may yet be saved, when
it is recollected that Gluck was already advanced in life before

[1] Gluck favoured his friend and correspondent, the Bailli du Rollet, with
many instances of his amusing partiality for his own performances. Of
" Alceste," he says, " I must own that it is very little short of perfection."
And a little further on, in the same letter, he observes: " There is a sort of
delicacy in ' Armida ' which there is not in ' Alceste;' for I have discovered a method of making the characters so express themselves, that
from the very first you may detect by their manner whether Armida is
speaking, or merely an attendant." With such fondness Gluck yearned
over his own productions.

he discovered the destiny of his genius, and associated his name with so many admirable and undying works. All the operas which as a young man be produced in Italy; all his attempts at symphony writing; and his solitary essay in church music, " De profundis; " have been overwhelmed by oblivion, because their style was conventional, and uninformed by the original genius of the master. But from the time that Gluck commenced reformer of the musical drama, as we learn from the admirable dedicatory epistle of the " Alceste," from the time that the analysis of his own truthful feelings, and reflection upon the dramatic abuses of poetry and music, enabled him to exhibit sentiment and situation in new and more forcible lights upon the stage; immortality placed her seal upon him. The enthusiasm which attended his progress was worthy of a revolution which promised to remove from operatic composition all the absurdities that had exposed it to the scorn of unmusical wit, and to make the art in future the vehicle of truth and nature. The full score of the " Alceste," which is among the earliest dramatic works ever published in that form, still remains a tribute to the great reputation of its author; whom Wieland compliments with truth, when he says that he had fulfilled one of the finest maxims of Pythagoras " in preferring the Muses to the Syrens."

Amidst all the admirers of this great master there was, however, not one who more deeply felt and appreciated the truth and beauty of style which he had derived from the contemplation of the purest models of classical antiquity, than Mozart, who professedly made the scores of Gluck his study. Still he could hardly have disguised from himself the fact, that the path of this musician was exceedingly confined. Give him some great situation or striking sentiment to express, and he did it in perfection; but in the mere luxury of music divested of action and in the numerous other ways in which music, though vaguely, addresses itself to the passions of the soul, he had no power. Haydn, though greatly inferior to Gluck in dramatic ability, occupied a much wider field, and came far nearer to Mozart in the abundance of his resources.

The acquaintance which Mozart's letter of the 7th of August shows to have been commencing between him and Gluck by a dinner invitation from the latter, never ripened into any great intimacy, still less into a cordial friendship. At first it may appear strange that two men who felt so much in common, should have been not quite at ease in each other's society; but their difference in years and circumstances, and, more than this, Gluck's enfeebled health, in which his mind participating, left him exposed to the influence of parasites and intriguers, will suggest many probable solutions of the difficulty.

That Mozart had already on several occasions handled the majestic pen of Gluck in dramatic choruses, and with as much success as at a later day he used the pens of Bach and Handel, often surpassing his models, is certain; and it may be questioned how far such a compliment could gratify a living composer. He had done this but too well in the second finale in D minor of "Idomeneo," *Corriamo fuggiamo;* in the sublime chorus *O voto tremendo;* and also in the march and priestly music of the same opera. He now gave more striking illustrations of his command of the heroic style, by producing the choruses and *entr'acte* music to the tragedy of "Thamos," by Freiherrn von Gebler; which compositions, of the date of 1782-3, now known to the public as the cantatas *Splendente te* and *Ne pulvis et cinis*, possess not only all the dignity of Gluck, but an instrumentation far more brilliant and spirited. The mere excellence of such performances would alone be sufficient to spur the malice of the *Dii minores* in the musical world of Vienna, and afford matter for unjust constructions and evil whisperings. The attempt to sow discord between Mozart and Haydn, by the exposure to each of some negligences or oversights in the works of the other, has been related by their biographers; and some such attempt may have succeeded in the case of Gluck; the more probably as he is known to have patronised a man so hostile to Mozart as Salieri. Musical history can scarcely parallel the animosity, the jealousy, and spirit of base intrigue which prevailed at this time among the composers of Vienna, of whom each was the guardian of his own little interests at the expense of everything else in life. To the numerous intrigues and repeated slanders of which Mozart was the subject, he had nothing to oppose but his rectitude of principle and transcendent genius; yet as the latter during his lifetime, through malicious arguments and ignorant judgment, was sometimes brought into question, his enemies not unfrequently gained their point by adding to the difficulties of his existence.

The profession of a dramatic composer seems to have been at this time one of incredible hardship. However successful an opera might be, the manager seldom increased the original sum agreed for with the composer; but left him to augment his stipend by arrangements of his work in "*harmonie*" for the public gardens, and in various other shapes for the music-sellers; so that the conclusion of an opera was but the commencement of his labour, if he wished to profit. But this was not all: musical property being entirely unprotected, and the score of a new opera left in the hands of the copyist, with liberty to dispose of as many transcripts on his own account as there might be a demand for, the composer was frequently forestalled and robbed of the fruits of his invention.

In the autumn of the year 1782, the Prussian ambassador, Baron von Reidesel, ordered a copy of the score of " Die Entführung aus dem Serail," to be sent to Berlin; and Mozart expressed his thanks that the commission was given to him, and not to the copyist. In writing to his father on this subject, he appears to be so dissatisfied with the state of dramatic rewards as they affected the composer, that he had some idea of engaging in a theatrical property on his own account. It would seem that the custom at that period was, as it has been since, to allow the copyist of the theatre to have the advantage, by way of perquisite, of furnishing copies of new music; and Mozart upon this occasion evidently felt that, however he might be warranted on every principle of reason and justice in disposing of a copy of his own work, he was committing a violation of established usage, which his enemies would be sure to bring against him on the first opportunity. It is to be feared that the whole transaction points not less to the vindication of his own right, than to pecuniary cares already commenced. He announced to his father in this letter, that his opera had just been performed before the Russian court at Vienna, on which occasion he sat again at the pianoforte, partly to rouse the orchestra from the slumber into which they had fallen, and partly to show himself to the visiting nobility, as the father of his child.

The novelties of form, as well as of style, in " Die Entführung aus dem Serail " continued to render it wonderfully popular. The three movements of the overture; the conclusion of the first act with a terzetto, of the second with a quartet, and of the third with a song which went round, each person singing a little verse in turn—thus avoiding the usual finale; were great and successful innovations, whose influence upon the lyric stage was not bounded by this opera. The stiffness and formalities of ancient custom now disappeared from the musical drama; and it acquired a vivacity and spirit to which it had hitherto been stranger. Concerted music, with brilliant accompaniments, combining variety of character and sentiment, began also to be enjoyed.

The age was certainly one of transition in operatic matters. Ten years before, Gluck had successfully opposed the corruptions introduced by the singers, and had cut off their organ-points, or cadences; Mozart now followed him as a reformer, by altering the conventional forms of pieces, and even venturing on some occasions to conclude *piano !* It is fortunate that these changes, which from that circumstance alone incurred enormous risk, were seconded by the efforts of admirable singers. Adamberger's expressive tenor, and the voluminous and full-toned bass of Fischer in " Osmin," aided the success by the perfect justice they did the music.

Mozart had peculiar associations with " Die Entführung," which always rendered it a favourite work in his eyes. He had written it as a bridegroom, and had given the name of his mistress to the heroine to whom he expressed his own feelings in the part of Belmont. There was thus a slight romance going forward, of which the audience were not in the secret, which, moreover, may now explain the singular excellence of the love songs.

He now lived in a delirium of invention, often working so hard that, as he happily expresses it, he does not know whether his head is on or off. Whatever extravagance may hereafter appear in his occasional diversions and relaxations, it would seem but a necessary consequence of such unexampled application.

Throughout this busy period his engagements were incessant. Count Rosenberg, in the midst of it all, persuaded him to undertake an Italian opera, and he sent to Italy for the newest subjects of *opera buffa*. Thus he describes the way in which his day is occupied:

" The whole morning, till two o'clock, is taken up with lesson-giving—then we dine. After dinner I am obliged to give my poor stomach a short hour for digestion; it is only in the evening that I can write anything, and this not always, on account of my being frequently invited to concerts." [1]

About this time he composed two concertos, in which he says he has preserved the medium between too great difficulty and too great facility.

[1] Let the reader think of the time thus irrecoverably lost in Mozart's short life, and then consult the catalogue of his works! Comment on such facts is quite superfluous.

"They are very brilliant, pleasing to the ear, and natur
without being vapid. Here and there are spots which co:
noisseurs will best appreciate, yet such as another class
hearers will like without knowing wherefore."

He was engaged at the same time upon the pianoforte arrang
ment of his opera, and the "Bard's Song," by Dennis, upc
Gibraltar, at the request of an Hungarian lady. Of this subjec
which he describes as difficult, he says:

"The ode is majestic—beautiful—what you will—but
my poor taste, however, rather overdone, and somewhat tum
and bombastic. But why complain?—the middle thing, whic
is the true thing in all matters, is no longer felt or appreciate
To gain applause, one must either write in so obvious ar
commonplace a style that one's productions may be caught ɩ
in the streets; or so unintelligibly, that, defying the utmo
power of sense to discover a meaning, we may please all tl
more on that very account."

At the beginning of the year 1783, Mozart was employed upc
a mass, of which he completed one half in January, and the
in the distraction of affairs, laid the rest aside to be finishe
at leisure. His reason for again entering upon the unprofitab
field of church music was a purely domestic one; but it d
honour to the goodness of his heart, and to his sense of religic
as a Catholic Christian.

This mass was a "labour of love" in more senses than on
To exercise his pen in the grand contrapuntal style of churc
music was at all times agreeable to him; and he was now fr
from the local restrictions under which he had written ł
numerous masses at Salzburg, where neither the style, tl
length of the pieces, nor their instrumentation, was left to ł
own discretion. Hence, making due allowance for the effe
of some few years in developing the composer's genius, tl
great superiority of "Davidde Penitente," by which title tł
mass was in the sequel better known, over all the earlier masse
as well for breadth of style as in true ecclesiastical solemnity.

Among the compositions of this period there are sor
concertos for the horn, which are too illustrative of the di
position and manners of Mozart, and of his connection with t
best performers of the orchestra, to be passed without notic
A correspondent of the *Harmonicon* [1] who had visite

[1] For March 1824.

[. André, at Bonn, to examine the MSS. of Mozart in his ossession, writes: " Besides many unpublished fragments of peras and sacred compositions, I saw a very curious MS. oncerto for the horn, with this droll superscription—' Mozart as compassion on that silly fool Leitgeb, and writes the fellow concerto for the horn.' " [1] He has given this player, with hom he seems to have been on a very intimate footing, a reat many other ludicrous epithets, which, however, do not ear translating. The manuscript of this concerto has all ie colours of the rainbow, and to some very difficult passages, ritten with blue ink, he has added queries like these, " What o you say to that, Master Leitgeb? "

Humour of this kind was, without doubt, well adapted to ie meridian of Master Leitgeb. He had got an excellent new oncerto wherewith to display his fine tone and execution; and iat the maestro condescended to have a laugh with him did ot detract from the value of the gift. The talent and good-umour of this horn player are obliquely complimented in nother concerto, of which the rondo contains a running accom-animent of drollery in the handwriting of the composer, from ie beginning to the end. Immediately on the entrance of the rst solo, we find: " *à lei Signor Asino. Animo—presto—su :a—da bravo—corraggio,*" and at the conclusion, " *Grazia al el! Basta, basta!* " As all these expressions were faithfully iven by the copyist, in writing out the part for performance, ie ludicrous effect of such a commentary read by the player, n the execution of each passage as it occurred, may be well onceived.

The instances in which Mozart performed acts of kindness) musical artists of all classes, by giving them compositions ithout any return or reward, are innumerable. His father ad counselled him to be on good terms with the men of his rchestra, that they might take pains with his works; but these rudential considerations had little weight with him. Wherever ε found talent united with a friendly character, his love for ιusic did the rest; and thus, however straitened or embarrassed ι his own circumstances, he would still be a benefactor to the ımblest follower of art.

[1] Mozart's words are: " *Wolfgang Amadé Mozart hat sich über den :itgeb, Esel, Ochs, und Narr erbarmt zu Wien den 27 Maij 1783.*" It will ıt be uninteresting to note, that the Leitgeb, to whom all these pleasantries are addressed, had formerly been one of the companions of his boyhood Salzburg.

The taste for the humorous displayed in the anecdote ju
related, may be possibly thought *infra dig.* But it is, howev
characteristic of the composer, who preserved in mature l
the same pleasure in the broadest and most extravagant pl:
of the imagination that he had shown when a boy. Usual
absorbed in the serious business of composition, he unbent l
mind with eagerness, and at times enjoyed such a holiday
sheer animal spirits as could scarcely have been tolerated in :
inferior person. He liked associates of this complexion; and
his love of sympathy, either overlooked, or cared not to s(
that a good jester and table companion may possess a hyp
critical and selfish character. In the end he discovered this
his cost; but his own humour was still the concomitant of
highly susceptible and tender nature, and might at any tir
have given place to tears.

Mozart had now for some time been enrolled ★ brother of
lodge of freemasons at Vienna, and had the honour to compc
the music for most of the remarkable solemnities and festiv&
of that order. The jollities of this club seem to have been mu
to his taste, and often raised his spirits when depressed by t
close attention to composition.

Towards the middle of the year 1783, Mozart was occupi
on the six quartets which two years afterwards he dedicat
to Joseph Haydn. He bestowed the highest pains on this wor
in order to render it an offering worthy of the great moc
upon which he always professed to have formed his style
quartet writing.[1]

Anfossi's opera, "Il Curioso Indiscreto," brought out
June 1783, excited a rather unusual interest in Vienna, fro
introducing the two celebrated German singers, Madame Lan
and Herr Adamberger, on the Italian stage for the first tim
Both had solicited Mozart to write something for them, ai
he accordingly gratified his sister-in-law with two airs, ai
Adamberger with a rondo. It was one of the most comm(
practices of the distinguished singers of that day to introdu
into any new part, in which they desired to make a favourab
impression, some composition written by a master who kn&

---

[1] He was employed on the second in D minor during the first accouch
ment of his wife, pursuing his occupation in the chamber of the inval
According to one of his German biographers, the minuet and trio we
composed immediately after her delivery. The various and profou
feelings displayed in that magnificent work afford internal evidence of t
truth of these domestic circumstances, and show the agitated state
mind in which it was produced.

nd could display their powers: in complying, therefore, with
ne wishes of the performers in this instance, there was nothing
nusual. But whether Italian jealousy was alarmed at the near
pproach, and feared the rivalry of German pretensions,—or
'hether the opportunity to prejudice the public against a young
nd rising composer, by representing him as dictatorial and
onceited, were thought too good to be lost,—certain it is that
ne report of Mozart's desire *to improve* Anfossi's opera was
1dustriously circulated.

In the account which Mozart gives his father of this trans-
ction, he says that he disappointed the malice of his enemies,
y causing a notice to be printed in the books of the opera,
hat the two airs sung by Madame Lange were composed by him,
nd not by Anfossi; so that there was no ground for charging
im with a design upon the reputation of that artist. And
nese two airs, one of which was encored, were the only parts
f the opera that pleased. Adamberger did not sing the rondo
Iozart had composed for him, having been tricked by Salieri
nto a belief that it would offend Count Rosenberg. " Adam-
erger, proud in the wrong place," observes Mozart, " was
etermined to show that he did not want introduction; he,
owever, repented of the resolution, and seeing his mistake,
ame to beg the rondo of me—but I would not let him have it."

Towards the end of July in this year, Mozart and his wife
isited their father at Salzburg. This journey had already been
ostponed some months from the want of money; and even
ow the circumstances of the composer appear to have been far
rom flourishing, for he was arrested on the step of the carriage
or a debt of thirty florins. After some difficulty, he was,
owever, liberated.

With what mingled feelings must the travellers have entered
pon this journey! There had now been some years' practical
xperience of the mode of life which Mozart had himself
oluntarily adopted. The brilliant reputation he had founded
1 the musical drama had brought with it no solid advantage,
or diminished the toil with which he earned his daily bread,
'hile it had sharpened the vigilance of his enemies, and increased
heir activity in contesting every step to his preferment. To
his life—the prospect a little softened, perhaps, by hope and
:cognised superiority—he was to return " to fight his battles
'er again." Still, if there were a dark spot in the vista of the
nagination, it did not affect the present, nor lessen the holiday

feelings and joy of heart with which he now revisited the scen
of his infancy and happy boyhood.[1]

But the travellers are arrived, and the imagination readi
pursues them to their retreat, partaking of the hospitalities
home, and the diversions usual on such occasions.[2]

Yet, if the Mozarts enjoyed themselves in these lovely solitud
—scenes which, viewed in youth and mingling in the bosom
the artist with the remembrance of life's uncertainty, awake
intensest feeling—it would seem that they must have borrowe
time from sleep; for never was the pen of the composer mo:
actively employed than during the interval of something le
than three months, which this visit occupied.

His first care was to complete the votive mass, of which
has been already mentioned that one half was ready in Januar
This mass was rehearsed on the 23rd of August, in the chape
house, and performed on the 25th at St. Peter's Church, his wi
singing the solos; probably at this time as a religious observanc
for we hear of her no more in the character of a public pe
former. But the solemnity was not allowed to pass withou
enhancing the mutual kindness of the young married pair.

The next work of the composer was to write two duets fc
the violin and viola for Michael Haydn, organist of St. Peter
at Salzburg. These duets, having originated in an office c
friendship and humanity, were never claimed by Mozart

[1] Of the effect of fine scenery upon Mozart, a characteristic anecdote
preserved which, though it does not relate to this journey, may not I
misplaced here. In travelling with his wife through a beautiful countr
he would first gaze attentively and in silence on the view before him; t
degrees, as the ordinary serious and even melancholy expression of h
countenance became enlivened and cheerful, he would begin to sing,
rather to hum, and at last exclaim, " Oh, if I had but the Thema c
paper! " On her answering that that might easily be, he would continu
" Yes, my treatment of it, no doubt. But how vexatious to be oblige
to hatch all one's conceptions within doors! " Mozart always compose
in the open air when he could. Thus " Don Giovanni " was compose
on a bowling-green, and the principal part of the " Requiem " in a garde
—two of his greatest works.

[2] Even during his own lifetime Salzburg derived a charm from i
association with Mozart, which enhanced the romance of its natural beaut
Kelly, not many years after the date of this visit, speaking of his approac
to the city, says, " As I viewed its lofty spires from a distance I felt a kir
of reverential awe; "—a becoming homage to the birthplace of the gre
musician. M. Beyle, the author of some charming letters on Haydn, date
Salzburg, in the spring of 1808, talks with rapture of his walks in the woo
there; and M. Mainzer, an intelligent correspondent of the *Gazette Musica
de Paris*, under the influence of the same feelings, gives a morning vie
of Salzburg in the taste of one of Claude's landscapes.

[3] They have since been published by André, of Offenbach, with the nan
of their real author.

heir history is short, but interesting. Poor Michael Haydn, t this time suffering from a severe attack of illness which endered him totally incompetent to work, had received the ommand of his prince to produce duets for the violin and viola gainst a certain day, and was threatened with the loss of his alary in case of failure. Such were the liberal dealings of the rchiepiscopal government with artists. Mozart, who was a aily visitor of Haydn, and saw his helpless circumstances, set o work for him so eagerly that in a short time the duets were ompleted, and ready for presentation in the name of Haydn, 7hom they benefited not less in purse than in reputation.

To this *holiday* period in Salzburg are also to be referred two talian operas, the very titles of which have as yet scarcely ranspired. The first, entitled "Lo Sposo deluso, ossia la ivalità di tre donne per un solo amante," an opera in two acts, he text by Varesco, the author of "Idomeneo," approached ompletion so nearly that its overture was written.[1] Of the econd, a comic opera, called "L'Oca del Cairo," the sketch nly of the first act in score was finished. From these pro-luctions it appears that the composer was addressing himself o the peculiar taste of the Viennese with the intention of con-irming the dramatic reputation he had commenced; but that n reviewing what he had done, he thought fit to suppress it. Nothing of importance has been lost by this proceeding; the best deas having been treated to greater advantage in other works.

On the 27th of October, Mozart set out on his return to 7ienna. One solitary cause of dissatisfaction between the ather and son arose out of this visit, which else had been all 1armony. It seems that the composer wished to present his vife with some of the trinkets given to him during his youthful rogress through the various European courts. This desire, 1owever, was not gratified; and M. Nissen [2] is of opinion, from he letters of Leopold Mozart to his daughter, who shortly after-vards married, that some coldness on the part of the father owards his son is perceptible. What the expectations of the ather were, has been already shown in various letters; he poked forward, at the least, to an old age of ease and religious neditation. Beaten from one ground of hope to another, until .t last no refuge was left, this coldness, if it existed at all, must 1ave been the natural effect of accumulated years and dis-

---

[1] The overture is the last piece produced in the composition of an opera.
[2] See the preface to the *Biographie, W. A. Mozart's*. Leipsic. 1828.

appointments. To these causes may be added the wide separ
tion of the two, and the now total independence of the son, wl
had been so long under the paternal wing and protection.

As for Mozart, who was the most disinterested of mankin
and whose even temper was scarcely ruffled by the gravest ac
of unkindness, it will be sufficient to read the letter addresse
by him to his sister on her marriage (which will appear in i
place) to prove that he never lost sight of the kind intentioi
of a good son towards his father, and that circumstances alor
prevented his realising them.

The travellers stayed at Linz on their journey homewar
stopping at the house of the old Count Thun, where they wei
treated with great politeness. At this place Mozart gave
concert, and not having a single symphony by him, he writes t
his father that he is over head and ears at a new one.[1] He hei
learned that his German opera, "Die Entführung aus dem Serail,
had been produced with much applause at Prague and Leipsi·

The spring of the year 1784 was unusually brilliant in respe(
of music at Vienna. Paesiello and Sarti, the one on his journe
from Russia, the other on his way thither, for a time enlivene
the city by their compositions and their presence. In additio
to these, an English party, consisting of Stephen Storace, h
sister, a celebrated singer fresh from Italy, and Michael Kell
an Irish youth, the pupil of Aprile, excited much attention, an
received the marked favour of the Emperor Joseph. To the las
mentioned individual we owe the best personal description (
Mozart now extant.

" I went one evening," he says, " to a concert of the celebrate
Kozeluch's, a great composer for the pianoforte, as well as
fine performer on that instrument. I saw there the composei
Vanhall and Baron Dittersdorf, and, what was to me one of th

[1] The symphony conceived and executed within four days, I take to k
the one in C, No. 6.

The dates of the other great symphonies are well ascertained, and th
origin of this alone remains to be determined. In the structure of th
slow movement, and in the astonishingly animated and impassioned final·
may be discovered such music as Mozart would write in haste—but sti
with a pen of fire that rescued him in the most hazardous straits, and und·
every disadvantage.

greatest gratifications of my musical life, was there introduced to that prodigy of genius, Mozart. He favoured the company by performing fantasias and capriccios on the pianoforte. His feeling, the rapidity of his fingers, the great execution and strength of his left hand, particularly, and the apparent inspiration of his modulations, astounded me. After this splendid performance we sat down to supper, and I had the pleasure to be placed at table between him and his wife, Madame Constance Weber, a German lady of whom he was passionately fond. . . . He conversed with me a good deal about Thomas Linley, the first Mrs. Sheridan's brother, with whom he was intimate at Florence, and spoke of him with great affection. He said that Linley was a true genius, and he felt that had he lived he would have been one of the greatest ornaments of the musical world. After supper the young branches of our host had a dance, and Mozart joined them. Madame Mozart told me that, great as his genius was, he was an enthusiast in dancing, and often said that his taste lay in that art, rather than in music.

" He was a remarkably small man, very thin and pale, with a profusion of fine fair hair, of which he was rather vain. He gave me a cordial invitation to his house, of which I availed myself, and passed a great part of my time there. He always received me with kindness and hospitality. He was remarkably fond of punch, of which beverage I have seen him take copious draughts. He was also fond of billiards and had an excellent billiard-table in his house. Many and many a game have I played with him, but always came off second best. He gave Sunday concerts, at which I never was missing. He was kind-hearted, and always ready to oblige, but so very particular when he played, that if the slightest noise were made, he instantly left off."—*Reminiscences*.

Kelly adds that Mozart advised him, when he talked of composing, to let well alone, and not to study counterpoint—a good-natured way of hinting that it would only be a waste of time.[1]

[1] The manners of the composer, and his views of composition, will be further illustrated by the following anecdote. During one of his journeys, Mozart was the guest of a musician whose son, a boy of twelve years old, already played the pianoforte very skilfully. " But, Herr Kapellmeister," said the boy, " I should like very much to compose something. How am I to begin?" " Pho, pho, *you must wait*." " You composed much earlier." " *But asked nothing about it. If one has the spirit of a composer, one writes because one cannot help it.*" At these words, which were uttered in a lively manner by Mozart, the boy looked downcast and ashamed. He, however, said, " I merely meant to ask if you could recommend me any

His engagements this spring were almost unexampled. H gives an account of his subscription concerts in a letter to hi father.

"Herewith you receive the list of my one hundred an seventy-four subscribers. I alone have thirty subscribers mor than Richter and Fischer together. I commence with thre subscription concerts in Trattner's-hall, on the three las Wednesdays in Lent, beginning on the 17th of March, the pric of the three is six florins. I shall also give two concerts in th theatre this year—and as I shall be obliged to play new thing you may imagine that I must write. The entire forenoon i taken up with pupils, and in the evening I have nearly every da to play. Here is a list of the concerts at which I am engaged:

"Thursday, February 26, at Gallitzin's.
"Monday, March 1, at Joseph Esterhazy's.
"Thursday, March 4, at Gallitzin's.
"Friday, March 5, at Esterhazy's.
"Monday, March 8, at Esterhazy's.
"Thursday, March 11, at Gallitzin's.
"Friday, March 12, at Esterhazy's.
"Monday, March 15, at Esterhazy's.
"Wednesday, March 17, my first private concert.
"Thursday, March 18, at Gallitzin's.
"Friday, March 19, at Esterhazy's.
"Saturday, March 20, at Richter's.
"Sunday, March 21, my first concert in the theatre.
"Monday, March 22, at Esterhazy's.
"Wednesday, March 24, my second private concert.
"Thursday, March 25, at Gallitzin's.
"Friday, March 26, at Esterhazy's.
"Saturday, March 27, at Richter's.
"Monday, March 29, at Esterhazy's.
"Wednesday, March 31, my third private concert.
"Thursday, April 1, my second concert in the theatre.
"Saturday, April 3, at Richter's.

"Have I not enough to do? At this rate, methinks, it wi be difficult for me to get out of practice.

"I must now very briefly tell you how it happens that I gi

book." "Come, come," returned Mozart, kindly patting the boy's chee "all that is of no use. Here, here, and here," pointing to the ear, tl head, and heart, "is your school. If all is right there, then you may tal the pen without delay."

concerts in a private saloon. The clavier teacher, Richter, is giving concerts in the same place on six successive Saturdays. When the nobility subscribed, they observed to him, that they had no wish to go if I did not play. Richter therefore engaged me—and I consented to play three times for him, but got up also three concerts for myself, to which all have subscribed. The first concert, on the 17th of March, went off well; the room was crammed; and the new concerto [1] which I played, pleased so extraordinarily, that wherever one goes one hears the praises of this concert."

In the month of February 1784, Mozart commenced a catalogue of his productions from that time onward; and suffered no distraction of affairs to interfere with his regularity in keeping it. As soon as he had finished a composition, he entered a few bars of its theme in a book, together with the date of its completion; and thus, in simply assisting his own memory to recognise the numerous offspring of his brain, left a document to posterity which is invaluable, as it affords a complete history of his genius throughout its most brilliant years.

M. André, who has published this catalogue, has given some anecdotes of the composer in the preface, which throw much light on his moral and social character. They also confirm the opinion that even at this time Mozart much wished to settle in England; a desire in which he was encouraged by Storace and his sister, by Kelly, and shortly afterwards by the persuasion of his pupil Attwood.

Allusion has been already made to some pecuniary embar-

[1] The concerto mentioned as such a favourite is the beautiful one in B flat, commencing in the Italian style—

Allegro. Oboi e Fag.

It was written only two days before the concert, and probably played in public by Mozart without having been once tried over—as was frequently the case.

rassment of Mozart, previous to his visit to Salzburg. This accident, unfortunately so frequent with him, was not the result of poverty so much as of an ill-regulated household economy, and, at that time, of inexperience. To live in a house in which it is not known how the money goes, has been at once the happiness and the misfortune of men of genius in all ages. But let us observe the strong, though most unwelcome effort, that this great man made to live with the reputation of a good citizen:

"At the time that he commenced this catalogue," says André, "he also commenced keeping a regular account of his receipts and expenses. His receipts, among which are comprised the produce of his concerts, of his instructions in distinguished families, and of the sale of some few of his works, were put down by him on an oblong piece of paper, commencing in March 1784, and extending to February of the year following. From that date, the account was handed over to his wife, who did not continue it long. The expenses were written in a little quarto book, which had before been appropriated to his studies in the English language, and which contains several letters translated by him into English."

The trifling disbursements which the composer thought fit to enter in his account, during this paroxysm of domestic prudence, may create a smile; while, at the same time, his purchases show the simplicity and elegance of his taste. On the first of May, he buys some flowers, which cost a kreutzer; this, though somewhat less than a farthing, forms an item in the musician's ledger. On the 27th, there appears to have been a more expensive purchase, in the shape of a bird—a starling, for which thirty-four kreutzers were paid. The tune which the starling had been taught to sing was so curious, that there is little doubt it occasioned the composer many a hearty laugh. Immediately under the entry of his purchase he has written its song, with the remark, "*Das war schön!*" How pretty![1]

[1] Cowper, the poet, writes on one of his tame hares:
　"I kept him for his humour's sake,
　　For he would oft beguile
　My heart of thoughts, that made it ache,
　　And force me to a smile."

These are the traits of an amiable and affectionate nature, but they have peculiar grace in connection with the great musician. His fondness for animals, but especially for birds, was a part of that original refinement—that feeling for the beauty of natural objects, which neither the artificial life of the theatre nor the influence of an absorbing profession were able to weaken, much less extinguish. It was his practice every summer to hire a little house and garden in the suburbs of Vienna. Here he enjoyed the air with his wife and friends, and often pursued his work in an arbour in the midst of their conversation. When the starling before mentioned, which became a great favourite, died, he buried it in his garden with due honours, and raised a monument and inscription to its memory.[1]

But to return to the catalogue. One of the most important productions of the spring of 1784 was the first of what are now known as a set of three pianoforte quartets. In its original form it was a quintet for the pianoforte, oboe, clarionet, horn, and bassoon. The author refers to this composition in the letter following:

VIENNA, *April* 10, 1784.

" I have gained great honour by my three subscription concerts. My concert at the theatre likewise went off very well. I have written two grand concertos, and in addition to these a quintet for the oboe, clarionet, horn, bassoon, and pianoforte, which has received extraordinary applause; and I myself hold it for the best that I ever yet wrote. How I wish that you could have heard it, and how beautifully it was performed! For the rest, I must confess that towards the end I was absolutely tired with mere playing, and it is not a little flattering to me that my hearers were not so."

This quintet was first performed at one of the Sunday concerts which Mozart was in the habit of giving at his own house, and a remarkable anecdote in Schlictegroll's narrative refers to it; but the identity of the particular composition is now first established.

" A Polish count, who was introduced on the occasion, was delighted, as were all the rest of the company, with this piece, and expressed his gratification to the composer, requesting that when he was at leisure he would compose for him a trio

---

[1] Cowper performed the same kind offices to his hares, whom he " sepulchred " with pomp, and even honoured with epitaphs.

for the flute. Mozart promised to do so, on condition that it should be at his own time. The count, on his return home, sent the composer one hundred gold demi-sovereigns (about £100), with a polite note, in which he thanked him for the pleasure he had enjoyed. Mozart sent him the original score of the piece for five instruments, which had appeared to please him. The count left Vienna. A year afterwards he called again upon Mozart, and inquired about his trio. ' Sir,' replied the composer, ' I have never felt myself in a disposition to write anything that I should esteem worthy of your acceptance.' ' Probably you will not feel more disposed,' replied the count, ' to return me the hundred demi-sovereigns which I paid you beforehand for the piece.' Mozart, indignant, immediately returned him his sovereigns; but the count said nothing about the original score of the piece for five instruments; and it was soon after published by Artaria, as a quatuor for the pianoforte, with an accompaniment for the violin, alto, and violoncello." [1]

Considering the unsettled nature of his employment, it could not well be otherwise than that Mozart must at all times have pursued composition with great irregularity. He was a bad composer " to order; " did not like to write *invitâ minervâ;* and was much indisposed to follow Johnson's recommendation to set to work " doggedly." But when the mood was on him, day and night were alike, and he wrote through both at a stretch.

Signora Strinasacchi,[2] a violin-player from Mantua, played before the court of Vienna this spring, and obtained the emperor's permission to give a concert in the royal opera-house. She soon made the acquaintance of Mozart, who undertook to write a sonata for her.

The composition of this sonata was by some means deferred until the night before the concert. Strinasacchi, anxious for a successful appearance, then pressed to have her violin part to study on the following morning, and received it; but this was

---

[1] In this unauthorised manner a great number of Mozart's compositions made their way into public.

[2] Strinasacchi, afterwards known as Madame Schlik, entered the service of the Duke of Saxe-Gotha, and continued in it till her death. Her violin passed into the hands of Spohr, who, I believe, played upon it at the Norwich Festival in 1839. The enjoyment of the hearers, on that occasion would have been enhanced had they known the historical interest attached to his instrument.

ll that there was time to write. Mozart could find no oppor-
unity to put his own part on paper. The players met in the
pera-house, and executed the sonata without any rehearsal,
o the high delight of the audience, both at composition and per-
ormance. The emperor, who was looking down on the stage
rom his box, through a lorgnette, suspecting that Mozart had
o notes before him, sent to him for the score. His astonish-
nent was great at finding the lines of the bars only on the paper.
' What! have you ventured that again? " said the emperor.
' May it please your majesty," returned Mozart, " there was not
. single note lost." [1]

The composer, in performing this surprising feat, had recourse
nly to a common expedient when pressed for time. He did
he same in the sonata written for himself and Brunetti in 1781,
vhich was produced in an hour—from eleven to twelve at night.
'hough nothing is more frequent than exhibitions of musical
nemory, there certainly is in the power to retain a *newly-invented*
omposition with accuracy, matter for very just and reasonable
.dmiration. It is almost as though we should ask a great
xtemporaneous performer, on his concluding a piece, to repeat
vhat he had played. Such anecdotes show the extraordinary
ompleteness of his conceptions, and prove that he could both
magine and retain the whole of a composition before putting
. single note upon paper.

On the 24th of May 1784, he wrote among other matters to his
ather:

" I really am unable to tell you which of the two concertos
in B flat and D, composed on the 15th and 22nd of March

[1] As it may be interesting to know the work which forms the subject of
his anecdote, two bars of the theme are subjoined.

This composition, conceived one day, and performed the next, without
laving been written down, is seventeen pages long!

1784) I prefer. I take them both to be concertos *die schwitzen machen* (that will make the player warm); but, as it regards difficulty, the one in B has certainly the advantage. I am, however, exceedingly anxious to know which among the three concertos in B, D, and G, major—the last written on the 12th of April—most pleases you and my sister; for that in E flat, of the 9th of February 1784, cannot be included among them, being a concerto of a peculiar kind, and written rather for a small than a great orchestra. As the talk at present is of nothing but these three concertos, I am desirous to know whether your opinion coincides with the *general* one and *mine* also. It is, indeed, necessary that they be well performed, and got up with all the parts. I can spare them till you have done with them; only take care not to let them go out of your hands, for I might have sold one for twenty-four ducats to-day; but I think it more to my advantage to keep them in my possession for a couple of years or so, and then publish them."

No author ever suffered such extensive injury by the surreptitious printing of his works as Mozart; and the injunctions which so frequently accompany the loan of a new composition to his friends—not to let it be seen, not to trust it out of their hands, etc,—were produced by the dishonesty which he had experienced in this respect. While at home, he preserved his MSS. in tolerable security; but during journeys and in giving concerts at the towns on his route, which some years later was a frequent resource with the composer, when his health or his purse were in bad condition, he could less easily be on his guard against the designs of unprincipled men. His manuscript compositions, if not stolen, were frequently copied and then printed, and the author thus deprived of all pecuniary advantage in them. The great memory of the composer now came to his assistance. The copy from which he used to play his concertos in travelling was such a mere outline of the original, and contained so few notes, that it could be of no value to the person who would take it. This method, while it secured him against depredations, must have been advantageous to those who heard him frequently, as it may be easily supposed that the great artist trusted much to impulse, and produced his works on every fresh occasion with some various reading, never condescending to repeat himself literally.[1]

[1] The brothers Hoffman, of Mayence, to one of whom we are indebted for some truly admirable duets for the violin and violoncello, observed at

Paesiello, though he had made a large fortune at Petersburg, was not permitted to remain unemployed at Vienna; he produced there his opera entitled " Il Re Teodoro," in which the English singer, Signora Storace, and Kelly, also appeared.[1] ' The Barber of Seville," of the same master, was likewise given at this time—the part of Rosina by Signora Storace. The Emperor and the nobility treated Paesiello with great distinction; and as his character possessed all the frankness and amiability of his own melody, Mozart became much attached to him. The two friends dined, walked, and drove out together. Mozart tells his father of having taken Paesiello with him into the country to hear Mademoiselle Babette, his pupil, and himself, perform a duet on two pianofortes. Of Sarti he also speaks as a man of worthy character, and adds that he had delighted him by making extempore variations on one of his airs. This was an elegant and peculiar art of complimenting much exercised by Mozart, but not always well received by composers.

With the exception of a single quartet for stringed instruments, produced towards the close of the year, the whole of 1784 was passed by Mozart in teaching, composing for, and playing on, the piano. The emolument of these occupations was considerable; and if such a destiny would have contented the great artist, he might have settled down in a very comfortable and flourishing condition as *music master !*

In August of this year, the Mozart family sustained a loss, which a few years earlier would have been deemed irreparable. The friar, Padre Martini, Kapellmeister to the church of St. Francis at Bologna, on whose friendly disposition, and powerful influence with the great, the family had founded all their hopes of advancement, expired during this month, at a great age.[2] Whether he fulfilled all that was expected from his interposition in favour of the Mozarts; whether absence made him lukewarm

concert at that city, that Mozart, in the performance of his own concertos, never confined himself to the precise melody before him, but varied : from time to time with singular grace and beauty according to the inspiration of the moment.

[1] The court of Vienna at this period was particularly gay and brilliant; and amongst the celebrities there was the Duke of York, who used to walk about the streets in the Windsor uniform.

[2] He was succeeded in his appointment by his pupil Mattei, a musician less learned than his master, but more melodious. Mattei retained the office till the suppression of the convent in 1798, when he resumed a secular life, and had the honour of instructing Rossini! How strange, to find such a descendant from a monastic school of severe counterpoint at only one remove from the Padre Martini!

towards them, or whether the kindest intentions and efforts in their behalf were merely unsuccessful; must now be left to conjecture. As the depositary, however, of the secrets of the poor Salzburg musicians, and as one whose amiable character had won their confidence, the good Cordelier is too important a person to be allowed to quit the scene unnoticed. The Padre Martini appears to owe his reputation rather to the age in which he lived, and to the great men with whom he became connected, than to anything actually accomplished by him. Jomelli, Metastasio, and others, have helped to extend his name; but, in fact, his labours, both literary and musical, as well in the history of music as in composition, form an accumulation of facts and principles, which, though curious enough for the research and industry they display, it has been left for others to arrange to advantage, and employ with profit. The fugues of Martini, which in their day served so well to illustrate the laws of counterpoint, are consigned to present silence, if not to perpetual oblivion.

During the same month, Anna Maria Mozart, the composer's sister, became Madame Sonnenburg. Previously to her change of condition she received a letter from her brother, accompanied by some verses, in which he endeavours to revive the gay and light-hearted tone of their youthful correspondence:

" VIENNA, *August* 18, 1784.

" MA TRÈS CHÈRE SŒUR!—*Potz sapperment !* I find that it is high time to write to you, if I mean to address you again in your vestal state. . . . My wife and I wish you all joy and happiness on this alteration of your condition, and heartily regret that we cannot have the pleasure of being present at the ceremony; we hope, however, early in the spring to embrace both you and your husband, and to see you at Salzburg and St. Gilgen. Our chief concern at present is about our dear father, who will now be forced to lead such a solitary life. You are not, indeed, at a great distance from him, and he may often take a drive over to see you; but he is now again tied to that abominable chapel-house. Were I in my father's place I would ask for some provision after so long a service, and, on getting my pension, would go and live quietly with my daughter. If the archbishop refused to listen to my request, I would resign my employment, and go to my son at Vienna: and this it is which I have principally in view in writing, to beg you to take

ll possible pains to persuade him to such a course; in fact, I
wrote to him to the same purport to-day. Farewell—live
together only as well as we do—we two. Meanwhile, accept
. little advice from the poetical casket of my brain. Just
listen: . . ."

The verses are suppressed. Whatever logic or forethought
Mozart may have exercised when his note-pen was in his hand,
he no sooner commences verse-maker than he loses all command of himself, and runs as mad a race, interspersed with as
many frisks and curvets, as a young horse turned loose in a
field. Rhyme was with him a vehicle of the ludicrous, and he
possessed a happy facility in it.

In the mere existence, however, of these long letters in verse,
evidence may be discerned of the passion with which the composer devoted himself to every pursuit, whether in the serious
business of his art, or in the lightest recreation. Returning only
to common life at intervals, as his abstracting fits of composition
subsided, and possessing a temperament at all times strongly
disposed for pleasure, it may be conceived how much a monitor
and guide within his own home—a second-conscience as it has
been humorously called—was necessary to him; and this duty
itly devolved upon his wife. She had been counselled by the
Baron von Swieten as to the most prudent course for the
management of a genius, whose life had become public property,
and she acted on this point as became her station; solicitous, in
the first place, for the health and welfare of her husband, and in
the next, for the punctual fulfilment of his engagements. But
if it were necessary when diverted from his composition by
friends, to remind him that this or that piece was waited for,
and so by a gentle remonstrance to send him again to his pen,
it as frequently happened that schemes and stratagems were
required to withdraw him from labour when tormented by
ideas, and in a state of feverish anxiety endeavouring to realise
some favourite plan. Under such influences he lost all consideration for himself; and in later years, when his constitution
was less able to answer the demands made upon it, by the
extreme irregularity of his life, he sometimes fainted at the
desk. It was the same when in the mood to improvise upon
the pianoforte, either alone, or in the society of a friend; when
he sat down to the instrument in the evening, he commonly
pursued the train of his fancies till long after midnight.

The delicate health of Mozart had already occasioned some inquietude to his family and acquaintance. Dr. Barisani, physician to the general hospital at Vienna, and probably Von Swieten himself, who formerly attended the Empress Maria Theresa in that capacity, had given him advice on this point. Both of these were men who directed their attentions to the composer on public grounds, and from a full appreciation of his artistical merits, as much as from motives of private friendship; and Mozart was thus doubly cared for in their hands. It was suggested, to prevent the evils of long-continued sitting, that he should *stand* at his desk to compose, and this method he now generally adopted. The billiard-table too, which has caused much scandal, and many unfair imputations on the memory of the composer, there is reason to believe, was not brought into his house so much out of an inordinate passion for the game, as from its affording an easy means of exercise and relaxation, accessible at all hours, and in all weathers.

The year 1785 brought no appointment with it; and while almost every other composer in Vienna could take his flights of imagination, and return, in case of failure, to the "sober certainty" of quarterly emoluments in right of some place or pension, Mozart alone was left to be provided for by chance. However, during the past year his diligence had been rewarded, and he had money in hand; but he had no sooner abandoned the practice of registering his expenses than the old vicissitudes of prosperity and adversity were renewed.

In January, he put the finishing hand to a work which had long deeply interested him, and had for some years employed much time, snatched from laborious duties—namely, the six violin quartets, dedicated in the autumn of 1785 to Joseph Haydn. The desire of transmitting to posterity a memorial of their friendship stimulated his industry far more than the probabilities of gain, which indeed, in the case of a work of such high art, were extremely remote. In one so situated as the composer—the production of these quartets was an act of pure sentiment, and romantic enthusiasm. It is not the less gratifying, however, to know that the work found a market, and that Artaria purchased the copyright for one hundred ducats.

The last of these quartets in C, finished on the 14th of January, commences with a few bars of slow introductory harmony, constructed on a point of imitation so close, and moreover so startling in its opposition to the canons of orthodox composition as to have revived within these few years a violent debate upon the continent.

The passage in question is the following: [1]

Adagio.

Sarti, of whom Mozart speaks in a letter of the 9th of June with so strong a personal predilection, published some severe strictures on this composition, in a pamphlet entitled "Osservazioni critiche sopra un Quartetto di Mozart." [2] He concludes his diatribe by asking, "Si può far di più per far stonare à professori?" The struggle for superiority between the Italian and German schools would hardly have been decided at this day if no one had astonished the professors. That was Mozart's business. Had it been permitted to Sarti, a disciple of the old vocal school of Italy, to decide *ex cathedrâ* upon the merits

[1] Reference to the original MS., in the possession of Mr. Stumpff, of Great Portland Street, settled the question. All these dissonances and *false relations* were re-asserted by the composer. The subject of the beautiful allegro, it may be added, appears in a very youthful composition; and was here first developed.

[2] Sarti was far from being the ingenuous character that Mozart thought him. Of the envy with which he saw the rising star of Germany, this pamphlet affords proof; for now having, as he conceived, good ground to carp, he even ventured to detract from Mozart's fame as a pianoforte player. He was about fifty-four years of age when he passed through Vienna, on his way to Russia, and became acquainted with the young man who was to reduce his dramatic reputation to nothing; and this was hard to one who had been a spoiled child of the public, and whose compositions had hitherto been termed *musica dell' altro mondo*. Of his numerous operatic pieces, Gerber remarks that there was nothing in them but what had been known twenty years before—namely, that he wrote good melodies for the singers, with a feeble and often incorrect harmony. In Russia he made a greater noise than ever. He there composed a psalm for Good Friday, in the native tongue, for eight voices—an orchestra, and the Russian horns; and in his *Te Deum* for the capture of Okzakow he added to these noisy horns, cannon, which were fired at particular intervals. in the court-yard of the palace. This might well be called music of another world. Such was Sarti, in whom the musician and the quack. seem to have been mingled in pretty equal proportions.

of German instrumental composition, Haydn and Beethove must have been proscribed as well as Mozart. Italian ears wei slow to approve the piquant chromatic harmony of the German or to perceive in it the source of unnumbered beautiful effec in instrumental music; and here an amusing and significar incident may be recorded, in reference to the six quartets i question. When Artaria sent the quartets to Italy they wei speedily returned with the excuse, "*the engraving is full (mistakes.*" Nissen relates that the Hungarian Prince Gra: salkowitsch was one day hearing them performed by tł musicians of his chapel, when he called out repeatedly, " Yo are playing wrong; " and on the parts being handed to convinc him of the contrary, he tore them up on the spot. Such is tł slavery to the conventional, by which the public at large ar enthralled. Parallel cases may be found in the sister arts t music, in which the self-love of the multitude being affronte by productions beyond their power to appreciate, they hav revenged themselves by treating with indignity and contemp the noblest efforts to enlarge the sphere of human enjoymen The bold inquirer after truth must often be content to wa till the accumulated opinions of years gradually reverse th verdict of contemporaries.

On Friday, the 11th of February, 1785, Mozart gave the fir: of six subscription concerts, and continued them on six Frida) in succession. They took place on the Mehlgrube. The pric of admission to the series was three ducats. The pianofori concerto in D minor, probably for its heroic and elevated sty: the finest of its author's productions of that kind, embellishe the first concert; and the time is altogether peculiarly interes ing on account of the presence of Leopold Mozart, of Salzbur; who was now the guest of his son, and whose observations, tran: mitted occasionally in letters to his daughter, give spirit an vivacity to the scene.

After informing her that the first concert went off admirabl] he communicates some circumstances of the secret history (the concerto in D minor, which will show to what a point Moza: had brought his practical skill and confidence in himself, eve before an accomplished audience.

"Wolfgang," he writes, "played a new and admirab] pianoforte concerto, on which the copyist was at work yeste day when we arrived, and your brother had not time to pla the rondo once through, because he was obliged to look over the copying. The concerto is in D minor."

If the idea of a concerto played without a single rehearsal or trial be surprising, how much more so must it appear when we remember the quantity the player wrote, and the little time that his fingers, cramped and contracted by holding the pen, had to recover their wonted freedom and agility.

There is little doubt but that rehearsals of the private concerts of Mozart, which would have exhausted more of time and money than the composer could well spare, seldom took place, at least, at Vienna, where he knew his orchestra; and that to examine the separate parts for the band was an ordinary practice with him. This precaution, with able readers and sight-players who apprehended his intentions at a glance, would, in some degree, supersede the necessity for rehearsal; but of the manner in which it heightened the labour, the risk, and the excitement, in the production of his concertos, the musician alone can judge. Let it not be imagined, that to create admiration at mechanical excellence in the rapidity and precision of his fingers was the principal object of Mozart; on the contrary, he kept closely within the original limit and signification of the term concerto, as a piece of combination for instruments, with a principal part for one in which all the bravura passages should subserve good musical ideas, and never be introduced for mere ostentation.

But there was one point in the old concerto in which the custom of the time obliged the artist to concentrate the whole energy of his being; to combine all the principal subjects in one magnificent *stretto* ; to exhibit his resources of fugue and canon; his mastery of effect, his promptitude of thought and action. The mark of the cadence ⌒ —discarded from the more mechanically difficult concertos of these degenerate times— when it ushered in, after a brief interval of silence, the improvisation of Mozart on the first performance of this concerto in D minor—how must it have exalted the fancy of his audience, and raised them on the tiptoe of expectation! It is not difficult to believe, that in these moments of extemporaneous invention the fingers of Mozart may have scattered even greater beauties than he has left in that great work—an effusion of passion and melancholy which from the first bar addresses the soul, like the opening of the overture to " Don Giovanni." [1]

[1] Of the coolness with which the renowned masters of the last century met the difficulties of the cadenza, an illustration may be given in the

A performer of these days, who was sufficiently an object o
interest to attract a large audience to six concerts in successior
would probably think it imprudent to weaken that interest b
exhibiting himself at the concerts of strangers. Such worldl
considerations, however, entered little into the theories c
Mozart, whose generous nature could not be induced to balanc
between prudence and friendship. Accordingly, the next da
after he had played with such success at the first of his ow:
subscription concerts—he performed another *new* concerto a
the Opera House for the benefit of Signora Laschi.

At this concert, the father, still an enthusiast in art, wa
not one of the least moved of the auditory. He thus describes it

"On the 12th of February, your brother played a magnifi
cent concerto which he has written for Paradies at Paris, at th
concert of Signora Laschi, in the Opera House. I was wel
placed in a good box, and had the pleasure to hear all th
changes in the instruments so admirably that the tears cam
into my eyes. On your brother's departure, the emperor too]
off his hat, complimented him, and cried, ' Bravo, Mozart!
As he went out after playing, the clapping and applause wer
without end."

We may conceive the composer to have been at this perioe
in the happiest disposition for music. There was a quarte
party at his house on the same evening, February 12, at whic]
Leopold Mozart and Joseph Haydn met for the first time
The father of Mozart, anxious to possess the opinion of th
most celebrated composer of the age, as soon as he found a:
opportunity of speaking privately to Haydn, inquired of hin
what he thought of his son. He refers to this in the followin
words:

"On the 12th, Joseph Haydn was with us. Three of th
latest of the new quartets were performed, namely, that in I
flat, A, and C major. They are certainly somewhat easier tha:
the three others, but admirably written. Haydn said to me
'I must tell you, before God and as an honest man, that
think your son the greatest composer I ever heard of—beside
his taste, he has a profound knowledge of compositions.'"

person of Handel. In setting " Il Penseroso " to music, and arriving a
the words, " There let the pealing organ blow! " he wrote the followin
directions for the organist: " Take the subject of the preceding chorus
and perform an extempore fugue upon it; " forgetting at the time, that t
do this well required a genius almost equal to his own.

It would be gratifying to know who were the performers on
ıis occasion. Mozart sometimes, though rarely, took up a
olin; his father, whom we know had been a good player in
ıe old school, was still equal to a second violin or tenor; and
aydn, though little of a practical musician, could sustain the
ınor part in a quartet. The two great composers were after-
ards heard to play together in a music party.

One of the friends with whom the composer was accustomed
ı play his four-handed pieces for the pianoforte was a Signora
artinas, an old lady, who kept house for her brother, a man
ı a great age. This ancient spinster, we are told by a con-
mporary, was reckoned a deep *blue*, and had even a reputation
r proficiency in the arts and sciences. The great poet
etastasio lived *sixty years* in her brother's house, upon the
ost friendly terms, and died in it. The colleges of Bologna
ıd Pavia gave her the title of *Dottoressa*, and deputations came
om both those places with her diploma. Although far advanced
 life, she still possessed the gaiety and vivacity of a girl. Mozart
as a constant attendant at her parties, and greatly admired
ır extraordinary musical taste, which Metastasio had had a
rge share in forming.

The visit of Mozart's father lasted six weeks. He was now
 declining health, much afflicted with the gout, and during his
hole stay almost constantly indisposed. However, what could
ı done to make the time pass cheerfully was done; he heard
usic at home and abroad; and was carried by his son to the
dge of the Freemasons, and initiated into the mysteries of that
aternity. But all the satisfaction that he could have derived
om witnessing the triumphs of his son and pupil, and from
alising, in one sense at least, the visions of success which had
ıunted him in former years, must have been sadly embittered
ɣ seeing that son still unappointed, unsettled, and left to the
.price and sport of accident. Leopold Mozart had long since
ıtered that poetical hell of Dante, which consists in ceasing to
ɔpe; but he could not cease to regret while he still felt the
·essure of injustice. The old musician, however, was still the
.me careful adviser and punctual correspondent. How anxious
 was that his daughter should participate in the news of
ienna, will be seen in the following fragments of his corre-
ondence.

" On the 14th of February your brother again played a
o

concerto at the Opera House. Concerts are going forwar
every day, and on the 15th he likewise played the new gran
concerto, in D minor, magnificently."

"February 21.—I attended your brother's second concer
which was again delightful. He plays to-day at Count Zichy's.

"March 12.—Your brother, who has also given an evenin
concert at the Opera House, made 559 florins by it, which w
did not expect, as he has a subscription list of more than 15
people, and has so often obliged others by playing in the
concerts as a favour."

"Since I have been here, your brother's pianoforte has bee
carried at least twelve times to the theatre, or to Princ
Kaunitz, or Count Zichy's. He has had a great *forte pian*
pedal made, which stands under the instrument, is about thre
spans long, and amazingly heavy."

"Torricella is engraving a pianoforte arrangement of 'D:
Entführung,' made by your brother, who up to this tim
however, has not completed his work. Torricella has alread
published three sonatas, but one only with the violin."

Leopold Mozart was continually pressing his son forwar
with this arrangement, fearful that some one else woul
anticipate him and reap the profit of his invention. The resu
justified his apprehensions. On the 16th of December 178.
he wrote to his daughter from Salzburg:

"That has now happened of which I had already warne
my son. A pianoforte arrangement of 'Die Entführung au
dem Serail' has been published at Augsburg, and one h
also been engraved at Mayence. Since March, when he con
menced, my son has not found time to complete the worl
He has therefore lost his labour and Torricella his expenses."

On the 19th of March he writes:

"I think that my son, if he have no debts to pay, migh
now place 2000 florins in the bank. The money has certainl
been earned; and the housekeeping, as it regards eating an
drinking, is in the highest degree economical."

Towards the end of March, Mozart's father returned t
Salzburg. When they shook hands and embraced at parting
it was for the last time. They never met again.

Shortly before this, the emperor had suppressed the institutio
for military music at Wartberg, over which Joseph Humme

father of the celebrated musician of that name, presided. Being thus left without any engagement, Hummel came to Vienna, where he soon succeeded in gaining the appointment of musical director to Schickaneder's theatre. His little son, scarcely seven years old, had already shown such talent for music, especially for the pianoforte, as to have attracted the favourable notice of the principal musicians at Vienna, and amongst others of Mozart. Whatever repugnance the great master may have felt towards the business of instruction, he was so pleased with the promising ability of this boy as to offer to superintend his education, provided he could have him in his house and continually under his eye. The proposal was accepted with gratitude: little Hummel was seated at Mozart's piano, and in two years made such progress as to delight every one with his smooth, brilliant, and rounded execution. His first public appearance was in a concert given by his master at Dresden.[1]

The adoption of this child into his family afforded fresh scope for the kindly workings of the musician's nature; his own childhood, and the anxious solicitude of his good father, must have recurred to his memory. His lessons we can imagine to have been rather desultory; but upon a mind disposed to learn, and capable in some degree of appreciating the greatness of the teacher, the fleeting observations of Mozart would make permanent impression. The master kept an eye on his pupil's progress, by deputing him to play any new music which he was desirous to hear, and which he would else have played himself. The following relation, derived from one of the members of the family, may give a view of the interior of the composer's abode, and at the same time show the manner in which Hummel profited.

At a late hour Mozart and his wife return home from a party. On entering their apartment the boy is discovered stretched on chairs, fast asleep. Some new pianoforte music has just arrived which they are both anxious to hear. Mozart, however, will not play it himself, but tells his wife (by her domestic name,

[1] Though Hummel afterwards became the pupil of Clementi, and in later years introduced a style of execution of his own, the original stamp of Mozart's school was too strong in his performance to be ever entirely effaced. In cantabile and scale passages, his playing seems to have greatly resembled that of his master. While a boy in Mozart's house he had made the acquaintance of Haydn, who much admired him. They both met in England in 1791, when Haydn wrote a beautiful pianoforte sonata in A flat for Master Hummel, who played it at the Hanover Square rooms, in the presence of the composer. Hummel, on a visit to this country a few years ago, still spoke of his boyish delight at having received from Haydn, on this occasion, his thanks, accompanied by a guinea!

Stänerl [1]) to wake up Hans, give him a glass of wine, and let him play. This is no sooner said than done; and now, should anything go wrong, there is an opportunity for suggestions. It is in fact a lesson, though given at the rather unusual hour of midnight.

Attwood, who at a somewhat later period was placed under the superintendence of Mozart, always spoke of his master with regard; but said of him, that he would at any time rather play a game at billiards with him than give him a lesson. This indeed, may be easily believed.

There was no end to the exertions which he made to advance those pupils who interested his friendship in their behalf. Whatever they wanted he wrote for them. The Abbé Stadler, the intimate friend and discerning admirer of the master, placed his niece under the care of Mozart, for instruction on the pianoforte and in the science of harmony. For her sake he commenced theorist, and actually wrote a treatise on thorough bass, which has been published, but is little known. The Abbé Stadler (whom the writer of these pages had the pleasure to meet at Vienna in 1827) seemed to cherish his personal recollections of the man, even more warmly than those of the artist.[2] He gave proof of this in the violent discussion which shortly afterwards arose in Germany respecting the authenticity of the "Requiem." Though at least eighty years of age, the venerable abbé grasped the pen in behalf of Mozart, and defended his fame with the vigour and earnestness of youth.[3]

The cantata "Davidde Penitente" was produced in the spring of 1785. The committee of the society for the relief of the widows and orphans of musicians wished to celebrate their festival by some new work, and engaged Mozart to compose an oratorio. As the time was short, he took the "Kyrie" and "Gloria" of his votive mass in C minor, and employed himself in placing Italian text under the music. The new pieces which

[1] The diminutive for Constantia in the Upper German dialect.

[2] The works entitled, *Fundament des General-Basses*, von W. A. Mozart, Berlin, 1822, and *Kurzgefasste General-Bass-Schule*, von W. A. Mozart, Steiner and Co., Vienna, were put together on the foundation of these MS. examples in composition, which were at the lady's death left as a memorial to her uncle. "Whenever I look over these pages," said the abbé, "I well remember the great master, and his manner of setting to work in giving instruction."

[3] The Abbé Stadler was originally professor of theology in the Benedictine Abbey of Mölk. He was an admirable organist, and is described by Gerber as one of the few who excelled in the conduct and treatment of an extempore fugue.

ιe wrote were an air for Adamberger, "A te frà tante affanni;"
ι bravura air, with introduction in C minor, for Mademoiselle
Cavallieri, "Tra l' oscure ombre funeste," and a trio for two
ιoprani and a tenor in E minor, a composition of the most
ιeautiful and original kind.

The entire work, with its additions, consists of ten movements;
ιnd, singular as it may appear, the oratorio which, originating
n this way, some might expect to be patched or bungled, is
ιonsidered by the best judges to exhibit one of the purest
ιxamples of Mozart's church style. In originality, and elevation,
n the various treatment of the subjects, and above all in *keeping*,
' Davidde Penitente " ranks among the greatest productions
ιf modern times.[1]

In the middle of this year he composed several songs, an
ιrchestral dirge for the Freemasons' Lodge, on occasion of the
leath of a distinguished brother of the house of Mecklenburg
ιnd Esterhazy, and the pianoforte quartet in G minor. This
ιork, which it may be thought would have formed an era in the
lomestic performances of the day, was intended as the first of
. set for which Hofmeister, a music publisher at Leipsic, had
ontracted. Its reception, however, was so unfavourable, that
Iofmeister freed himself from his obligation with respect to
he rest by making the composer a pecuniary compensation.
Iozart wrote the second of the set now known under his name
bout a year later, immediately after the composition of
Figaro; " the first of that set, as has already been stated, is
n arrangement from a quintet. Two original pianoforte
uartets are therefore all that we possess from his hand.[2]

Before Weber, Ries, and Mendelssohn had contributed to
ιe stock of chamber music for the pianoforte, violin, viola, and
ioloncello, the pianoforte quartets of Mozart formed the sole
ιsource of musical families who found pleasure in that kind
f instrumental combination. Thus, during a long series of
ears, they were reiterated and hackneyed, until it has fared in
ιrtain quarters with them as in others with some of the finest
ιssages of Shakspeare, debased by vulgar use and association;

[1] This work, hitherto only partially made known in England, through
ιe exertions of amateur societies, will, it is to be hoped, be shortly intro-
ιced to the same general notice at our festivals as it has received in
ιrmany. It is interesting to contrast its style and form with those of
s earlier masses, and even with the " Requiem." The final chorus is
teemed by continental critics as the " queen of vocal fugues."
[2] Five are stated in the catalogue, but they are unknown in England.

their original beauty has been obscured by familiarity. But those who bring sensibility, taste, and unprejudiced organs to the hearing of these works, will confess that compositions of more exquisite refinement and purity of style never fell from the pen of musician.

It was the misfortune of Mozart, that his genius was in advance of his age.

Compelled by his necessities to produce, and, at the same time, by his conscience towards the art to write up to his own standard of excellence, he never enjoyed an amount of sympathy adequate to his unlimited faculty of invention. This want of sympathy, amongst other evils, brought poverty in its train; and he who, above all other composers, must have been conscious of his power of creative beauty, and confident of his reception with posterity, found it a difficult matter to live without degrading himself to the vulgar taste.

From July to November 1785, three entire months, the catalogue affords no evidence of composition, and all we can attribute to that period is the correction of the engraving of the quartets dedicated to Haydn. In November, Mozart wrote a quartet and terzet; the latter, the admirable "Mandina amabile," for the opera of "La Villanella rapita;" and on the 28th of December following, he informs his father, at Salzburg, that he has been obliged to get up three subscription concerts in haste, that he has 120 subscribers, and that he has composed a new concerto in C minor for the occasion, the andante of which he was obliged to repeat.

It is necessary to observe, as a peculiarity of the concerts at Vienna in Mozart's time, that the audience were entertained with minuets and trios like those of symphonies played by an orchestra between the intervals in the appearance of the singers and solo-performers. This fact, for which M. André is the authority, accounts for some compositions of this kind found among the MSS. of Mozart, and not belonging to any symphony

From a letter of Leopold Mozart to his daughter, dated November 11, 1785, we learn that the composer was already engaged in preparations for his opera, "Le nozze di Figaro;" but they were only preparations, as other engagements intervened; and the actual score was not commenced until the April following.

The musical history of Vienna, for some few years, may now be said to have formed an epoch in that of the art itself. The

unexampled confluence of high genius and decided talent in
composition, the presence of numerous singers of rare powers,
any one of whom might alone have occupied the attention of
the public, and the energy of production conspicuous in the
lyric drama, render the traditions of the time highly interesting.
Although Gluck had resigned the pen, yet his tragic operas,
' Alceste," " Iphigenia," etc., were performed, from time to
time, with great splendour and effect; and the superintendence
of the rehearsals drew the veteran musician from his retirement
—amusing him, without exposing his feeble health to the
injurious excitement of original composition. Salieri, who was
obsequious to Gluck, and as his professed disciple hoped to
inherit some of his laurels, added to his industrious efforts in
composition the most strenuous exertions to oppose the growing fame of Mozart. This, his position of Kapellmeister to the
court, and consequent influence with the singers his countrymen, gave him many opportunities of doing; but when he had
exhausted all the resources of cabal and intrigue,—when he had
done his utmost to raise a party in his favour among the ladies
who surrounded the emperor—there remained for him but one
effort more, which was to bring out a new work by himself,
or some one of his party, to compete with any new work of
Mozart's; and in this way to divide and distract public attention. Thus Martini's opera, " Una Cosa Rara," brought
forward at the same time with " Figaro," being light and
superficial music, created a *furore*—which, with respect to the
latter, was only partially the case; and when Mozart, highly
disgusted with the reception of his music at Vienna, and driven
thence to Prague in quest of a fitter audience, returned with
the score of " Don Giovanni," he found Salieri ready to oppose
him with " Tarrare," or " Axur," as it was then called. Party
is the natural offspring of party; but it would be unjust as
well as degrading to the league of amity in which Mozart,
Paesiello, and Storace lived, mutually attracted by their
sympathy in art, and by their candid natures, to refer their
association to any origin of this kind. Their friend Haydn,
sheltered at least from the storms of theatrical life, wrote on in
his peaceful study, in the green seclusion of Prince Esterhazy's
country residence—almost realising the patriarchal idea of the
shade of his own vine and fig-tree.

It is highly to the credit of England that Storace was enabled
to make so good a figure as he did among his celebrated con-

temporaries. He was by no means an idle man at Vienna—a hanger-on in the train of his sister, content to depend for notice on her adventitious superiority; on the contrary, he had claims of his own which he exerted. The first opera that he brought out at Vienna was produced on the occasion of the Duke of York's first visit to the theatre, and failed from a singular accident. In the middle of the piece, Signora Storace suddenly lost her voice, and could not utter a note. In this state of incapacity she remained for five months; but on her recovery she made her brother ample amends by performing in another opera of his, called the "Equivoci," adapted by Da Ponte from the "Comedy of Errors." This opera, which had a long and brilliant career, established the musical reputation of Storace at Vienna.[1]

The very early age at which these laurels were won must not pass unnoticed. Storace was at this time but two-and-twenty; his friend Mozart was seven years older. Independently of their musical enthusiasm, a strong congeniality of temperament and mutual inclination for the pleasures of society attached them to each other. Mozart selected Signora Storace for the *prima donna* of his forthcoming opera of "Figaro." Storace highly admired Madame Lange, Mozart's sister-in-law, and thought her execution the most brilliant he had ever heard— surpassing even that of Bastardella herself. Among the points of sympathy in the two musicians, their juvenile passion for arithmetic is one of the most remarkable.

It is related of Storace, that when a boy, studying music under his father, he received a bravura song of Bastardella's to copy. He was so astonished that fifty guineas should be paid for *singing a song*, that he counted the notes in it, and calculated the amount of each note at 4s. 10d. He valued one of the divisions running up and down at £18 11s. There is a lurking satire in this whimsical estimate, betokening talent, and worthy of the powers which Sheridan thought fit to praise.

The adventures of the English party must have afforded infinite merriment to the private circle of their friends. The laughter-loving, good-humoured Signora Storace was always committing some *guacherie* in the etiquette of high life, or involving herself in some ludicrous distress. Even the Emperor

---

[1] The composer introduced some of the music of the "Equivoci" into the opera of the "Pirates," and into the after-piece, "No Song, no Supper."

'oseph, whose numerous oddities of behaviour made sober
pectators laugh, was himself unable to resist her *naïveté*.[1]

The goodness of heart and generous qualities of this lady
night be celebrated in as many instances as her eccentricities,
.nd they must have rendered her society, whether musical or
itherwise, extremely agreeable.[2] In the parties given by the
itoraces, the music was sometimes of a remarkable character,
.s will appear by the list of performers at a quartet entertain-
nent described by Kelly.

First violin	.	.	. Haydn.
Second violin	.	.	. Baron Dittersdorf.
Tenor	.	.	. Mozart.
Violoncello	.	.	. Vanhall.[3]

An equally celebrated audience, among whom were Paesiello
.nd the poet Casti, honoured this quartet of composers by
iving them their attention. At the supper which followed,
here is no doubt but that Kelly displayed symptoms of that
enial temperament, and nice discrimination in the art of good
.ving, in which he afterwards rose to such eminence when
oasting oysters and drinking champagne with Sheridan.

The powers of mimickry with which the " beardless stripling "
s Kelly calls himself, was gifted, were mainly instrumental to
.is success on the stage, and must have contributed much to his
avourable reception in private society. Paesiello, he informs
.s, was much " diverted by his monkey tricks." Among the
·ersons upon whom this talent in mimickry had been exerted
/as one who was well known to all the company at Storace's.
'his was the Abbé da Ponte, the author of the *libretti* of " Don

---

[1] One day she was driving in the Faubourg to witness a fête, when the
mperor rode up, asked if she was amused, and if he could do anything
ir her. Storace, with her characteristic bluntness, said, " Why, Sir, I am
ery thirsty, will your majesty be so good as to order me a glass of water? "
'he emperor turned round and directed one of his attendants to bring it;
ut one can easily imagine the consternation of her companions at this
ompliment to the sincerity of the Emperor of Austria.

[2] We remember with pleasure the monument she helped to erect in the
.bbey Church at Bath, to her master Rauzzini, and the legacy of £1000
·hich she bequeathed to the Royal Society of Musicians.

[3] Whether Kelly's memory did not deceive him with respect to the
·lative positions of Haydn and Mozart in this memorable quartet, may
e questioned. Haydn played the tenor very well, but it is doubtful
·hether he was sufficiently master of the violin to lead a quartet. Mozart,
n the contrary, had been a concerto player. While, however, we have
ie interesting fact of a quartet performance by this assemblage of sym-
honists, accuracy in the details of the anecdote is a matter of minor
nsideration.

Giovanni," " Figaro," and some other works made immortal by music. Kelly describes his life as one of singular transition. By birth a Venetian, and originally a Jew, he turned Christian, dubbed himself an abbé, and then became a great dramatic writer. The profession of Da Ponte, and his situation of poet to the opera, where he was well known as a lounger, made him a favourable mark for Kelly, who, though so young, was particularly successful in hitting off every variety of old age and oddity, and who accordingly brought Da Ponte on the stage the first opportunity that presented itself.

" My friend, the poet," he says, " had a remarkably awkward gait, a habit of throwing himself (as he thought) into a graceful attitude by putting his stick behind his back, and leaning on it; he had also a very peculiar dandyish way of dressing; for in sooth the abbé stood mighty well with himself, and had the character of a consummate coxcomb. He had also a strong lisp and broad Venetian dialect."

It must be added that the abbé recognised himself in the caricature; and what is more, saw that every one else, including the emperor, knew him; but yet he took the ridicule in good part, and with a forbearance not unbecoming the Christianity he had assumed.

The satisfaction with which Mozart participated in all that interested or amused his English friends, may be conceived from the fact that during the following year of their acquaintance he had been fully persuaded to make preparations for rejoining them in England. Of this more in its place.

During his subscription concerts of the winter of 1785-6 he appears to have produced selections from the opera of " Idomeneo." At all events that work was not unknown to the higher musical circles of Vienna; indeed it would appear, by the evidence of the catalogue, that " Idomeneo " was given at this time in some private society of amateurs; as Madame von Puffendorf, Baron Pulini, and Count Hatzfeldt performed in it.

The first production of the year 1786 was " Der Schauspiel Director," composed by desire of the Emperor Joseph for the entertainment of the court at Schönbrun. Mozart calls it " a comedy with music," and his work consists of an overture, two airs, a terzetto, and vaudeville. Supported by such singers as Madame Lange, Mademoiselle Cavallieri, and Adamberger, this piece, which is intended to display the embarrassments of the director of a theatre in dealing with rival candidates for favour, must have afforded considerable amusement. It was the business of the composer here simply to exhibit in an apt and humorous musical form the extraordinary compass and execution of the singers for whom he wrote; and no one certainly could execute a task of the kind with more dexterity and tact. But all interest in the " Schauspiel Director " departed with the occasion for which it was produced, and the original performers. The overture alone remains, an agreeable and spirited composition in the Italian style.

The all-engrossing subject of Mozart's thoughts during the spring of the year was " Le Nozze di Figaro," an opera likewise undertaken at the suggestion of the Emperor Joseph. This work, which has maintained its place on the stage and in the drawing-room for nearly sixty years in continuation is justly considered, for its extraordinary wealth of melody, the variety of its syle, and the perfection of its concerted music, as one of the most wonderful trophies of human skill.

The libretto adapted by Da Ponte from the well-known comedy of Beaumarchais seems to have satisfied Mozart, and the subject to have possessed unusual charms for him, if we may judge by the rate at which he worked. The whole opera was written in the course of April. The marvellous finale of the second act, consisting of six grand pieces, occupied him for two nights and a day, during which he wrote without intermission. In the course of the second night he was seized with an illness which compelled him to stop; but there remained a few pages only of the last piece to instrument. During the month of May the composer was occupied in teaching the singers and superintending the rehearsals. It is remarkable that the experienced friends of Mozart trembled for the reception of this opera; and the father, who well knew the musical politics of Vienna, and the state of parties there, writes to his daughter, April 1786, in these doubtful terms:

" The first stage rehearsal of ' Le Nozze di Figaro' will take place on the 28th. It will be fortunate if the opera succeeds, for I know that there are immensely strong intrigues against it; Salieri and all his tribe will move heaven and earth to put it down. Duschek lately said to me that the reason of your brother's having such strong cabals against him, is the high estimation which he has gained by his uncommon talents and skill."[1]

Salieri and Righini, being at this time ready with operas, were both competitors with Mozart for preference; and the contest between the composers was so warm that the emperor was obliged to interpose, and he decided for " Figaro." Some eagerness of rivalry seems to have been pardonable on an occasion which is rendered memorable by the unequalled talent of the singers, and the extraordinary congress of composers assembled at Vienna. Rarely, if ever, has it happened to a musician to submit his composition to such an ordeal as Mozart did " Figaro,"—and few have been the instances in dramatic annals in which men of such renown as Haydn, Mozart, Gluck, Paesiello, Storace, Salieri, Righini, Anfossi, etc., have been collected under one roof to witness the first performance of an opera, as it is no improbable surmise that they were on this occasion.

The rehearsals went off favourably;[2] but on the first night

[1] The Duschek, or Dussek, here mentioned, was a musician of Prague, and a pupil of that Wagenseil who " *understood the thing.*" His wife, one of the most celebrated singers of Germany, was also an admirable performer on the piano and harp, and a thoroughly scientific musician. The acquaintance of the Dusseks with the Mozart family was of old standing, the composer having begun to write for Madame Dussek before his journey to Munich in 1777. The connection of these musicians with the opera of " Don Giovanni," which will hereafter appear, gives them a certain prominence in the history of the composer, independently of the great talents of the lady, which inspired Mozart with some of the finest productions of his genius.

[2] Kelly, who claims to have sung " Crudel perché " with the composer, just as it had fallen fresh from the pen, gives a lively account of the first rehearsal. Alluding to this occasion, he observes: " I remember Mozart was on the stage with his crimson pelisse and gold-laced cocked hat, giving the time of the music to the orchestra. Figaro's song, ' Non più andrai, farfallone amoroso,' Benucci gave with the greatest animation and power of voice. I was standing close to Mozart, who, *sotte voce*, was repeating, ' Bravo, bravo! Benucci; ' and when Benucci came to the fine passage, ' Cherubino, alla vittoria, alla gloria militar,' which he gave out with stentorian lungs, the effect was electricity itself, for the whole of the performers on the stage, and those in the orchestra, as if actuated by one feeling of delight, vociferated ' Bravo! bravo! maestro. Viva! viva grande Mozart! ' Those in the orchestra I thought would never have ceased applauding, by beating the bows of the violins against the music desks. The little man acknowledged, by repeated obeisances, his thanks for the distinguished mark of enthusiastic applause bestowed upon him." What a transition this, from the midnight solitudes in which, animated by a great idea, he could not rest till he had delivered himself of it! Had it been the acclamation of a crowded house at a performance, instead of a spirited scene at a rehearsal, it might have been better; still, it was the voice of truth, which he seldom heard save in his own music.

if the performance there was a cabal among the singers, which
obliged Mozart to go between the first and second acts to the
box of the emperor, where he pointed out in great agitation
the danger his music was incurring. The refractory performers
were brought back to their duty by royal interference. For
an account of the opera during the second and third nights we
must extract a sentence from a letter of the composer's father,
dated May 18th, 1786.

"At the second representation of 'Le Nozze di Figaro' at
Vienna there were five, and at the third, seven pieces encored
—and among them a little duet which was sung three times."

These encores, which seem indicative of the growing popularity
of the opera, were, notwithstanding, of transient effect, and the
balance of parties was decidedly adverse to Mozart.

It is well ascertained that the profits of the third representation, which were to reward his labour, proved so inconsiderable
as in no degree to ameliorate his circumstances; and so discouraged was he with the reception of "Figaro" that he
resolved never more to produce an opera at Vienna. This
resolution he indeed waived through change of circumstances
and motives of private benevolence, but his dissatisfaction with
the musical taste of that city is well known.[1]

Among the performers who sustained the original cast of
characters in "Figaro," Mozart could certainly reckon upon
some friends. According to his memorandum on this opera
they consisted of the following female singers—Storace, Laschi,
Mandini, Bassani, and Nanina; the men were Benucci, Mandini,
Ochely, and Bassani. We may be curious to know who of this
party were enthralled by sinister influences; but the facts
cannot now be ascertained. The intrigues of the day may well
give place to a few considerations on the work itself. What the
lyric drama gained by this opera in elegance of melody, in
models of love songs, in rich concerted music, and varied finales,
is the question at present; and that we are well able to
determine. While all the popular melodies of the comic operas
coeval with "Figaro" (tunes which were regularly transferred
from the theatre to the street musicians) are lost, not a note of
that composition has faded; and when reproduced it still finds
as many enthusiastic admirers as a comedy of Shakspeare. The

[1] To expect nothing became a habit with him. On completing a great
work he would say, "I shall gain but little by this; but I have pleased
myself, and that must be my recompense."

combination of playfulness and grace which predominates in i
imparts to " Figaro," according to some critics, a more decide
Mozartean character than any other of his works.   Every on
may certainly find in it something to please.   The musiciar
for instance, listens with delight to the bass of the first due
or to the admirable instrumentation of the song in which th
page is trying on the cap.   What wealth of beauty in place
comparatively unnoticed!   Those who like to combine deligh
ful music with a laugh, may find both in the duet in whic
Susanna describes the behaviour of the count when her brid
groom is gone on his travels.   The deprecatory interjections (
poor Figaro, " *Susanna pian pian*," call up the most pleasar
recollections.   It were endless to pursue this opera through a
its materials for pleasure.

The favourite piece of the composer was the sestett
" Riconosci in questo amplesso."

" Le Nozze di Figaro " is the third dramatic piece which i
composer had produced by desire of the Emperor Joseph, th
whole of whose splendid patronage had hitherto consisted i
setting Mozart to work, and in repaying him by an occasion:
bow in public; by granting him a general facility of acces
and treating him with a great store of what Parson Evans in th
play contemptuously calls " *good worts*."   It is worth while i
contrast the two patrons of the composer, the Emperor Josep
and the Archbishop of Salzburg, for the sake of the light the
reflect upon his character.   The emperor, who spoke respec
fully of his art, but gave him nothing, inspired him with a degre
of attachment that almost brought his understanding int
question; while the archbishop, who provided him with son
means of existence, coupled with insults and degradations, w;
the object of his unmitigated dislike.

Throughout the remainder of the year in which " Figaro
was produced, Mozart appears to have been full of a plan f
settling in England.   At the commencement of 1787 the fath
of the composer writes to his daughter:

" Wolfgang proposes to me certain terms to undertake tl
care of his two children, as he is desirous of making, in tl
course of next spring, a tour through Germany to Englan
where he seems not disinclined to settle.   His scholar, Attwoo
however, who is to precede him in London, is to assure him
some certainty in advance, either through an engagement f

an opera, or by subscription concerts. Madame Storon (Storace) appears to have made his mouth water, and the whole plan has been set on foot through her conversation and that of his scholar (Attwood). As I have, however, written to him a fatherly letter, telling him that he will make nothing by a journey in summer; that he will arrive at an improper season in England, and be certainly 2000 florins out of pocket, which may involve him in distress—Storace being positively engaged to write the first opera—he may possibly be disheartened."

Notwithstanding these representations, it appears that the scheme of a journey to England proceeded so far that, after loitering over it for several months, they at last determined to go, and everything was packed up for their departure, when the appointment of Mozart as chamber composer to the emperor, accompanied by a pension, took place, and broke up his plans.

It will be seen that the English musicians now at Vienna were not exempt from the nationality which is so characteristic a foible of our travellers, and that they had not omitted to describe their own country as the true home of the artist, and the centre of all possible perfection. In persuading him to join them on their return they obeyed the impulses of enthusiastic friendship —Stephen Storace generously postponing his own claims as a composer, to the pleasure of introducing Mozart personally in England. If prosperity were ever reasonably augured in the life of an artist, it would appear to be so on this projected expedition. The death of John Christian Bach had left a void at court which it required a man of genius to supply; the Italian opera languished for the pen of Mozart, while from the pianoforte-playing world he might have richly shared in the patronage bestowed on Clementi and Dussek. What impediment, indeed, would there have been to his following up the career of Handel?

Mozart's winter concerts, in 1786, were distinguished by the first production of some of the finest of his compositions, and it was at this time that Beethoven, then a youth just entering on his musical career, came on a visit to Vienna, where a few years after Mozart's death he finally settled. He was introduced to the composer, and became for a short time his pupil. Seyfried, who has recorded some particulars of the interview, remembers that Mozart gave Beethoven a subject to extemporise upon, and while he was working it, said to some persons, who were standing near him in an adjoining apartment: " Listen to that young

man; he will some day make a noise in the world." [1] After
intermitting the composition of symphonies for three years,
Mozart now produced his symphony in D (with the introductory
adagio), a work in which we first notice a certain elevated
character in the slow movements, as peculiar to the composer,
and at times reaching the sublime.[2] At these concerts also
were first heard the grand pianoforte concerto in C, known as the
posthumous concerto, and the scena and rondo, "Non temer,"
with pianoforte obligato, which last was sung by Signora
Storace. His approaching separation from the Storaces, who
were to set off for England early in the next year made him
desirous to commemorate their friendship by some acceptable
memorial. He accordingly produced this work, and, in inserting
it in his catalogue, placed the names of the performers in friendly
conjunction—"for Mademoiselle Storace and myself." To
have inspired so inimitable a production is a lasting credit to the
singer and to English art.

Early in February 1787, Mozart saw these friends on their
way to England, and was moved to tears in bidding them adieu.
He furnished them with an introduction to his father, by whom
they were shown all the curiosities of Salzburg. They found
Raff still alive, and heard him sing; and the archbishop's
orchestra was much improved.[3]

[1] Beethoven esteemed Mozart and Handel most of all composers, and
next to them Sebastian Bach. If ever I found him with music in his hand,
or on his desk, it was sure to be that of one of these mighty men.—Schindler's *Life of Beethoven*, vol. ii. p. 291.

[2] It is claimed for Mozart to have first raised the symphony to its true
standard, by his impassioned and poetical effects; of which a *decrescendo*
in the andante of the present one affords a striking example. Chronology
"the eye of history," awards him this distinction.

[3] From this tour Storace brought to England, and introduced into the
orchestras of our English theatres, the German effects of wind-instruments
and a method of instrumentation before unknown. He survived his friend

In the very same week that he parted from his English friends, Mozart himself set out upon a journey to Prague, whither he had been very cordially invited by a distinguished nobleman and connoisseur, Count John Joseph Thun, who maintained in his service an excellent private band. This was the first professional expedition of any consequence in which he had engaged since his settlement in Vienna; it was prosecuted under the most favourable auspices, and with glowing anticipations of that pleasure for which he so ardently longed, but so imperfectly realised at home—the entire sympathy of the public. Nor was he disappointed. On the same evening that he alighted at the castle of his noble entertainer, his opera of ' Figaro ' was given at the theatre, and Mozart found himself for the first time in the midst of that Bohemian audience of whose enthusiasm and taste he had heard so much. The news of his presence in the theatre quickly ran through the parterre, and the overture was no sooner ended than the whole audience rose and gave him a general acclamation of welcome, amidst deafening salvos of applause.

The success of " Le Nozze di Figaro," so unsatisfactory at Vienna, was unexampled at Prague, where it amounted to absolute intoxication and frenzy. Having run through the whole previous winter without interruption, and rescued the treasury of the theatre from ruinous embarrassments, the opera was arranged in every possible form; for the pianoforte, for wind-instruments (garden music), as violin quintets for the chamber, and German dances; in short, the melodies of " Figaro " re-echoed in every street and every garden; nay, even the blind harper himself, at the door of the beer-house, was obliged to strike up " Non più andrai " if he wished to gain an audience, or earn a kreutzer. Such was the effect of the popular parts of the opera on the public at large; its more refined beauties exercised an equal influence on musicians. The director of the orchestra, Strobach, under whose superintendence " Figaro " was executed at Prague, often declared the excitement and emotion of the band in accompanying this work to have been such, that there was not a man among them, himself included, who, when the performance was finished, would not have cheerfully recommenced and played the whole through again.[1]

Mozart five years; dying in 1796, in his thirty-third year, of a cold caught being carried from a sick-bed to attend the rehearsal of the " Iron Chest " Drury Lane Theatre.

[1] In the good old times of the opera in London, before long ballets and

Finding himself, at length, in a region of sympathy so gen
and delightful, a new era in the existence of the composer seem
to open, and he abandoned himself without reserve to
pleasures.   In retracing a life so ill-rewarded by contemporari
and so chequered by calamity, it is pleasant to dally awhile
the primrose path, and enjoy the opening prospects of go
fortune.

In a few days he was called upon to give a grand concert
the opera house.   This was in reality his first public appearan
and many circumstances conspire to render it memorable; b
chiefly that every piece throughout the performance was of l
own composition.   The concert ended by an improvisation
the pianoforte.   Having preluded and played a fantasia, whi
lasted a good half-hour, Mozart rose; but the stormy and ou
rageous applause of his Bohemian audience was not to
appeased, and he again sat down.   His second fantasia, whi
was of an entirely different character, met with the same succe:
the applause was without end, and long after he had retir
to the withdrawing-room he heard the people in the thea
thundering for his re-appearance.   Inwardly delighted, he p:
sented himself for the third time.   Just as he was about to beg
when every noise was hushed, and the stillness of death reign
throughout the theatre, a voice in the pit cried " *from Figar*
He took the hint, and ended this triumphant display of skill
extemporising a dozen of the most interesting and scienti
variations upon the air " Non più andrai."   It is needless
mention the uproar that followed.   The concert was altogetl
found so delightful that a second, upon the same plan, so
followed.   A sonnet was written in his honour, and his p
formances brought him one thousand florins.   Wherever
appeared in public it was to meet testimonies of esteem a
affection.   His emotion at the reception of " Figaro " in Prag
was so great that he could not help saying to the manag
Bondini, " As the Bohemians understand me so well, I m
write an opera on purpose for them."   Bondini took him at

the reiteration of the flimsy compositions of modern Italy had lowered
animal spirits of the performers, there was not less enthusiasm here.
recollect to have heard, on the conclusion of a rehearsal of " Figaro,"
first bassoon express precisely the same thing.   It was an especial fe
to the leader and the first bass: Spagnoletti and Dragonetti revelled in
accompaniments, and gave a tone of enjoyment to the orchestra.   W
pleasure has Mozart dispersed among musicians alone!   And as long as
natural and healthy sensations at musical beauty last, this pleasure
all its freshness, will be revived from time to time.

word, and entered with him, on the spot, into a contract to furnish his theatre with an opera for the ensuing winter. Thus was laid the foundation of " Il Don Giovanni."

The remaining few weeks which this journey occupied were given to pleasure. Many balls took place; Mozart's pen was in requisition for the music, and in this act of kindness the great musician's career as the Strauss and Lanner of his day appears to have commenced. For the future not a carnival passed without numerous contributions to its dance music from his pen; and, unfortunately, such was the degraded state of patronage, that he found in this unworthy resource the surest means of subsistence.[1]

On returning to Vienna he lost no time in writing to the members of the opera orchestra at Prague, ascribing the greater part of his late success to their able execution of his music, and thanking the director, M. Strobach, very gratefully for the attentions he had received. This slight incident shows that pride and ingratitude formed no part of his nature.

The new and busy life on which he had entered since quitting Salzburg, and the great fame which his compositions were establishing, in no respect altered the original simplicity of his character. Filial piety had always distinguished him, and the following letter of April 4, 1787, written on occasion of the intelligence of the alarming illness of his father, shows that the feeling remained unaltered.

" MON TRÈS CHER PÈRE!—I have just received some news which has given me a sad blow; the more so, as your last letter left me reason to suppose that you were in perfect health. I now, however, learn that you are really very ill. How anxiously I await and hope for some comforting intelligence from you I need hardly say, although I have long since accustomed myself in all things to expect the worst. As death, rightly considered,

---

[1] His easy manner of dispatching these things is seen in a story, which may remind the reader of Sheridan. A certain count, master of the ceremonies at Prague, had requested Mozart to write some country-dances; and had been promised them, but by some accident they were not forthcoming. The count had recourse to a trick. He invited the composer to dinner, informing him that on this occasion it would be served an hour earlier than usual. On his arrival at the appointed time, the master of the house ordered the necessary writing materials to be brought, and pressed him to fulfil his promise for a ball that was to take place on the following day. Thus ungenerously entrapped, Mozart set to work, and in less than half an hour was ready with four country-dances for a full orchestra.

fulfils the real design of our life, I have for the last two year
made myself so well acquainted with this true friend of man
kind, that his image has no longer any terrors for me, but mucl
that is peaceful and consoling; and I thank God that he has giver
me the opportunity to know him as the key to our true felicity
I never lie down in bed without reflecting that, perhaps (young
as I am), I may never see another day; yet no one who know:
me will say that I am gloomy or morose in society. For thi:
blessing I daily thank my Creator, and from my heart wish it
participated by my fellow-men.

" I hope and trust that while I write you are getting better
but should this, in spite of all our hopes, not be the case,]
beg that you will not conceal it from me, but write, or lei
some one write to me the real truth, in order that I may be
with all possible speed in your arms. I conjure you to do this
by everything that we esteem holy. Meantime, I trust that]
shall soon receive a more favourable letter from you."

As the composer did not make this journey, it is likely that
a favourable change occurred in the condition of the invalid;
but a fatal turn shortly afterwards took place, and on the 28th
of May, 1787, Mozart lost his father. He died at Salzburg, in
his 68th year, a solitary man, and in a condition which the
exertions of his children were not able to remove many degrees
from absolute necessity. The clouds which lowered over his
declining days were of darker hue than ordinary, even in the
history of artists; and it is impossible to recall to mind his
simple and irreproachable life, his numerous virtues, his refined
tastes and quiet enthusiasm, without affording him the deepest
sympathy. His estimation in the eye of posterity, as the father
and instructor of such a son, will always be great, and not less
certainly than it deserves to be, when it is considered how much
of Mozart's perfection was the result of judicious education.

From the time that the first parental tears of joy and wonder
bedewed his cheeks, his whole life was a course of self-sacrifice,
anxiety, and forethought; animated by high religious principle,
he believed himself to be discharging a sacred trust. But the
successful result of his labour demanded a strenuous exertion
of faith; for, in educating a man of the greatest genius he had
only produced an unfortunate being far in advance of his age,
and the more exposed to envy and malevolence, and a subject of
more bitter persecution on that very account. Had he looked

hrough the history of the world to examine the strange circum-
tances in which men of the highest influence on the intellectual
rogress of mankind often fulfil their destiny—themselves
uffering the hardship and injustice—others reaping the delight
nd the profit of their lives—he could not have found a more
erplexing chapter than that furnished by his own son.   Nothing
ertainly could equal his disappointment.   He had been so much
nterested in the youthful performances of his son, that at one
ime he intended to write the narrative of his life, and desired
hat all the letters to which his tours gave occasion should be
arefully preserved for that purpose.   But as time wore on, this
ask, which promised to revive unpleasant recollections, was
bandoned.   The musical part of his correspondence alone has
een made public; but many of his letters, particularly those
rom Italy, abound in statistical and descriptive passages, and
bservations on manners and customs, which are the more
nteresting from their reference to a period when that country
ras not the trite theme of tourists.   The passages relating to his
rivate affairs and intentions were written in a cipher which
ecured them from the spies of the archbishop.   In his last years
eopold Mozart became no very encouraging correspondent;
nd the hasty letters of a few lines each which he received from
me to time from his son at Vienna, were no longer to be found
t his death.
In reviewing the compositions of the most prolific years of
Iozart, we are struck, not merely with the number of fine
iinor productions which cluster round his greatest works and
iow the activity to which his genius was excited—but that so
iany of these productions are still landmarks to the artist,
xhibiting excellence achieved in totally new paths.   Thus,
efore " Le Nozze di Figaro," we find the concerto in C minor;
onspicuous for its fine combination of the wind instruments
nd the pianoforte; immediately after it a pianoforte quartet,
t that time a new combination in chamber music, and written
i a style which found little favour with the musicsellers.
hen came, at no great interval, the magnificent pianoforte
uet in F major; in which the ideas are orchestral, and of greater
ignity than had ever been displayed in music for that instru-
ent.   These are not merely new compositions, but important
ages in the advancement of the art.
Thus also, in a short month from April to May 1787, stringed
strument music for the chamber acquired fresh distinction

from the two quintets in C major and G minor, in which two tenors beautify the score and add richness to the harmony. These works show the variety of powers that Mozart brought to composition; the great organist and contrapuntist—the profound master of harmony and rhythm are there—but taste and imagination ever preside. The quality of these productions can, in fact, only be estimated by the attempts which musicians have been making ever since to attain some credit in the same path.[1]

Mozart was obliged to suspend all application to his art during the month of July, in consequence of an illness which threatened his life. That he had had more than one attack of this character since his settlement in Vienna may be ascertained from his own testimony.

His friend, Dr. Siegmund Barisani, first physician to the general hospital at Vienna, who, it seems, was a connoisseur in music, had written some verses in the album or memorandum book of the composer. After complimenting him on his masterly pianoforte playing, and the variety and magnificence of his genius, the writer gives a very elegant and affectionate turn to his address: in the midst of all a composer's triumphs, he is not to forget one who recollects with alternate pride and pleasure that he has twice served him in the capacity of physician, and prolonged a life which contributes to the pleasure of the world—but whose greatest pride is still to be called his friend. In the autumn of 1787, the doctor was suddenly carried off, and the composer wrote immediately under the lines paraphrased:

" To-day, the 2nd of September, I have had the misfortune to lose, through an unexpected death, this honourable man, my best and dearest friend, and the preserver of my life. He is happy!—but I—we, and all who thoroughly knew him cannot again be so—till we have the felicity to meet him in a better world, never again to separate. MOZART."

The want of the kind attentions of this benevolent physician may have hastened a state of things which led to the premature dissolution of the composer, whose health, tried by frequent night-watching and fits of excessive application, began at this

[1] Mingled with these great productions we find songs and other trifles of which the titles are sufficient to excite curiosity as to their secret history. Among them are " The Concealment," " The Parting," " Louisa Burning the Letters of her Faithless Lover," " Evening Feelings," etc.

ne to experience a material change. He was well aware of his ɪgile tenure of existence, and we learn from the letter which : wrote to his father, April 4, 1787, that death was much in s thoughts. He was, however, by no means so familiar with e countenance of " the great queen of sepulchres " as to be :tirely at ease in contemplating it; on the contrary, those ›out him knew that he was at times much disquieted by the ᴏught of death. In this weakness he shared with many ɪaginative people of more robust organisation.

In September 1787, we find him in the country, composing ʀenades and sonatas for piano and violin. The summer- ›use in a garden continued to be his favourite resort for com- ›sition, as numerous inscriptions on his MSS. evince. He dates ɪrious pieces from the country-house of his friend, M. Gottfried ›n Jacquin, for whom he wrote the fine scena, " Mentre ti scio."

Having now completed all his arrangements for " Don iovanni," he set off on a second expedition to Prague, accom- ɪnied by his wife. Not a note of the music of his opera was as ːt upon paper, but he had thoroughly digested the subject in s mind. The original libretto, entitled " Il Dissoluto punito ːsià Il Don Giovanni," was adapted by Da Ponte from the ɔanish tale, " El combidado de piedra," of Tirso de Molina; ɪd of all the dramatic subjects treated by Mozart, this appears › have taken the strongest hold on his imagination; from the ːginning to the end he has sustained it without a symptom ː fatigue. On reaching Prague, he first took up his quarters ː the inn called the Three Lions, in the Coal Market; but sub- ːquently removed to his friend Dussek's, who resided at a ɪneyard at Kosohitz, in the picturesque suburbs of the city. ꞁere, on an elevated site, which commanded a view of the ntique magnificence of Prague, its faded castles, ruined cloisters, nd other majestic remains of feudal times; under the mild ɪys of an autumnal sun, and in the open air, " Don Giovanni " ·as written.[1] Dussek's house was a scene of great resort and

---

[1] While this work was in progress, he was called upon to conduct " Le ˙ozze di Figaro " in the presence of Prince Antony of Saxony and his wife ꞇaria Theresa, sister to the Emperor Francis. The rehearsals took place ɴder the personal superintendence of the composer, and they gave occa- ᴏn to show his management of the lady performers. Onᵉ of these, at ɪe rehearsal of " Figaro," did not sing in a voice that satisfied Mozart; e obliged her to use more power, and exert herself to a degree that made er somewhat angry. When the song was ended, he did not apologise to er, but perfectly restored her good-humour by a " *Brava Donzella !* "

revelry while Mozart was his guest; and it is remembered, that there was often considerable playing at bowls in his grounds In the midst of all the talk and laughter with which this amusement was attended, the composer pursued his work, but rose from time to time when it came to his turn to take part in the game.[1]

"Il Don Giovanni " was finally completed, excepting the overture, on the 28th of October 1787, about six weeks after Mozart's arrival at Prague. The parts were given out to the singers as they were finished, and the composer rehearsed them privately with each, while the rest of his work was in course of completion. A week only was left for stage rehearsals; from which fact, much previous study, and a good general notion of the business of the drama, are to be presupposed.[2]

[1] The original score of this opera is written on various kinds of music-paper, apparently the first that came to hand. Nothing more happily illustrates the decision of Mozart, who never made sketches, or retouched compositions; though we now and then find him improving a thought in the act of writing.

[2] In directing the first rehearsal of his opera, he was obliged to stop the orchestra at the scene in the cemetery, " Di rider finirai," " Ribaldo audace," etc., as one of the trombone players did not execute his part correctly. The scene was originally accompanied by three trombones only. As the passage after repeated attempts had no better success Mozart went to the desk of the player and explained to him how he would have it done. The man, who was a crusty fellow, answered with some rudeness, " It is impossible to play; and if I can't play it, I am sure you can't teach me." " Heaven forbid," returned the composer, smiling, " that I should attempt to teach you the trombone; here, give me your part, and I will soon alter it." He did so on the spot, and added two oboes, two clarionets, and two bassoons. The coincidence of the modulation in this celebrated scene, and of the oracle in the " Alceste " of Gluck, is remarkable. Mozart has, however, strikingly improved upon his model, and increased the solemn and unearthly effect of the voice of the commendatore by terminating on the fifth of the key. The original Zerlina of the opera was Signora Bondini, daughter of the manager. In rehearsing that part of the finale of the first act, where she is seized by Don Giovanni, there was some difficulty in getting her to scream in the right manner and place. It was tried repeatedly, and failed. At length, Mozart desiring the orchestra to repeat the piece, went quietly on the stage, and awaiting the time that she was to make the exclamation, grasped her so suddenly and so forcibly that, really alarmed, she shrieked in good earnest. He was now content. " That's the way," said he, praising her, " you must cry out just in that manner."
He gave at this time a fresh instance of his extraordinary memory. The drum and trumpet parts to the finale of the second act of " Don Giovanni " were written by him without the score—from mere recollection. He brought them himself into the orchestra, and giving them to the players, said, " Pray, gentlemen, be particularly attentive at this place," pointing to one, " as I believe that there are four bars either too few or too many." It proved to be as he had said. The brass-instruments have frequently no place in the original scores of Mozart. He wrote them continually on a separate paper, carrying the composition in his memory at the time.

Everything went so smoothly and comfortably in the production of this opera, that the time was one of great enjoyment to the composer. At the conclusion of the first rehearsal, he went out walking with the organist and orchestra-director, Kucharz. Among other confidential talk, the discourse fell upon the new opera, and Mozart asked, " What is your opinion of ' Don Giovanni? ' It is quite of a different character to Figaro: ' do you think that it will please as much? "

On receiving an encouraging reply he continued:—" Your assurance quiets me; it comes from a connoisseur. But, indeed, I have spared neither labour nor pains to produce something extraordinary for Prague. It is a very great error to suppose that my art has become so exceedingly easy to me. I assure you there is scarcely any one who has so worked at the study of composition as I have. You could hardly mention any famous composer whose writings I have not diligently and repeatedly studied throughout."

The people of Prague were charmed by his affability of manners and unassuming demeanour. Niemtschek, his biographer, who remembered him well, says, " His friends at Prague think with joy on the delightful hours they have passed in his society, and can never sufficiently extol his kind, innocent heart. They might have entirely forgotten that they were in the presence of Mozart, the great composer."

The time passed in festivities of various kinds, and the composition of the overture to " Don Giovanni " was entirely neglected until the night of the 3rd of November 1787. This was the eve of his great triumph. A large party was assembled at Dussek's, and Mozart was enjoying himself with them, apparently thoughtless of the overture. As usual overflowing with ideas, he had that day been at work for his hostess, Madame Dussek, and had produced for her the exquisitely scientific scena, " Bella mia fiamma: " a composition by which her style

Recit. Andante.

and attainments as a singer are effectually characterised. His friends, however, became uneasy, and one of them said to him, " Mozart, the first performance of ' Don Giovanni ' is to-morrow, and you have not yet written the overture." He appeared to consider awhile, and about midnight retired to his apartment, desiring his wife to make him some punch, and to stay with him to keep him awake.[1] The overture was ready by the morning; but the copyists were less diligent or less successful with their work. The opera should have commenced at seven in the evening; but there was no overture, and the crowded theatre was kept waiting until a quarter to eight, when the parts were hastily brought into the orchestra covered with sand, and with them entered Mozart to take his place as conductor. His appearance was greeted by the general applause of the theatre, and the un-rehearsed overture was then commenced. During its perform-ance the audience gave many signs of repressed pleasure, which at length broke out into a loud exclamation. When the curtain rose, and the first scene of the opera was going forward, Mozart said to some of the musicians near him, " The overture went off very well on the whole, although a good many notes certainly fell under the desks." He was well acquainted with the talent of the orchestra of Prague, and it is not unlikely that this most unusual exhibition of an overture played without rehearsal was a designed compliment to it.[2]

Thus, with no other inducement than love for his art, and attachment and gratitude to his audience at Prague, Mozart produced another great work, combining the labour of the greatest melodist, symphonist, and master of dramatic ex-pression ever united in the same individual. Whether we regard the mixture of passions in its concerted music, the pro-found expression of melancholy, the variety of its situations,

[1] Schlictegroll thus records the circumstance, which has been confirmed by the widow herself: " She accordingly began to tell him fairy tales, and odd stories, which made him laugh till the tears came. The punch, however, occasioned such a drowsiness, that he could only go on while his wife was talking; as soon as she ceased, he dropped asleep. The efforts which he made to keep himself awake, the continual alternation of sleep and watching, so fatigued him, that his wife persuaded him to take some rest, promising to awake him in an hour's time. He slept so pro-foundly that she suffered him to repose for two hours. At five o'clock in the morning she awoke him. He had appointed the music-copiers to come at seven, and by the time they arrived the overture was finished."

[2] The original cast of the characters was as follows:—Don Giovanni, Signor Bassi; Donna Anna, Signora Saporiti; Donna Elvira, Signora Micelli; Don Ottavio, Signor Baglioni; Leporello, Signor Felice Ponziani: Don Pedro ed Masetto, Signor Lolli; Zerlina, Signora Bondini.

he beauty of its accompaniment, or the grandeur of its heighten-
ng and protracted scene of terror—the finale of the second act—
' Don Giovanni " stands alone in dramatic eminence. Of all
nusical romances it is certainly the first.

He received about one hundred ducats for this opera—a
lender consideration, which was a little augmented by the sale
f scores to the theatres of Vienna and Warsaw; but when he
ound how badly his opera was got up at Vienna, he regretted
hat his necessities had prevailed with him to let it be played.
' ' Don Giovanni,' " said he, " was rather written for Prague
han Vienna, but chiefly for myself and my friends." It is an
xtraordinary fact that the " Tarrare " of Salieri, which was
rought forward at Vienna with Mozart's new opera, far out-
tripped it in popularity.[1]

The criticism which the Viennese made upon his last operas
ried his forbearance to the utmost. He had heard it said
f " Figaro," that it was " too difficult," and " too much spun
ut for a comic opera; " and now he heard of " Don Giovanni,"
hat for a romantic opera it was ", too learned — too much
rowded with effects of scientific harmony."

Criticism of this kind—" faint praise " qualified with blame,
vas bestowed on " Don Giovanni " by an assembly of com-
osers and dilettanti at the house of Prince Radziwill, where
hat work was performed soon after its production. Haydn,
vho had long sat silent at this party, was at length appealed to.
' It is difficult to decide," said he, " among your various
pinions. All I know is," he added with vivacity, " that Mozart
s the greatest composer now existing."

He expressed himself yet more strongly in a letter dated
December 1787. Bondini, the manager at Prague, who had
rospered considerably with " Don Giovanni," now wished for
n opera buffa by another great composer, and commissioned
. friend to write to Haydn on the subject. In reply, Haydn
hinks it would be possible only with an entirely new libretto,
nd adds—

" Even then it would be a bold attempt, as scarcely any one
an stand by the side of the great Mozart. For were it possible

---

[1] At this distance of time, it appears strange that an opera known only
or one tolerable round should have had the success described. But the
ortune of works, when backed by the influence of living composers, and
vhen submitted afterwards to the tribunal of posterity, is often very
lifferent. " Tararre " is now only named with a smile, or to provoke the
nquiry, " What was it all about? "

that I could impress every friend of music, particularly among the great, with that deep musical intelligence of the inimitable works of Mozart—that emotion of the soul with which they affect me, and in which I both comprehend and feel them, the nations would contend together for the possession of such a gem.   Prague ought to retain him, and reward him well too; else the history of great genius is melancholy, and offers posterity but slight encouragement to exertion, which is the reason, alas! that many hopeful and aspiring spirits are repressed. I feel indignant that this *unique* Mozart is not yet engaged at some royal or imperial court.   Forgive me if I stray from the subject—but I love the man too much."

The Emperor Joseph himself, who saw Mozart in a most unsettled state, bringing out his operas in remote places, and likely to abandon Vienna altogether, thought it now high time to interpose with some solid testimony of favour, and accordingly sent him the appointment of chamber composer to the court, with a promise that in future his interest should be cared for.   There was not the least intention of acting upon this promise; but it was deemed fitting to grace the miserable sinecure with something in prospect.   Before the emperor could make up his mind what to give, he consulted his page, Strak, as to the sum necessary for the sphere of life in which Mozart moved.   This M. von Strak had been repeatedly at musical entertainments at the composer's house, and it might be thought would have seized the occasion to place him at his ease.   He was, however, too good a courtier to alarm the parsimonious monarch by naming a liberal sum;   and therefore boldly answered eight hundred florins.   This paltry pension, which barely defrayed the rent of the apartments of Mozart, commenced towards the end of the year 1787.   In writing to his sister at this time, he endeavours to make as favourable a representation of his *munificent* patron as he can.

" With regard to your question respecting my appointment, I must inform you that I now belong to the imperial chamber, and am regularly and formally installed, but *for the present* with eight hundred florins only;   there is, however, no other musician of the chamber who receives so much."

The first announcement of the composer in his new office appeared on the play bills of " Don Giovanni " at Vienna.   In in age when a free artist—a composer living solely by the resources of his talent, was a most unusual spectacle—even this trivial distinction might and did give pleasure. But Mozart soon found that his condition was substantially unaltered; he was mortified at having an appointment void of duties, and from which no reputation could possibly accrue. He accompanied one of the receipts of his stipend with a sealed note containing the words, " Too much for what I do—too little for what I could do: " a stinging epigrammatic remonstrance, which, however, produced no effect.

About this time, shortly after his return to Vienna, the long and eventful career of Gluck was brought to a close by a renewed attack of apoplexy. In dramatic accent, as well as in harmony and melody, this composer had so much in common with Mozart as to render it somewhat surprising that his works are now almost confined to the cabinet of the musician, while those of his contemporary still keep possession of the stage. But the reason will become obvious when it is considered that the interest in the operas of Gluck is maintained by short airs and short choruses, which form inseparable parts of a great whole; and artfully contrived scenes, in which he moves no step without the immediate inspiration of the poetry and situation; while Mozart, on the contrary, fills up the scantiest outline from his invention, wandering at will, as he somewhere describes himself, in the mere luxury of imagination. How then does it happen that the one who requires the theatre and an entire connected representation, should no longer keep possession of the stage, while the other, who furnishes such exquisite morsels for the concert-room and the chamber, still exercises his sovereignty there? For this simple reason, that in order to preserve popularity on the stage it is necessary to supply the audience with music which they can carry out of the theatre—music which can be retained alone, and can charm by itself without the help of dramatic auxiliaries. It is because Mozart's operas are crowded with passages that wing their flight into the concert room, and the chamber, that they have always maintained their influence on the stage. Another circumstance may also be referred to as giving them continual freshness—the choice of subjects; which are almost invariably derived from the romance of real life, affording greater scope for variety of style and contrasts of passion; while Gluck's operas are exclusively founded on remote and barbaric themes. Mozart, with his

nervous and playful genius, keeps within the range of ou
sympathies—Gluck deals with materials that lie beyond then

During the year 1788, Mozart made no excursion, bu
remained at Vienna, patiently waiting some of the benefit
to be anticipated from his new office. The rumour of a wa
with Turkey, which now filled the puplic mind, and formed
very popular subject of allusion in the minor theatres, altogethe
depressed the interests of music, and enabled him the better t
bear his proportion of the general neglect. At the commence
ment and close of the year, we find him writing orchestra
minuets, waltzes, and country-dances, for the court balls—
works which were of a better market value than operas, and t
which he could fortunately have recourse when pressed for th
means of existence. Meanwhile, it is extraordinary that h
nature was not " subdued to that it worked in; " and that in th
intervals of this inferior occupation, his genius so soon regaine
its wonted elasticity. His compositions this year were unusuall
numerous: and though their occasional insignificance preclude
the idea of his having written them from his own choice, the
seem little calculated for extensive popularity. Composin
gratuitously to supply the wants of a large acquaintance, it :
difficult to tell whence he drew his means of subsistence; an
the inquiry now would be the more useless, since it is prett
certain that he hardly knew himself.

The distinguishing feature of the year 1788 was the pro
duction of the three symphonies:—in E flat, G minor, and th
Jupiter, which rapidly succeeded each other during the spac
of about six weeks from the 26th of June, and were the last of h
productions of this kind. When he collects his powers for som
grand effort, and throws the whole of his strength, fancy, feelin
and invention into a congenial work, then we see Mozart in h
true character. We discern him especially in these symphoni
which are as dissimilar from themselves as they are distinc
from everything else; which exhibit a mind making constar
advances, yet not content to produce, without at the same tin
giving an impulse to the art. Wonderful was the faculty whic
enabled him to dismiss from memory the composition ju:
finished; to disengage himself from the throng of pleasin
recollections, and bring forward a new face for each successivel
The family likeness is there—

——— facies non omnibus una
Nec diversa tamen;

but it is in an elegance and perfection elsewhere undiscernible
that we discover the parent.[1]   Instrumental music is so vague a
subject without notes to revive our pleasurable sensations, that
we gladly select a passage which shows the individuality of
Mozart in his method of bringing several subjects together, and
returning to his original theme by a sequence.   The whole of this
return (from the second part of the andante of the G minor symphony) is never heard but with renewed astonishment and delight.

For producing such music as this he suffered the usual penalty
attendant on bold innovation and anticipation of the future:
he was neither understood nor, of course, rewarded.   The

[1] The genius of instrumental music, of Mozart's especially, is beautifully
characterised in the following passage:—" The present strain seems not
only to recall, but almost to renew some past movement, another, and yet
the same!   Each present movement bringing back, as it were, and embody-
ing the spirit of some melody that had gone before, anticipates and seems
trying to overtake something that is to come; and the musician has
reached the summit of his art, when having thus modified the present by
the past, he at the same time weds the past in the present to some prepared
and corresponsive future.   The auditor's thoughts and feelings move
under the same influence, retrospection blends with anticipation, and hope,
and memory, a female Janus, become one power with a double aspect."—
Coleridge, *The Friend*, p. 170.

composers of instrumental commonplace immediately preceding, or contemporary with him, were provided for. Dr. Burney found Vanhall, though somewhat crazed in intellect, living at Vienna in comfortable retirement: his symphonies, which had been engraved in Holland, established his fortune. Dittersdorf, another symphonist of the day, who produced a series of works illustrative of Ovid's *Metamorphoses*, was rewarded by an addition of nobility to his name, and a post under the Austrian government.[1] Mozart alone was turned over to that unfailing patron of the muse—necessity. The pleasure he had in this kind of writing is apparent. He lingered with fondness over those productions, upon which he chiefly calculated for his reception with posterity. Of this the symphony in G minor affords an example: he returned to it, and made a second score, in which he added two clarinets to the two oboes, and, to make room for these instruments, altered the original in several places. In the adagio to the " Jupiter Symphony " he profited by an afterthought. That movement was originally intended to conclude at the cadence which precedes the last introduction of the subject; but the master, on reviewing his work, appended a coda, in which he reproduced the affecting and passionate strain of melody with which it now dies away upon the ear. If in haste to commit his ideas to paper he omitted anything, his review was decisive.

We may here take a picture of two great symphonists with a work still undergoing the process of gestation. Mozart when he washed his hands in the morning could never remain quiet, but traversed his chamber, knocking one heel against the other, immersed in thought. At table he would fasten the corners of his napkin, and, while drawing it backwards and forwards on his mouth, make grimaces, apparently " lost in meditation." Beethoven, in a fit of abstraction, would pour several jugs of water on his hands, " humming and roaring." After wetting his clothes through, he would pace up and down the room with a vacant expression of countenance, and eyes frightfully dis-

---

[1] The public taste for commonplace, and the composers who pandered to it, were satirised by Mozart in a composition which, though in its exterior a symphony consisting of an allegro, minuet and trio, adagio and finale, is only a joke (Musikalischer Spass), sounding " the basest string of humility." It must have cost him some pains so completely to divest himself of his genius, as he seems to have done in this production. He sometimes, though rarely, played with his art. The Germans possess a method of composing waltzes mechanically by means of throwing dice, the invention of which is ascribed to him. This principle of the musical kaleidoscope is thought to have been applied ere now to graver compositions.

ended.[1] Schlictegroll has observed that Mozart's physiog-
nomy was remarkable for its extreme mobility. The expression
changed every moment. His body also was in perpetual
motion; he was either playing with his hands, or beating the
ground with his foot.

Throughout this year of incessant occupation, discourage-
ment was gaining ground upon him, and the thinness of his
catalogue during 1789-90, when compositions appear only at
the rate of one a month, or even at longer intervals, affords con-
clusive evidence of the fact. The music-shops, as a source of
income, were almost closed to him, as he could not submit his
genius to the dictates of fashion. Hofmeister, the publisher,
having once advised him to write in a more *popular* style, or he
could not continue to purchase his compositions, he answered
with unusual bitterness, " Then I can make no more by my
pen, and I had better starve, and go to destruction at once."
The fits of dejection which he experienced were partly the effect
of bodily ailments, but more of a weariness with the perplexity
of affairs, and of a prospect which afforded him but one object
on which he could gaze with certainty of relief, and that was—
death. Constant disappointment introduced him to indulgence
which he had not before permitted himself.

He became wild in the pursuit of pleasure; whatever changed
the scene was delightful to him, and the more extravagant the
better. His associates, and the frequent guests at his table,
were recommended by their animal spirits and capacity as boon
companions. They were stage-players and orchestral musicians,
low and unprincipled persons, whose acquaintance injured him
still more in reputation than in purse. Two of these men,
Schickaneder, the director of a theatre (for whom Mozart wrote
the " Zauberflöte "), and Stadler, a clarionet-player, are known
to have behaved with gross dishonesty towards the composer;
and yet he forgave them, and continued their benefactor. The
society of Schickaneder, a man of grotesque humour, often in
difficulties, but of inexhaustible cheerfulness and good-fellowship,
had attractions for Mozart, and led him into some excesses that
contributed to the disorder of his health, as he was obliged to
retrieve at night the hours lost in the day. A long-continued
irregularity of income, also, disposed him to make the most of any
favourable moment; and when a few rouleaus of gold brought
the means of enjoyment, the champagne and tokay began to

[1] Schindler's *Life*, vol. ii. p. 178.

flow.[1] This course is unhappily no novelty in the shifting li
of genius, overworked and ill-rewarded, and seeking to thro
off its cares in the pursuits and excitements of vulgar existenc
It is necessary to know the composer as a man of pleasure,
order to understand certain allusions in the correspondence
his last years, when his affairs were in the most embarrass
condition, and his absence from Vienna frequently caused l
the pressure of creditors. He appears at this time to ha
experienced moments of poignant self-reproach. His love
dancing, masquerades, masked balls, etc., was so great, that l
did not willingly forego an opportunity of joining any one
those assemblies, whether public or private. He dressed han
somely, and wished to make a favourable impression in socie
independently of his music. He was sensitive with regard
his figure, and was annoyed when he heard that the Prussi
ambassador had said to some one, " You must not estimate tl
genius of Mozart by the insignificance of his exterior." Tl
extremity of his animal spirits may occasion surprise. I
composed pantomimes and ballets, and danced in them himse
and at the carnival balls sometimes assumed a character. I
was actually incomparable in Arlequin and Pierrot.[2] Tl
public masquerades at Vienna, during the carnival, were su
ported with all the vivacity of Italy; the emperor occasional
mingled in them, and his example was generally followed. V
are not, therefore, to measure these enjoyments by our cold
northern notions.

That these scenes of extravagant delight seduced him in
occasional indulgences, which cannot be reconciled with tl
purity of his earlier life, it would be the worst affectation in l
biographer to deny. Nor is it necessary to the vindication
Mozart that such temporary errors should be suppressed by
feeling of mistaken delicacy. Living in such a round of excit
ments, and tortured by perpetual misfortunes, there is nothi
very surprising in the fact that he should sometimes have be

[1] What effects even an occasional indulgence of this kind, when combin
with night-watching and composition, must have had upon his nervo
system, may be easily imagined. It was, indeed, to borrow a vulgar b
expressive metaphor—lighting the candle at both ends. The vice
ebriety was not, however, among Mozart's failings. His sister-in-la
Sophia, who has contributed the best anecdotes of his domestic li
testifies that she never saw him intoxicated;—he drank to the point
exhilaration, but not beyond.

[2] There is a tradition of his having also excelled in the character ol
quack doctor, in which he acquitted himself in prescriptions to his numerc
patients with great address and promptness of wit.

drawn into the dangerous vortex; but he redeemed the true nobility of his nature by preserving, in the midst of his hasty inconstancies, the most earnest and unfailing attachment to his home. It is a curious illustration of his real character, that he always confessed his transgressions to his wife, who had the wise generosity to pardon them, from that confidence in his truth which survived alike the troubles and temptations of their chequered lives.

But Mozart must be seen in quieter moods, and with other companions. One of his great favourites was Benedict Schack, an opera singer, and a devoted student to ecclesiastical composition. Their friendship had a pleasant trait. When Mozart called upon him that they might walk out together, and Schack retired to dress for the purpose, leaving the mass that he was composing unfinished on his desk, Mozart would take the pen and proceed with it.

He was still surrounded by his poorer brethren of the profession, to whom he was liberal of his time and labour even to excess. The quantity he wrote to oblige, could it be seen in the aggregate, would create astonishment. A volume of the airs, scenas, etc., written for various performers, his friends, to introduce into their parts in operas, has been published by Breitkopf and Härtel, of Leipsic, and is known to contain some of his finest things. These, however, form but a small part of his contributions to the cause of friendship and benevolence. A host of concertos, sonatas, and other instrumental productions, sufficient to have founded a lasting fame in that department of the art, remain to be placed in the same category of gratuitous labour. The works already referred to, under the date of 1783, as *entr'acts* to the tragedy of " König Thamos in Egypten," now better known as the motets "Splendente te " and " Ne pulvis et cinis," and generally employed as offertories and graduals in the Roman Catholic Church, were originally of this description. He wrote them for a manager at Vienna, named Schwerlich, reserving, however, the MSS. for himself; and three years afterwards he transmitted copies of the same work gratuitously to the distressed manager of the German theatre at Prague, whom they greatly assisted. In this manner the ill-rewarded Mozart was a constant benefactor to his indigent contemporaries. ' Nothing," says his biographer, Schlictegroll, " could extinguish his compassion for the unfortunate." He himself received many testimonies of esteem from persons unconnected with his

profession, in which the effects of his genius, or amiable dispos
tion, or both, are to be traced. One of his chief friends in time
of pecuniary difficulty was M. von Puchberg, a merchant o
Vienna, who continually lent him money. This gentlema
appears to have been an amateur performer on the double bass
and it is gratifying to trace his name in the catalogue of th
composer, as an evidence of the relation in which they stoo
The bass air, "Per questa bella mano," with its unique accompan
ment of contra basso obligato, was written for M. Puchberg.[1] Th
Baron von Swieten also afforded him assistance of the same kind

But one of the most remarkable instances of enthusiasr
awakened by his genius was exhibited in an humble station i
life, by one who had the advantage of knowing Mozart person
ally. A citizen of Vienna, named Rindum, excited by the mer
admiration of music, received the sick wife of the composer int
his house, where she had full opportunity, from the nature o
his business, to apply a remedy prescribed by physicians for
lameness which afflicted her. The cure was tedious, but Rindur
supplied everything necessary, and would receive nothin
for lodging or expenses. In estimating the immense musica
public whom Mozart has gratified, it would be unjust to om
those who have a purely natural taste, without pretensio
to connoisseurship. His operas are continually attended b
amateurs, who concentrate the pleasure of an evening in two o
three favourite melodies; no professedly scientific composer ha
ever embraced so large a class of this kind among his audience

With his own relations he lived like the most insignificant o
mankind; and his home, unfortunately, afforded but to
many opportunities for his sympathy in painful circumstance
During the year 1788, the principal scene of his labours seem
to have been the chamber of his sick wife, whose sister ha
commemorated his soothing attentions and anxiety to reliev
suffering, in an anecdote.

"I well remember a long illness, during which I attende
her for full eight months. I was at her bedside and Mozar
likewise, composing—both of us as silent as the grave; for afte
much suffering she had just sank into a sweet and refreshin
slumber. On a sudden a noisy messenger entered the apart
ment. Mozart, alarmed lest his wife should be disturbec

[1] Mozart, at the time of his death, was indebted 1000 florins to th
gentleman; this claim remained unsettled for some years, but was finall
liquidated by the widow.

ushed his chair back and rose hastily, when the penknife, which was open in his hand, slipped and buried itself in his oot. Although very sensitive to pain on ordinary occasions, e was now silent; but beckoned me to follow him into another oom, where I found that the wound was really a very serious ne. Johannisöl, the surgeon, attended him, and he was cured without his wife's knowing that an accident had happened; lthough the pain made him for some time lame in walking." [1]

The females of his wife's family, it is to be observed, all joined 1 his commendation as a husband and brother, and one reason f this certainly was the unselfishness which they perceived in im. In any turn of good fortune they all shared. They saw is genius, his application, and its rewards, and could not eproach him even with his errors; among the rest, with his nhappy choice of familiar companions, though this occasioned 1any a cause of secret regret.

Having glanced at some of the circumstances connected with the disorder and agitation of the last years of Mozart's ife, when melancholy, relieved only by an occasional extrava- ance of humour that heightened and confirmed the disease, ad become habitual to him, it is necessary to revert briefly to he history of his compositions during the year 1788, while the opes encouraged by the promises of the emperor, and by the nconsiderable appointment he had received as the earnest of uture favours, were yet fresh. His solo pianoforte music of his date is extraordinary from the character of the ideas which e thought fit to employ upon it. The sonata in F, from its peautiful style, fine counterpoint, and the regularity of the arts in which it is written, might pass as a quartet for stringed nstruments.

Allegro.

---

[1] The custom of attending an invalid had by this time grown so familiar o him, that he found a difficulty in discontinuing habits suitable only to he sick chamber. While his wife was ill, he met every one who came to ee her with his finger on his lips, as an intimation to them not to make . noise. For some time after her recovery this practice still remained; e spoke in a subdued tone of voice; and his abstraction was so great, that e even accosted his acquaintances in the street with his finger on his nouth, and with hushing whispers.

An adagio for the pianoforte solo in B minor, which is as elevated and severe in its style as anything in the " Passione " of Haydn, sets speculation to work as to its origin. The fine compositions in the appendix to " Don Giovanni " also distinguish the year 1788.[1]

After the completion of the three symphonies, the remainder of the original compositions of the year 1788 were but light work for the composer, and require no detailed observation. Their diversity is, as usual, interesting. A war song, two sets of canons for four and three voices, a divertimento, and a terzetto for instruments, and some country dances, bring us down to November, in which month he was occupied in putting additional accompaniments to Handel's " Acis and Galatea " for the Baron von Swieten. The original score of his work has never met the public eye, but remains to the present day in the archives of an amateur at Berlin; curiosity to view the first touches of this novel and, in ruder hands, hazardous process, cannot therefore be gratified. Mosel, the editor of the popular German version of Handel, states that Mozart made Handel's choruses the principal object of his study from the year 1788 to 1790. His opinion of that master is well known. " Handel," said he, " understands effect better than any of us; when he chooses, he strikes like a thunderbolt."

In commencing his delicate task, Mozart seems to have proceeded tenderly and with diffidence, for in the correspondence which passed between him and the Baron von Swieten, while engaged on it, he hopes to be encouraged and confirmed by his favourable opinion. The answer of the baron is dated March 21, 1789. The " Messiah " was then in hand.

" Your idea of changing the text of the frigid air into a recitative is excellent; and in the uncertainty whether you have received the words, I again send you the copy of them. He who can arrange Handel with such taste and solemnity as to accommodate him to the day, without detracting from the majesty of his compositions, must have felt and understood

---

[1] In this he introduced some of the singers who thought themselves neglected with regard to songs into more prominent situations in that opera. The fine song of Don Ottavio, " Dalla sua pace," was composed for Mr. Morella; the duet between Zerlina and Leporello, " Per quelle tue manine," for Madame Mombelli and Signor Benucci; and the recitative and aria of Elvira, " Mi tradi," for Mademoiselle Cavallieri. We are thus furnished with the names of the original representatives of these characters at Vienna, and the pieces he now supplied for them are in no respect inferior to those written in the first heat of production.

:m, and reached the very source of his inspiration. This is
' opinion of what you have done; it is not necessary for me to
' more than merely to express my wish to receive the recitative
soon as posible."

[t is probable that Mozart's first labours on Handel were
:h as we observe in the " Alexander's Feast," confined chiefly
 improvements of the effect—the substitution of one voice
: another—of air for recitative, or the contrary; avoiding,
 fact, the monotony which the old master did not care to
un, and enriching his harmonies, without adding new features.
it in the " Messiah " he grew bolder. The clarionet and the
ssoon parts in the air " Every Valley," introduced in passages
ere Handel had formerly accompanied the voice by a single
ss—and more remarkably still, in the bass song, " The People
at walked in Darkness "—are examples of innovation which
ually astonish and delight by their intrepidity and their
ccess. Here, doubtless, something is added beyond what
andel could have done, had he been familiar with the modern
ıployment of wind instruments—effects of harmony which
e certainly neither of his age nor style, and the propriety of
iich has been discussed by the critics for the last half century.
it the beauty of these additions has finally triumphed over
'ejudice; they are now generally adopted, and Mozart is
sociated with Handel in undying conjunction.
Though meditating on the grandeur of Handel in the winter
 1788, it was still important that he should not neglect his
d and kind patrons, the masters of the ceremonies at the
ıurt and carnival balls, who gave him employment, and re-
·mpensed him liberally for it. Between his operations on
Acis and Galatea " and the " Messiah," he wrote minuets
ıd waltzes for the full orchestra by the dozen, and probably
it better through the winter by this means than had he
:pended on appointments from the emperor.
In April 1789, Mozart left Vienna on a tour, in the company
 his pupil the Prince von Lichnowsky, who accommodated
m with a seat in his carriage as far as Berlin. The King of
russia had expressed himself favourably towards Mozart on
veral occasions; and the uncertainty of the composer's position
 the Austrian capital made it desirable that he should not
nit the chance of finding a new and more generous patron.
his was his first visit to those more northern capitals of

Germany in which the science of Sebastian Bach, and the
traditions of his school, flourished; and as everything strange
and beautiful which he heard influenced his genius, he collected
at this time many new views and designs of composition.

On the 10th of April he wrote to his wife from Prague:

"We arrived here to-day at half-past eleven o'clock, in
perfect safety.   Now, with respect to affairs at Prague—I went
immediately to Guardassoni, who has all but agreed to give me
200 ducats for the opera next autumn, besides fifty ducats for
travelling expenses.   Ramm left this place a week ago on his
road home.   He came here from Berlin, and said that the king
had spoken of me frequently and with great earnestness, and
as I had not arrived, he said again, *I fear that he won't come.*
Ramm was quite concerned, and endeavoured to assure him to
the contrary.   From this account it would appear that I shall
not do badly."

The opera referred to in this letter is "Cosi fan tutte."   How
much Mozart's fame had advanced since the composition of
"Don Giovanni" may be inferred from the fact of his now
being able to command a double price for his labour.   Guardassoni, with whom he engaged, was a contractor in theatres
and had several dramatic speculations on his hands at the
same time in the different capitals of Europe, from Vienna to
Warsaw.   This is the reason why the opera was agreed for at
one place and produced at another.

At Leipsic, where Mozart stayed to give concerts, he was
closely observed by an intelligent youth, who, with a presentiment of the famous master before him, preserved the
memorabilia of the time.   This was afterwards the celebrated
critic Rochlitz, whose authority confirms what is already known
of the ingenious method pursued by Mozart on his journeys
and with strange orchestras, to make his music go well.   We
have seen him ruffling the plumes of a fair singer at Prague;
he now angers an orchestra by design, to rouse their attention.
One evening he had been heard declaiming in a very animated
manner on the injury his compositions received by hurrying
the time.   "They think," said he, "to impart spirit and fire
by that means; but if there is no fire in the composition, it will
never get it by quick playing."

"The next morning at rehearsal Rochlitz remarked that he

took the first movement of one of his symphonies at a rapid rate. Scarcely twenty bars had been played before the musicians held the time back, and dragged. Mozart stopped them, explained what was wrong, then resumed the baton, cried *ancora*, and recommenced at the same rate of speed. The result was as before. He did everything in his power to keep up the time, and once stamped the bar with such force that his shoe-buckle flew in pieces. But all to no purpose. He laughed at his misfortune, let the fragments lie, again cried *ancora*, and recommenced for the third time in the same *tempo*. The orchestra, now thoroughly incensed with the little pale man who drove them on at such a rate, at length exerted themselves in earnest, and the movement went well.

"All that followed he took more moderately. And now it became the object of the composer to recover the good-will of the irritated orchestra, without, however, compromising the good effects to which his zeal had been directed. He praised the accompanying, and said, 'When gentlemen play in this manner, it can be of no use to rehearse my concerto, for the parts are all correctly written. You play right, and I too; what more can be done?' And at the performance the orchestra accompanied an uncommonly difficult and intricate concerto at sight with perfect correctness. After the rehearsal he said to some connoisseurs, 'Don't be surprised at me; it was not caprice. I saw that the greater number of the performers were men in years, and there would have been no end of the *dragging*, if I had not put some warmth into them by making them angry. Mere vexation at last made them do their best.'"

He played his posthumous concerto, and accompanied Madame Dussek in "Non temer," charming the hearer by the "melting tenderness of his execution." Strange concerts must these German concerts have been, at which the programme was so utterly disregarded. After performing two concertos, and accompanying for a couple of hours, some one wished to hear him play alone, and he began afresh in order to please everybody. There was little money in the house, and so all his acquaintance received a free admission, the chorus singers (an interesting class of enthusiasts) came by dozens, though there was nothing for them to do. When the Herr Kapellmeister was appealed to, "Oh, let them in; let them in!"

was the reply. A clever violin-player in the orchestra attracted
his notice. At the conclusion of the performance he takes this
musician aside, " Come home with me, ' dear Berger,' and I will
play a little more to you; you understand it better than most
of those who have just been applauding." They went away
together, and after supper Mozart extemporised fantasias till
midnight, then suddenly springing up, as was his custom, he
exclaimed, " Well! are you pleased?   Now you have heard
Mozart for the first time."

His reception by Frederick William II., of Prussia, was highly
favourable, and that monarch, who, though no great connoisseur, was a tasteful amateur of the arts, listened almost
daily to his extemporaneous fantasias, or engaged him in
quartet performances with the choicest artists of his private
band. From the letters of the composer, while sojourning at
Berlin, it would appear that he had been at Potsdam, thence
had returned to Leipsic, visited Dresden, and was back again
at Berlin. He writes from this place to his wife, on the 23rd
of May:

" The queen will hear me on Tuesday—*but there is not much
to be made.* I announced myself, because it is customary,
and she might else have taken offence. You must prepare
at my return to find your pleasure rather in me, than in the
money I shall bring. A hundred Friedrichs-d'or (*which he
appears to have received from the king*) are seven hundred of
the Vienna gulden. Lichnowsky was obliged to hasten away;
consequently my purse has been emptied at Potsdam, which
is a dear place; and I have besides been obliged to lend a
hundred florins to a person whom I could not refuse. Add
to this the failure of the concert at Leipsic, which I always
prophesied; but Lichnowsky would give me no rest, and I was
constrained to acquiesce in it. Here at Berlin there is little
to be made by concerts, as the king is not friendly to them.
You must, therefore, be content with getting me, together with
this good news, that I am in high favour with his majesty.
What I have written to you on this head is, however, between
ourselves."

This letter was written about a week before his return to
Vienna. But the numerous adventures and characteristic
anecdotes connected with the visits of the composer to Leipsic
and Dresden, render it incumbent on us to retrace our steps

nd somewhat invert the order of events in this place. One
f the warmest of his admirers at Leipsic was Doles, cantor
o St. Thomas's school, a pupil of Sebastian Bach's, and his
uccessor at that institution. In the company of this musician,
ιe went privately one afternoon to the organ in the church
ιf St. Thomas, at which Bach formerly officiated, and though
ιe had long omitted organ practice, played in so masterly a
tyle, that Doles, who was standing behind him, declared with
:motion that he could have believed old Bach to have risen
rom the grave. These accidental visits to the organ were
ιerhaps serviceable to him as a preparation for a famous en-
:ounter, hereafter to be noticed. The excellent organists of
ιutheran Germany—men "well up" in Bach's fugues and
rios, with obligato pedal, came about him with the humble
ubmission of their mechanical skill to the might of his science
ιnd invention. In the album of M. Engel, organist of Leipsic,
ιe wrote a little sportive fugue in G $\frac{6}{8}$, in Sebastian Bach's
ιanner, which he entitles in his own catalogue, "Eine kleine
ïigue" (a little jig).

The impression he received on first hearing the motets of
ïebastian Bach for a double choir was striking. Doles had the
ιleasure of astonishing Mozart by an admirable performance of
he eight-part motet, "Sing to the Lord a new Song," from the
ιupils of his own school, a chorus of about forty voices. Scarcely
ιad the music proceeded before Mozart started with an exclama-
ion, and then was absorbed in attention. At the conclusion
ιe expressed his delight, and said, "That now is something
rom which a man may learn." On being informed that Bach
ιas cantor to this school, and that his motets were venerated
here as reliques, he was eager to see them. No score being to
ιe obtained, they handed him the separate parts, and it was
ιteresting to observe his manner of reading them, holding some
ιn his hands, some on his knees, placing some on chairs around
ιim; seeming thoroughly lost to everything, and not rising till
ιe had thoroughly satisfied his curiosity. He requested to have
. copy of the motet which he had so much enjoyed. A young
ιan among the bass singers happening to attract his favourable
ιotice, he entered into conversation with him after the music,
ιnd taking an opportunity when unobserved, slipped a con-
iderable present into his hand.

It was now Mozart's turn to astonish Doles, with whom he
upped in high spirits the night before his journey to Dresden.

It was at the house of this friend that he most enjoyed himself, for there he found his own free and unconstrained behaviour reciprocated. About the time of separation, Doles said in a melancholy tone, "Who knows whether we shall ever meet again?—leave me a line or two from your hand." Mozart, who was rather more inclined to sleep than to write, did not at first comply; however, he said at last, "Well, papa, then give me a piece of paper." This was soon brought, and Mozart, tearing it in halves, sat down and wrote for five or six minutes. He then gave one half to Doles and the other half to his son. Upon the first leaf there was a three-part canon in long notes, without words. "We sang the notes," says Rochlitz, "and found it an excellent canon of a very mournful expression. Upon the second leaf there was also a three-part canon in short notes, without words; we sang this, too, and found it also excellent and very droll. We now remarked with pleasure that both of them could be sung together. 'Now for the words,' said Mozart; and wrote under the first, *Lebet wohl, wir sehn uns wieder* (Farewell, we shall meet again); and under the second, *Heult nicht gar wie alte Weiber* (Don't be crying like old women). We now sang it through again, and it is impossible to describe what a laughable, and yet profound—I may almost say, majestically comic—effect it had upon us, and, if I mistake not, upon himself too; for, exclaiming in a wild tone of voice, ' *Adieu, kinder !* ' he was gone."

He had peculiar gratification in shaking the diaphragm of " old Doles " by startling and extravagant jokes. Whether his canon, " Bona nox bista rechta ox " (in which we may depose on oath to Mozart's text as well as music), was sung at these Leipsic parties, is matter of speculation; but he certainly contrived to exhibit his just and ready criticism in a most humorous scene at the house of the cantor. Doles tolerated brilliant accompaniments in church music, and praised the mass of a composer who, with a decided talent for comic opera, had attempted to treat ecclesiastical composition in the same light manner. Mozart borrowed the score of this mass for a short time, and brought it back with fresh words under the music— some whimsical sentences of his own invention. The parts were distributed, and it was sung amidst the " zealous laughter profound " of the vocalists and of Mozart himself, who accompanied, calling out as well as he could, " Now—doesn't that go better? " He excused himself, however, to Doles for taking this somewhat free method of displaying the reasons for which music, good in itself, might yet be unfit for ecclesiastical purposes.

Whatever compositions he heard or read, instantly brought his critical faculty into exercise; and even some of his own music had scarcely grown four or five years old before his improving judgment discovered places in which alteration would be desirable. Thus, in playing an air from " Die Ent-führung " in private society, he was no longer satisfied with it for the theatre. " It may do well enough in this form for the chamber," said he; " but on the stage it is too long. At the time I wrote it I was never tired of hearing myself, and did not know how to bring my work to a conclusion."

His table talk in the musical society at Leipsic, of which he was the centre of attraction, affords many happy illustrations of his just discrimination. Discoursing on the merits of composers and composition, Paesiello was mentioned, and Mozart, who knew his works well, spoke very favourably of them. " Whoever seeks for light and pleasurable sensations in music," said he, " cannot be recommended to anything better."

His admiration of Handel was not confined to his choruses; he had a high opinion of many of his airs and solos. " However he may linger in the fashion of his day," said he, " there is always something in him."

Jomelli was a favourite. " The man has a path of his own, in which he shines; but he should not have quitted it to attempt to write church music in the old style. None of them all," he continued, " can be jocose or serious, raise laughter or create profound emotion, and both with equal success, like Joseph Haydn." The nicer qualities of the style of these masters were so well known to him that he could imitate them even to deception.

On this journey he appears to have formed the acquaintance of a certain baron, an amateur composer, who forwarded to him sundry compositions for the benefit of his opinion, accompanying them with what was probably more to the taste of Mozart—a present from his cellar. This gives occasion to an inimitable letter, characterised by extraordinary contrasts. Levity and sense, humour and melancholy, the most profound observations upon art, and the happiest turns of thought, are here mixed up with incoherent eccentricity and irresistible nonsense. Mozart is the same person that we have known from boyhood, but more masterly and rapid in his mode of dealing with composition:

"To the Baron V——.

"Herewith I return you, my good baron, your scores; and if you perceive that in my hand there are more *nota benes*[1] than notes, you will find from the sequel of this letter how that has happened. Your symphony has pleased me, on account of its ideas, more than the other pieces, and yet I think that it will produce the least effect. It is too much crowded, and to hear it partially or piecemeal (*stückweise*) would be, by your permission, like beholding an ant-hill (*Ameisen haufen*). I mean to say, that it is as if Eppes, the devil, were in it.

"You must not snap your fingers at me, my dearest friend for I would not for all the world have spoken out so candidly if I could have supposed that it would give you offence. Nor need you wonder at this; for it is so with all composers who without having from their infancy, as it were, been trained by the whip and the curses (*Donnerwetter*) of the maestro, pretend to do everything with natural talent alone. Some compose fairly enough, but with other people's ideas, not possessing any themselves; others, who have ideas of their own, do not understand how to treat and master them. This last is your case. Only do not be angry, pray! for St. Cecilia's sake, not angry that I break out so abruptly. But your song has a beautiful cantabile, and your dear *Fraenzl*[2] ought to sing it very often to you, which I should like as much to see as to hear. The minuet in the quartet is also pleasing enough, particularly from the place I have marked. The *coda*, however, may well clatter or tinkle, but it will never produce *music ; sapienti sat*, and also to the *nihil sapienti*, by whom I mean myself. I am not very expert in writing on such subjects; I rather show at once how it ought to be done.[3]

---

[1] "In the original stands *fenster*, windows, which signify passages marked ♯ for the sake of drawing particular attention to them."—*Note by the Translator.*

[2] The Baron's daughter.

[3] In illustration of this passage, which recalls one of the famous sayings of antiquity, I insert an anecdote of Mozart, preserved by the late Mr. Attwood. Soon after Attwood's arrival at Vienna, he showed a book of sonatas or lessons to the great composer, who glanced at them, and said, "I should have begun thus;" in another place, "this would have been my mode of proceeding;" writing on the spot new passages, which were exquisite improvements. Attwood always preserved this book as a trophy of the masterly skill of Mozart.

" You cannot imagine with what joy I read your letter; only you ought not to have praised me so much. We may get accustomed to the hearing of such things, but to read them is not quite so well. You good people make too much of me; I do not deserve it, nor my compositions either. And what shall I say to your present, my dearest baron, that came like a star in a dark night, or like a flower in winter, or like a cordial in sickness? God knows how I am obliged, at times, to toil and labour to gain a wretched livelihood, and Stänerl, too, must get something.

" To him who has told you that I am growing idle, I request you sincerely (and a baron may well do such a thing) to give him a good box on the ear. How gladly would I work and work, if it were only left me to write always such music as I please, and as I can write; such, I mean to say, as I myself set some value upon. Thus I composed three weeks ago an orchestral symphony, and by to-morrow's post I write again to Hoffmeister (the musicseller) to offer him three pianoforte quatuors, supposing that he is able to pay. Oh heavens! were I a wealthy man, I would say, ' Mozart, compose what you please, and as well as you can; but till you offer me something finished, you shall not get a single kreutzer. I'll buy of you every MS., and you shall not be obliged to go about and offer it for sale like a hawker. Good God! how sad all this makes me, and then again how angry and savage, and it is in such a state of mind that I do things which ought not to be done. You see, my dear good friend, so it is, and not as stupid or vile wretches (*lumpen*) may have told you. Let this, however, go *a cassa del diavolo*.

" I now come to the most difficult part of your letter, which I would willingly pass over in silence, for here my pen denies me its service. Still I will try, even at the risk of being well laughed at. You say, you should like to know my way of composing, and what method I follow in writing works of some extent. I can really say no more on this subject than the following; for I myself know no more about it, and cannot account for it. When I am, as it were, completely myself, entirely alone, and of good cheer—say, travelling in a carriage, or walking after a good meal, or during the night when I cannot sleep; it is on such occasions that my ideas flow best and most abundantly. *Whence* and *how* they come, I know not; nor can I force them. Those ideas that please me I retain in memory, and am accustomed, as I have been told, to hum them to myself. If I continue in this way, it soon occurs to me how I may turn this or that morsel to account, so as to make a good dish of it, that is to say, agreeably to the rules of counterpoint, to the peculiarities of the various instruments, etc.

" All this fires my soul, and, provided I am not disturbed, my subject enlarges itself, becomes methodised and defined, and the whole, though it be long, stands almost complete and finished in my mind, so that I can survey it, like a fine picture or a beautiful statue, at a glance. Nor do I hear in my imagination the parts *successively*, but I hear them, as it were, all at once (*gleich alles zusammen*). What a delight this is I cannot tell! All this inventing, this producing, takes place in a pleasing lively dream. Still the actual hearing of the *tout ensemble* is after all the best. What has been thus produced I do not easily forget, and this is perhaps the best gift I have my Divine Maker to thank for.

" When I proceed to write down my ideas, I take out of the bag of my memory, if I may use that phrase, what has previously been collected into it in the way I have mentioned. For this reason the committing to paper is done quickly enough, for everything is, as I said before, already finished; and it rarely differs on paper from what it was in my imagination. At this occupation I can therefore suffer myself to be disturbed; for whatever may be going on around me, I write, and even talk, but only of fowls and geese, or of Gretel or Bärbel, or some such matters. But why my productions take from my hand that particular form and style that makes them *Mozartish*, and different from the works of other composers, is probably owing to the same cause which renders my nose so or so large, so aquiline, or, in short, makes it Mozart's, and different from those of other people. For I really do not study or aim at any originality; I should, in fact, not be able to describe in what mine consists, though I think it quite natural that persons who have really an individual appearance of their own, are also differently organised from others, both externally and internally. At least I know that I have constituted myself neither one way nor the other.

" May this suffice, and never, my best friend, never again trouble me with such subjects. I also beg you will not believe that I break off for any other reason, but because I have nothing further to say on that point. To others I should not ιave answered, but have thought: *mutschi, butschi, quittle, etche, nolape, newing.*[1]

" In Dresden I have not been eminently successful. The Ɔresden people fancy themselves to be even yet in possession ɪf everything that is good, merely because they had formerly ο boast of a great deal. Two or three good souls excepted, he people here hardly knew anything further about me than hat I had been playing at concerts in Paris and London in a ;hild's cap. The Italian opera I did not hear, the court being n the country for the summer season. Naumann treated me n the church with one of his masses, which was beautiful, well ιarmonised, and in good keeping, though too much spread, ɪnd, as your C—— would say, rather cold (*e bieszle kühlig*). t was somewhat like Hasse, but without his fire, and with a ɪore modern *cantilena*. I played a great deal to these gentleɪen, but I could not warm their hearts, and excepting *wischi, ɪaschi*, they said nothing at all to me. They asked me to ɪlay on the organ, and they have most magnificent instruments. told them, what is the real truth, that I had but little practice ɪn the organ; notwithstanding, I went with them to the church. Ɪere now it showed itself that they had *in petto* another foreign ɪrtist, a professed organ-player, who was to kill me, if I may ay so, by his playing (*todt spielen*). I did not immediately ɪnow him, and he played very well, but without much ɪriginality or imagination. I therefore aimed directly at this tranger, and exerted myself well. I concluded with a double ugue, in the perfectly strict style, and played it very slowly, ɪoth that I might conduct it properly to the end, and that he hearers might be able to follow me through all the parts. Ɪow all was over. No one would play after this. Hässler, owever (this was the stranger's name—who has written some ood things, in the style of the Hamburg Bach), was the most ood-natured and sincere of them all, though it was he whom had endeavoured to punish. He jumped about with joy, nd did not know how to express his delight. Afterwards he ɪent with me to the hotel, and enjoyed himself at my table; ɪut the other gentlemen *excused* themselves, when I gave them friendly invitation; upon which my jolly companion Hässler aid nothing but ' *Tausend Sapperment!* ' [2]

[1] Such language as this was certainly never heard but by Panurge, in ɪe island of Lanterns.

[2] The Hässler who figures so pleasantly in this gladiatorial exhibition, fterwards came to London, and was introduced by his friend, Mr. Baum-

R

"Here, my best friend and well-wisher, the pages are full
and the bottle of your wine, which has done the duty of this
day, is nearly empty. But since the letter which I wrote to
my father-in-law, to request the hand of my wife, I hardly ever
have written such an enormously long one. Pray take nothing
ill. In speaking, as in writing, I must show myself as I am
or I must hold my tongue, and throw my pen aside. My last
word shall be—my dearest friend, keep me in kind remembrance
Would to God I could one day be the cause of so much joy to
you as you have been to me. Well! I drink to you in this
glass: long live my good and faithful ——.

"W. A. MOZART."[1]

On the return of the composer from Dresden to Berlin, it
was evening as he reached the door of his hotel. He had
scarcely alighted before he inquired, "Is there any music going
forward here to-night?" "O yes," said the waiter, "the
German opera has just begun." "Indeed! and what do they
give to-day?" "'Die Entführung aus dem Serail.'" "Charming!" cried Mozart, laughing with delight. "Yes," said the
man, "it is a very pretty piece indeed—let me see—who composed it?—His name is——" Meantime Mozart was gone
Entering the theatre in his travelling dress, he at first established
himself at the entrance of the pit, that he might listen unobserved; now pleased with the execution of certain passages
now dissatisfied with the time of the pieces, or with the *fioriture*
of the singers; advancing insensibly as the interest gained upon
him, towards the bar of the orchestra, humming this or that
phrase, sometimes in a subdued, sometimes in a louder tone
and unconsciously exciting the general wonder at the eccentric
behaviour of the little man in the old greatcoat. He was close
behind the musicians when they came to Pedrillo's air, "Frisch
zum Kampfe, frische zum streit." The manager had either employed an incorrect score, or some one had been making attempts

garten, organist of the Lutheran church in the Savoy, to the notice o
connoisseurs. His performance on the fine instrument in that church
was much admired.
[1] From the *Harmonicon* for November 1825. The original letter is in
the possession of Mr. Moscheles. It is without date, and the translator
supposes it to have been written from Prague, in 1783; but his conjecture
is evidently erroneous, as the quartets mentioned were not composed till
some years later. The internal evidence of the letter favours the sup
position that it was written from Berlin, in 1789; it is not the production
of a man commencing a career with hope, as Mozart was in 1783, but o
one experienced in life and battered by misfortune.

to improve the harmony, for at the frequently repeated passage, *Nur ein feiger tropf verzagt*, the second violins always played a D sharp instead of a D natural. This was too much for the patience of Mozart, who now called out aloud—" Confound it! —play D natural! " Everybody stared, and particularly the musicians in the orchestra, some of whom recognised him, and now " *Mozart is in the house !* " ran like wildfire from the orchestra to the stage. The singers were in great agitation at the intelligence, and one of them, who played the part of Blondine, could not be prevailed on to reappear. The music-director, aware of the embarrassment, informed Mozart of it, who was in an instant behind the scenes. " What are you alarmed at, madam? " said he to the singer. " You have sung capitally—capitally—and if you wish to give the part still more effect, I will study it with you myself."

On the last occasion that the composer was in private with the King of Prussia, that monarch inquired his opinion of the royal orchestra at Berlin. Mozart, at no time a flatterer, replied—" You have the greatest assemblage of fine performers in the world; and such quartet playing I never heard before; but when the gentlemen are all together they might, perhaps, make better music." The king was pleased with his frankness, and, smiling, said to him, " Stay with me, then, and improve them—I will give you a pension of three thousand dollars a-year." " Can I leave my good emperor? " said Mozart, with emotion, remaining silent and thoughtful. The king himself appeared not wholly unmoved at this instance of attachment, and shortly added—" Consider my proposal: I shall keep my promise, even should it be a year and a day before you return to claim it."

Encouraged by this prospect, Mozart returned to his family at Vienna, on the 4th of June. His first work was to evince gratitude towards his royal patron by writing stringed quartets especially adapted to the artists of the Berlin chapel, who preferred music allied with difficulty of execution, at once fanciful and contrapuntal; and here again we see his flexile genius accommodating itself to the progress of the mechanism of music.

At the first view it may appear surprising that a man who led so harassed a life at Vienna should not instantly have closed with the advantageous offers of the King of Prussia. But among the circumstances unfavourable to this arrangement, the principal one was Salomon's arrival at Vienna, for the purpose of engaging Haydn and Mozart for his London concerts Had not death intervened, Mozart would have succeeded Haydn in London, and, doubtless, have also produced *his* twelve grand symphonies for Salomon's concerts.[1] With this change of life in prospect, the interest in the Berlin scheme was probably weakened.

Now came his separation from Haydn—the man to whom habit and sympathy had strongly attached him, and who was so to speak, an artist-father.[2] It was a grievous trial, and Mozart, in his declining health, saw in it only evil omens— disaster and death. At the parting he was much agitated, and shed tears. " I fear," said he, in bidding Haydn adieu, " that we see each other for the last time; " a presentiment but too fatally confirmed.

With regard to his settlement at Berlin it is probable that however he might esteem the liberality of his Prussian majesty the mode of living in the north of Germany had no charms for him. " I am fond of Vienna," said he one day to a friend who was blaming him for neglecting the King of Prussia's proposals " the emperor treats me kindly, and I care little about money."

Some intrigues against him at court, however, at length determined him to go and tender the resignation of his appoint- ment. The emperor listened to his complaints, and when he had finished, said to him in a tone of kindness, " My dear Mozart, you know my opinion of the Italians, and will you leave me? " These condescending words altered the already wavering resolution of the composer, and induced him to remain.[3] When he arrived at home with this intelligence, and

---

[1] Haydn was so enamoured of the quiet life he led at Esterhazy, that it is thought he would hardly have complied with the proposals of Salomon if the death of Mademoiselle Boselli, which left a void in his days, had not occurred. He stipulated only to precede Mozart, and without disguising his reason for it. The journey turned out prosperously; it brought some of his best works to light, and founded the fortune on which he retired from public life. Its most striking effect, however, was, to have silenced professional enmity. Haydn described himself on his return as for the first time free from the malevolence of rivals. If the life of Haydn, up to the age of sixty, was embittered by professional jealousies, we may form some estimate of what Mozart had to endure from the same cause.

[2] In an affectionate and playful spirit Mozart always called Haydn father

[3] M. Fétis, in his *Biographie des Musiciens*, doubts whether these words were ever spoken by the emperor; but they certainly agree with that insincerity of character which history ascribes to him. His partiality to the Italians was notorious. He was fond of hearing the opinion of one artist upon another, and thought, after gratifying himself in this way, to

·elated to one of his friends the particulars of his interview
vith the emperor, " At least," said his hearer, " you should have
:eized the favourable moment to stipulate for some better
)rovision than you have at present." Mozart was annoyed
ιt this reflection on his want of prudence. " Satan himself,"
ιe replied, " would hardly have thought of bargaining at such
ι moment."

This conversation, so decisive of the composer's fate, was
)ne of the last which ever passed between him and the emperor,
vhose death followed at the distance of a few months. This
vas a fresh calamity; at least so it seemed to Mozart, who to
:he last believed that he had in this monarch a protector and
)atron awaiting only the opportunity to advance him. He,
ιowever, did better without the emperor, and wanted nothing
:o be prosperous but an unimpaired constitution and " sixty
.·ears on his shoulders."

From the time of the composer's agreement to remain in the
:ervice of the Emperor Joseph in the autumn of 1789 to the
ιutumn following, may be dated the epoch of his life in which
ιis temporal affairs reached the crisis of misfortune. His pen
vas peculiarly unproductive during this period, although it
;ave birth to an opera, two quartets, a quintet, several airs, etc.
—work, in bulk alone, to say nothing of its quality, sufficient
:o have redeemed any other composer from the charge of in-
lolence or misspent time, but not enough to satisfy Mozart, who
ιas left under his own hand, while suffering from some calamity
)rought on by himself, his own self-accusation of neglect.

" Cosi fan tutte," an *opera buffa* in two acts, was brought upon
:he stage in January 1790. Guardassoni, the dramatic con-
:ractor to whom we owe it, after engaging Mozart, left both the
;ubject of the work and the place of its production in doubt, and
vhen both were made known gave satisfaction to the composer
n neither. The interest of the libretto, which turns upon a
:rivial incident in the taste of the French stage, would not have
nduced Mozart, had he been at liberty to consult his own

xercise an unbiassed judgment of his own; but he was deceived. His
entiments were always influenced by the parties with whom he conversed.
Ie took Dittersdorf to his counsel in forming a comparative estimate of
:lementi and Mozart as pianoforte players, and of Mozart and Haydn as
omposers. But his musical advisers were sometimes unsound. He
·referred a blunt to a fawning and sycophantic address, and placed artists
·n an easy footing in their intercourse with him; but his liberality in
·ublic compliments destroyed their value, as they ceased to be recognitions
·f individual eminence.

feelings, to set it to music; and the opera was now to be produced on the Italian stage at Vienna, a theatre detested by him from the remembrance of its intrigues. By this measure he also lost all the pleasure and collateral advantage to be expected from visiting some foreign city free of expense, to superintend its performance. The music of the opera corroborates this account of its origin. From the introduction for seven or eight pieces there is a characteristic grace, animation, and enthusiasm; but this high excellence is not sustained; and the composition, though undeniably Mozart's, is carried out with less than his accustomed vigour. Of the success of the first representation the records are wanting; but it may be suspected to have been the reverse of distinguished. We do not find the composer returning to this opera to write new things for it as his manner was with favourite and successful works. He commemorates it in his catalogue by a single inscription, and we hear no more of it.

During six months after the completion of " Cosi fan tutte," he completed nothing but two stringed quartets, the remainder of a set of three, which he dedicated to the King of Prussia, who acknowledged the compliment by a hundred Fredericks d'or in a gold box.

In July of the same year, 1790, Mozart was employed on Handel's " Alexander's Feast " and " Ode on Cecilia's Day," for the Baron von Swieten. These were the last works of Handel that received finishing touches from his pen, and the embellishment of his exquisite wind-instrument parts. The score of " Alexander's Feast " displays alterations and reduplications, rather than added novelties; — efforts directed towards improving the effect and connection of the piece rather than new features. Thus we find the air " Softly sweet in Lydian Measures " given to a soprano voice instead of a tenor, for the sake of a more beautiful combination with a violoncello obligato; —and now and then a chord accompanying the recitative more effectively dispersed among the instruments, while the harmony of the choruses generally is enriched. Such is principally the nature of Mozart's additions; in one air only, " The Prince unable to conceal his Pain," has he ventured to occupy certain interstitial places with phrases of his own for a flute and bassoon obligato.

To remodel and beautify Handel must have been a gratifying task to the composer, to whom good music *not his own* was always welcome as a respite to his ever-working invention. His wife could not give him a more agreeable surprise on the occasion of any family holiday than by getting up in private some new church work by Michael or Joseph Haydn.

The ceremony of electing the new emperor took place at Frankfort in the autumn of the year 1790, attracting, as usual, a concourse of nobility, and giving occasion to many festivities. Mozart, who was at this time in great pecuniary difficulty, went to Frankfort in the hope of retrieving himself. His misfortune seems to have been sudden, and his finances were reduced so low, that before he could raise funds for the journey his wife was obliged to part with the most valuable articles of her toilet. Thus furnished he set off, carrying with him his brother-in-law, Hofer, a needy man and an excellent violin player attached to Schickaneder's orchestra. Hofer studied the first violin of Mozart's quartets under the direction of the composer, who made him his companion with the friendly view of putting opportunities of advancement in his way. The journey was performed in a chaise, rather a perilous enterprise in the then state of the German roads; but it rendered the travellers independent; enabling them to stop where they pleased, and take advantage of circumstances. Mozart was in high spirits, and in his correspondence with his wife speaks of dining magnificently at Ratisbon, of hearing divine music at table, of being treated with English hospitality, and drinking admirable Moselle. He looked forward with great hope to the issue of his journey, and pledging himself to *work, work, work,* promised his wife that the results would prevent all embarrassments for the future; and then he adds, " What a delicious life will we lead! " The slightest gleam of success, through a life of disappointments, with the invincible consciousness of genius, always threw him into ecstasies, but they were of short duration

Of Mozart's performances at Frankfort, all that is known is that he played a pianoforte concerto for four hands with M. von Becke, a personage who filled the joint offices of music-director and groom of the bed-chamber to the Prince of Oettingen-Wallerstein. This Becke [1] Mozart was wont to term the father of all pianoforte players.

It appears that a proposal had been made to him at Vienna for liquidating his debts, by advancing him 1000 florins on Hoffmeister's account. This scheme largely occupied his thoughts during the visit to Frankfort.

[1] The reader has met with this performer before in Mozart's letters from Augsburg.

He experienced hours of deep dejection, not sufficiently accounted for by his pecuniary troubles, but as though these were embittered by some latent cause of self-reproach. In a letter addressed to his wife at this time, it will be seen that he advises her, while arranging money matters, to suppress the true cause of the difficulties under which they are labouring.

" I should certainly prefer, for security's sake, raising 2000 florins on Hoffmeister's account, but you must allege some other than the actual reason; for example: that I had a speculation in hand which you were unacquainted with. I shall make something here without doubt, though not quite so much as you and other friends anticipate. Here I am well known and admired enough; so we shall see. But in order to play a sure game, I would rather that the business were transacted with Hoffmeister, because then I get money with nothing to pay back, but have merely to work, and that will I most willingly do, from love, my little wife, to thee. I am as happy as a child at the thought of returning to you. If the people here could see into my heart I should be almost ashamed. I am cold to everything,—cold as ice. Were you with me, indeed, then perhaps the kind attentions I receive might give more pleasure; but now they are all lost.

" P.S. In writing the foregoing page many tears fell on the paper. Now let us be merry. Prepare yourself; the kisses begin to fly about amazingly. *Teufel !* here's a crowd of them. Ha! ha! I just now caught three that were delicious."

A flash of the old spirit that used to scatter such sunshine over the letters of his boyhood.

From Frankfort he continued his journey over the familiar ground through Mannheim to Munich; a scene associated with many sweet and bitter recollections, in which thirteen years before he had commenced his first practical acquaintance with life, and its disappointments, in futile efforts to obtain an appointment in the service of the elector; but at a time when youth made cares sit lightly, and when the consciousness of the dawning magnificence of his genius, and the delightful society of his Mannheim friends, Cannabich, the Wendlings, the Webers, of M. de la Pottrie (*our Indian*), to whom he used to play the organ, and even of the priggish Abbé Vogler himself, compensated for everything. Thirteen years had elapsed since Mozart had been at Mannheim in the first spring of hope and ambition: and what a change had taken place in the interval. It is true he had " achieved greatness," but the sere and yellow leaf had set in upon the very summer of his life. There needs not the melancholy gaiety of such a postscript as that to the letter just given, to prove how low was the tone of Mozart's spirits during this journey. He returned home towards the beginning of December, very inconsiderably benefited by this tour, and began to redeem his promise by an activity beyond all example. The death-year of Mozart, 1791, was the most wonderful of his life; it was an end crowning the work, in every way worthy of his extraordinary career.

On reaching home, it became an early object with him to release some of the valuables that his wife had parted with, to prevent his paying the exorbitant interest on which alone he could have raised money. This, however, his gains permitted him for the present only to accomplish in part;—and Stadler, the clarionet player,[1] was entrusted with the commission to redeem some articles, and renew the term of others. The tickets, or duplicates, now received, were soon afterwards stolen from an unlocked cabinet in Mozart's house, under circumstances that left no doubt of their having been purloined by Stadler. This man was the familiar acquaintance of the composer—his intimate at all times, fed at his table, employed by him in business, and enabled to turn the knowledge thus gained to his own advantage. His unprincipled character, and the incredible forbearance of Mozart, will appear from another anecdote. He was constantly lurking about, on the watch to discover the best opportunity of borrowing money. The emperor, on a certain occasion, sent Mozart fifty ducats, which as soon as Stadler knew, he came to the composer, representing that he should be utterly ruined if he could not borrow that sum. Mozart wanted the money himself;—but, never proof against a tale of distress, he gave him two valuable watches (repeaters) to raise money upon, with the words: " There—go and bring me the ticket, and take care to have them out at the right time." Stadler neglecting to do this, Mozart, in order to save his watches, was obliged to advance him the fifty ducats with interest—which the fellow actually kept! Mozart gave him a severe reprimand for his base and dishonest conduct—but continued, as usual, to receive him at his table and to be his benefactor. In other men, mercy like this to such a monster of perfidy would be highly culpable; but

[1] This person must not be confounded with the Abbé Stadler.

in Mozart it sprang from that exalted quality of his nature which literally rendered him incapable of resentments, and always led him to return good for evil. One of the last acts of his life was for the benefit of this very Stadler, who wished to try his fortune at Prague. Towards this expedition, he furnished him with a new concerto for the clarionet—money for his travelling expenses, and a letter that procured him an engagement on his arrival.[1]

Notwithstanding the vulgar exigencies in which this great man passed much of his life, he was gradually working his way to fame and fortune. The age, however tardily, was beginning to acknowledge the genius so much misplaced in it—but its rewards and encouragements unhappily came too late.

Most of the compositions produced by Mozart, from the time of his return to Vienna, have, in their several kinds, the melancholy interest which attaches to the last touches of a great master. He began work again in December with a quintet in D major, for two violins, two tenors and bass—but immediately after this his thoughts were directed into a new channel.

A powerful self-acting organ, to which a clock seems to have been appended, and the machinery of which was to regulate the times of playing, was in course of erection at the country house of a nobleman, and Mozart received a commission to furnish the music. Nothing could have been more agreeable to him than this employment, which brought with it recollections of the grand organ fugues and preludes of Sebastian Bach, heard on his visits to Leipsic and Berlin, and afforded him the opportunity of emulating them. For this instrument he pro-

[1] His well known disinterestedness was particularly abused by musicsellers and managers of theatres. The greater part of his compositions for the piano brought him not a single penny—being written chiefly to oblige acquaintances desirous of possessing some piece in his handwriting for their private use. Hence may be discovered the reason for the inferiority of some of his *solo* pieces for the piano; as he was obliged to conform in them to the taste, proficiency, etc., of the persons for whom they were written. The musicsellers found means to possess themselves of copies of these productions, and published them without hesitation. Artaria, of Vienna, was a great offender in this way. A lady one day called upon the composer: " Artaria has again been publishing some variations of yours for the piano—do you know anything about it? " she inquired. " No." " Will you not remonstrate with him? " " Oh, no—what is the good of talking?—the man's a wretch; " returned Mozart. " But this is not a mere money matter—it is one in which your fame is concerned." " Well—whoever forms his judgment of me from such trifles must be a wretch too—let us say no more about it." In the abrupt exclamation *Der lump!* (the wretch!) his resentment of very grave injuries frequently evaporated.

duced two companion pieces of surpassing excellence—the first
in F major in Handel's manner—the second in F minor in that of
Bach. A comparison of his work with that of his predecessors
is in no respect unfavourable, but gives him that advantage
which the progress of the art and the peculiarity of his genius
lead us to expect. These pieces appear to have given so much
satisfaction, as to have procured for him the patronage of the
organ builders; for, in the spring of 1791, we find him writing
an andante for a barrel or cylinder in a little organ, and acquit-
ting himself in this trifle with all the simplicity and propriety of
one who had reached the limit of his powers.

It was now long since Mozart had presented himself before
the public of Vienna as a pianoforte-player. He had a strong
repugnance to resume this course, arising from his dislike to the
frivolous audiences of that city; but debts and difficulties left
him little choice. For the concerts which he gave in January
1791 he wrote a new pianoforte concerto; of which, as his
final work of that description, the subject will not be thought
devoid of interest in this place.

The opportunity of one of his last appearances in public as
a pianoforte-player may be well taken to describe all that

remains to be told respecting his person. Mozart, though born of beautiful parents, possessed beauty himself as a child only; in his later years he retained nothing of his early look but its pleasing expression. His features were marked, and had a strong individuality of character that rendered them as impossible to be mistaken as those of Socrates, or Frederick the Great. The outward man of the composer presented no index to his genius. His eyes, which were rather large and prominent, had more of a languid than a brilliant and animated character; the eyebrows were well arched, and the eyelashes long and handsome. His sight was on all occasions sharp and strong, notwithstanding his frequent and laborious application in the night. There was wandering and abstraction in his eye except when seated at the piano, when the whole expression and character of the face seemed altered. His unsteady gaze became then earnest and concentrated, and every muscle of his countenance betrayed the influence of those feelings on himself which he was seeking to awaken in others.

His head was comparatively too large for his body; but the body itself, and the hands and feet, were formed in exact proportion, of which he was rather vain. The easy, natural, and elegant movement of his small hands on the piano, rendered it interesting to overlook him when playing; while the power which he occasionally exhibited raised astonishment. His nose, which had been handsome, became so prominent a feature in the last years of his life, from the emaciation of his countenance, that a scribbler in one of the journals of the day, the *Morgenblatte* of Vienna, honoured him with the epithet " enormous-nosed."

It has been stated that he never attained his natural growth; and the reason assigned for this is—his want of exercise in childhood. But both assertions may be questioned. Mozart's parents were small persons; and the best proof that Leopold Mozart, though he did not permit his children to lose their time, cared sufficiently for their health, may be found in the long life of Madame Sonnenberg, whose youth was passed in the same industrious culture of excellence as her brother's.

The house in which Mozart resided during his last years at Vienna, and in which he died, was called the *Kaiser-Haus* (the imperial house), and was at one time a building belonging to the government. The simplicity and kindliness of his domestic habits may be illustrated by a passage in one of the letters of his sister-in-law, Sophie:

" Mozart daily became dearer to our deceased mother, and she to him. He used to come running to our house on the Wieden with little parcels of coffee and sugar under his arm, and would present them with the words, ' Here, dear mamma; I have brought you a little collation.' [1] He never came to us empty-handed."

Madame Weber and her daughter reciprocated these acts of kindness, and Mozart accepted their offerings with the joy of one to whom no testimony of affection was unwelcome. They were at work for him in his last illness, wholly unsuspicious of the fatal termination at hand; they prepared for him the cloth by which he was drawn forward in his bed, when helpless and unable to turn on account of the weakness and swelling that accompanied his disorder; and had also in readiness against his recovery a wadded night-gown, in the hope of enjoying which he was much cheered. These are slight things; but nothing is unimportant that reveals glimpses of the domestic life of such a man.

In the year 1791, when he pledged himself to work so hard, he accomplished far more than he could have himself anticipated.

For the carnival of the year 1791 he composed no fewer than five-and-thirty minuets, *Teutsche* and other dances of full orchestral parts, during the month of February and a part of January. Among the labours of these remarkable six weeks will be found the waltzes commonly known as Mozart's, which were danced to at the balls of Vienna, under the designation of *Landlerische*. This resort to the ball-room, however little creditable to the then existing state of musical patronage, had the good effect of restoring him to comparative ease in his circumstances, and of enabling him again to oblige his friends, and to write for fame.

He wrote also, during the spring, his last quintet for violins (in E flat $\frac{6}{8}$), and a final chorus to Sarti's opera, " Le Gelosie Vilane," which was at that time in preparation by a company of amateurs.

The plan of the " Zauberflöte " originated about May in this year, with Schickaneder, Mozart's old acquaintance, and the companion of his revels. The theatre of which this man was the manager was fast falling into a ruinous condition; partly from his own carelessness, partly from the absence of public patronage;

[1] Hier, liebe Mama, haben Sie eine kleine Jause.

and in a half-distracted state he came to Mozart, telling him that
he was the only man who could relieve him from his embarrassment. " I," replied Mozart, " how can that be? " " By composing for me an opera to suit the taste of the description of
people who attend my theatre. To a certain point you may
consult that of the connoisseurs, and your own glory; but have
a particular regard to that class of persons who are not judges
of good music. I will take care that you shall have the poem
shortly, and that the decorations shall be handsome; in a word,
that everything shall be agreeable to the present mode."
Touched by the entreaties of Schickaneder, Mozart promised to
undertake the business for him. " What remuneration do you
require? " asked the manager. " Why, it seems that you have
nothing to give me," returned Mozart; " however, we will so
arrange the matter that I may not quite lose my labour, and
yet enable you to extricate yourself from your difficultes. You
shall have the score, and give me what you please for it, on
condition that you will not allow any copies to be taken. If the
opera succeeds, I will dispose of it to other theatres, and that
will repay me."

The delighted manager closed this advantageous bargain with
the most solemn assurances of good faith. Mozart soon set to
work, and so far kindly consulted the taste, or rather interest
of Schickaneder, who was constantly with him during the progress of the " Zauberflöte," as to strike out whole scenes that
displeased him, and to compose one duet five times over in order
to satisfy him. In a few weeks the opera was produced; its
reputation spread throughout Germany, and it was soon performed by several provincial companies; but, alas! not one
of them received the score from Mozart! The cruelty which
Schickaneder in this instance superadded to his black ingratitude
was chiefly shown in his being fully aware of the necessitous
condition of the man whom he thus basely defrauded. Mozart
did not permit conduct of this kind to disturb his equanimity.
When made fully aware of the manager's treachery, he exclaimed, " The wretch! " and dismissed the matter from his
thoughts.

It was during the composition of the " Zauberflöte " that
the eruption of those symptoms which portend decay of the
vital powers, and a general breaking-up of the constitution, first
appeared. As usual, he grew interested in his work, and wrote
by day and night; but not, as formerly, with impunity. He

sunk over this composition into frequent swoons, in which he
remained for several minutes before consciousness returned.
His health suffered so much, that in the month of June he suspended for a time his labours on the " Zauberflöte " and made a
short excursion to Baden.   There he produced his " Ave verum
corpus," a strain of such calm but exalted religious feeling, as
may well interpret his sensations in sickness and solitude.   The
" Zauberflöte " is entered in his catalogue as finished in July,
though it was not performed till the 30th of September, after the
composer's return from Prague.   That it was not quite finished,
however, at that time, but submitted to various alterations and
additions, which rendered the " Zauberflöte," " La Clemenza
di Tito," and the " Requiem " contemporaneous subjects of
thought, will presently appear.

And now comes one of the most curious incidents in his life.
Early in August, the composer was one day surprised by the
entrance of a stranger, who brought him a letter without any
signature, the purport of which was to inquire whether he would
undertake the composition of a requiem, by what time he could
be ready with it, and his price.   The unknown expressed himself
on this occasion in a manner as flattering as it was mysterious.
Mozart, who was never accustomed to engage in any undertaking without consulting his wife, related to her the singular
proposition made to him, adding, that he should much like to
try his hand in a work of that character, as the elevated and
the pathetic in church music was his favourite style.   She
advised him to accept the engagement; and he accordingly
wrote an answer, stating his terms for the composition, excusing
himself from naming the precise time of its completion, but
desiring to know where it should be sent when finished.   In a
few days the messenger returned, paid twenty-five ducats, half
the price required, in advance, and informed the composer that
as his demand was so moderate, he might expect a considerable
present on completing the score.   He was to follow the bent
of his own genius in the work, but to give himself no trouble
to discover who employed him, as it would be in vain.   On the
departure of the stranger he fell into a profound reverie; then,
suddenly calling for pen, ink, and paper, began to write.   He
had not proceeded far, before his further progress was interrupted by the commission to compose the opera for the
coronation of the Emperor Leopold, at Prague.   The subject
proposed by the council of the Bohemian nobility was " La

Clemenza di Tito." The whole idea of this opera seems to have
been unreasonably deferred, and the work was now to be completed on an emergency. About the 18th of August he set off
for Prague, accompanied by his wife, and his pupil Süssmayer;
he commenced the composition in his travelling carriage, and
finished it at Prague in eighteen days. He carried with him
at this time a number of little slips of ruled paper, on which he
noted various subjects to be afterwards amplified. Such was
the nature of his travelling labours, now, from the great diversion
of his thoughts, unusually necessary as an aid to memory. The
unaccompanied recitative, that is to say, the dialogue merely
accompanied by a pianoforte, was wholly committed to
Süssmayer.

Just as Mozart and his wife were entering their travelling
carriage for Prague, the stranger who had brought the commission for the requiem suddenly re-appeared. " How will
the requiem proceed now? " he inquired. Mozart excused himself on account of the necessity of the journey, and the impossibility of giving intelligence of it to his anonymous employer; but
expressed his determination to make the work his first care
on his return. This assurance gave satisfaction, and they
separated.[1]

Throughout the whole of his visit to Prague Mozart was ill,
and took medicine incessantly. An unusual paleness overspread
his countenance, and its expression was languid and melancholy,
though in the cheerful society of friends his spirits occasionally
revived.

In composing " La Clemenza di Tito " he evinced the masterly
decision to which he had attained in treating the subjects submitted to him. Metastasio's drama on this subject contains
three acts; but finding that the action would be more rapid
and the interest more concentrated, by the abridgment of the
original, he at once struck out the second act as superfluous,
and united the first and the third. He made other alterations
in the libretto that discovered his knowledge of audiences, and
better adapted the work for a festival in which tedium was

[1] In this anecdote, which it must be admitted is abundantly mysterious
and provocative, we have the source of the supernatural origin to which
the " Requiem " is popularly ascribed. To a man in Mozart's condition
of weakness and melancholy, which by degrees filled him with prepos-
sessions approaching insanity, the unexpected appearance of the bearer
of this ghostly commission from a concealed hand, might easily suggest
that it was a communication from the other world.

unlikely to be tolerated. The plan of an opera, abounding in airs, to be completed in little more than a fortnight, would be usually considered of the most difficult execution; but Mozart was so fertile in melodies, that it favoured his rapidity by permitting most of the movements of the work to be studied in succession as they were finished. It was thus that " La Clemenza di Tito " was produced; Mozart was unable to see his whole score until he had finished the last note. And what a surprising work—how new in its character—how full of a certain Roman grandeur and magnanimity was thus hastily put together!

But hurried as the composer was in " La Clemenza di Tito," his thoughts were not wholly engrossed by it. He was at this time in the daily habit of visiting a neighbouring coffee-house with some friends, for the purpose of recreating himself with billiards. One day, they observed that he drew a book at intervals from his pocket in the midst of his game, and humming as he made some hasty memoranda in it, pursued his play. The company at Dussek's house were soon after astonished to hear him perform the beautiful quintet in the first act of the " Zauberflöte," *Hm, hm, hm,* which he had completed in this manner.[1]

" La Clemenza di Tito " was finished on the 5th of September 1791, and produced on the 6th.[2] It had less success during the course of its first representations than the merit of the composition deserved. But the audiences of Prague were at this

[1] One or two anecdotes of this last visit to Prague remain to be told. The pianoforte player Woelfl was giving concerts at this time, and advertised himself in his programme as the " Pupil of Mozart." When this was shown to the composer, he mildly replied, " The young man plays admirably, but he owes nothing to me—perhaps he may have profited by my sister."

The humbler class of musical retainers—the choristers at Leipsic, for example, sometimes displayed a very just appreciation of the greatness of his genius. An old harpsichord tuner came to put some strings to his travelling pianoforte, " Well, my good old fellow," says Mozart to him, " what do I owe you? " The poor man regarding him as a sort of deity, replied, stammering and confounded, " Imperial Majesty! Mr. the *maître de chapelle* of his imperial majesty!—I cannot—it is true that I have waited on you several times. You shall give me a crown." " A crown! " replied Mozart, " a worthy fellow like you ought not to be put out of his way for a crown," and he gave him some ducats. The honest man, as he withdrew, continued to repeat, with low bows, " Ah! Imperial Majesty! "

[2] The opera is thus entered by Mozart in his catalogue: " LA CLEMENZA DI TITO," opera seria in due Atti, per l'incoronazione di sua Maesta, l'imperatore Leopoldo II. ridotta à vera opera dal Signora Marroli, Poeta di sua A. S. L'Elettore di Sassonia. Attrici—Signore Marchette Fantozi, Signora Antonini. Attori—Signore Bedini, Signora Carolina Perini (da uomo) Signore Baglione, Signore Campi e cori. 24 Pezzi."

season intoxicated with the revelry of a coronation; balls, festivities, and amusements of various kinds, had stupefied their faculties, and rendered them for a time incapable of the pleasures of sentiment, or of tasting the noble simplicity that prevails in this music. The composer appears to have been little disturbed by the cold reception of his work, for he ascribed it to the right cause, and could foresee the time when its deserts would be more truly acknowledged. He stayed with his friends, the Dusseks, till near the end of the month, enjoying, as well as his ill-health would permit, the cheerful and congenial musical society which they drew around him. On taking leave of the circle of his acquaintance at Prague he was unusually affected, and shed tears, for it was with a strong presentiment of his approaching death, and that he should see them no more.

Towards the close of September he was again at Vienna, where the " Zauberflöte " only awaited the last touches to be quite ready for representation. On the 28th of this month he composed the memorable overture, and a priests' march, in which he seems to have cast a retrospective glance on a similar subject in " Idomeneo." The opera was produced on the 30th with a success which fully warranted the manager's prediction.

That Mozart was pleased with this his first creation on enchanted ground, and that, with the taste of a poet, he " loved fairies, genii, giants, and monsters, to gaze on the magnificence of golden palaces, and to repose by the waterfalls of Elysian gardens," there is no doubt; but still his pleasure in the music of this opera was a divided pleasure. He could not follow it as he did his favourite works, " Idomeneo " and " Don Giovanni," from the beginning to the end with constant satisfaction; for though he had availed himself largely of the permission to write for the connoisseur in the priest-music, and other movements of the opera, yet every now and then there was a sacrifice to the vulgar, and the parts incessantly applauded by the public were little to his taste. The contrast between the high solemnity of some parts of the " Zauberflöte " and the farcical levity of others, renders this work less delightful to the musician than it might have been; however, he may here and there cull specimens of the best manner of the master.[1]

[1] How full his mind was of Handel and Bach during these his last years is well worthy of notice, and so also is the noble ambition which made him seek opportunities of trying his strength with them. In " Don Giovanni " he had written a song in Handel's manner, and in " La Clemenza di Tito "

But he had causes of pleasure, independently of the music, in the success of the " Zauberflöte." He saw himself surrounded by friends whom this effort had benefited; on the stage were his friend Schack the original Tamino, the manager Schicka- neder (his treachery yet unknown) as Papageno, Madame Hofer, his wife's sister; and in the orchestra was her husband. There was a numerous company in this theatre with whom Mozart was on familiar terms, and thus in conducting his opera he had more of the charm of private sympathy and was more emphatically " at home." [1]

When confined to his house, and no longer able to attend the performances of the " Zauberflöte," he would place his watch by his side, and follow it in imagination. "Now the first act is over," he would say; " now they are singing such an air," etc., and then the thought of his approaching end would strike him with melancholy. It was in this state of mind that he worked at the " Requiem," partly at home, but more frequently at the Laimgrube in Trattner's garden. Schack and Süssmayer were much with him during the progress of this work; and it was his custom as soon as he had finished a move- ment to have it sung, while he played over the orchestral part on the pianoforte. His application to the " Requiem " was accompanied by unusual silence and dejection; he was, in fact, brooding over one idea till it assumed a character of monomania. He thought, though he did not confess it, that he had been poisoned. In the hope of distracting him from his melancholy, his wife engaged his most intimate friends to call, as if by chance, at times when, after many hours' applica- tion, he ought naturally to have thought of resting. Though pleased with their visits he did not cease writing; they talked

a chorus. In the " Zauberflöte " he wrote upon a *canto fermo*, remem- bering doubtless the motets for a double choir of Sebastian Bach, which he had heard at Leipsic. The melody sung in unison to Tamino by the two men in armour, strengthened by bassoons, oboes, and flutes, is an ancient church tune, ascribed to Martin Luther: *Ach Gott vom Himmel sieh darein, und lass dich doch erbarmen.* This choral covered by Mozart's learned counterpoint, seems long to have escaped detection; but Gerber, an excellent writer on music, penetrated the composer's design. We may well imagine Mozart's enjoyment of this astonishingly fine movement, while directing the orchestra during nine or ten representations, which were all that his weak state permitted him to attend.

[1] Mozart's note of the original performers in the " Zauberflöte " is as follows: Ladies—Mademoiselle Gottlieb, Madame Hofer, Madame Görl, Mademoiselle Klöpfter, Mademoiselle Hofmann. Gentlemen—M. Schack, M. Görl, M. Schickaneder, Sen., M. Klöpfter, M. Schickaneder, Jun., M. Nouseul.

and endeavoured to engage him in the conversation, but he took no interest in it; they addressed themselves particularly to him: he uttered a few inconsequential words, and pursued his occupation.

One fine day in the autumn his wife drove with him to the Prater. As soon as they had reached a solitary spot, and were seated together, Mozart began to speak of death, and said that he was writing this " Requiem " for himself. She tried to talk him out of these gloomy fancies, but in vain, and his eyes filled with tears as he answered her, " No, no, I am but too well convinced that I cannot last long. I have certainly been poisoned. I cannot rid myself of this idea."

Shocked to hear him talk thus, yet unable herself to persuade him how groundless were his suspicions, or to administer effectual consolation, she determined to consult a physician; and with his approbation the score of the " Requiem " was taken away. This, for a time, had a good effect; the removal of the work which so fatally excited his imagination caused a sensible improvement in his health, and by the middle of November he was so far recovered as to be able to attend a meeting of his old friends the Freemasons. Their joy at seeing him again among them, and the excellent performance of a little cantata which he had just written for them, entitled " The Praise of Friendship " (" Das Lob der Freundschaft "), greatly revived his spirits. On reaching home after this festival he said to his wife, " Oh, Stänerl, how madly they have gone on about my cantata. If I did not know that I had written better things, I should have thought that my best composition." He now entreated to have his " Requiem " restored, that he might complete it as soon as possible, and his wife, no longer seeing any objection, complied.

The favourable turn of his fortune within the last few months heightens the interest of the catastrophe in this strange drama of life. On returning from Prague he found awaiting him the appointment of kapellmeister to the cathedral church of St. Stephen, with all its emoluments, besides extensive commissions from Holland and Hungary for works to be periodically delivered. This, with his engagements for the theatres of Prague and Vienna, assured him of a competent income for the future, exempt from all necessity for degrading employment. But prospects of worldly happiness were now phantoms that only came to mock his helplessness and embitter his parting hour.

With the "Requiem" his former illness returned. About the 21st of November his hands and feet began to swell, he was seized with sudden sickness, and an almost total incapacity of motion. In this state he was removed to the bed from which he never rose again. During the fourteen days in which he lay thus, his intellectual faculties remained unimpaired; he had a strong desire for life, though little expectation of it, and his behaviour was generally tranquil and resigned. But sometimes the singular concurrence of events at this juncture, and the thought of the unprotected condition of his wife and children overpowered him, and he could not restrain passionate lamentations. "Now must I go," he would exclaim, "just as I should be able to live in peace: now leave my art when, no longer the slave of fashion, nor the tool of speculators, I could follow the dictates of my own feeling, and write whatever my heart prompts. I must leave my family—my poor children, at the very instant in which I should have been able to provide for their welfare!" Sometimes he spoke more cheerfully. His sister-in-law Sophie, who visited him daily, and did all that affectionate attention could suggest to alleviate his sufferings, found him on the day before his death apparently much improved—hoping for, and even anticipating, recovery. He now sent a message to Madame Weber—"Tell mamma that I am getting better, and that I shall come during the octave of her fête day to wish her joy." This was followed by a fearful night, in which his attendants were in momentary apprehension of his dissolution.

Throughout his illness music was still a subject of the greatest interest to him. The "Requiem" lay almost continually on his bed, and Süssmayer was frequently at his side receiving instructions as to effects, the production of which by an orchestra he could never expect to superintend personally. One of his last efforts was an attempt to explain to Süssmayer an effect of the drums in the "Requiem;" he was observed in doing this to blow out his cheeks, and express his meaning by a noise intelligible to the musician.

At two o'clock on the same day, which was that of his death, he had been visited by some performers of Schickaneder's theatre, his intimate friends. The ruling passion was now strongly exemplified. He desired the score of the "Requiem" to be brought, and it was sung by his visitors round his bed; himself taking the alto part. Schack sang the soprano, Hofer, his brother-in-law, the tenor, and Gorl the bass. They had proceeded as far as the first bars of the "Lacrymosa," when Mozart was seized with a violent fit of weeping, and the score was put aside.[1] Throughout this day he was possessed with a strong presentiment of the near approach of death, and now gave himself up, relinquishing every hope that he had hitherto occasionally cherished. His physicians, indeed, thought unfavourably of his case from the first—and one of them, Dr. Sallaba, some days previously, had pronounced him beyond all human aid. It is remarkable that Mozart, notwithstanding the religious principles in which he had been educated, and which it is believed he always preserved, made no application for spiritual aid in this extremity; nor did the priests offer to bestow the last sacraments of their church upon the dying man. As he had not solicited their attendance, they left him to depart without the *viaticum*.

It was late in the evening of December 5, 1791, that his sister-in-law returned, but only to witness his dissolution. She had left him so much better that she did not hasten to him. Her own account may now be given. "How shocked was I, when my sister, usually so calm and self-possessed, met me at the door, and in a half-distracted manner said, ' God be thanked that you are here. Since you left him he has been so ill that I never expected him to outlive this day. Should he be so again he will die to-night. Go to him, and see how he is.' As I approached his bed he called to me—' It is well that you are here: you must stay to-night and see me die.' I tried as far as I was able to banish this impression, but he replied, ' The taste of death is already on my tongue—*I taste death;* and who will be near to support my Constance if you go away?' I returned to my mother for a few moments to give her intelligence, for she was anxiously waiting, as she might else have supposed the fatal event already over; and then hurried back to my disconsolate sister. Süssmayer was standing by the bedside,

[1] It may appear incredible that Mozart should be in a condition to sing after an illness of a fortnight's duration, in which his weakness was such that he was obliged to be drawn forward whenever he required to sit up in his bed. But there is no reason to doubt the fact; for, besides the circumstantial testimony of Schack, to whom we owe this anecdote, it is well known that other musicians, whose death was caused by some one of the insidious forms of consumption, have sung a few hours before their departure. Two instances have occurred within our own knowledge: viz. in Kiesewetter, the violin player, and Weippert, the pianist—names still fresh in the memory of the musical circles.

and on the counterpane lay the 'Requiem,' concerning which
Mozart was still speaking and giving directions. He now called
his wife, and made her promise to keep his death secret for a
time from every one but Albrechtsberger, that he might thus
have an advantage over other candidates for the vacant office
of kapellmeister to St. Stephen's. His desire in this respect was
gratified, for Albrechtsberger received the appointment. As
he looked over the pages of the 'Requiem' for the last time,
he said, with tears in his eyes, 'Did I not tell you that I was
writing this for myself?'

" On the arrival of the physician, Dr. Closset, cold applica-
tions were ordered to his burning head, a process endured by
the patient with extreme shuddering, and which brought on the
delirium from which he never recovered. He remained in this
state for two hours, and at midnight expired." [1]

Thus died Wolfgang Amadeus Mozart, at the age of thirty-
five years and ten months. The funeral, with the arrangements
for which Baron von Swieten charged himself, was unostenta-
tious to meanness, and far from such as befitted the obsequies
of so great a man. The mortal remains of the composer were
deposited in the cemetery of St. Marxer Linie, near Vienna;
the same in which his intimate friends Albrechtsberger and
Joseph Haydn were afterwards buried. A common undis-
tinguished grave received the coffin, which was then left without
memorial—almost forgotten—for nearly twenty years; and
when, in 1808, some inquiries were made as to the precise spot
of the interment, all that the sexton could tell was that, at
the latter end of 1791, the space about the third and fourth
row from the cross was being occupied with graves; but the
contents of these graves being from time to time exhumed,
nothing could be determined concerning that which was once
Mozart.

---

[1] The disease which carried off Mozart was variously characterised by
the physicians; it was by turns a miliary fever, a rheumatic inflammatory
fever—consumption. Mozart's notion that he had been poisoned was
always treated by those about him as a fantastic idea; and in fact the
post mortem examination discovered nothing extraordinary beyond inflammation of the brain. The tale of poisoning, however, having transpired, Salieri, the known inveterate foe of Mozart, was fixed upon as the
imaginary criminal. It is a singular fact that Salieri, who died in the
public hospital at Vienna, thought fit on his deathbed to make a solemn
deposition of his innocence before witnesses, and that the document thus
duly signed and attested was made public. The story is not without its
moral. Salieri was aspersed—but to the humiliating necessity for his
formal contradiction, the violence of party spirit had reduced him.

Of six children born to the composer—four boys and two girls—two boys alone survived infancy. The elder, Carl, was early established, and is, I believe, still engaged in some mercantile pursuit at Milan; the younger, Wolfgang Amadeus, followed the profession of his father. He was long established at Lemberg, in Gallicia, but afterwards removed to Vienna. He died a few months ago, much beloved for the sweetness and gentleness of his disposition, but, as an artist, totally overwhelmed by the splendour of the family name.

The widow of Mozart had a long and arduous struggle to surmount the difficulties of her position. Unskilled as her husband in the knowledge of business, she was particularly unfortunate in her attempts to bring out various pieces of music; of which an arrangement of " Idomeneo," and a piano-forte concerto (dedicated to Prince Louis of Prussia) were offered by subscription.[1] The publication of these compositions was delayed from year to year, until the subscribers were no longer to be found. The malignity of the enemies of Mozart did not cease even when he was in the grave. The ear of the Emperor Leopold was abused by tales of his extravagance, and his debts were magnified to three times their amount. But in an audience to which the widow was admitted, she vindicated her husband; and showed that an uncertain income, combined with sickness and the expenses of a family, were the real cause of his debts; undertaking, at the same time, to settle any claim with about three thousand *gulden*. The emperor patronised a concert on her behalf; the example was followed at Prague, Leipsic, Berlin, etc., and with the receipt of these performances she performed her promise. Not a debt remained unpaid.

After many years of widowhood, Madame Mozart entered into second nuptials with M. von Nissen, aulic counsellor to the King of Denmark, with whom she resided at Copenhagen. They subsequently removed to Salzburg, where Nissen died, and his tomb testifies that he was the benefactor to Mozart's family. At Salzburg also lived Madame Sonnenberg, a widow, advanced in age, and in narrow circumstances. This is an

---

[1] Süssmayer, who had obtained possession of one transcript of the " Requiem," the other having been delivered to the stranger immediately after Mozart's decease, published the score some years afterwards, claiming to have composed from the *Sanctus* to the end. As there was no one to contradict this extraordinary story, it found partial credit until 1839, when a full score of the " Requiem " in Mozart's handwriting was discovered.

affecting picture of the last days of poor Nannerl, the devoted sister of Mozart:

" We found Madame Sonnenberg, lodged in a small but clean room, bedridden and quite blind. Hers is a complete decay of nature; suffering no pain, she lies like one awaiting the stroke of death, and will probably expire in her sleep. . . . Her voice was scarcely above a whisper, so that I was forced to lean my face close to hers to catch the sound. In the sitting-room still remained the old clavichord, on which the brother and sister had frequently played duets together; and on its desk were some pieces of his composition, which were the last things his sister had played over previous to her illness." [1]

The death of Madame Sonnenberg occurred in the spring of 1830, and twelve years later followed that of her sister-in-law, Madame Nissen. All the intimate friends and connections of Mozart are now removed; but the works of the composer, in various modes of republication, or first printed from the MSS., are, at the distance of half a century, continually springing into life. This is the fame he sought with the most earnest devotion and self-sacrifice. Estimated by the universality of his power— the rapidity of his production, and its permanent influence on art, the models he created, and the constantly advancing march of his genius, arrested in full career, and in the bloom of life, Mozart certainly stands alone among musicians.

The attempt to determine his exact position amongst the greatest composers would be fruitless, as opinions must always be expected to differ upon questions of taste and sensibility; but of his title to the highest honours which posterity can award, there cannot be a doubt.

His works remain the " star-y-pointing pyramid " of one who excelled in every species of composition—from the impassioned elevation of the tragic opera, to the familiar melody of the birth-day song; nor will they cease to command universal admiration while music retains its power as the exponent of sentiment and passion.

[1] From some papers contributed by Mrs. Novello to the *Musical World*. The distinguished musical family of this name, being on a tour to Salzburg in 1829, aware of the necessitous and infirm condition of Mozart's sister, provided themselves with a subscription raised among their friends in London. It should be added that this timely offering was, with characteristic forethought and delicacy, presented to the aged lady, as a remembrance on her name-day from some friends of her brother.

I am indebted to the same source for some original sayings of Mozart, and traits of his character.

APPENDIX

THE WORKS OF MOZART

:.—Catalogue of the Compositions produced by Mozart
between his Seventh and Twelfth Year.

1. Sonates pour le clavecin avec l'accomp. de violon, dédiées
   à Madame Victoire de France, par W. Mozart, agé de
   sept ans. Paris, Oeuvre 1, 1764.
2. Sonates pour le clavecin, etc., dédiées à Madame la Comtesse
   de Tessé, etc. Oeuvre 2, 1764.
3. Six Sonates pour le clavecin avec l'accomp., etc., dédiées
   à sa Maj. Charlotte, Reine de la Grande Bretagne, par
   W. Mozart agé de huit ans. A Londres, Oeuvre 3, 1765.
4. Six Sonates pour le clavecin avec l'accomp. dédiées à
   Madame la Princesse de Nassau Weilburg, née Princesse
   d'Orange, par W. Mozart, agé de neuf ans. A la Haye,
   Oeuvre 4, 1766.
5. Variations for the clavier engraved at the Hague, 1766.
6. Other variations for the clavier engraved at Amsterdam,
   1766.
7. Fifteen Italian airs, written partly in London and partly at
   the Hague.
8. A quodlibet entitled, "Galimathias Musicum," for two
   violins, tenor and bass, two oboes, two horns, two
   bassoons and harpsichord *obligato.*
9. Thirteen symphonies for two violins, tenor and bass, two
   oboes, and two horns.
10. An oratorio for five principal singers. The original contains
    208 pages.
11. Another oratorio for two soprani and a tenor, with accom-
    paniments for an orchestra. Written in Holland.[1]
12. Kyrie for soprano, alto, tenor, and bass, with accompani-
    ments for stringed instruments. Paris.[1]
13. Music to a Latin comedy called "Apollo and Hyacinth,"
    for five principal singers. Composed for the University
    of Salzburg. The original score contains 162 pages. 1767.

---

[1] The works thus distinguished are additions to the catalogue furnished
by Nissen, and have been collected from the MSS. in the possession of
M. André.

14. Six Divertimentos in four parts, for various instruments, viz., violin, trumpet, horn, flute, bassoon, trombone, viola, violoncello, etc.
15. Six trios for two violins and violoncello.
16. A cantata on the Passion, for two principal singers. It consists of two airs, a recitative, and a duet.
17. A short Stabat Mater for voices alone.
18. Various solos for the violin—for the violoncello (for the Prince of Fürstenberg) for the viol di gamba—and for the flauto traverso (for Duke Louis of Würtemberg).
19. Several pieces for two trumpets, two horns, and two corni di bassetto.
20. Several minuets for the orchestra.
21. Various passages for trumpets and drums.
22. A collection of marches—some for an orchestra, some for military instruments, and others for two violins and bass.
23. Two MSS. books containing numerous pieces for the clavier, composed from time to time in London, Holland, etc.
24. A Fugue for the clavier.
25. A Fugue for four voices.
26. Veni sancte spiritus for four voices, and accompaniments for an orchestra. 1768.
27. A German operetta. "Bastien and Bastienne." 1768.
28. An opera buffa, "La Finta Semplice." 1768. The Score 558 pages.
29. A grand mass for four voices, two violins, two oboes, two violas, four trumpets, drums, etc. 1768.
30. A shorter mass for four voices, two violins, etc. 1768.
31. A grand offertorium for four voices, two violins, two trumpets, etc.
32. Four concertos for the clavier, with accompaniments for an orchestra.[1]

II.—CATALOGUE OF WORKS COMPOSED BY MOZART FROM FEBRUARY 9, 1784, TO NOVEMBER 15, 1791, ACCORDING TO THE THEMES PRESERVED BY HIMSELF, AND AS SINCE PUBLISHED BY ANDRÉ, OF OFFENBACH.

1784

February—Concerto for the pianoforte in E flat, 3-4.
March—Concerto for pianoforte in B flat, 4-4. Concerto for

pianoforte in D, 4-4. Quintetto for piano and wind instruments in E flat, 4-4.

April—Concerto for pianoforte in G, 4-4, Sonata for piano and violin in B flat, 4-4.

August—Ten variations for the pianoforte alone.

September—Concerto for the pianoforte in B flat, 4-4.

October—Sonata for the pianoforte in C minor.

November—Quartet for two violins, tenor, and bass in B flat, 6-8.

December—Concerto for pianoforte in F, 4-4.

1785

January—Quartet for two violins, tenor, and bass in A, 3-4. Quartet for the same instruments in C, 3-4.

February—Concerto for pianoforte in D minor, 4-4.

March—Aria, " A te frà tanti affanni." Concerto for pianoforte in C, 4-4. Aria, " Fra l'oscure." A masonic song for voice and piano.

April—Andante to a violin concerto in A, 3-4. A cantata, " The Joy of Freemasons."

May—Three German songs. Fantasia for the pianoforte in C minor.

June—Song, " The Violet."

July—Masonic funeral music. Pianoforte quartet in G minor, 4-4.

November—Quartet for the opera. " La Villanella rapita,"—terzetto for the same opera.

December—Sonata for piano and violin in E flat, 3-4. Concerto for pianoforte in E flat, 4-4.

1786

February—Music to the comedy, " Der Schauspiel Director."

March—Concerto for pianoforte in A, 4-4. Duet for " Idomeneo." Scena and rondo for the same with violin obligato. Concerto for the pianoforte in C minor, 3-4.

April—The opera, " Le Nozze di Figaro."

June—Pianoforte quartet in E flat, 4-4. Rondo for the piano alone in F, 4-4. Concerto for the horn.

July—Trio for piano, violin, and violoncello in G, 4-4.

August—Sonata for four hands in F, 3-4. Trio for the pianoforte, clarionet, and tenor, in E flat, 6-8. Quartet for two violins, tenor, and violoncello, in D, 4-4.

September—Variations for pianoforte.

November—Variations for four hands. Trio for piano, violin, and violoncello, in B flat, 4-4.
December—Concerto for pianoforte, in C, 4-4. Symphony for the orchestra in D, 4-4. Scena with pianoforte obligato.

1787

February—Six German dances.
March—Rondo for the pianoforte. Scena ed aria, " Non sò d'onde viene." Aria, " Mentre te lascio."
April—Quintet for two tenors, two violins, and bass, in C, 4-4.
May—Quintet for the same instruments, in G minor, 4-4. Four German songs. Sonata for four hands, in C.
June—A musical joke. Two songs.
August—A little serenade for two violins, alto, and bass. Sonata for piano and violin, in A, 6-8.
October—The opera, " Il dissoluto punito, ossia il Don Giovanni."
November—Scena, " Bella mia fiamma." Two songs.
December—A song.

1788

January—Sonata for the pianoforte. Two country dances. Six German dances.
February—Concerto for the pianoforte, in D, 4-4.
March—Aria, " Ah scia ciel." Song, " Ich möchte wohl der Kaiser seyn." Adagio for the piano, in B minor.
April—Air for the opera, " Don Giovanni," " Dalla sua pace." Duetto for the same, " Per quelle tue manine." Scena and rondo for the same, " Mi tradi."
May—Arietta, " Un bacio di mano."
June—Trio for piano, violin, and violoncello, in E, 3-4. Symphony for the orchestra, in E flat, 4-4. A little march for the orchestra. A little easy sonata for beginners. Introductory adagio to a quartet fugue, in C minor.
July—Sonatina for piano and violin, in F, 4-4. Trio for piano, violin, and violoncello, in C, 4-4. Canzonet for two soprani and bass. Symphony, for the orchestra, in G minor, 4-4.
August—Symphony for the orchestra, in C, 4-4. War song.
September—Eight four-part canons. Two three-part canons. Divertimento for violin, alto, and violoncello, in E flat, 4-4.

October—Trio for pianoforte, violin, and violoncello, in G, 4-4. Two country dances.

November—Instrumentation of Handel's " Acis and Galatea."

December—Six German dances. Twelve minuets.

1789

January—A German song.

February—Sonata for pianoforte, in B flat, 3-4. Six German dances.

March—Instrumentation of Handel's " Messiah."

April—Variations on a minuet, by Duport.

May—A little gigue, for the clavier.

June—Quartet for two violins, tenor, and violoncello, in D, 4-4.

July—Sonata for the pianoforte, in D, 6-8. Rondo for the opera of " Figaro."

August—Aria, " Alma grande."

September—German air. Quintet for clarionet, two violins, alto, and violoncello, in A, 4-4.

October—Aria, " Chi sà, chi sà." Aria, " Vado, ma dove? "

December—Aria, " Rivolgeti à me." Twelve minuets. Twelve German dances.

1790

January—The opera, " Cosi fan tutte."

May—Quartet for two violins, alto, and violoncello, in B flat, 3-4. Quartet for the same instruments in F.

July—Instrumentation of Handel's " Alexander's Feast," and ode on " St. Cecilia's Day."

December—Quintet for two violins, two altos, and bass, in D, 3-4. A piece for an organ in a clock.

1791

January—Concerto for pianoforte, in B flat, 4-4. Three German songs. Six minuets. Six German dances.

February—Four minuets and four German dances. Two country dances. Two minuets and two German dances. A country dance and six waltzes.

March—A piece for an organ in a clock, in F minor, 4-4. Two dances. A song, with obligato double bass. Variations for the piano.

April—Quintetto for two violins, two altos, and violoncello, E flat, 6-8. Final chorus to Sarti's opera, " Le Gelosie vilane."

May—Andante to a waltz for a little organ. Quintet for the harmonica.

June—" Ave verum Corpus."

July—A short German cantata. The opera, " Die Zauberflöte."

September—The opera, " La Clemenza di Tito." Overture and priest's march for the " Zauberflöte." Concerto for the clarionet.

November—A cantata for the freemasons.

Note—The " Requiem," which should have closed the catalogue of works in this year, necessarily omitted; as are likewise a great many compositions of which he reserved no copy, presented by Mozart to various friends.

III.—Catalogue of Musical Fragments and Sketches found among Mozart's papers, with a description of them by the Abbé Stadler.

A.—*Fragments for the Clavier.*

1. Concerto for the piano and violin, in D major, begun in 1778, at Mannheim. The ritornello is one of the most beautiful he had ever written at that time. The violins begin *piano*, and the tenors, violoncelli, and basses, accompany for eleven bars *pizzicato ;* to this succeeds a magnificent *forte* of sixty-five bars, accompanied by flutes, oboes, horns, trumpets, and drums, and interspersed with the most agreeable *piano*. The principal violin has the first solo for eleven bars, then the piano a solo for eleven bars; a short *forte*, with all the instruments, follows. At last the principal violin and piano enter together, and interchange concerto passages by turns for twenty-one bars. To these solos the accompaniment is wanting; in other respects they are entirely completed.

2. Concerto for the piano, in D major. Of this twenty-one bars only for the principal instrument are written; the space for the accompaniment is empty.

3. Concerto for the piano, in D major, 3-4. The ritornello is merely indicated by the violin and bass without any accompaniment, for a flute, two clarionets, two horns, two bassoons, etc.

4. Concerto for the piano, in C major, 3-4, with accompaniments for two violins, viola, flute, two oboes, two horns, etc. The introduction consists of twenty-five bars, but is

not fully instrumented. To this succeeds a solo for the piano of eight bars length, and then four bars for the instruments.

5. Concerto for the piano, in C major, with two violins, viola, flute, oboes, horns, trumpets, and drums. The introductory symphony is indicated in the first violin and bass part for nineteen bars.

6. Concerto for the piano in D minor with two violins, viola, flute, oboes, corni di bassetto, horns, bassoons, etc. Of this there are only six bars for the violin and bass.

7. Commencement of a rondo to a pianoforte concerto in E flat, major. It consists of three bars only, without accompaniment.

8. Rondo in A to a pianoforte concerto. The piano commences *alla breve* for eight bars, and the violin and bass continue for fifteen bars. The other accompaniments are wanting.

9. Rondo in A, 6-8, to a pianoforte concerto. The principal instruments begin alone for four bars; the clarionet has then four bars, which are again mutually interchanged. The violins then enter, but the accompaniments are not written.

10. A quintet for the piano, in B major, 6-8, with oboe, clarionet, corno di bassetto, and bassoon. Thirty-five bars only are written, but they are completely in the Mozart style.

11. Commencement of a piece for the piano, in D major, with two violins, two horns, and bass. It consists of twenty-nine bars.

12. Commencement of a trio for the piano, violin, and violoncello, in B major. Twenty-five bars.

13. Commencement of a trio for the same instruments in G. Nineteen bars.

14. Beginning of an andantino, in G minor, for piano and violoncello. Thirty-three bars.

15. Ditto of a sonata for piano and violin, in B. Thirty-one bars.

16. Another of the same, in A. Thirty-four bars.

17. Another of the same, in A, 3-4. Fifteen bars.

18. Commencement of a fantasia for the piano, in F minor. Fourteen bars.

19. Commencement of a clavier sonata, in F. Seven bars.

20. Commencement of a clavier sonata, *alla breve*. Fifteen bars.

T

21. Commencement of an allegro for the piano, in F, 6-8. Sixteen bars.
22. A rondo, in F, 6-8. Thirty-three bars.
23. An adagio, in D minor. Four bars, and the first part of a minuet in the major.
24. The opening of a sonata, in B. Nineteen bars.
25. A very short andante, in E flat. The first part contains eight, and the second twelve bars.
26. Thema for variations, in C major.
27. Adagio in D minor. Nine bars.
28. Commencement of an allegro, in C minor, for two pianos. Twenty-two bars.
29. Ditto of a sonata for two pianos. The adagio contains eight, and the presto forty-four bars.
30. Another of the same, in B. Fifteen bars.
31. Beginning of a fugue, in G. Thirty-three bars.
32. Forty half sheets, containing various themes for fugues, canons, and exercises in counterpoint
33. A sonata for piano and violin, in C. Andante followed by an allegro. The first allegro and andante are completed by Mozart, the allegretto is the work of another.
34. Sonata in A for piano and violin. It begins with a beautiful andante, which is entirely Mozart's work, but of the following fugue in A minor, only one half is by him.
35. An allegro in D minor. A Tempo di Menuetto in G. Another allegro in D, 6-8 for clavier, violin, and violoncello, not quite completed. It has been finished by an amateur, and together forms a trio.
36. A beautiful allegro for the piano in B. It has been finished by an amateur.
37. Commencement of a clavier sonata in B with a violin. Completed by an amateur.
38. A short fugue for violin, viola, and violoncello in G.
39. A prelude or short fantasia in C major, composed for his sister. It begins with an allegretto, which is succeeded by a capriccio and an andantino. A cantabile and capriccio allegro form the conclusion. It is completed.
40. A concerto for three claviers with violins, oboes, horns, viola, and bass in F. The introduction is an allegro in F. Then follows an adagio in B flat, a movement in minuet time and a rondo in F. Of this composition there are the parts for the first clavier, the first and

second violin, viola, and bass. It may have been composed in the year 1777. That it was completed is proved not only by the relation of its performance at Augsburg, October 24, 1777, given by Mozart in a letter to his father (see page 90), but by the elegantly ornamented title page, on which appears in the handwriting of the father, " Dedicatio al incomparabile merito di sua Excellenza la Sigra. Contessa Lodron, nata Contessa d'Arco, e delle sue figlie—le Sigre. Contesse Aloisia e Giuseppe,

"In F . . . dal loro devotissimo servo,

" WOLFGANGO MOZART."

Mozart's handwriting was probably not thought good enough for such a dedication.

41. A variety of his earliest compositions.

B.—*Fragments for the violin.*

1. Commencement of a symphony in E flat, with violins, viola, flute, oboes, horns, bassoons, violoncello, and bass. The adagio of fourteen bars is entirely instrumented and quite complete. The first part of the allegro, consisting of eighty-three bars, is likewise concluded, and for the most part instrumented. The second part is wanting.

2. A fragment apparently belonging to an opera. It is in D minor, of sixty-four bars length, and is complete, with accompaniments for an orchestra.

3. Introduction to an overture, andante in E flat, with violins, viola, flutes, oboes, clarinets, bassoons, horns, drums, and bass. It is of eight bars length, and is followed by an allegro, of which eighteen bars are written in the violin part, but without accompaniment for the other instruments.

4. " Chasse," in A, 6-8, with two violins, viola, two flutes, two horns, aboe, and bass. The first part contains eight bars, and the second likewise. Both are entirely completed and instrumented. To these succeed a *minore* in two parts, of eight bars length; but the accompaniment is wanting.

5. Sinfonie concertante a tre instrumenti, violino, viola, violoncello. In A major with two oboes, two horns, two violins, and bass. The introductory symphony of forty-three bars is completed. The concerto passages for

the other instruments contain eighty-three bars, mostly without accompaniment.

6. Commencement of a symphony in G major. Ten bars without accompaniment.

7. Minuet for violins, two oboes, bassoon, two horns, flauto piccolo, and tamburin, in A. The first part of eight bars is finished; the second has only three bars.

8. Commencement of a rondo in B, for violins, flute, oboe, bassoon, horn, alto, and bass. Twenty-five bars; the accompaniment wanting.

9. Rondon in F, for two violins, viola, two horns, and bass. It is of three parts only, each of which has eight bars, but no accompaniment.

10. Quintet for violin, tenor, clarionet, corno di bassetto, and violoncello, in F major. 102 bars; the accompaniment mostly complete.

11. Quintet for two violins, two tenors, and violoncello. Allegro in A flat. Seventy-two bars.

12. Ditto   ditto   in B *alle breve.* 102 bars.

13. Ditto   ditto   in E flat, 3-4. The allegro contains seventy-one bars, but is unfinished.

14. Ditto   ditto   in E flat. Nineteen bars.

15. Ditto   ditto   in D major. Eighteen bars.

16. Rondo to a quintet in G minor, 6-8. Eight bars.

17. Ditto   in F major, 6-8. Ten bars.

18. Larghetto for the same instruments in C major. Sixteen bars.

19. Violin quintet in E minor. The first part of the allegro of seventy-four bars is finished.

20. Ditto   in G minor. Twenty-four bars.

21. Ditto   in B. *Allegretto.* Fifty-six bars.

22. Rondo for the same instruments in B. Ten bars.

23. Ditto   ditto   in A, 6-8. 139 bars.

24. Adagio for the same instruments in F major. Eight bars.

25. Rondo   ditto   in F 6-8. Sixteen bars.

26. Another beginning with a minuet. Nine bars.

27. Trio in G, 3-4, for violin, viola, and violoncello. The first part of ninety-one bars is finished. Of the second part there are nine bars.

Note.—Among these fragments, No. 1, 2, 3, 5, 10, 11, 12, 13, 19, 23, and 27 may be especially distinguished for originality of design, melody, harmony, and masterly accompaniment.

Appendix 293

C.—*Fragments for Wind Instruments.*

1. Adagio for the harmonica, with flute, oboe, viola, and violoncello. Ten bars.
2. Introduction to a horn concerto.
3. Ditto   ditto.
4. Quintet for Clarionet, two violins, viola, and bass in B flat. The first part of ninety bars in completed. The second part has only three bars.
5. Quintet for the same instruments in A; contains eighty-nine bars, but is incomplete, the accompaniment being only indicated here and there.
6. Allegro for two oboes, two horns, two clarionets, and two bassoons in B flat. Sixteen bars.
7. Adagio in F for a clarionet and three corni di bassetto. Six bars.
8. Allegro for the same instruments. Twenty-two bars.
9. Adagio for a "Corno Inglese," two violins and bass. The first part of twenty-three bars is finished. The second part of thirty-six bars is also finished, but without accompaniment.

D.—*Fragments of Vocal Composition.*

1. Commencement of a Kyrie in E flat, 4-4, *largo*, for four voices, two violins, two violas, two oboes, two horns, two trumpets, drums, and two bassoons. Twenty-two bars full of religious feeling and in the true church style. The most agreeable melody, with various accompaniments in the harmony, prevails. The "Christe" contains short solos for the soprano and alto.
2. Kyrie in C major, for four voices, two violins, two trumpets, drums, and organ. Nine bars.
3. Kyrie in D major, four voices, two violins, viola, two oboes, etc. Eleven bars, completely in the church style, and remarkably beautiful.
4. Fragment of a Kyrie. Four voices with orchestra, in a majestic style. Thirty-seven bars.
5. Ditto, commencing with an adagio in G, to which a fugued andante succeeds. Thirty-four bars.
6. Ditto, in D major. A fugued allegro. Thirty-two bars.
7. Ditto, in C, commencing with an adagio of fourteen bars, and then an allegro, of which there are thirty-five bars.
8. Fragment of a Gloria in C. Twenty-six bars.

9. A psalm, " Memento, Domine, David," etc., for four voices, in F. Thirty-two bars.

10. A German cantata " Die Seele des Weltalls, o Sonne! " etc., for two tenors and bass. The first chorus in E flat is complete. It commences with a magnificent *unisono*, and a simple, noble, and agreeable melody prevails throughout it. At the words, " From thee come fruitfulness, warmth, light," etc., the word *light* is brought out by a *forte* on the chord of the seventh, which must have much effect were the accompaniment for the instruments in the score, flutes, oboes, clarionets, bassoons, etc., not wanting. A tenor air in B flat of the tenderest melody, and magnificently accompanied by the double bass, succeeds this chorus. But the other accompanying instruments are here deficient, the space being left for them. A second tenor air in F follows. Seventeen bars.

11. Duet for two soprani, " I speak thy name unconsciously," with accompaniment for the piano. Twenty-seven bars.

12. A recitative, " O Calpe," with accompaniment for the piano. Imperfect.

13. Air in D minor, " Lonely am I." Eight bars.

14. Another, " V'amo di core." Eight bars.

15. Sined's (Denis) Bard's song on Gibraltar.

16. An Italian operetta, in which the personages are Bettina, Don Astrubale, Pulcherio, and Bocconio. Incomplete.

17. A German operetta, somewhat similar in design to the " Entführung aus dem Serail," in which the names of H. von Dummkopf (Baron Thickskull), Rosaura, Trautel, Leander, Casperl, etc., appear. Incomplete.

18. A cradle song in three verses, with accompaniment for the piano. It is entirely in Mozart's manner, perfectly naïve and original.

19. An air, " Dentro il mio petto." Allegro maestoso. Imperfect.[1]

IV.—CATALOGUES OF THE COMPOSITIONS WHICH, IN ADDITION TO THOSE HERE MENTIONED, MOZART LEFT COMPLETE.

1. An oratorio, " Davidde penitente." 1783.
2. Thirty various church compositions—masses, litanies,

[1] To this list of Fragments should be added two Italian operas, " Lo Sposo Deluso, Ossia la Rivalità di tre Donne per un solo Amante," and " l'Oca del Cairo."

offertories, motets, hymns, cantatas, etc., and among them a requiem. Of these a *stabat mater* for three soprani, consisting entirely of canons, and an antiphona in four parts, which he wrote at Bologna in 1770, for reception into the Philharmonic Society of that city, deserve especial notice. The greatest work of all is, however, the requiem.

3. Four choruses for four voices and orchestra.
4. Forty-three Italian airs, duets, trios, with and without recitative accompaniments for a full orchestra. Written for particular singers and voices of various kinds.
5. Sixteen canons with and without words, for three and four voices.
6. Some *solfeggi* for practice.
7. Thirty-four songs with accompaniment for the piano.
8. Thirty-three symphonies for the orchestra. Of these several have been published at Vienna and Offenbach.
9. Fifteen opera overtures. Seven of them have been published at Offenbach.
10. Forty-one divertisements for various instruments more or fewer. Among these are several *suites* of pieces for wind instruments.
11. Eight quintets for two violins, two tenors, and bass. The whole engraved at Leipsic, Vienna, and Offenbach.
12. Twenty-eight quartets; twenty-six are for two violins, tenor, and bass; one is for the oboe and one for the flute.
13. Ten violin trios.
14. Four ballets and pantomimes.
15. Five violin concertos. Some of them have been engraved at Offenbach.
16. Six horn concertos. Three have been published at Offenbach.
17. One bassoon concerto. Published at Offenbach.
18. Fifteen pianoforte concertos besides those already mentioned In the whole he composed twenty-nine concertos for the piano: of these Breitkopf and Härtel have published twenty-one, and André twenty-three.
19. Five pianoforte quartets.
20. Twenty-three pianoforte trios. They are all in Breitkopf and Härtel's edition of " Œuvr. Compl."
21. Thirty-one pianoforte solos.
22. Four sonatas for four hands on the piano.
23. Two pieces for two pianos, namely, a sonata and a fugue.

24. Several themes varied for two and four hands on the piano.
25. Four rondos for the piano.
26. " Mitridate." Opera seria. Milan, 1770.
27. " Ascanio in Alba." Dramatic serenata. Milan, 1771.
28. " Il Sogno di Scipione." Serenata for the Installation of the Archbishop of Salzburg, 1772.
29. " Lucio Silla." Opera seria. Milan, 1773.
30. " La-finta Giardiniera. Opera buffa. Munich, 1774.
31. " Il Re Pastore." Pastorale Salzburg, 1775.
32. " Zaide." Melodramatic opera in two acts.
33. " Idomeneo, Ri di Creta." Opera seria in three acts. Munich, 1780.
34. " Die Entführung aus dem Serail; or, Constance and Belmont." Comic opera. Vienna, 1782.
35. Choruses and entr'acte music to the tragedy, " Thamos von Egypten," for four voices and orchestra.
36. A brief system of thorough bass. Kurz gefasste general bass-schule.

Two little Pieces, as specimens of Mozart's composition at six years of age.

PRINCEPS CAETERIQUE

ACADEMICI PHILHARMONICI

Omnibus, et singulis praesentes Literas lecturis, felicitatem

Quamvis ipsa Virtus sibi, suisque Sectatoribus gloriosum comparet Nomen, attamen pro majori ejusdem majestate publicam in notitiam decuit propagari. Hinc est quod hujusce nostrae PHILHARMONICAE ACADEMIAE existimationi, et incremento consulere, singulorumque Academicorum Scientiam, et profectum patefacere intendentes, testamur Domin. Wolfgangum Amadeum Mozart e Salisburgo—sub die 9 Mensis Octobris Anni 1770. inter Academiae nostrae MAGISTROS Compositores adscriptum fuisse. Tanti igitur Coacademici virtutem, et merita perenni benevolentiae monumento prosequentes, hasce Patentes, Literas subscriptas, nostrique Consessus Sigillo impresso obsignatas dedimus.

Bononiae ex nostra Residentia die 10 Mensis Octobris Anni 1770.

' PRINCEPS PETRONIUS LANZI.

Registr. in Libro Campl. G. pag. 147.   ALOYSIUS XAV. FERRI, *a Secretis.*
               CAMPLONERIUS, *Cajetanus Croci.*

Copy of the *Antiphona* given to W. A. Mozart, for treatment by the *Princeps* and the censors of the Philharmonic Academy. It is from the "Antiphonarium Romanum"—*Antiph. ad Magnificat. Dom. XIV., post Pentecost et in Festo Cajetani*—and as follows:

INDEX

ABEL, CHARLES, 25
Adamberger, Valentine, 157, 167, 174, 185, 188-9, 213, 218
Affligio, 39-42
Aix-la-Chapelle, 19
Albert, M., 79, 81
Albrechtsberger, 279
Aloys, Francis, 79
Aman, Herr von, 50, 52
Amelia, Princess, 19, 161
André, Johann, 1, 43 n., 73 n., 187, 190 n., 195, 214
Anfossi, Pasquale, 180, 188-9, 220
Angerbauer, M., 155
Antony, Prince of Saxony, 231 n.
Aprile, Giuseppe, 49, 57, 192
Arbaur, Joseph Felix, 106
Arco, Count, 154, 157, 159
Arnaud, Abbé, 111
Artaria, Brothers, 198, 206, 266 n.
Attwood, Mr., 162 n., 195, 212, 222-3, 254
Augsburg, 3, 17, 29, 79, 80, 85, 87, 91, 210, 263 n.

Bach, Charles, 171 n.
Bach, Emanuel, 5, 34, 171 and n.
Bach, Friedemann, 5, 161 and n., 171 and n.
Bach, John Christian, 24, 96 and n., 109 n., 171 n., 223
Bach, John Christopher, 171 n.
Bach, J. Sebastian, 73, 76 n., 96 n., 161-2, 170-1, 183, 224 n., 248, 251, 266, 274 n.
Bachmann, 34
Baden, 271
Baglioni, Signor, 234 n.
Barisani, Dr., 204, 230
Barrington, Hon. Daines, 27, 34 n.
Bassani, 221
Bassi, Signor, 234 n.
Bastardella (Agujare), 216
Baumgarten, Countess, 144
Bavaria, Elector of, 141
Beaumarchais, Pierre, 219
Becché, 89, 90, 120
Becke, Von, 136, 147, 263 and n.

Beethoven, L. von, 89 n., 173, 206, 223, 224 n.
Belmont, 166-8
Benda, George, 5, 134, 140, 161, 174
Benucci, 220 n., 221
Berlin, 5, 161 and n., 246-8, 250, 258-60, 280
Bernasconi, Antonia, 58, 61, 62
Bertlina, Anna (afterwards Mrs. Leopold Mozart), 4, 121-7
Beyle, M., 1, 190 n.
Bioley, M., 79
Boenecke, 154
Bologna, 50, 52, 58-60, 67, 77, 96, 201, 209
Bondini, M., 225, 235
Bondini, Signora, 232 n., 234 n.
Bonn, 19
Boselli, Mademoiselle, 172 n., 260 n.
Bourbon, Duchess de, 112
Braganza, Duke of, 41
Braun, Counsellor, 155
Brescia, 62
Bretzner, 174
Brunetti, Gaetano, 80, 149, 153-7, 199
Brunswick, Crown Prince of, 32
Brussels, 24
Bullinger, M., 78, 103, 121, 126-7
" Buona figliuola," 41, 42
Burney, Dr., 240

Cajetan, 18
Calais, 24
Cambini, Giuseppe, 114, 115
Cannabich, 92-5, 143, 146-7, 153, 264
Cannabich, Mademoiselle, 99
Capua, 55
Carattoli, 39, 40, 42, 56 n.
Caribaldi, 39, 40, 42
Carignan, Princess, 20
Carlotti, Marchese, 45-6
Carmontelle, M. von, 24
Carraccioli, 110 n.
Caseli, M., 48
Casti, Battista, 217
Cavalieri, Mademoiselle, 167, 174, 213, 218, 246 n.

Ceccarelli, 143, 153, 157
Charlotte, Queen, 27
Chartres, Duke de, 23
Chiemsee, Bishop of, 72, 81, 82
Chiemsee, Prince von, 80
Chobert, 87
Clement, Prince, 16
Clementi, Muzio, 164-5, 211 *n.* 223, 261 *n.*
Clermont, Madame de, 23
Cobentzel, Prince de, 163
Colloredo, Prince, 156
Coltellini, Ecleste, 42
Consoli, Signor, 80
Conti, Prince, 24
Cordelier, 202
Corilla, Signora, 54
Cowper, William, 196-7 *n.*
Crosa, 62

D'Aguillon, Duchess, 24
D'Alembert, J. le R., 111
Dallberg, M. von, 134
Dauer, 174
Daun, Field-Marshal, 13
Davis, Cecilia, 71 *n.*
De Amicis, Signora, 54, 57, 67, 68, 116
Degenfeld, Count von, 39
Demler, M., 90, 91
Dennis, 186
D'Epinay, Madame, 112, 128
De Pompadour, Madame, 20, 22
Diderot, Denis, 19
Dittersdorf, Baron, 174, 192, 217, 240, 261 *n.*
Doles, 251-2
Donauwörth, 91
"Don Giovanni," 227-36, 246
Dresden, 250-1, 257-8
Duschek, John Louis, 219-23, 231-3, 273-4
Duschek, Madame, 220 *n.;* 249

Eberlin, Joh. Ernst, 3, 34, 88
Eckard, 23
Edelmann, 86
Emily, Conti Carlo, 45
Engel, M., 251
Esser, M., 149
Esterhazy, Prince Antony, 66
Esterhazy, Prince Nicholas, 171, 215, 260 *n.*

Farinelli (Broschi), 17 *n.,* 52
Ferdinand, Archduke, 63
Ferraris, General Count, 19
Fétis, M., 151 *n.,* 251

Fiala, 149 and *n.*
Fingerl, M., 79
Firmian, Count, 49, 63, 64, 67
Fischer, J. C., 99, 100, 113, 166, 174, 185
Florence, 52, 54, 69
Francis, Emperor, 13, 231 *n.*
Frankfort, 18, 24, 79, 263
Fränzl, M., 98, 134

Gabrielli, Caterina, 64, 65 *n.*
"Galimathias Musicum," 30 *n.*
Gallitzin, Prince, 154-5
Galuppi, Baldassare, 62
Gasparini, the Abbé, 62
Gasser, M., 79
Gavard, Mr., 54
Gebler, Freiherrn von, 183
Gellert, Christian, 5, 48
Gemmingen, M. von, 135
Gerber, H. N., 160, 205 *n.,* 212 *n.,* 275 *n.*
Gilowsky, M. von, 177
Ginguené, Peter L., 111
Glatz, M., 79
Gluck, Christopher, 38, 58, 110-11, 129-30, 140, 161, 177, 180-5, 215, 220, 232 *n.,* 237-8
Gossec, Francis, 111
Grassalkowitsch, Prince, 206
Gretry, André, 115
Grimm, Baron de, 19, 24, 33 *n.,* 73-4, 112-3, 118-9, 123-5, 128
Grua, 144
Gschwender, M., 136
Guardassoni, 248, 261
Guari, Signora, 50
Guines, Duc de, 116, 117 *n.*

Haarlem, 31
Hafeneder, 149
Hagenauer, M., 10, 11 *n.,* 18, 67
Hagenauer, Madame, 11 *n.,* 20, 21 *n.*
Hague, the, 28
Haine, M., 121
Hamilton, Lady, 55
Hamilton, Sir William, 55
Handel, G. F., 24, 25, 34, 44, 65, 73, 133 *n.,* 162, 170, 181, 183, 208 *n.,* 223, 224 *n.,* 246-7, 253, 262, 267, 274 *n.*
Hardegg, Count, 12
Harrach, Count, 12
Haslang, Count, 27
Hasse, J. A., 17 *n.,* 34, 41 *n.,* 62, 63-5, 257
Hässler, 257 and *n.*
Hatzfeldt, Count, 218

Hay (afterwards Bishop of Königs-
  gräz), 35
Haydn, Joseph, 66, 70, 74, 80, 151 *n.*,
  155 *n.*, 162, 171-2, 182, 188, 204-11,
  214-17, 220, 235, 246, 253, 260-1,
  279
Haydn, Michael, 3, 52, 76, 139, 149,
  171, 190-1
Heffner, Elizabeth, 75
Heffner, M., 71, 79
Heidelberg, 18
Herbenstein, Count, 11
Hieronymus, Archbishop, 65
Hilber, M., 80
Hochenaltheim, 91
Hoffman, the brothers, 200 *n.*
Hofmeister, M., 213, 241, 255, 264
Holzbauer, 92-3, 96-7, 131-2, 142
Huber, Professor, 81, 85
Hummel, Johann-Nepomuck, 173,
  211
Hummel, Joseph, 210-11

" Idomeneo," 18 *n.*
Innsprück, 79
Jacquin, Gottfried von, 231
Johannisöl, 245
Jomelli, Nicolo, 17 and *n.*, 56 and *n.*,
  57, 92 *n.*, 202, 253
Joseph, Emperor, 14, 155 *n.*, 163-4,
  178 and *n.*, 181, 192, 199, 217-22,
  236, 261

Kaunitz, Prince, 40, 175, 210
Kauniz, Count, 12
Kaysersheim, 135
Keiserin, 84
Kelly, Michael, 192-5, 201, 217-8,
  220 *n.*
Kinsky, Countess Leopold, 13
Kirchheim-Poland, 103-5
Kirnberger, Joh. Philip, 5
Kleinmayern, Herr von, 154-5
Kozeluch, Leopold, 192
Krönner, Johannes, 81 *n.*

" La Cashina," 41
La Harpe, 111
Lampugnani, Maestro, 61
Lang, 92, 147
Lange, M., 136 *n.*
Langenmantel, M. von, 79, 86
Laschi, Signora, 42, 208, 221
Lasso, Orlando di, 73
Laugier, 39, 42
Legrand, 143
Le Gros, M., 112, 114, 129
Leipsic, 192, 248-53, 273 *n.*, 280

Leitgeb, 18, 187
Lemberg, 280
Leopold, Archduke (afterwards Em-
  peror), 11, 271, 280
Lichnowsky, Prince von, 247, 250
Ligneville, Marquis of, 52
Lille, 28
Linley, Rev. Ozias, 54 *n.*
Linley, Thomas, 54 and *n.*, 193
Linz, 11, 192
Linz, Bishop of, 10
Lodi, 68
Lodron, Countess Theresa, 13, 75,
  90 *n.*
Lolli, Signor, 130, 234 *n.*
London, 24, 28, 33, 257, 260
Ludwigsburg, 17
Luggiati, Signor, 45
Luxemberg, 175

Mainzer, M., 190
Majo, Ciccio di, 56 and *n.*
Mandini, M., 221
Mannheim, 83, 90 *n.*, 92, 97-109,
  132-5, 142, 148, 153, 169, 264
Mantua, 47, 48
Manzuoli, 27, 54, 64
Maria Theresa, 63, 231 *n.*
Marie Antoinette (afterwards Queen
  of France), 14, 111
Marmontel, 110-11
Marpurg, F. W., 5
Martinas, Signora, 209
Martini, Vicenté, 180
Martini, Padre, 44, 52, 59, 76, 77, 82,
  96, 105, 129, 201 and *n.*, 202, 215
Maschi, M., 48
Mattei, Stanislas, 201 *n.*
Matthausen, 11
Maximilian, Archduke, 12, 73
Mayence, 18, 83, 210
Mayence, Elector of, 18
Mayer, Mr., 106
Mechel, M. de, 24
Mechlin, Archbishop of (Count
  Frankenburg), 19, 32
Mendelssohn, 213
Mesmer, Dr., 35, 71, 81, 153
Metastasio, Pietro, 17 *n.*, 58, 65, 66,
  202, 209, 272
Micelli, Signora, 234
Michl, 131
Milan, 47-50, 58-66, 96
Misliwetschek, 65 and *n.*
Mizerl, Mademoiselle, 72
Mölk, Herr von, 34, 47, 50
Mölk, Mademoiselle, 72 *n.*
Morella, Mr., 246 *n.*

Mosel, M., 246
Mozart, Leopold, 3-9, 17-22, 26, 30-3, 37-9, 44, 49, 58, 62, 69-70, 75, 105, 109, 117-9, 124, 129-35, 147-9, 161, 191, 208-10, 214, 224, 228-9, 268
Mozart, Maria Anna (Nannerl) (afterwards Mme. Sonnenberg), 4, 12, 18-24, 36, 55, 79, 103, 126-7, 202, 210, 268, 280-1
Munich, 6, 9, 16, 71, 76-86, 95, 102-3, 131-53, 220 n., 264

Naples, 17 n., 55-7
Naples, King of, 34, 58
Nardini, 17, 54
Naumann, John, 257
Nissen, M. von, 1, 9 n., 191, 206, 280-1
Nördlingen, 91
Novello, Mrs., 281 n.
Noverre, 112, 117, 128, 132 n.
Nymphenburg, 16, 82

Ochely, M., 221
Olmütz, 35
Orange, Prince of, 28, 30
Orange, Princess of, 103
Orleans, Duke of, 24
Ottini, M., 48

Paar, Count, 12
Padua, 63
Paesiello, Giovanni, 165, 192, 201, 215, 217, 220, 253
Palavicini, Field-Marshal, 59
Pallavicini, Cardinal, 53
Palmini, Signor, 77
Paradies, Pietro D., 24, 73
Paris, 19-24, 29-33, 105-32, 159 n., 160, 257
Parma, 50
Passau, 10
Pedrillo, 258
Piccinelli, Madame, 49
Piccini, Nicolo, 84, 110, 115, 129
Pick, Herr, 49
Piozzi, Mrs., 58 n., 164 n.
Podstatsky, Count, 35
Poggi, 40, 42
Ponte, Abbé da, 217-219
Ponziani, Signor Felice, 234 n.
Porpora, Nicolo, 65
Potsdam, 250
Pottrie, M. de la, 264
Prague, 192, 215, 225-36, 243, 248, 258 n., 266, 271-80
Prato, Del, 141, 143, 145, 150

Prussia, Frederick William II. of, 247, 250, 259-60, 262
Puchberg, M. von, 244
Puffendorf, Madame von, 218
Pulini, Baron, 218

Quaglio, Lozenzo, 143

Radziwill, Prince, 235
Raff, 109 n., 141, 143-45, 147, 224
Ramm, 92, 114 n., 147, 248
Randall, Mr., 27
Ranelagh, 26
Raupach, M., 33
Reichardt, J. F., 174
Reidesel, Baron von, 184
Richter, 194-5
Ries, Ferdinand, 213
Righini, Vincenzo, 180, 220
Rindum, M., 244
Robinnig, Madame, 136
Rochlitz, J. F., 248, 252
Roessler, M., 46
Rombeck, Countess, 156, 164
Rome, 52-8, 65 n., 73
Rosa, Madame, 50
Rosenberg, Count, 185, 189
Rossini, G. A., 201 n.
Rousseau, J. J., 24, 159
Rudolph, 118
Rumling, Baron, 85

St. Gilgen, 4
St. Marxer Linie, 279
St. Petersburg, 33
Salern, Count, 83
Salieri, Antonio, 180 and n., 183, 189, 215, 219, 220, 235
Salzburg, 3-19, 25-49, 55, 65-83, 102, 120-1, 129-33, 138-49, 154, 158-60, 187-91, 210, 214, 224, 228, 280-1 n.
Salzburg, Archbishop of, 3, 19, 55 n., 119, 143 n., 148, 149 n., 153, 222, 224
Salzburg, Prince of, 94
Saporiti, Signora, 234 n.
Sarti, Giuseppe, 192, 201, 204-5 n., 269
Savioli, Count, 92-5, 99-101
Saxe-Gotha, Duke of, 198 n.
Schachtner, Andreas, 7, 10, 14
Schack, Benedict, 243, 275-8 n.
Schickaneder, 145, 241, 269-70, 275-7
Schidenofen, Herr von, 50, 55, 59
Schlick, Count, 11
Schlictegroll, 1, 197, 234 n., 241
Schwenkel, Professor, 29
Schwerlich, 243

Schwetzingen, 17, 18
Seau, Count, 80-5, 142-5, 149-53
Seiler, 134
Seinsheim, Count, 80, 147
Sigl, M., 86
Sonnenfels, M. von, 164
Spagnoletta, 48
Spolverini, Marchese, 45
Spork, Count von, 41
Stadler, Abbé, 135 n., 212
Stadler, M., 241, 265-6
Stamitz, 91, 115
Starnberg, Count, 119
Starzer, M., 156
Steffani, Agostino, 73
Stein, M., 79, 80, 86-91, 156
Stephani, M., 166, 168
Storace, Signora, 180 n., 192, 195, 201, 215-7, 221-4
Storace, Stephen, 192, 195, 215-7, 220, 223
Strak, M. von, 163 n., 164, 236
Strasburg, 133, 147 n.
Strauss, 227
Streicher, M., 89 n.
Strinasacchi, Signora, 198 and n.
Strobach, M., 225, 227
Stumpff, Mr., 205 n.
Stuttgard, 17, 135
Suard, 111
Sussmayer, 272, 275, 277, 280 n.
Swieten, Baron von, 39, 41, 162, and n., 170-1, 203-4, 244, 246, 262

Tartini, Giuseppe, 5
Tayber, Mademoiselle, 174
Tessé, Countess, 20
Thanet, Lord, 26
Thorwart, M. von, 177
Thun, Count, 192, 225
Thun, Countess, 155-7, 163-5
Thurn, Count von, 3
Tibaldi, 64
Tölpel, Herr, 59
Torricella, 210
Trattner, Madame von, 164
Trier, 83
Turin, 58, 62, 67

Valesi, 84
Valotti, Padre, 63, 96
Vanhall, 192, 217, 240
Varesco, Abbate, 141, 142, 191
Venice, 62, 73

Verona, 48, 62, 77
Versailles, 20-4, 118, 138
Vetter, M., 86
Victoire, Madame, 20
Vienna, 9-12, 16, 24, 34-8, 70, 119, 153-69, 191, 197-250, 254 n., 259-62, 266-8, 274-9
Vieregg, Baron, 147
Villeneuve, Mr., 133
Vogler, the Abbé, 90 n., 92, 93, 96-8, 103, 104, 264
Vogt, Karl von, 18, 59

Wagenseil, G. C., 14, 25, 220 n.
Waldstädter, Baroness, 164
Waldstetten, Baroness, 177
Wallerstein, Prince of, 91
Wartberg, 210
Wasserburg, 16
Weber, Aloysia (afterwards Mme. Lange), 103-4, 128-38, 170, 188-9, 216-8
Weber, Constance (afterwards Mme. Mozart), 136-8, 141 n., 169-70, 176-7, 193, 212, 255, 281
Weber, Fridolin, 103, 135, 138, 213
Weber, Sophie, 150 n., 268, 277
Weigl, Joseph, 157
Weilburg, Princess von, 28, 29, 30, 105
Wendling, M., 18 and n., 98, 101, 115, 143 n., 150, 153
Wendling, Dorothea, 143, 145
Wendling, Lisetta, 145
Wenzl, 10, 18
Wieland, 182
Williamson, Mr., 24
Woelfl, 273 n.
Wolfegg, Count, 90, 106
Wotschika, M., 82, 83
Wurtemburg, Duke of, 17 n., 151 n.
Wurzburg, 80

York, Duke of, 201 n., 216

Zabuesnig, Christoph von, 79
" Zauberflöte," 275 and n.
Zeil, Prince, 82
Zeschinger, 88
Zetti, Herr, 154
Zetto, Landrath von, 177
Zitchi, Count, 175, 210
Zweibrucken, Prince Max of, 16, 17, 18, 133

THE TEMPLE PRESS, PRINTERS, LETCHWORTH

CPSIA information can be obtained at www.ICGtesting.com
Printed in the USA
LVOW121723310112

266405LV00007B/55/A